GROWING INTO RESIL.

Sexual and Gender Minority Youth in Canada

Best Wishes
André P. Grace

Despite recent progress in civil rights for sexual and gender minorities (SGM), ensuring SGM youth experience fairness, justice, inclusion, safety, and security in their schools and communities remains an ongoing challenge. In *Growing into Resilience*, André P. Grace and Kristopher Wells – co-founders of Camp fYrefly, a summer leadership camp for SGM youth – investigate how teachers, health-care workers, and other professionals can help SGM youth build the human and material assets that will empower them to be happy, healthy, and resilient.

Grace and Wells investigate the comprehensive (physical, mental, emotional, social, spiritual, and sexual) health of SGM youth, emphasizing the role of caring professionals in an approach that recognizes and accommodates SGM youth. Throughout, the authors draw upon the personal narratives of SGM youth, emphasizing how research, policy, and practice must act together for SGM youth to be able to thrive and be at promise.

Both a resource for those professionally engaged in work with sexual and gender minorities and a comprehensive text for use in courses on working with vulnerable youth populations, *Growing into Resilience* is a timely and transdisciplinary book.

ANDRÉ P. GRACE is Canada Research Chair in Sexual and Gender Minority Studies and a professor in the Department of Educational Psychology at the University of Alberta.

KRISTOPHER WELLS is an assistant professor in the Department of Educational Policy Studies and the Director of Programs and Services, Institute for Sexual Minority Studies and Services, University of Alberta.

Growing into Resilience

Sexual and Gender Minority
Youth in Canada

ANDRÉ P. GRACE

WITH KRISTOPHER WELLS

UNIVERSITY OF TORONTO PRESS
Toronto Buffalo London

© University of Toronto Press 2015
Toronto Buffalo London
www.utppublishing.com
Printed in the U.S.A.

ISBN 978-1-4426-3757-3 (cloth)
ISBN 978-1-4426-2904-2 (paper)

Printed on acid-free, 100% post-consumer recycled paper.

Library and Archives Canada Cataloguing in Publication

Grace, André P., 1954–, author
Growing into resilience : sexual and gender minority youth in Canada /
André P. Grace with Kristopher Wells.

Includes bibliographical references and index.
ISBN 978-1-4426-3757-3 (bound).   ISBN 978-1-4426-2904-2 (paperback)

1. Sexual minorities – Canada.   2. Youth – Canada.   3. Resilience
(Personality trait) – Canada.   4. Gender identity – Canada.   I. Wells,
Kristopher, 1971–, author   II. Title.

HQ73.3.C3G73 2015   306.760835   C2015-903006-4

University of Toronto Press acknowledges the financial assistance to its
publishing program of the Canada Council for the Arts and the Ontario Arts
Council, an agency of the Government of Ontario.

This book is dedicated to Dr Fern Snart, Dean of Education at the University of Alberta. As an inclusive educator and mother, Fern intellectually and lovingly gets what it means to be there for sexual and gender minority children and youth. Few people in our life circles are kindred spirits who leave a deep impact personally, professionally, and socially. Fern is one of those rare, truly caring people. She has inspired and supported us fully and completely in our work to build the Institute for Sexual Minority Studies and Services as a place where research meets advocacy in our outreach to sexual and gender minority children and youth and their parents, caregivers, and other significant adults. Fern emphasizes the integrity of each child and youth, all of whom deserve to be at promise. We are forever grateful to her for standing tall with us.

Contents

Preface

Remembering the *Vriend* Decision

Teachers' associations or federations, provincial and territorial ministries of education, and other educational interest groups would no doubt agree: the safety and security of children and youth as students in Canadian schools must be a primary focus of educational policymaking and implemented practices. Indeed all students, despite linguistic, ethnocultural, sexual, gender, and other differences, should feel safe and protected in classrooms, corridors, gyms, washrooms, and anywhere else on school grounds. They should also feel safe using school buses or other public transportation, walking between the school they attend and where they live, and hanging out in parks and other public spaces off school grounds. However, sexual and gender minority (SGM) students, a diverse group that includes lesbian, gay, bisexual, intersexual, trans-identified, gender-nonconforming, Two-Spirit, and queer students, are among vulnerable youth subpopulations that often feel unsafe and prone to violence in these environments. More and more, they are relying on the force of Canadian law to acknowledge their right to experience safe and caring schools that respect and accommodate their identities, differences, and needs (Grace, 2007a; Grace & Wells, 2005; Wells, 2008).

Canadian law upholds equality provisions enshrined in Section 15 of the Canadian Charter of Rights and Freedoms (Grace, 2007a). In 2010 Canadians celebrated the twenty-fifth anniversary of the implementation of this section of the Charter. As a tenet advancing social inclusion, Section 15 guarantees individual rights and protections for minorities, including sexual minorities. In 1995 in *Egan v. Canada*, the Supreme Court of Canada ruled that *sexual orientation* was a character of a person analogous to other characteristics like race and gender, as listed in Section 15. Building on this recognition, in 1998 in *Vriend v. Alberta*, the Supreme Court of Canada confirmed equality rights for gay and lesbian citizens. *Vriend* did more than require provinces and territories to acknowledge sexual orientation as a prohibited ground of discrimination in their human rights legislation. It also challenged the Canadian citizenry to develop a broader social, cultural, and political mindset that views members of sexual minorities as true citizens who ought to be able to live, learn, and work free from discrimination in safe and secure surroundings. In truth, *Vriend* has brought Canada to the forefront of a worldwide movement to ensure civil equity and human rights for sexual minority and, at least in the spirit of the Charter as a living document, gender minority persons. It has led to monumental outcomes. Perhaps most notably, the Government of Canada legalized same-sex civil marriage in 2005, making Canada the fourth country in the world to do so after the Netherlands, Belgium, and Spain. These progressive changes represent a move towards a more just and inclusive society for sexual-minority Canadians, a move that must be fully reflected in recasting Canadian education as a more inclusive social institution for transmitting knowledge and values in our society and multiculture. Here the drive to be more inclusive must also encompass recognition and accommodation of gender minority Canadians who do not neatly fit the binary classification of biological male or female.

In this preface, I want to focus on the *Vriend* decision, noting its stunning, positive impact on the quest of sexual-minority Canadians to enjoy the rights and privileges of full citizenship. It is the recent history of Supreme Court decisions like *Vriend*, and the preceding history of sexual-minority stigmatization and exclusion, that all students should learn about as they study the history of Canada. They should know that Canadians categorized as *homosexuals* were considered criminals until 1969, when homosexuality was decriminalized thanks to the daring initiative taken by Pierre Elliot Trudeau in 1967 when he was federal Minister of Justice. It took another 31 years for sexual-minority Canadians to have the force of law deem them citizens with equal benefit and equal protection of the law. Students ought to learn how heroes such as Delwin Vriend and Pierre Elliott Trudeau stood their ground to make Canadian society more inclusive for sexual minorities. Knowing this part of Canadian history is integral to efforts to make Canadian schools more encompassing so all children and youth, especially vulnerable SGM youth, can be open, visible, protected, and accommodated as they grow and develop.

On 6 April 2008, a large number of SGM citizens and their allies gathered at City Hall in Edmonton to celebrate the tenth anniversary of the Supreme Court of Canada decision in *Vriend v. Alberta*. Those present included lesbians, gay men, bisexuals, trans-identified persons, Two-Spirit persons, queers, and others who constitute the spectrum of differences marking sexual orientation and gender identity. Partners, families, friends, and allies were there as well. Such a gathering at City Hall would have been unthinkable in Alberta 10 years earlier. There was electricity in the air as Mayor Stephen Mandel welcomed everyone into a civic space where we now have a presence and a place. What follows is my personal account of this historical day. As someone who was a teenager still in junior high school when homosexuality was decriminalized, I found the experience deeply moving. Here I recall and reflect on this important anniversary as I consider what the *Vriend* decision means for Canadian culture, society, and education.

Moderator and lawyer Julie Lloyd opened the event by referring to the *Vriend* decision as "that spectacular thing that happened ten years ago." Indeed the Supreme Court of Canada decision was amazing: it changed the fabric of Canadian society by providing equal benefit and equal protection of the law to sexual-minority Canadians. This was unequivocal recognition of our inherent dignity, recognition that said Canadian law would not tolerate assaults on our integrity in workplaces or in the other social and cultural contexts in which we live and mediate our lives. We are now legally able to sustain ourselves as citizens and social beings. Moreover, we can make provision for those in our constructions of family to whom we are committed and for whom we are responsible. As Lloyd related, we can now redress discrimination and enjoy the rights and privileges of Canadian citizenship. Since the *Vriend* decision, changes in law and legislation have provided such basics of civility as same-sex partner benefits for employees, spousal pensions, and, since 2005, recognition of same-sex civil marriage. In keeping with the inclusive spirit inherent in the Canadian Charter of Rights and Freedoms, the Canadian mosaic now contains the vibrant rainbow colours that symbolize sexual-minority diversity and presence in our culture and society.

What led to the striking Supreme Court of Canada decision in *Vriend v. Alberta*? In essence, as Lloyd noted, it was the courage and tenacity of one gay man who fought a seven-year battle in the courts for himself and for other sexual-minority persons. As organizers of the tenth anniversary celebration noted in advertising the City Hall event, this fight constituted "Alberta's Stonewall." This was a reference to the Stonewall Inn in New York where the global battle for gay liberation began in 1969 (D'Emilio, 1992). Lloyd declared that Delwin Vriend's personal and political battle provided testament to *the power of one* to refuse to back down or retreat from injustice. His battle inspired a galvanizing grass-roots phenomenon. It became a rallying point for sexual-minority people who had historically experienced exclusion from the Canadian mosaic, which has long been a metaphor for the apparent value placed on recognizing and accommodating human differences in constituting Canadian democracy.

Vriend's battle began when he was fired from his position as a laboratory instructor in introductory chemistry at King's College (now King's University College), a conservative Christian college in Edmonton where he had been employed since 1987. Before he was fired, Vriend had not been out (openly gay) at work, saying his personal paranoia had led to a self-imposed exile in his workplace. He had told his parents about a year before his dismissal. At the City Hall gathering, Vriend described telling them as a relief-filled process that took an incredible few days. He related that although they were members of the Dutch Reformed Church and had questions, his parents also had a caring bottom line: "You are our son." Having grown up in a family culture that did not put up with injustice, Vriend found strength in the support of his accepting family.

Vriend was also out at his church, and he was visible in Edmonton's gay community. At one point he and his parents attended a Gay and Lesbian Awareness conference, which led to his name appearing in an *Edmonton Journal* article about the conference. Vriend described this exposure as the beginning of the end. When the college president confronted Vriend about his same-sex orientation, he acknowledged that he was gay. As Vriend recounted, the president responded by telling him that the practice and promotion of homosexuality was not consistent with the Christian mission of King's College. Appallingly, this educational leader, in the sorry fashion of so many who take an anti-gay stance, reduced Vriend's being and integrity to what he perceived as some sinful sexual act. Vriend's disclosure led to the college's Board of Governors to enact a policy culminating in Vriend being asked to sign a letter of resignation on 28 January 1992. He refused and was fired. Unfortunately, as Vriend soon found out, he had no protection under the human rights legislation in Alberta. In fact, Vriend told the audience, the Alberta Human Rights Commission had received instructions from the Conservative government of the day not to help him.

In the face of such iniquity, the Gay and Lesbian Awareness Society of Edmonton (GALA) mobilized a supportive constituency of citizens for justice for Vriend. GALA was spurred on by what invited discussant and GALA member Murray Billett described as the collective will and just anger of the city's sexual-minority community. As Vriend related, GALA provided him with the moral and financial support to move his case forward. Vriend persisted with the case, following two tenets learned from his parents: stand up for what is right and speak your mind. Vriend won his case in the Alberta Court of Queen's Bench. However, the Alberta Court of Appeal subsequently overturned that ruling. Vriend then appealed his case to the Supreme Court of Canada. Supportive interveners included the Alberta Civil Liberties Association, the Canadian Bar Association, the Canadian Human Rights Commission, and the Canadian Jewish Congress. Lawyer Lyle Kanee, another invited discussant at the City Hall gathering, related that the Canadian Jewish Congress was there because its members were deeply concerned about Vriend's experience of intolerance and lack of protection due to under-inclusive legislation. The Congress feared that what had happened to Vriend in his job could happen to any member of any minority, including Jewish Canadians, who compose about 1 per cent of the national population.

The Supreme Court of Canada began hearing the case on 4 November 1997, issuing its decision in *Vriend v. Alberta* on 2 April 1998. It found that the Individual Rights Protection Act, Alberta's human rights legislation at the time, violated the Canadian Charter of Rights and Freedoms. The Supreme Court ruled that sexual-minority individuals could not be excluded from provincial or territorial human rights legislation. In effect, the Supreme Court ruling granted equality rights to sexual-minority Canadians. This decision was groundbreaking. Yet for Vriend, to whom all Canadians valuing equality are indebted, the lengthy court case had taken a tremendous personal toll. Remembering that 2 April day, he declared, "It was a hell of a morning." He said that everyone had gathered at his lawyer Sheila Greckol's office to await the decision. However, he could not go into the office. Vriend heard the cheer from outside, and he cried. He just knew that he would experience more social malice, more days of hell in the wake of the decision. His premonition became an actuality in the subsequent media frenzy and the vitriolic backlash of so many Albertans, including members of the provincial Conservative cabinet who made hateful comments about sexual minorities. This bigoted contingent was not ready for, and as a matter of fact rejected, the new Charter-induced Canadian reality of providing equal benefit and equal protection of the law to sexual-minority Canadians. Billett remarked that their overt public vitriol provided clear evidence that homophobia was rampant in Alberta. For Vriend, a reserved person drawn into the vortex of gay activism, the toll was cumulative. He had carried the personal and professional burden of the province's failure to protect him in his workplace, and he had also carried the weight of seven years of court proceedings. The backlash following the Supreme Court decision was probably the last straw. Vriend moved away to seek anonymity and a private life in San Francisco. Home in Edmonton wasn't home anymore.

The public hell that Vriend experienced exists in other forms today. Despite significant changes in law and legislation that protect sexual minorities, changes in Canadian society and its schools, which replicate a heteronormative and genderist status quo, have been slow. Beauchamp (2008) provided evidence of this in a report for the Canadian Centre for Justice Statistics. Drawing primarily on results from Statistics Canada's 2004 General Social Survey (GSS), she related that lesbians, gays, and bisexuals – the GSS focused only on these three sexual minorities – were 3 times more likely than heterosexuals to have experienced discrimination. Indeed 44 per cent of gays and lesbians and 41 per cent of bisexuals indicated they had experienced some form of discrimination in the previous five years compared to 14 per cent of heterosexuals. Furthermore, these sexual-minority groups had experienced violent victimization including physical assault, sexual assault, and robbery at a rate nearly 2.5 times higher for gays and lesbians and 4 times higher for bisexuals than the rate for heterosexuals. Beauchamp's analysis also related that age was an important relationship of power in this case: 15- to 24-year-old youth were 6 times more likely to be a victim of a violent crime than individuals aged 55 and over. Beauchamp noted that some of the factors contributing to the violent victimization of youth were more common among lesbian, gay, and bisexual youth. Comparative contemporary statistics from diverse sources are presented throughout this book.

At the City Hall event, Vriend alluded to the vulnerability of youth to violent victimization from a personal perspective. He said that he worried about his nieces and nephews in light of the media coverage of the tenth anniversary of the Supreme Court decision in his case. He was concerned about what might happen to them because there will be those in their schools who will know that he is their uncle. Vriend was right to worry. Schools remain dangerous places for so many students, including SGM children and youth, those perceived to be members of sexual and gender minorities, and children and youth with SGM parents or relatives. Most schools in Alberta and across Canada continue to replicate a heteronormative and genderist status quo that finds a particular manifestation in the silence and inaction that surround unchecked sexism, heterosexism, genderism, and homo/bi/transphobia. The substantial work that remains to be done was brought home to me in a most profound way when a teachers' association conducted a complaint appeal committee review of a case in which a student was violated by incessant homophobic bullying that was particularly virulent at his school when the student was in grades 6 and 7. I had been called as an expert witness during this review. Our goal was to redress the injustice the student experienced because the bullying had continued unchecked. Following is an excerpt from the impact statement that the student read at the review, shared here with his and his mom's permission. The brave youth's heartfelt words speak profoundly to the need for school boards, schools, principals, and teachers to be held accountable (1) to develop policies that respect and accommodate SGM students and (2) to implement these policies so they find expression in everyday schooling, including curricular, instructional, and other social and cultural practices.

They told me, "Sticks and stones may break my bones, but names would never hurt me." Whoever wrote that was definitely not in my shoes. I never got a "hello." Instead I got "faggot," and for four years that word was something I tried to ignore – but years of torment are hard to forget. I smiled, I laughed, but most of the time I'd cry. I'd cry before school, at school, and after school. I'd cry before I even got home so my parents wouldn't have to ask me what was wrong. I told myself I wasn't who they belittled me to be, but confidence doesn't come easy for a kid. I was always watching my back and keeping note of all the things they'd say to me in class. When the coach asked for the class to split up into boys and girls, I didn't fit in with those two categories: "Hey fag, what are you doing in the boys' line? You're not a boy." It was even worse when my so-called "friends" wouldn't even stand up for me. Being at my school was absolutely, positively the worst experience of my teenage life. Transitioning from elementary to junior high with the same kids every year made it impossible to get away from the names. As the years progressed, the names from their mouths became bruises from their hands. I remember vividly the shoving into lockers and sand kicked in my face.

I remember getting garbage thrown at me during lunchtime, and I remember the blank look on the teachers' faces when I was being harassed. I feel like this experience robbed me of the person I could have become. This entire process has ruined family vacations, relationships, and just overall my faith in people. I hated myself for the longest time. I was insecure, depressed, and I just longed for a way out. Yet even now, to this day, those memories cross my mind and I still shudder at the horrific names I hear that remind me of my time there.

Sadly, the complaint appeal committee felt the case did not warrant a hearing. Subsequently, the mother and her son, by then a high school student, filed a complaint with the human rights commission in their province. While the investigation indicated that the student had been deeply affected by homophobic bullying and discrimination, and should receive damages for the assault on his integrity, there were no real consequences for the school, school board, or those who had violated the student's identity as a sexual and gendered person. As is too often the case with such complaints, the school board as a respondent agrees to pay the complainant a small financial settlement in return for the victim's silence and a release from all liability. In this and similar cases, such an inconsequential settlement is little recompense for years of experiencing symbolic (such as name-calling) and physical (such as bruising) violence. It accentuates the importance of making schools a focal point and a frontier in the civil rights movement for sexual and gender minorities in Canada. Despite the strength of the Canadian Charter of Rights and Freedoms, and the laws and legislation it has engendered to provide sexual-minority Canadians with many rights and protections, there is still much work to do to ensure SGM children and youth are treated as persons and full citizens in our schools. In this regard, schools and the groups with a vested interest that shape their cultures and climates have a duty to respect these students, to ease their hurt and pain, and to help them grow into resilience as functional and functioning, loved and lovable human beings. Moreover, they have an obligation to exercise an ethic of care, teaching SGM children and youth in age-appropriate ways that Canadian law and legislation provide protections for *all* citizens, even the youngest and most vulnerable. In a country where individuals rights and institutional rights are subject to Charter respect and protection, let's hope that those involved in schooling will work with that reality and fulfil their duties and obligations so SGM students will fully experience fairness, justice, inclusion, safety, and security.

A Postscript: Fifteenth Anniversary of the *Vriend* Decision

On 10 October 2013, Delwin Vriend returned to Edmonton to mark the fifteenth anniversary of the decision in *Vriend v. Alberta*. He participated in a panel discussion moderated by lawyer Julie Lloyd and hosted by the Centre for Constitutional Studies, University of Alberta. Recounting the aftermath of being fired, Delwin stated that he managed to get through it somehow after he cleared out his college office and went home. Much of what Delwin shared was really about steeling his life as he ran an anti-gay gauntlet for much of the 1990s. The media barrage appeared incessant. He related how the ringing of a telephone can still trigger intense anxiety for him and how he has a history of migraines. Still he felt he has gained from his adversity and trauma, with the "bad thing" of being fired producing much good. He described his firing as the ultimate "outing" experience, which was ultimately wonderfully freeing. Today he keeps his gay character visible, and he does not hold his tongue about being who he is. He had this advice for SGM persons in the audience: choose visibility, take responsibility, and follow through. When a situation warrants it, file a complaint with a human rights commission and be done with relative anonymity. Truly, Vriend's journey exemplifies steeling life and becoming resilient through determination and persistence.

While the *Vriend* decision is, at its core, about citizenship, it is also about personhood, humanity, and feelings of being, becoming, and belonging for SGM Canadians. The ruling made it clear that a particular sexual orientation and, by inference, a particular gender identity are not qualifications for citizenship but characters of persons to be recognized, respected, and accommodated. The *Vriend* decision emphasizes this: SGM citizens, regardless of sex, sexual, and gender differences, are Canadians, with the rights and responsibilities of citizenship in our nation. The *Vriend* decision is now a substantial part of Canadian history. For sexual-minority Canadians, the *Vriend* decision is now a primary marker in deliberations that link our full citizenship to the preservation of our dignity, integrity, and worth as human beings, persons, and citizens. The spirit of inclusion it has engendered should permeate classrooms and corridors so SGM students know hope and the possibility of better and safer schools. This will take more than the incremental educational policymaking requiring Canadian principals, teachers, and other interest groups to be there for SGM students. Unfortunately, there is still a pervasive disconnection between written policies and lived inclusive and ethical practices in many of our schools. While this huge gap remains, there is still much work to do to ensure Canadian schooling truly includes and accommodates sexual and gender minorities.

About This Book

In Canada, teacher education programs and in-service professional development have historically failed to provide sufficient attention to topics including sexual orientation, heterosexism, gender identity, genderism, heteronormativity, homo/bi/transphobia, and the sexual and mental health of SGM youth (CPHO, 2011; Luecke, 2011). Indeed most training programs in education, counselling, public health, and medicine fail to use core curricula as pedagogical sites to prepare caring professionals to work competently with SGM youth in professional contexts and as allies (Case & Meier, 2014). One can argue that medical education, and health care by default, do harm to sexual and gender minorities as a result of ignorance of and inattention to this population. Shelton (2013) provides this evidence: "In 2011 the Stanford School of Medicine's Lesbian, Gay, Bisexual, and Transgender Medical Education Research Group surveyed 175 medical schools in the United States and Canada and found that 33.3 percent of respondents spent zero instructional hours on LGBT health and that, on average, these institutions offered five hours on LGBT issues" (p. 90). Moreover, there has been little research focused on SGM comprehensive – physical, mental, and sexual – health issues, with SGM youth, the rural and suburban SGM population, SGM persons of colour, low-income SGM individuals, bisexuals, and transpeople among those under-researched (Shelton, 2013). This vacuousness in training and research disengages the notion of caring from professionalism, jeopardizing comprehensive health for a diverse and underserved SGM population.

Recognizing this dire scenario, this book provides knowledge and understanding of SGM issues and concerns that can assist caring professionals to become inclusive practitioners who act ethically in relation to the SGM children and youth who need them. Matters of policymaking and its monitored implementation in caring professional practices are core concerns of this book about SGM youth in Canada. In addition to being a resource for those professionally engaged in contemporary work with sexual and gender minorities, *Growing into Resilience* is a timely transdisciplinary text for use in caring professional preparation. It is a comprehensive text for use in university and college courses that focus on the policy and practice dimensions of working with vulnerable youth populations, especially historically disenfranchised SGM youth.

The book is an encompassing text, highlighting complex systemic and structural issues that impact the inclusive education and comprehensive health of this population. It is also a useful text that school boards, teachers' associations, and other caring professional associations can use to guide professional development of staff working with the increasingly visible, multivariate SGM youth population in schooling, health care, and other institutional and professional contexts. Focusing on stressors, forms of risk taking, assets, signs of thriving, and their impacts on SGM youth, the text is instructive for courses in education, psychology, social work, nursing, and other areas of study and practice that train caring professionals to work with youth presenting an array of needs and concerns. It is also informative for courses focused on ethics and social justice in education, health care, and other institutional contexts. *Growing into Resilience* is an insightful resource for those concerned with the social, cultural, and political impacts of systems and structures on the individual development and socialization of SGM youth as they struggle for recognition and accommodation in education and health care as core Canadian social institutions. The book provides critical perspectives as it challenges readers to be there for SGM youth to help them steel life, grow into resilience, and be at promise as citizens who will move Canada forward as a truly inclusive social democracy. In the end, I hope the book inspires each reader's own critical action in relation to each of these life dynamics. For vulnerable youth like SGM youth, steeling life is learning from experience and building an arsenal of individual, caregiver, family, and community assets to help them deal with future adversity and trauma. Growing into resilience is using this arsenal of assets to enable thriving as the pinnacle of learning to cope with stressors and the consequences of risk taking. Being at promise is mobilizing one's abilities and capacities while recognizing that being at risk is not an end point but a starting point, where challenges can be met by garnering resources and supports to help make life better *now*. Enabling these life dynamics is at the heart of what it means to be a caring professional.

André P. Grace, PhD
Canada Research Chair in Sexual and
Gender Minority Studies (Tier 1)
Professor, Department of Educational Psychology (EDPY) and
Director, Institute for Sexual Minority
Studies and Services in EDPY
Faculty of Education
University of Alberta

Acknowledgments

I would like to acknowledge the support of the Social Sciences and Humanities Research Council of Canada in enabling me to write this book based upon research conducted with standard research grant support. One profound way in which that support has been actualized is in the substantive efforts of the committed graduate and undergraduate students who worked with me as research assistants. For their enthusiasm and dedication, I would like to thank Alexis Hillyard, Cory Dawson, Kelcey Pregizer, Lindsay Herriot, Jeffrey Hankey, and Kristopher Wells. Kris, who assisted me in writing the chapters in part 2 of this book, is now an assistant professor working in the Institute for Sexual Minority Studies and Services.

GROWING INTO RESILIENCE

Sexual and Gender Minority Youth in Canada

PART 1

Steeling Life in the Face of Adversity

Part 1 of this book positions growing into resilience as an ecological process influenced by experiences in personal, social, and environmental contexts. In examining this process, it considers how sexual and gender minority (SGM) youth navigate stressors and risk taking, build human and material assets, and show signs of thriving. In sum, it explores how SGM youth steel life in the face of adversity. As the following four chapters indicate, the process of growing into resilience is complex and non-linear, still requiring much empirical research to clarify its dimensions. To help build understanding of this process, the chapters are accompanied by an appendix that presents an emergent typology, providing a synopsis of research on resilience from the 1980s to the present. With understandings of resilience as a concept, construct, process, and outcome still emerging, the appendix provides a synopsis of developing knowledge about stressors, risks, assets, and indicators of thriving using an ecological framework that surveys complexities impacting how vulnerable youth grow into resilience.

To understand resilience as a dynamic, interactive process today, Rutter (2012) suggests we start by recognizing that there is immense heterogeneity in individual responses to physical, psychosocial, and cultural adversity, with some people doing better than others as they mediate a comparable level of difficulty and distress in navigating an environment. Moreover, he maintains that a negative individual experience can have either a sensitizing effect, increasing vulnerabilities, or a steeling effect, reducing vulnerabilities. Rutter asserts that having a steeling effect is linked to feeling one can succeed, which can result in a better coping response and opportunities for problem solving in the face of a future experience of adversity or distress. From these perspectives, steeling life is about building an arsenal of assets that enable SGM youth to cope successfully and thrive as they deal with difficulties in everyday life. As a dynamic, steeling life is about becoming less vulnerable in the face of historical, social, cultural, political, and economic factors that can relegate individuals to the social periphery, where marginalization, stigmatization, and disenfranchisement are common markers of vulnerability. Steeling life is about transgression and transformation of individual, social, and environmental conditions that feed nihilism, which is a sense of helplessness and hopelessness that stifles the desired outcome of individuals attempting to live a full and satisfying life. In the case of SGM youth as a complex and vulnerable population, steeling life is about promoting and advancing their self-efficacy, which involves having a strong belief in their abilities and capacities to do better and to be relatively successful change agents wherever possible in their own lives, in the lives of their peers, and in the family, school, health-care, and other sociocultural environments they inhabit (Rutter, 2012). As they steel their lives, SGM youth can grow into resilience.

For an overview, chapter 1 discusses sexual and gender minorities as a multivariate population. It provides a synopsis of how this population has been positioned in historical and cultural contexts in Canadian society. The chapter positions resilience as a concept, a construct, a process, and an outcome, laying the foundation for the discussion of growing into resilience in the rest of part 1. The chapter closes with a synopsis of the qualitative methodology used with SGM youth as research participants and key contributors to knowledge building in this book. Chapter 2 provides a detailed discussion of gender identity and its spectral nature or endless variations within a male/female continuum. It discuss how this contemporary topic is in urgent need of extensive empirical research as we witness a gender surge in education, health care, and community programming such as that which the Institute for Sexual Minority Studies and Services (iSMSS), University of Alberta, offers. The chapter compares conservative (generally deficit-based) and progressive (affirmative) treatment modalities for children and their families, and it deals with social, legal, and other complexities marking the construction of gender today. With education, health care, and other institutions historically providing little or fragmented attention to SGM youth, as chapter 2 and other chapters demonstrate, chapter 3 discusses iSMSS's flagship youth program, Camp fYrefly, which, for more than a decade, has provided community-based social and health education that SGM youth have historically not received in schools and other social institutional contexts. The chapter on Camp fYrefly exemplifies our solutions-based approach to programming for SGM youth in the face of the failure of school districts and schools to do an adequate job of recognizing and accommodating SGM youth. This discussion sets up chapter 4, which explicates the need for school districts and schools (as a composite, contemporary civil rights frontier) to be proactive in initiating stand-alone SGM policymaking and its implementation in caring educational practices that make schools safe spaces for SGM students. Chapter 4 also examines policymaking in health care as well as education, and it provides guidelines for ethical practices across these caring professions.

Found narratives, which I created from transcripts of interviews with SGM youth involved in iSMSS programming, are strategically interspersed as "InterTexts" throughout the book to introduce readers to themes, issues, and concerns that youth emphasized in conversations with iSMSS researchers. The InterTexts, which can be used as case studies in coursework, are positioned as triggers interplaying with chapter discussions of research, policy, and caring practices.

InterText 1

Mara: *Learning to Own Gay*

Mara came out as a lesbian at 14, telling her friends as a prelude to telling her parents. She is a strong, vibrant, and very articulate person who is able to think on her feet. She saw the aftermath of coming out to her parents as an affirming process. Mara has a supportive network that includes her family and friends. She doesn't include teachers as an integral part of that network, doubting their capacity to deal with gayness. She takes great strength and direction from the arts, which she sees as a support and an asset in steeling life. For Mara, the arts can be a means of catharsis and a coping mechanism. When she talks about coming out, Mara situates it as an ecological process that has been about her, her school environment, and her family, friends, and a special mentor. When she talks about growing into resilience, she speaks to the importance of having people that care about her and love her regardless as the foundation for moving forward.

I was aware that I was definitely interested in women at a very young age. It is something that never bothered me. I never thought I was abnormal, and I never thought of hiding. My parents always indulged me with very sexless toys. I always had a lot of Lego. From a young age, I loved science and animals. I still love animals. I'm wearing my animal T-shirt right now. For me, there were never gender constructs. I was very lucky that I have a liberal family who raised me in a very conscientious way. When you reach the age of puberty, you see that everyone is noticing people. I think it was at that point that I really came to terms with the fact that I am a lesbian. It never really bothered me. Still I knew I had to put it into context and figure out how to address it with the people around me. I wasn't so worried about my parents because they were good and fairly open. After all, I'm their kid. Maybe there were signs, but I'm not entirely sure.

I came out to my parents at 14. I was going on a date and I needed a ride. I just blurted it out. I love my parents dearly, and I know they love me very much. Still I was confirming a facet of my personality I had not addressed before. I was really throwing them a curveball. I had told friends first because I felt that it was very important to have a social network to support me. I had read that you should have a place to stay for a few days because there are situations where you are asked to leave. I really do trust my parents, but I wanted a safety net. Plus I could test the waters by telling friends. It was definitely in anticipation. When I did tell my mother, she just looked at me and said, "Really?" I don't think that she was surprised. Still I gave her no warning. She was brushing her teeth and I came up behind her and said, "I need a ride." She asked, "For what?" I said, "So I can see my girlfriend." She was just blank. She was trying to take it in and, for all intents and purposes, I was still a child – her child. And maybe it was a little bit earlier than she had expected me to date. After a while, she said, "Well alright then, but this is new to us." I thought it probably shouldn't have been. Yet, for the most part, she took it very well. A few weeks later she was still trying to get her head around it, and she still needed to talk to me.

I felt guilty for not telling my parents earlier, and I'm still trying to come to terms with that. I feel that I owed them a better explanation because I just came out in a way that was really quick, really dirty, and really nonchalant. I really should have sat down with them and made sure they were comfortable. I should have been there to answer questions that night. I felt selfish. Later I did have good chat with my mother. She asked a lot of questions, which I tried to answer to the best of my ability. I didn't come out to my father. My mother told him, and that's actually what I asked her to do. I felt that he would take it better from her. Fortunately, he took it very well, too. And then my mother did a lot of research, which is her way of dealing with something new. She bookmarked websites, she got me pamphlets, and she called friends. That's just how she works. That's just how she operates. I saw all this as a process. I saw my father helping out, which was amazing because he's a very quiet person who finds it hard to address really serious issues. But he was involved, too. To see all this happening was such a validation. It showed me that they want to understand. They want to support me. They want to make sure that I feel comfortable. I think that I am just so unbelievably lucky because I know this is not the case for everyone who comes out.

My family and friends have supported me. Beyond that, the most influential person in my life was actually a summer camp counsellor. No teacher helped me like he did. Still I had an all right time with middle school in Ontario where I was in an enrichment program. It was super academic, and it was something that, for me, was quite indulgent because it allowed me to learn a lot in a short period of time. That being said, my school was a very low budget facility. The school was understaffed. For the most part, I felt that my teachers were fairly absent. There was a lot of homophobia, which wasn't really addressed until my eighth grade year. For me, how they addressed it was absolutely bizarre. A teacher was leading us through a school survey, which was not an anonymous survey. I guess the teachers were expecting students to put ridiculous things down because we were 12-year-olds. One of the questions was "How do you identify sexually?" This question really took me aback because I was well aware that I identified as a lesbian in the eighth grade. Yet I thought, "Do I really want to share this with the faculty here?" While I felt that the faculty had been very considerate of my academic needs, they had not really dealt with my social needs. So I left the space after that question blank. It was not something I regret doing, even though I am always one for filling out forms and giving as much information as possible. I felt they might not be able to deal with me as a young student who already identified as a lesbian. They might not have training to do that. So I didn't let them know who I was in middle school.

Now I'm in high school. I am tremendously lucky to go to an arts high school and one that has a very prominent GSA [gay-straight alliance] and very out gay teachers. Even so, gay topics tend to be addressed in the GSA, but not so much in the classroom setting. While the school is known as the "gay school," there are issues. For the most part though, gay is something that is quite tolerated, but there are always exceptions. Still the school generally works for me because of the focus on the arts. In fact, my sense of belonging there has everything to do with the arts, which I have always found quite compelling.

Earlier I mentioned a camp counsellor who was quite influential in my life from age 8 to age 13. I consider him to be a role model. He was an alumnus of my high school. He had a tremendous effect on me. He was a fascinating man and I got to meet his partner. He was openly gay, even in the community setting working with children. I had never seen this before. He introduced me to writing. He was always lending me books. He would tell me, "If you ever get the chance to go to the arts high school, do the writing program. You will love it. I see a lot of myself in you." That was really nice. That experience was a good gateway into the arts. As well, getting involved in arts programs has always been encouraged in my family. My sister is in musical theatre. I've always loved the visual arts and literary arts. They have been the two things that I always fall back on, and it makes such a difference. For me, the arts are a coping mechanism. There is a lot of anxiety with coming out, accepting yourself, and dealing with people and the community around you. Whether it is regarding sexual issues or not, writing is a way of decompressing. It is a form of catharsis. Whether it's a social issue or a queer issue, it lets you get a problem out of your head. When I put something on paper, I feel like I've accomplished something. Then I can keep on going. It's always been that way for me because I'm a perfectionist. Writing lets me take something up and put it down. I can reconstruct an issue and look it over with a fine-toothed comb. It helps me to turn things around. It gives me a greater sense of who I am.

Camp fYrefly has been a space where I can say out loud what I write. I can't say that I have been necessarily comfortable sharing some things, but I don't mind bringing them up because of the situation. It feels safe here. There is a definite sense of learning from other people's experiences. Still you can feel guilty for just kind of putting it out there and putting it on everyone's conscience. I worry about that. Maybe that's because, by nature, I'm an introverted person. If I had it my way, I would be holed up all day with a book. Still I remember my days in middle school. Being alone there, being quiet, and being in my own world were some of the most miserable times in my life. Though being like this made me feel safer and more comfortable, I was without people. And regardless of how much I chose to spend time on my own, we are social animals. At this camp, I am making an effort to meet as many people as I can. I am trying to come across as friendly and positive because you need to know that people think well of you. You want people to have your back and care about you, even in the smallest way. As far as being resilient goes, you have to know that people care about you and love you regardless.

In the future, I would like to help queer children and youth to be resilient. I am really interested in child psychiatry. Even as I read now, I am really interested in helping children who identify as being born in the wrong body. There is a serious backlog of issues in medicine when it comes to dealing with the queer community. For me, psychiatry is fascinating, and paediatrics is fascinating. There is this huge debate going on right now about children who are younger and younger coming out and identifying as the opposite gender. There is this huge ethical and moral debate regarding how you deal with that. There are many questions. What should medical professionals be expected to do? What is the right thing to do? What are you determining for your child? What is your child determining? Who is listening? It is just so fascinating. I've done a lot of research about this. It's something that I want to pursue because there is no hard and fast answer. Obviously, going through medical school, going through what seems to be two specialties to get to a single, very focused point of research is a lot of work and a very high and mighty goal. But it is something very important. There is just no answer for these children right now. It's something that needs to be addressed, and something I would love to do. In the end, it is important for me to be a compassionate person. I feel for other people and, for the most part, I have a lot of faith in other people. In my darkest moments I need to know that there is always something good about the people around you, and I need to know that you can always find that good.

InterText 2
Vincent: *I'm Passing*

Vincent is a 19-year-old trans male who likes to play with gender and appear androgynous. He is growing comfortable with the person he is, and he is less affected by what other people think. As he begins his transition using hormone blockers, Vincent is happy with his progress, especially changes in his voice as it drops. He has clinical and social supports on his journey to becoming and being male. He is mediating a life where he is living independently, going to school full-time, and working many hours to sustain himself. Vincent is a strong person who is building a male identity that involves physical, physiological, and emotional changes for him. Although it is not easy for him, he deals with the dynamics surrounding acceptance and accommodation in family, work, and university as he steels life in the primary social sites in his everyday life.

I am transitioning to male, but I don't like being hyper-masculine. I find I dress really girly, but I don't act really girly. I like to be seen as kind of a gay boy. It's really funny because, at work, I'm in uniform and I get "sir" about 85 per cent of the time and "ma'am" the rest of the time. Before it would have upset me, but now it's kind of amusing. For the most part I'm passing as male these days, and I like it. During the last month my voice has really started to drop. I think that's the main indicator of maleness for people. Sometimes customers will come up to me and address me as female, but once they hear my voice, they often say, "Oh, I'm sorry." I find this so interesting because I'm still dressing the same and wearing the same clothes. Now that I'm passing more, I'm more comfortable. Before when people didn't take me as male at all, it would upset me. Even when I wasn't on hormones, I was always working towards being male.

Right now I have some supports. There are a couple of doctors I see at this general clinic. It's more of a walk-in clinic, but I always make appointments. I don't have time to attend a youth group because I go to university full-time, I live on my own, and I have to work a lot of hours to pay my rent. I used to see a psychiatrist and I did go to youth group, but I've kind of grown beyond these supports. Because I'm quite busy, one of the doctors I see is helping me get a hook-up with a teleconference to learn more about top surgery. Just that alone, even though it's a small thing for her, is really helpful for me. It's nice that she is there to do that – to look out for me and help me through the steps.

Because I'm so busy, I can't plan ahead for anything. It all happens as it happens. My mind is always very occupied. But work is great. I have a manager who is really chill. I still have my legal name, the birth name that my parents gave me. It shows up on my paycheques. I'm sure he's noticed it, but he's never asked me about it. I don't think it's a case of him thinking, "Oh, it's too awkward for me to ask." I just think he doesn't really care. I'm a good employee. He calls me Vince because that's what other people at work call me. And he calls me *he*. I like that who I am is not something I have to worry about at work.

It's important to have supports, to have people that I can talk to as I transition. There's a youth worker I can always go to when I really need to talk. Most of the time though, I usually go to see my mom when I am upset about something. Sometimes just being around her makes me feel better. She's a comfortable person to be around and I feel I can talk to her. Still it was weird when I first came out to her as trans. She said, "Oh yeah, I could see it. I've always known." Then about a year later when I started getting serious and wanted to go on hormone blockers, she had a little freak out. She told me, "Well, I thought it was just a phase." We got into this huge fight where she said, "No matter how much you transition, I will never call you 'he.'" It's been a while now and she's finally calmer about it. Early on, she told a psychiatrist in a session, "Oh, it's like my child has died and I guess I'm mourning." Now that it's been a while and she sees that I'm still me, that I'm still here, she's definitely more chilled out about it. She's even calling me *he* sometimes now. And she calls me Vincent, which is good. That's the name I want to be called now. My dad is still more "la, la, la" about it. He calls me Vincent, but he still uses the female pronoun. I just let it slide because he's different from my mom. I have to deal with him differently.

This year it's really nice to be at Camp fYrefly because I've been locked up in my suite doing homework when I'm not working. So this is like my vacation. I love it because I haven't been around many people for a while. I first came to camp when I was 15. I was an insecure kid shy about getting involved in the workshops. This year though I'm definitely into being a part of them. Last year when I was a pod leader, I had a youth in my group who was really nervous at first. I encouraged him and eventually he really opened up. It was really great. I'm still trying to be a cheerleader this year. To be totally submersed in this experience with so many people for four days is a great experience. You need to take in as much as possible while you have the chance. For me this year, it was really important to talk to some of the other trans guys because I know some of them have already had some surgery. Since I'm going for my assessment soon, I wanted to know about the kind of questions I might have to answer. Even though I already have some idea of what's going to happen, getting that insight is helpful because I'm nervous about having to go for an interview. I know it won't be a problem because I'm already on hormones and I'm coping. Plus I'm doing a lot with my life without a lot of outside support day to day. However, it feels like they're going to ask me questions and judge me. I know it's something I shouldn't worry about, but it's a natural thing to worry.

I have lots of dreams for the next few years. I want to go to a different city and a different university, hopefully a better one. I want to get my undergraduate degree in fine arts, and I want to go on and get my master's degree. Hopefully, I can make it as an artist. However, even some of the professors I know who are doing amazingly well in their careers as artists still have to teach. So maybe I'll do some teaching, which is fine by me since I see it as a kind of leadership. I would be supporting the next generation of students. Maybe they can have better experiences than I've had. For example, I'm in the process of legally changing my name right now. However, at my university, the name that my parents gave me at birth appears on class lists. Even though I'm known by my preferred name, Vincent, I've had a number of incidents in my classes where the instructor calls out my current legal name when going down a class list. I would just be there frozen in class because I have no idea what to say. I don't want to put my hand up in front of everyone and say, "Yeah, that's me!" I'm trying to go by Vincent.

Even though I'm sometimes exhausted and sometimes frustrated these days, I'd still say I'm doing pretty good. Sometimes I just want a break because I haven't had a day off in months. But it's not that bad. I feel I've been gaining a comfort zone, which I think is very important because at one time I was in a psychiatric ward for self-harm. I was 16 or 17. At that time I wanted nothing more than to have hormone blockers. It was a huge thing and I was absolutely fraught over not having it. There's a thing in the medical system that if you're suicidal or depressed they won't give you anything until you prove you're stable. At the same time it was not having hormone blockers that made me unstable. Once I was on them, once that ball was rolling, I just picked up speed. I became much happier. I have a plan and now that plan is being fulfilled.

1 Making It Better *Now* for Sexual and Gender Minority Youth

Sexual and gender minorities comprise a demographically complex and multivariate population, as indicated by the LGBTTIQQ2SA acronym used by WorldPride 2014 organizers in Toronto (Armstrong, 2014). The acronym, which stands for "lesbian, gay, bisexual, transgender, transsexual, intersex, questioning, queer, two-spirited and allies," is the current iteration of an ever elongating list of descriptors that becomes harder to remember as the politics of naming extend who is included (Armstrong, 2014, p. A1). Acronym constituents, and as yet unnamed others in this spectral population, have minority status because of differences in sexual orientation or variations in gender identity and expression that fall outside heteronormative categorizations of sex, sexuality, and gender, as well as outside the dichotomies of the male/female and heterosexual/homosexual binaries (Grace, 2009a, 2013a). Countering this long-standing, lockstep way of compartmentalizing sexual and gender minorities in heteronormative, genderist culture and society, in this book sexual orientation basically refers to one's sexual feelings and affection for one or more persons that can change over time, while gender identity is understood as one's self-identification, self-affirmation, and expression of gender that either fits or transgresses conventional male and female gender categories (D'Augelli, 1994; Ehrensaft, 2011, 2012, 2013; Grossman & D'Augelli, 2007; Perrin, Cohen, Gold, Ryan, Savin-Williams, & Schorzman, 2004; Savin-Williams, 2005, 2008).

As the research shared in this book demonstrates, we live with a paradox in our country: although there is a persistent stereotype that Canadians are nice people living in a peaceful nation, it is pitted against the realities of incessant heterosexism, sexism, genderism, and homo/bi/transphobia in everyday culture and society. Youth like Mara and

Vincent, as well as other youth introduced in the InterTexts, wonder who they can trust and how they can navigate family, workplace, health-care, and other social environments where sexual and gender differences meet a dominant and entrenched sociality. Still there is a trend to make changes in legislation and in educational, health, and other institutional policies that respect and accommodate sexual and gender minority individuals in living, learning, and working contexts in our country (Grace, 2005a, 2007a, 2008a; Grace & Wells, 2005; Lahey, 1999; MacDougall, 2000; Rayside, 2008). This trend notwithstanding, heterosexism, sexism, genderism, and homo/bi/transphobia are still pervasive retrograde antisocial forces that threaten the safety and security of SGM individuals and do damage to our health and well-being in Canadian culture and society. In fact, backlash against us is a usual corollary to our legal, legislative, and institutional progress. Mainstreaming queer can be costly in individual and social terms. Even SGM activists and cultural workers with the time and privilege to politicize queer must interrogate ways their efforts contribute to the backlash, putting the more marginal members of the SGM community at risk. This backlash may be particularly virulent in local communities where anti-SGM narrow-mindedness can be rampant. Shelton (2013) explains, "Indeed, the more LGBT men and women make strides at the national level, the less safe many individuals feel in their own communities. These advances turn the spotlight on many families [with SGM parents and/or children], and the unwanted recognition is complicating their lives, and for some even exposing them to danger" (p. 14). Clearly then, headway in lawmaking and institutional policymaking does not dismantle hate, with SGM families providing a focal point for the virulence of homo/bi/transphobia (Shelton, 2013). Safety and inclusion of a queer sociality as an accepted part of a larger sociality of recognition, respect, and accommodation may even be forfeited as homonegativity – discrimination, contempt, and hatred targeting sexual and gender minorities – escalates. For example, as Shelton (2013) relates in a US context, progress in the national gay civil rights movement runs parallel with the emergence of anti-SGM splinter professional organizations. This is also the case in Canada. For example, REAL (Realistic, Equal, Active, for Life) Women of Canada (2014), which is a pro-family conservative women's interest group formed in 1983, exclusively supports the traditional heteronormative family and considers variation from this norm to be a threat to society, albeit the heterosexist and genderist one they value. In recent years, they have set their sights on transpeople,

reducing the ontological state of being trans – or occasionally trans*
in this book, both of which are used as shorthand for the spectrum
of trans-identity categories (Marx, 2011) – to something fantastical or
pathological. In opposing Bill C-279, the trans human rights bill, in a 4
June 2013 media release, REAL Women of Canada (2013) erroneously
reduced trans identity to a problematic sexual activity, conflating gender identity and being in the world with engaging in sexual acts. In
their misinformed declaration opposing trans civil rights in Canada,
they included the usual rightist comparison to paedophilia, which is
a common rightist bullet fired in the culture wars on queer in general.
With transpeople so maligned, Shelton (2013) points out that the real
danger to children is systemic. In Canada, it comes from organizations
like REAL Women of Canada that disparage trans citizens. Shelton
adds that disadvantage and negative consequences for transpeople are
compounded when they are poor, undereducated, persons of colour,
or marked by other subjugating relational differences. As well, Shelton
notes that factors like the lack of community support systems and the
parochialism endemic to small-town and rural communities exacerbate
difficulties that transpeople face as they and their children navigate life
in schools and communities.

Such realities are indeed problematic for SGM youth, whose age and
sexual and gender differences render them vulnerable and targeted in
a homo/bi/transphobic culture. Furthermore, these realities are fed
by ignorance and fear that can lead to symbolic violence (such as stereotyping and anti-SGM name calling and graffiti) as well as physical
violence (such as bullying, including assault and battery). In considering these realities, this book focuses specifically on the multivariate
SGM youth population and their space and place in institutional and
community contexts in Canada. It considers stressors, risk taking, asset
building, and signs of thriving – see the emergent research typology
in the appendix – that mark the lives of SGM youth in their quest for
recognition, respect, safety, and accommodation in families, schools,
health-care settings, and other life spaces where they mediate everyday living. The book explores contemporary realities of SGM youth in
a post-Charter Canada, where SGM citizens still struggle to ascertain
individual rights that the Canadian Charter of Rights and Freedoms
guarantees. It examines the challenges that SGM youth face in mediating life and its complexities in the Canadian culture-knowledge-
language-power nexus. However, it does so within a politics of hope
and possibility that insists life can be better *now* for SGM youth as they

steel life by building assets to grow into resilience. These politics constitute a much needed counter-force to what can be perceived as the death
of hope in the wake of the rash of completed gay male youth suicides
in Canada and the United States in recent years (Grace, 2013b). When
there are too many stressors and risks to deal with, it is fodder for SGM
youth to ideate about, attempt, or complete suicide as an ending to an
unhappy and unbearable existence, however unchangeable that ending
would be.

The ongoing *It Gets Better* campaign has been trying to address this
dilemma (Savage, 2012). However, this campaign may only be a signifier that it is not really getting better in culture and society and in our
schools, which are expected to replicate the hetero-patriarchal, genderist status quo. What the phenomenal growth and impact of the It Gets
Better Project (www.itgetsbetter.org) indicates is the pervasiveness of
the problem of youth suicide. Started by Dan Savage (2012) in response
to the suicide completions of two teenage males – one gay and one perceived to be gay – the initiative was intended as a project of hope, with
thriving queer adults reaching out to joyless, despondent teenagers
who wondered how they might survive to live another day. The ongoing project is about keeping SGM youth alive. It is about exposing and
smashing homo/bi/transphobic bullying and not letting it continue to
be a silent, unnoticed killer. It is about helping SGM youth to transgress
the pain that is part of living with queer differences, which too many
citizens still perceive to be cancerous anomalies of the human condition. It is about being able to imagine and being able to think about possible and desired futures. It is about caring SGM and allied adults no
longer waiting for the permission that schools have long denied those
who wish to speak to and mentor SGM youth. It is about transgressing heteronormativity, heterosexism, sexism, genderism, and homo/
bi/transphobia in all their exclusionary complexities. It is about being
there for *every* SGM youth, especially when they are vulnerable and
feeling isolated. Savage (2012) provides a synopsis describing how,
historically, an anti-SGM culture works, damaging sexual and gender
minorities and holding us hostage as youth and as adults:

> The culture used to offer this deal to lesbian, gay, bisexual, and transgender
> people: You're ours to torture until you're eighteen. You will be bullied
> and tormented at school, at home, at church – until you're eighteen. Then,
> you can do what you want. You can come out, you can move away, and
> maybe, if the damage we've done isn't too severe, you can recover and

build a life for yourself. There's just one thing you can't do after you turn eighteen. You can't talk to the kids we're still torturing, the LGBT teenagers being assaulted emotionally, physically, and spiritually in the same cities, schools, and churches you escaped from. And, if you do attempt to talk to the kids we're still torturing, we'll impugn your motives, we'll accuse you of being a pedophile or pederast, we'll claim you're trying to recruit children into "the gay lifestyle." (pp. 5–6)

To counteract the damage from this torture, teachers, health-care workers, and other caring professionals have an obligation to meet the needs of SGM youth as a vulnerable population. In the work to help these youth lead full and satisfying lives, this duty has to be grounded in a professional ethics that sets aside private morals tied to hetero-centrism, genderism, and homo/bi/transphobia. Indeed our collec-tive goal should be to help SGM youth to grow into resilience and be at promise. This book locates growing into resilience as a non-linear, asset-building process of steeling life and eventually thriving through experiencing ups and downs. So they can become resilient and at prom-ise, SGM youth need mentoring and support to (1) develop a sense of purpose focused on thriving in the face of adversity and trauma; (2) engage in an ecology of learning whereby they develop a sense of commitment to self, others, and their living environments; (3) enhance their comprehensive – physical, mental, emotional, sexual, social, and spiritual – health; and (4) counter a damaging kind of individualism caught up in nihilism (a profound sense of hopelessness and helpless-ness) and the neoliberal tendency to blame individuals rather than systems and structures (Grace, 2013a, 2013b, 2013c). The latter focus is important because SGM persons are still suspect and are subject to systemic fracturing which is morally scripted within a conservative cultural disposition that uses tradition as a mask for homo/bi/trans-phobia. This fracturing is exacerbated by heteronormative and gender-ist structures, strictures, assumptions, prescriptions, and stereotypes that are reinforced by ignorance and fear of sexual and gender differ-ences. As a barrage, these are the systemic bullets that increasing num-bers of today's SGM youth deflect with determination and certitude that are inspirational, transgressive, and potentially transformative, enabling them to steel life and be at promise. This expanding contin-gent of at-promise SGM youth is getting the support and resources they need to grow into resilience and thrive. However, there are still many vulnerable SGM youth who are trying to muster the energy and assets needed to survive in core life spaces that are unsafe and unsupportive. They need resources and supports, including peer support from the growing cohort of proactive, creative, and engaged SGM youth, propelled by resistance to histories of hurt and the desire for better lives. This book shares some of their stories as interview excerpts and as illuminating found narratives included as InterTexts between chapters.

The book takes up the issue of peer support in chapter 3, which examines Camp fYrefly. The summer leadership camp for SGM youth that Kristopher Wells and I co-founded in 2004 emulates the ideal of truly inclusive schools. Youth peers and adult mentors work with campers, fortifying them in word and in action to help them deal with stressors and risk taking. Camp fYrefly sends a clear and important message to SGM youth: each of you is at promise, and you can be, become, belong, and behave as a person whose sex, sexual, and gender differences are gifts adding texture and beauty to the person you are inside and in the world. To make this message real, the camp employs a model that focuses on asset building and affirming youth as at-promise individuals with abilities and capacities. This focus on being at promise challenges us to interrogate the notion of being at risk. Indeed the preponderance of research on SGM youth has been focused on the impact of stigmatization and associated negative health and educational risk factors (Russell, Muraco, Subramaniam, & Laub, 2009). However, there is a void in research understanding the mechanisms and contexts shaping risk as a concept and as an outcome to overcome (Russell, 2005). With the mainstream cultural tendency to stereotype at-risk youth as deficient, delinquent, disenfranchised, and disaffected, the "at-risk" label has been symbolically violent and dismissive, although many youth do not internalize the label or see it as personally meaningful or accurate (Foster & Spencer, 2011).

What is all too frequently ignored in practice and research, and what this book takes up, is the potential and desire of SGM youth to be at promise so they can be, become, belong, and thrive as agents of change in their own lives and in their social environments. At the end of the day, youth want to be strong navigators of ecologies where they interact with community members and environments. As they grow into resilience, two key engines driving this process are a sense of purpose and self-esteem (Galligan, Barnett, Brennan, & Israel, 2010). Today there is more research investigating those SGM youth who thrive despite negative or hostile home, school, faith, or family environments (D'Augelli, 1998; Friend, 1998; Goldstein & Brooks, 2005a, 2005b; Grace, 2009a;

Grace, Dawson, & Hillyard, 2010; Grace & Wells, 2005, 2007a, 2007b, 2007c, 2009; Savin-Williams, 1994, 2005). This newer trend in research is important. Continually positioning SGM youth as at risk has tended to pathologize these youth as victims. Certainly, deficit discourses have been limiting, keeping the focus solely on SGM youth as vulnerable and in need of being saved from themselves (e.g., as victims of suicide ideation and drug and alcohol abuse) and from others (e.g., as victims of homo/bi/transphobic bullying). This negative focus is detrimental to youth agency and to possibilities for transformation of the heteronormative and genderist social environments they have to navigate (Marshall, 2010; Rasmussen, Rofes, & Talburt, 2004; Russell, 2005). It erroneously positions vulnerable SGM youth as the problem.

Historically, SGM youth have been blamed for simply being who they are because their sexual and gender identities and expressions do not fit the hetero-patriarchal casting of sexuality and gender. However, it is hetero-patriarchy itself that is to blame, inculcating heterosexism, sexism, genderism, and homo/bi/transphobia as everyday dangers for SGM youth. These days we need to tear down hetero-patriarchal systems and structures that damage and even destroy SGM youth as they mediate their lives in homes, schools, health-care facilities, and communities. This is urgent work, as indicated in chapter 7, which discusses the comprehensive health of SGM youth who are coming out and coming to terms with their differences at younger ages. In this regard, families, group homes and other alternative living spaces, public and faith-based schools, health-care facilities, and communities have a clear social responsibility to provide these youth with the amenities and supports they need to grow, develop, and be healthy, happy, and hopeful. Historically, these social institutions have acted to hold youth accountable. However, they should only expect youth accountability when they have respected youth and given them room to grow and develop within the context of the sexual, gender, and other relational characteristics that make them whole and special. There are dire consequences when core social institutions attempt to package SGM youth in heteronormative acceptability. Rather than blame SGM youth for their queer existence and social predicaments, families, schools, health care, and other institutions might begin by examining ways that they have collectively harmed, hurt, and even humiliated these youth. The way forward begins with institutional knowledge building, understanding, and transformation that abet youth development and their transformation through recognizing, respecting, and accommodating their personal differences.

The Canadian Culture Wars

I live in Alberta, a province where, historically, the forces of social and political conservatism have been relentless in targeting sexual and gender minorities. As social and cultural outsiders and castaways, we have perennially struggled to live with the torment and fragility that mark our existence in the intersection of the moral and the political. For us, everyday living has involved mediation of the stereotypes, rumours, presumptions, exclusions, and hostilities that mark us as unwanted and unwelcome in hetero-patriarchal society and its heterosexualizing, genderist culture. The disadvantage that sexual and gender minorities have experienced in Alberta has been replicated in comparable insidious forms across the country. Recently, for example, as discussed in chapter 8, which focuses on establishing gay-straight alliance (GSA) clubs in Canadian schools, the Catholic Church unsuccessfully led resistance to Bill 13, the Accepting Schools Act, which passed in the Ontario Legislature on 5 June 2012 (Artuso, 2012; Canadian Press [CP], 2012a). This anti-bullying bill requires public schools and publicly funded Catholic schools to permit students to establish GSAs (Howlett, 2012). What the Catholic Church's disdain for Bill 13 demonstrated is a limited sociality in its schools as well as the operation of a politics of cultural invisibility that erases gay, motivating youth resistance and activism. Advocating for one-size-fits-all social policymaking and rejecting the idea of a stand-alone SGM policy so Catholic school districts could provide direct protection and accommodation for SGM students, the Catholic Church hierarchy and its school trustees attempted to minimize or erase the need to focus explicitly on homophobia and transphobia in schooling. In an effort to dissociate itself from homo/bi/transphobic violence, the Catholic Church persisted in using the "antigay lite" tactic (Shelton, 2013, p. 25), which is "to annihilate *homosexuality*, not homosexuals themselves" (Shelton, 2013, p. 24, italics in original). In the end, the Bill 13 episode highlighted the conundrum of gay for Catholic schools, which are publicly funded but not public in the sense of being fully SGM-inclusive. Within Catholic theocracy committed to a restrictive heterosexist and genderist sociality, it appears impossible to reconcile the integrity of a heteronormative faith that valorizes social action with the integrity of "homosexuals" whose individual rights are protected in Canada, as stated in Section 15 of the Canadian Charter of Rights and Freedoms (Grace, 2007a). Although the term "homosexual" has a long-standing history of being associated with pathology in medicine and culture, the Catholic Church still uses this term and refuses to use the descriptor "gay," although the church recognizes sexual minorities, referring to us as persons with same-sex attractions. The church also works within the restrictions of the male/female binary, refusing to acknowledge gender minorities and their affirmed (as opposed to assigned) genders. This dismissal of trans is addressed in chapter 2. As shown in this chapter, social institutions have often blamed transgender and gender-nonconforming individuals for what they see as the predicament of not choosing to belong within the confines of the male/female binary, as though one's gender identity can be refused or eradicated. This modus operandi denying the spectrum of gender possibilities is creating great challenges if not crises for education and health care today. Acknowledging what now seems to be "a gender swell," Ehrensaft (2013, p. 9) speaks to the importance of children and youth being able to deal with gender conundrums so they can emerge as authentic and affirmed gender selves. She maintains it is vital that gender-nonconforming and trans individuals be gender healthy and supported by nuclear and extended families, therapists, endocrinologists, school principals, teachers, and other significant adults who protect and advocate for them.

Social conservatives in the Catholic Church hierarchy could take a lesson in inclusive Christian teaching from Bishop Gene Robinson, an openly gay bishop who was elected to lead the Episcopal Diocese of New Hampshire in 2003. Bishop Robinson (2012) advocates for SGM youth who want to live in the fullness of their spirituality and SGM differences. He tells them, "God loves you the way you are. God doesn't want you to change. God doesn't want you to be cured or healed, because there's nothing to be healed from. You are the way you are, the way God made you. And the way God loves you" (p. 31). Such messages value youth so they can be strong and at promise.

Symbolic violence in a religious context has been complemented by pronounced symbolic and physical violence in the larger Canadian culture. This violence has left many SGM citizens emotionally and psychologically damaged, injured, maimed, or dead (Janoff, 2005). Today enough is enough. SGM activists and cultural workers now refuse the life-eroding boundedness of living in the intersection of the moral and the political where communities and ostensibly caring institutions in the realms of education, health care, and religion still largely fail to accept and accommodate us in the fullness of our humanity (Grace, 2007a, 2008a, 2008b). As a spectrum of disenfranchised groups, sexual and gender minorities seek to transgress and transform life in this intersection as we confront the complexities of change, institutional and community cultures, and civil society in order to have full and satisfying lives (Grace, 2013a, 2013b, 2013c). In this regard, the efforts of so many determined SGM youth have been spectacular. For example, chapter 6 provides insights into how three Canadian gay and bisexual male youth mediated their identities in transgressive and transformative processes of being, becoming, belonging, and acting in their schools and communities. Each youth created a democratic space where SGM peers could engage in a politics of voice and visibility as they countered an engrained hetero-patriarchal school culture marked by rampant and dangerous homo/bi/transphobia. These youth engaged in queer critical praxis to counter anti-SGM forces and affirm their identities. This was a strategic process of planning action, building allies, reflecting on the outcomes of actions taken, and regrouping (as necessary) to act again.

Still, that SGM youth survive and thrive is a miracle. They have been perennially and variously unsafe in family, school, health-care, and community environments in this country. Their nemeses have included conservative governments and churches that give them little status as persons, citizens, students, Christians (or other faith designators), and human beings. In my home province, for example, this was made clear in the debacle in 2009 surrounding efforts of the provincial Conservative government to entrench Bill 44, which amended provincial human rights legislation to include sexual orientation as a specifically named category. While this particular amendment was progressive, Bill 44 also included a regressive parental rights clause, which was added on as an olive branch to appease social conservatives. As Simons (2009) summarizes, this meant that the bill had the potential to "allow parents to pull their children out of any classes dealing with religion, sex education, or sexual orientation, and to receive advance notice of any classroom material dealing with such topics" (para. 6). In other words, Bill 44 served as a legislative control inhibiting diversity in schooling. It created endless possible scenarios for the strangulation of public education in Alberta. Simons (2009) asserts that this happened because social conservatives engaged in "fearmongering, plain and simple" (para. 10). In her estimation, this perceptibly positioned socially conservative politicians and religious leaders as bullies interfering in the democratic process by which Bill 44 would recognize, once and for all, that sexual minority Albertans are persons and citizens, too. Certainly, Bill 44 has not threatened religious freedom, as social conservatives who apparently are not Charter savvy conjectured. By now, as the chapter 5 discussion of the

Marc Hall prom predicament and its politicization indicates, it should be crystal clear, based on Supreme Court of Canada pronouncements, that the Canadian Charter of Rights and Freedoms unequivocally protects religious freedom in our country. Alongside this protection of institutional rights, the Charter also protects individual rights. And in keeping with Section 1 of the Charter, one does not have primacy over the other. This creates a dilemma for the Catholic Church, which has always upheld its constitutional right to institutionalized Catholic schooling in Canada. As noted in chapter 5, the Catholic Church's constitutional right to have its own schools has intensified deliberations regarding the individual rights of students in those publicly funded schools. Indeed this positions Catholic schools as a contemporary frontier in the queer civil rights movement in Canada, where separation of church and state is a core democratic principle. Thus those Catholics committed to denominational schooling will continue to be challenged.

As mentioned in the preface, lesbian and gay Canadians and, in the spirit of the Charter as a living document, all SGM Canadians have equality rights emanating from the Supreme Court of Canada decision in *Vriend v. Alberta* in 1998 (Grace, 2007a). In the wake of this decision and culminating changes in federal and provincial/territorial laws, all that sexual and gender minorities want is accommodation of our rights as Canadian citizens to be safe in our life, learning, work, and worship spaces, and to be free from prejudice and discrimination. In sum, beyond the concerns, fears, and even moral apprehensions that culture, society, and various interest groups may have, it is becoming quite clear that queer or gay is not going to go away and that Canada's educational, health-care, and other institutions have to become more responsive and responsible in meeting the needs of SGM youth. Therefore, chapter 4, which discusses the importance of policymaking and its implementation in caring practices in education and health, shows an urgent need for more and better institutional policies that attend to sexual and gender differences in ways synchronized with the tide of positive legislative changes recognizing, respecting, and accommodating the rights of sexual and gender minorities in Canada (CPHO, 2011, 2012; Grace, 2007a, 2013b). Moreover, there is a pressing need to ensure that these policies are implemented in safe, caring, and inclusive practices.

Resilience: A Concept, a Construct, a Process, and an Outcome

Ryan2: I just decided it was easier to shake it off than worry about it. I don't know when I decided that, and I don't know how I decided that.

It's just something that I did. Ever since then, if people don't understand being gay I can try to help them understand, if they're willing to listen. But if all they're going to do is make judgments, I don't need that. I'm better than that.

Locating resilience as an emergent concept in my research, I understand it to be a multidimensional, non-linear, and fluid construct, and I develop the notion of *growing into resilience* to indicate its changing nature. This process is about capacity building, successful adaptation, and sustained competence in the face of stressors and risk taking; it involves building assets and mobilizing strategies to enhance signs of thriving in the everyday lives of vulnerable youth who have had to deal with stressors, threat, adversity, and trauma (Bogar & Hulse-Killacky, 2006; Bowleg, Huang, Brooks, Black, & Burkholder, 2003; DiFulvio, 2011; Hauser, 1999; Luthar, Cicchetti, & Becker, 2000; Masten, 2001; Masten, Best, & Garmezy, 1990; O'Grady & Metz, 1987; Rutter, 1987, 1999; Testa, Jimenez, & Rankin, 2014; Werner, 1995; Wexler, DiFulvio, & Burke, 2009; Yates, Egeland, & Sroufe, 2003). Growing into resilience "is a dynamic developmental process" that "is clearly not a static state" (Luthar et al., 2000, pp. 546, 552). It "is never an all-or-nothing phenomenon" (Luthar & Zelazo, 2003, p. 516). The process can be viewed as ecological since growing into resilience means individuals increase their capacities and abilities to deal with biopsychosocial aspects of development, situational barriers, and environmental (climate and cultural) contexts (Herrenkohl, Herrenkohl, & Egolf, 1994; Luthar & Zelazo, 2003; Masten, 2001; Ungar, Brown, Liebenberg, & Othman, 2007).

There is a growing volume of interdisciplinary research from psychology, social work, education, and other fields that investigates resilience as a multifaceted concept, process, and outcome (D'Augelli, 1998; Goldstein & Brooks, 2005a, 2005b; Grace, 2013a; Savin-Williams, 2005; Testa et al., 2014; Ungar, 2010, 2011; Wexler et al., 2009). Emerging research on growing into resilience has located resilience as a more intricate process that accounts for individual development in the intersection of relationships of power. This research highlights how SGM individuals build strengths, capacities, and assets, which are influenced by biopsychosocial factors, the dynamics of advocacy, policy and practice interventions, and protective factors that enable processes of steeling life and growing into resilience (Bottrell, 2007; Brokenleg, 2010; Brown & Colbourne, 2005; DiFulvio, 2011; Foster & Spencer, 2011; Gabarino, 2005; Galligan et al., 2010; Gastic & Johnson, 2009; Glicken, 2006;

Goldstein & Brooks, 2005a, 2005b; Masten, 2001; Mustanski, Newcomb, & Garofalo, 2011; Reyes & Elias, 2011; Thompson, 2006). Here resilience as a construct and process "can be understood as the capacity ... to deal effectively with stress and pressure, to cope with everyday challenges, to rebound from disappointments, mistakes, trauma, and adversity, to develop clear and realistic goals, to solve problems, to interact comfortably with others, and to treat oneself and others with respect and dignity" (Brooks, 2005, p. 297). For Ungar et al. (2007), steeling life "is about finding a way to 'hit your stride' and live with relative comfort despite contradictions and conflicts: to continue to negotiate and navigate one's way through the challenges one is experiencing" (p. 301). These researchers, like Rivers and Cowie (2006), see steeling life and growing into resilience as involving multiple pathways that individuals traverse depending on their social and cultural locations.

There is an array of internal psychological resiliency factors associated with self-understanding, self-labelling, self-acceptance, and self-reflexivity that enable youth to grow into resilience. These factors are associated with coping, quicker recovery in the face of stressors and challenges, and better physical and mental health; they include happiness, hopefulness, self-esteem, self-confidence, spirituality, a sense of humour, and believing that one can control one's unique life and solve problems (Bowleg et al., 2003). When present and coupled with environmental factors such as access to educational, health-care, and other social resources and information and a sense of value and support in community settings, they assist SGM youth in engaging in head-on problem solving, which helps them become healthier (Lock & Steiner, 1999). As well, healthy mentors or role models from outside the family, including SGM-identified teachers, counsellors, health-care workers, social workers, and clergy, can be buffers for vulnerable SGM youth, who can emulate their strengths, social skills, good behaviours, and abilities to mediate different environments (Cagle, 2007; Gastic & Johnson, 2009; McCabe, 2014; Pepper, 2012; Rak & Patterson, 1996; Scharrón-del Río, Dragowski, & Phillips, 2014; Southwick, Morgan, Vythilingam, & Charney, 2007).

Increasingly, research on resilience explores the self-confidence, social competence, and other characteristics of resilient youth as well as the assets – including a strong internal locus of control and social problem-solving abilities – that these youth need in order to recognize and deal with adversity and trauma (Anderson, 1998; Brooks, 2005; DiFulvio, 2011; Elias, Parker, & Rosenblatt, 2005; Luthar, 1993; Pianta & Walsh,

1998; Reyes & Elias, 2011; Russell, 2005; Rutter, 1985; Testa et al., 2014; Ungar, 2010, 2011). Contemporary research has three important aspects: (1) it views growing into resilience as a non-linear process; (2) it recognizes that youth may experience stress and setbacks along the way; and (3) it indicates that subsequent exposure to and successful mediation of stressors and challenges can have steeling effects (Carbonell, Reinherz, & Giaconia, 1998; Lock & Steiner, 1999; Masten et al., 1990; Meyer, 2007; Rak & Patterson, 1996; Rutter, 1985, 1987, 1993, 1999, 2006; Scourfield, Roen, & McDermott, 2008; Ungar, 2010, 2011). To be sure, there is a significant relationship between growing into resilience and positive SGM identity development (Adams, 2006; Reyes & Elias, 2011). However, more research is needed to help us understand how variously positioned SGM youth discursively negotiate the meaning of resilience by identifying what they count as stressors, risks, assets, and positive outcomes (D'Augelli, 2002, 2003; D'Augelli, Grossman, & Starks, 2006; Fergusson & Horwood, 2003; Grossman & D'Augelli, 2007; Grossman et al., 2009). More research is also needed to help us understand how an ecological approach to researching resilience locates growing into resilience as an intricate process affected by the culture and contexts in which SGM youth live (Brokenleg, 2010; Este, Sitter, & MacLaurin, 2009; Goldstein & Brooks, 2005a; Liebenberg & Ungar, 2008, 2009; O'Dougherty Wright & Masten, 2005; Reyes & Elias, 2011; Ungar, 2008, 2010, 2011). Speaking to the need to study ways a cultural context can innervate growing into resilience, Ungar (2010) challenges us to ask a core question: "Whose definition of privilege is most privileged?" (p. 434). This requires us to look at resilience as a multivariate cultural construct that can involve "many different paths to [adaptive skill building and] positive development in stressful social ecologies" like families and local communities (p. 434). As he conceptualizes it, an ecological approach is one that decentres the individual as the problem and focuses on cultural, structural, and systemic factors that influence vulnerable children and youth and impede their comprehensive health and development. Relatedly, an ecological approach requires more research exploring the impacts of proximal and distal environments on growing into resilience and more research on why the majority of SGM individuals grow up to be healthy and productive despite variously mediating heterosexism, sexism, genderism, homo/bi/transphobia, and the expectation of heterosexuality (Filbert & Flynn, 2010; Freitas & Downey, 1998; Case & Meier, 2014; Hall, 2007; Heck, Lindquist, Machek, & Cochran, 2014; Pepper, 2012; Russell, 2005; Sharkey, You, & Schnoebelen, 2008).

Further research is needed to investigate the efficacy of a resilience framework for working with SGM youth navigating different social ecologies (Alessi, 2014; Mustanski, Newcomb, & Garofalo, 2011; Wexler et al., 2009). This should demonstrate how resilience may be different in the academic, personal, social, emotional, and other spheres of an individual's life (Gastic & Johnson, 2009; Herrenkohl et al., 1994; Hill & Menvielle, 2009; Luthar, 1993; Marx, 2011; McCabe, 2014; Shelton, 2013). Since growing into resilience is not something that can be indicated in some all-or-nothing way, it can be presumed that SGM youth, like other vulnerable youth, may be successful in some adjustment domains but unsuccessful in others as they navigate life in various contexts (Cicchetti & Rogosch, 1997; Freitas & Downey, 1998; Jaffee & Gallop, 2007; Luthar, 1993; Luthar & Zelazo, 2003; Reyes & Elias, 2011). Luthar et al. (2000) conclude that the reality that vulnerable youth might "excel within particular adjustment domains should never obscure the possibility of significant problems within other spheres" (p. 554). Thus, in gauging growth into resilience, it is important to examine multiple domains, including personal adjustment, mental health, interpersonal relationships, and social competence as discrete albeit interrelated entities in gauging how SGM youth are doing in terms of everyday coping (Herrenkohl et al., 1994; Luthar, 1993).

The dire state of affairs created by the compounding effects of stressors and risk taking in the lives of SGM youth requires greater synchronicity among research, policy, and practice whereby stakeholders collectively help this multivariate population to build capacity (a solutions approach), moving away from unconstructive strategies focused on stigmatizing or fixing these youth as a source of social disorder (a problems approach) (Liebenberg & Ungar, 2009; Marshall & Leadbeater, 2008). This kind of institutional – health, educational, and governmental – and community synergy can help SGM youth to transgress adversity and grow into resilience. Interdisciplinary research frames resilience as a multifaceted concept, construct, process, and outcome, demonstrating that growing into resilience involves helping SGM youth to discern the personal, social, and environmental assets needed to develop the dexterity to survive and thrive (Brooks, 2005; Deater-Deckard, Ivy, & Smith, 2005; Elias et al., 2005; Fine & Weis, 2005; Gabarino, 2005; Glicken, 2006; Goldstein & Brooks, 2005a, 2005b; Grace, 2013a; Jordan, 2005; Liebenberg & Ungar, 2009; Masten, 2001; Pollack, 2005; Ungar, 2005, 2008, 2010, 2011). Growing into resilience can be viewed as transactional: "In this model, resilience refers to a process in which specific protective influences [or assets] moderate the effect of risk processes within both individual and environment over time in order to foster adaptive outcomes" (Elias et al., 2005, p. 317). Here the emphasis is on building individual, family, community, and environmental strengths so persons can survive and thrive (Fergusson & Horwood, 2003).

Research on growing into resilience evidences that there are certain homogeneous factors – like senses of self-worth and hope, belongingness and dependable attachments, and safety and security – that affect how all youth grow into resilience; it also indicates that there are heterogeneous factors impacting this growth process in SGM youth that are culturally and contextually grounded, including interactions at school and in families, faith groups, and the larger community (Alfonso, Diaz, Andujar-Bello, & Rosa, 2006; Anderson, 1998; Angell, 2000; Bowleg et al., 2003; Carbonell et al., 1998; Carbonell et al., 2002; Clauss-Ehlers, 2008; Este et al., 2009; Fieland, Walters, & Simoni, 2007; Holmes & Cahill, 2004; Liebenberg & Ungar, 2009; McCready, 2004; Meyer, 2007; Munns, 2007; Russell, 2005; Safren & Pantalone, 2006; Sanders & Kroll, 2000; Scourfield et al., 2008; Sesma, Mannes, & Scales, 2005; Timmons, 2006). In other words, SGM youth experience homogeneous stressors, those that mark adolescence in general, and heterogeneous stressors, those particular to their historically disenfranchised and stigmatized locations based on their sexual and gender differences (Fassinger & Arseneau, 2007; Hunter & Mallon, 2000). Regarding the latter, Fassinger and Arseneau (2007) say,

[There is] a constellation of influences on LGBT identity trajectories that are rooted in people's locations along various demographic dimensions … [including] such factors as religion, disability, geographic location, race and ethnicity, and socioeconomic status and social class … These cultural variables interact and serve to differentiate among members within each of the LGBT reference groups because each individual's particular pattern of influences is highly specific and creates a unique context for identity development and expression. (p. 32)

Russell (2005) points out that little is known about these ecological dimensions shaping how sexual and gender minorities grow into resilience. With this in mind, there is a need to investigate the contextual, relational, and ecological factors shaping how SGM individuals mediate their everyday lives (Grace, 2013a; Luthar et al., 2000; Russell, 2005).

It has certainly been challenging to conceptualize and work with resilience as a construct, process, phenomenon, and outcome. As Luthar et al. (2000) relate, "Theoretical and research literature on resilience reflects little consensus about definitions, with substantial variations in operationalization and measurement of key constructs" (p. 544). They add, "There also is little consensus around central terms used within models of resilience. Researchers use terms such as 'protective' or 'vulnerability' factors in varied and inconsistent ways" (p. 546). Thus more research is needed to understand this complexity of contextual and relational factors affecting the balance between risk and resilience and its effects on the individual development, socialization, and comprehensive health of SGM youth. Russell (2005) states, "Research on risk among sexual minorities has been too narrowly focused on specific individual-level negative outcomes. There has been ... very little attention to risk per se (the contexts, experiences, characteristics, or life statuses that lead to risk factors and outcomes) and almost no attention to protective factors or resilience" (p. 8). I would argue that the same goes for gender minorities. Johnson (2008) concludes that we need to place greater emphasis on researching resilience as a protective process whereby individuals build the arsenal of assets and capacities needed to mediate threats and risks to their health and well-being.

In this regard, in exploring growing into resilience as a dynamic and complex contextual, relational, and ecological process, it is important to remember that multivariate SGM identities and their lived expressions are not inevitable precursors to nihilism, depression, suicidal tendencies, or other mental health problems that continue to affect so many SGM youth. Instead it is the interplay of ignorance and fear of these identities in cultures, institutions, and systems that impedes positive identity development, comprehensive health, and well-being by provoking stigmatization, prejudice, discrimination, marginalization, disenfranchisement, and victimization (Brokenleg, 2010; CPHO, 2011, 2012; Filbert & Flynn, 2010; Grace, 2008a, 2008b; Grossman & D'Augelli, 2007; Hunter & Mallon, 2000; Savin-Williams, 2008; Savin-Williams & Ream, 2003; Singh, 2012; te Riele, 2006). As SGM youth grow and develop, they deal with heterocentric and genderist intolerance and bigotry that often frame and permeate cultural and politico-religious reactions to their differences. In immediate ways, SGM youth experience this derision in such damaging forms as internalized homo/bi/transphobia, untenable family and community relationships, and intimidating school and faith environments (D'Augelli, 2002; Meyer,

2007; Russell, 2005). Consequently, SGM youth can experience harm and negative or impeded development as uneven risk outcomes when compared to normatively (as traditionally understood) sexed and gendered youth (Russell, 2005). Signifiers of the impaired individual and social development of maltreated youth include poor self-concept, bad conduct, and negative or dysfunctional peer relationships, which often result in youth being variously unhappy, confused, depressed, anxious, aggressive, and lacking the abilities to cope, adapt, and have control over their successes and failures (Bolger & Patterson, 2003; Bottrell, 2007; Lock & Steiner, 1999). With SGM youth experiencing so much emotional turmoil, it is clearly challenging for them to develop and implement stable working models for mediating life experiences in personal and social contexts (Freitas & Downey, 1998; DiFulvio, 2011; Minter, 2012; White Holman & Goldberg, 2006).

Although considerable empirical data documents the unhealthy and unhappy predicaments of so many SGM youth, more positive change and outcomes are happening. Increasingly, many SGM youth are finding ways to rise like phoenixes from the ashes of stressors, adversity, and trauma. Having been variously debilitated by heterosexism, sexism, genderism, and homo/bi/transphobia, they find ways to transgress systemic and structural forces that impede their development to grow into resilience as a non-linear process of recoupment. While their "experiences with adversity may ... [have precipitated setbacks, they can also lead to] significant personal growth through increasing the depth and complexity in one's life" (Savin-Williams, 2008, p. 137). Thus resilient SGM youth are literally steeling a life. Here significant adults in their lives can enhance their processes of growing into resilience by (1) affirming SGM youths' wholeness caught up in the differences that define them, (2) accentuating their positive individual accomplishments, and (3) complimenting and nurturing their abilities and capacities that contribute to their arsenal of assets, enabling change for the better.

The Research Process: A Synopsis

In engaging SGM youth in research on growing into resilience, I have framed the process using queer critical ethics that interrogate power, oppression, and privilege in the study of societal systems and structures, exclusion, erasure, hurt, history, politics, equity, justice, collaboration, and radical democracy (Cannella & Lincoln, 2011; Grace, 2013a; Greene, 2007; Kincheloe, McLaren, & Steinberg, 2011; Leech, 2010).

These queer critical ethics guided analysis throughout this book. Incorporated interview excerpts and InterTexts emerged from open-ended interviewing that involved follow-up with participants, who had final say during editing of their transcripts. Interview data were analysed and contextualized using the resilience typology – stressors, risk taking, assets, and signs of thriving – delineated in the appendix (Este et al., 2009; Grace, 2013a; Marshall & Leadbeater, 2008).

To conduct this research, I worked with graduate research assistants to engage SGM youth in open conversations to produce knowledge and understanding as ethical and political co-constructions (Foley & Valenzuela, 2005; Kincheloe & McLaren, 2005; Plummer, 2005). Interviewing has been used to good effect in qualitative research focused on SGM research participants, investigating diversity, inclusion and exclusion, justice, and emancipation (Fine & Weis, 2005; Fontana & Frey, 2005; Kamberelis & Dimitriadis, 2005; Morgan, 2001). For more than a decade, a reflexive queering of the interview has occurred in SGM research, in which styles of interviewing and analysis/interpretation recognize particularities of SGM identities, the multivariate nature and complexity of SGM experiences, and the importance of addressing systemic exclusion, including transgressing heterosexism and homo/bi/transphobia (Grace, 2013b; Kong, Mahoney, & Plummer, 2001; Plummer, 2011a, 2011b). This approach informed the nature of questions constructed for interviewing the SGM youth who participated in this research. The focus on queer critical ethics was complemented by a focus (emerging in researching resilience) on including disenfranchised SGM youth voices on ethical grounds within a participatory and iterative process sensitive to the influences of culture and contexts (Grace, 2013a; Liebenberg & Ungar, 2009). From a queer critical ethical standpoint, this means including SGM youth in researching resilience so they might benefit from what is learned from the research process. Here researchers have an ethical responsibility to advocate for these youth as participants with differences who have been historically disenfranchised in institutional and larger community contexts.

The overall research project that I developed to investigate growing into resilience also included (1) autoethnographic research in which the research team examined their interests and biases and (2) policy analysis of documents from education, health care, and federal and provincial/territorial governments (Grace, 2005a, 2007a, 2008c, 2009a, 2013a; Grace et al., 2010). Research shows that employing multiple methods contributes to rigour by producing different kinds of data and providing opportunities to check data for plausibility, authenticity, credibility, and relevance (Denzin & Lincoln, 2011; Este et al., 2009; Fontana & Frey, 2005; Richardson & St. Pierre, 2005). Using multiple methods in research with youth, especially vulnerable youth, helps comprehensively frame research with them; it also helps understand their ways of knowing and representing themselves as they transgress deficit-based frameworks and practices to grow into resilience as creative change agents (Hilfinger Messias, Jennings, Fore, McLoughlin, & Parra-Medina, 2008; Koro-Ljungberg, Bussing, & Cornwell, 2010; Marshall, 2010). It enabled my research team to gather the kind of detail that made possible the range of interview excerpts and InterTexts that support the themes developed throughout this book.

The InterTexts: Narratives on Steeling Life and Growing into Resilience

The InterTexts in this book provide opportunities to explore the individual pathways that 10 of the SGM youth research participants navigated in mediating the ups and downs of steeling life and growing into resilience. The narratives incorporate richly textured accounts of the conversational exchanges recorded in the interview transcripts. The InterTexts offer opportunities to reflect on the complexities and variations marking steeling life and growing into resilience as inextricably linked processes in flux. They are powerful stories, variously recounting stressors, risk taking, assets, and signs of thriving that, in unique combination, mark each youth's account as a story of the particular. Ultimately, the InterTexts are stories of the composite search for self-recognition and recognition by others, self-respect and respect from others, and accommodation in home, school, and community contexts. Along with providing informed consent, research participants wanted their first names used as part of a politics of visibility and agency associated with growing into resilience, a mutable process of steeling life and showing signs of thriving. These SGM youth are brave and insightful individuals who needed to share how stressors, risk taking, and systems and structures in education, health-care, family, community, and other contexts have affected them for worse and for better. As their stories reveal, sometimes these youth are still dealing with adversity and trauma, and sometimes they are moving forward and thriving. These ups and downs all influence growing into resilience. This process may be incremental and, at times, even stalled, but it is a process that moves forward because SGM youth, like all youth, want to be happy, healthy, and hopeful about the future.

InterText 3
Sean: *I'm a Man, Yes I Am*

When I interviewed Sean, I had an extraordinary personal and pedagogical encounter with trans humanity. Sean is a happy constellation of spectral points that shake and stir gender. He is very clear: his core person is a man, and he identifies as a heterosexual male. Still he told me he would always be queer since he is trans. When I asked him to teach me Sean 101, he talked about being a self-directed learner as he absorbed everything he could about female-to-male transsexuality. Sean is strong, focused, proactive, and persistent, and he has a loving family. He recounts how his coming-out letter to his parents provided them with their first trans resource book. He describes his transition as a threefold process: mental, social, and physical. When Sean decided to be himself, he felt time was of the essence. The Internet became his gateway to learning about all things trans, albeit as a cautious engagement. In the narrative that follows, Sean teaches us about trans agency, desire, and acting in the world. He speaks about the importance of having a supportive and accommodating family doctor. He also discusses what he sees as the profound ignorance of trans among medical professionals in general. Regarding schooling, he critiques the value of GSAs for trans youth. Sean is an educator and cultural worker for social transformation so transpeople can have the rights, freedoms, protections, and supports that are part of full citizenship. He has thrived to become a resilient trans youth steeling life in the face of adversity and trauma. Sean is now a very present, self-assured person who wants a career helping others mediate their trans journeys. Here is his story.

It was three years ago, I'd say, when Sean became Sean. I had always felt different from probably the youngest age I can remember. I knew that I felt like a boy. Elementary school wasn't too bad until they started segregating male and female. You have to change for gym class. You're a girl, so you have to go into the girls' change room. It always felt a little strange for me because I just didn't feel like I belonged there. High school was really awkward, super awkward. I started dressing more androgynous, and I kind of dabbled with a boyfriend for about six months. Since all the girls were doing that, I decided that I should probably conform to society and try that out. And yeah, it was different. It was interesting, I guess. And then we went our separate ways. After that I just decided that I wasn't attracted to men. That was grade 9. As high school went by, I realized that I was attracted to women. I never did come out as a lesbian, because I didn't feel like a lesbian. I wanted to have a girlfriend, but I didn't want to be her girlfriend. I wanted to be her boyfriend. In high school no one really talked about that kind of stuff. Even homosexuality was not really discussed.

We had a GSA in our high school, but I never joined it because it was a Gay-Straight Alliance and I didn't feel that I was gay. Clearly I wasn't straight, so it didn't really include how I felt. I didn't really know about trans until 2009 when I stumbled on it on YouTube. I don't know how I came across it, but I discovered my first video of another trans guy. He was pretty much pre-transition at that point and he talked about his experiences, saying he was going to transition. It was like he was sitting there talking about my life. Suddenly, it all made sense. So I started looking into this thing they call transition. I guess I had been exposed to it a little bit prior to this. Male-to-female transsexuals were definitely in the media, but you got the Jerry Springer version. So they were portrayed to me as strange. I never thought, "Oh, they're doing it; maybe it could go the other way from female to male."

After stumbling on this video, I did about a year of research. I used pretty much every spare moment I could find. I read about all the different things that were available to you. It was hard to find Canada-based information, like local Saskatoon stuff, but there were tons of resources in the United States. I pretty much planned everything out – what I wanted to do, what I was going to do, how I was going to go about doing it, and how I was going to come out to my friends and my family. Then I decided that I would write my family a letter. That took me about a month or two. I really wanted to emphasize that my parents weren't at fault for me feeling the way that I feel. I wanted them to know that they were great parents and that I couldn't have asked for a better childhood. I thought writing a letter was a good idea because I was pretty confident that my parents were going to be okay with it. Also, I felt that if I sat down and told my parents, "So I think I'm a boy," then that sentence right there and then would interrupt everything they had known about me. So I wrote them a letter that they could sit down and read numerous times, over and over again if they wanted to do that. I tried to spell everything out in a basic way: what I wanted to do, how I felt, and why I felt this way. I finally gave it to my parents. I guess if they had reacted negatively at first and could be supportive some point down the road, then, by not being in the room when they read it, I couldn't hold their initial reaction against them. Still it went really well, I would say. They said, "We'd like to see you now." When I went upstairs, my mom was crying. She stood up and gave me a hug. She said, "I love you." In that moment I think I realized that I'd taken those three words for granted every single day until then. And so, my transition had begun. That was February 2010 – Family Day in fact. My dad was working in Fort McMurray at the time. He was home for that day, and then he was going away for about two weeks. So I thought, "I'm going to do it now."

My family has been very supportive. I actually have a younger sister, and I came out to her before I came out to my parents. About two weeks before I came out, as I found out afterwards, my sister had asked my mother, "So when do you think she's going to come out as a lesbian?" At this point I was almost a year into researching trans, so I started presenting more masculine. My mom actually said to my sister, "I think she's a boy stuck in a girl's body." She didn't know what the terminology was for it, but she had the general idea. When I did come out to them, I stated in my letter that I wanted to be very open about the transition process with them, that I'd answer any question they had and, if they needed any resources, that I'd be available to provide them either through the Internet, books, or other people I've talked to that are trans in the city. My parents were really cool about it. My dad doesn't say a lot, but my mom actually told me later on that the letter I wrote her was really a good thing to do. She said that as we progressed forward with my journey, she could go back and read the letter. It helped her to make more sense of what was going on. It also helped that I was more open to talking about what was actually going on with me. My mother and I have a much better relationship now because trans is not like this awkward elephant in the room that no one wants to talk about. My learning about trans helped us both.

What drove me to do the learning? Many things. Honestly, once I found out that transition was possible, the size of my chest was a factor. I had a large chest, probably about a D-cup chest, and that was what stopped me from doing so many things when I was younger. It's also a character thing. Usually once I get something stuck in my head, it has to happen yesterday. So I learned because I was frustrated and motivated. Some people wait for others to tell them what to do next, but I never wanted to wait. I found out I could do it. I came out to my family, and they were fine. Then it all started to happen. I mean I did my whole medical transition in less than a year, essentially, which is very fast compared to some people. I was a self-activist.

In June, a few months after telling my family, I had my name changed and I started the process of my physical transition. I saw my GP [general practitioner or family doctor] whom I actually had told prior to telling my family. He wanted to send me for a psych evaluation. I did lots of research before going to my GP, and I basically spelled it out for him: "This is what I want to do. This is how I am going to do it. Are you going to help me?" He had absolutely no idea about anything trans related, so he said, "I don't know anything about it. I'll be up front with you. If I don't think it's going to harm you in any way, I'm on board with helping you reach whatever goal you'd like." That's the answer I wanted, so I told him that I would like to see the gender therapist in Saskatchewan that I had learned about. Then we would go from there. I got a referral sent to her, but it came back that she wasn't even accepting referrals at the time. That left me in a stuck spot, so I asked my GP, "How about we just do it ourselves and see how that goes?" He said, "Well, you still need a psychological evaluation." My GP, whom I had only been seeing for a short time, was helpful in the fact that I was shitting bricks when I first went to see him about this. He was basically the first person I really came out to about being trans. I had no idea about how he would react. And there was the fear of rejection. You don't want the first person that you tell to refuse to see you. He was really helpful. I feel I owe him pretty much the last two years of my life because he was so accommodating. You can't do this without someone who has an MD after their name.

I did see this psychiatrist who knew absolutely nothing about gender in itself. He was of the opinion that this was a sexual preference. I saw him twice and decided that wasn't going to work. However, the psychiatrist did say, "You're clear to do whatever you want. You're mentally competent to make your own decisions." From there I was expecting my doctor to refer me to an endocrinologist, but he seemed to be dragging his feet on making the referral. The top surgeon whom I decided to see for my chest surgery didn't require a psych evaluation, so I saved up the money myself and paid out of pocket for the whole thing. I went to Toronto with my mom, and we were there for two and a half weeks. The trip cost me $9,000, but it's the best money I've ever spent. When I came back, I saw my doctor, who then found an endocrinologist who had no problem with what I wanted. On January 31st, 2011, I had my first prescription for testosterone. That's when my hormone journey began. I had had my top surgery on November 3rd, 2010, so I kind of did everything backwards. Things continued to move forward. I got on a waiting list to have a hysterectomy because I wanted to get that out of the way. I had that operation in October 2011. Then I finally got to see the gender therapist for the first time on November 15th, 2011. So I really did do everything backwards, but it was honestly the best way for me to do it. I don't regret doing it that way at all. It was my choice to go forward. That's pretty much my transition history in a nutshell.

Throughout the whole thing, I definitely faced some drama with medical professionals. I definitely made lots of phone calls to make sure people were doing what they were supposed to be doing, and to make sure referrals were getting sent out. I just took charge of my own transition and was proactive with it. The worst thing that I've experienced with medical professionals throughout this process is probably just sheer ignorance of trans. It also bothers me when doctors have support staff who drag their feet in helping you go through the transition process. For example, when I went to see a doctor in Regina about my hysterectomy, he said he could arrange for me to have the operation in about three months. After three months, I had heard nothing. When I checked with the people who manage the waitlist for the surgery, I found out that the doctor's assistant had not submitted the necessary paperwork. She did submit it after I called her, but when I checked with the people keeping the waitlist for the surgery, it now looked like I would have to wait a year. I was mad. When I called the doctor's assistant again, she wouldn't take my call. So I said to myself, "To hell with you then." I called the doctor's receptionist and left a message directly for the doctor saying, "Honestly, I don't know if you can do anything about it, but here's what's happened." He must have intervened because when I called three weeks later to check where I was on the surgical waitlist, they said, "Oh yeah, your hysterectomy should be in about two weeks." He had obviously made a call and fast-tracked things. I got in on a cancellation three days later. So it worked out because I acted on my own behalf. However, I shouldn't have to check to see if medical professionals are doing their jobs.

Now I'm Sean. Every time I do a workshop, people ask, "Why did you pick the name Sean?" When I was choosing a name, I wanted to stick with my birth initials – A.M.H. – since that's what my parents named me. I chose Aidan for a little while. I didn't use it at home before I came out. I just used it with a few friends to try it out. It didn't work for me, so then I picked Sean. I don't know why. It was a toss up between that and Shane, which are similar I guess. When I did come out to my parents, actually my mom had said, "Have you thought about a name or anything?" I said, "Well, I do like the name Sean, but I want your opinion on it because you should have some say in it." I told them I was thinking about Aidan, but my mom said, " No, I actually like Sean better." That made it a unanimous decision.

The Internet was very important to me throughout my transitioning process. There are definitely pros and cons to using it. As I mentioned, I stumbled on transpeople through the YouTube community. For the past three years, I've been giving back to that community by doing video logs. I started off with pre-transition things and I talked about physical transition. I've moved on to discuss deeper issues like my mental health before I came out to people. I tell people that my transition was first mental, then social, then physical. It's important to talk about all three parts because most people only want to talk about the physical like how much facial hair I have. That's nice, but I mean I'm taking hormones so these things are expected. I want to talk about the more personal side of things so people understand what's going on with me as a person, and not just what's happening to my body. So sharing information on the Internet is a pro. You can find all sorts of information using YouTube, Wikipedia, and Google. The con to this is there's a lot of misinformation spread around on the Internet. So I guess it's like in school when teachers tell you not to just take one source and run wild with it. You need to look at more sources and hopefully get more trusted information. I watched probably 50 YouTube videos of different people going through different stages of their transitions. Then I started doing text research down to reading about taking testosterone and its effects. That learning was super handy because there's a lot of medical professionals that know nothing about transition or the process, or the side effects of hormones, or the side effects of different surgeries. Learning that information on your own is helpful to give someone in the medical profession a baseline to start. Then they can do their own research using probably more trusted references and resource materials to help you make decisions during transition. As far as YouTube and the Internet go, I've talked a lot to trans guys who say, "Oh, I want to take testosterone. It's going to be so wonderful. How do I do it? It sounds cool." Well, yeah, it's cool, but you need to do your research on it. You need to know about the side effects of taking testosterone like your blood pressure going up, cholesterol going up, and liver problems. If you have a hysterectomy and have no estrogen, you can have bone density problems when you get older. Many people don't want to hear about these things. The point though is you need to think about these things before you make changes because it's not just physical appearance that's changing, but it's also everything inside, too. You're ingesting chemicals, synthetically made drugs, and those have effects. Not every drug reacts the same with all people. I try to stress those points when I'm telling people about transition. So I guess the pro is that you can find all sorts of information on the Internet to educate yourself, but the con is that some of those references you're using don't always give you the full story.

I've been out of school for five years now. It was hard to think about trans or to learn about trans in school. Honestly, when I was in high school I would say I was a little bit homophobic, just because I didn't identify as a lesbian. If you were gay, or if you were a lesbian, you go to the GSA group, but I really didn't want to be identified as a lesbian. I didn't want to go to the gay group essentially because I wasn't gay. You walk by it and you kind of peek your head in to see who's in there – the turnout wasn't really ever that good – and you definitely feel you don't quite fit. Of course, I was still figuring out the whole trans thing. It would have been so much better had someone mentioned that trans was possible, like in health class, but no one ever said anything about it. There was nothing about gender identity at all. All I got in high school was basic Gay 101: if you're a girl, and you like girls, you're a lesbian; if you're a guy and you like guys, you're gay; if not, you're straight. That was the extent of the queer education I had in high school. If someone in the GSA had said, "You know what, you can transition," then I probably would've gone to the club because saying that would have acknowledged what I felt like. I think the GSA itself is probably fine. You can call it whatever you like – Queer Alliance, Rainbow Alliance, Gay-Straight Alliance – but it's the fact that many high school youth don't know that there's other possibilities. There are other identities you can take on besides gay or straight.

As I said, I see my transition as having different parts that describe what I've been through. First, there was my mental transition, which is basically the process of coming out to me. It is realizing that you are trans, that this is possible, that there's actually a word for what you're feeling, and that you're not crazy. It's being okay with that and knowing the world is not going to crash. Everyone's been bullied in life, so it's getting over all of that. I think the biggest step for me in my mental transition before coming out was coming to terms with being a man. I realized I felt like a guy and could pass as a guy. However, I asked myself, "Can I be a man in society with all the gender stereotypes like sons are supposed to follow in their father's footsteps?" For example, my dad is a carpenter, but I don't know anything about building a fence or a deck. I know how to drive a car moderately well, but if I get a flat tyre, I'll call CAA [Canadian Automobile Association]. So I wondered if I could pull off being a man in society. I don't know why, but one day it dawned on me: I don't care. I'm going to be interested in what I'm interested in. If I want to pretend to fit all the stereotypes and be this hyper-masculine person, then I may as well not transition because I'm not being true to myself. Going through my mental transition was probably the hardest part, but working through these things was really empowering.

Then there was my social transition. I don't ever want to use the word "lifestyle," but I had to realize that not everyone is okay with trans, with this journey that I'm on. So I had to be okay with potentially losing friends, family, and whoever else wasn't supportive. Getting to a comfortable place with that took a while. Then finally it came to me that I don't care if no one's going to be supportive. I'm going to do it. It's something I need to do. However, I also realized that transitioning is not just something I'm going through. My parents and everyone around me are going to go through it as well. However, it is still something that I need to do for myself. The social transition is all about coming out to people and telling them, "So I'm trans, I'm going to go by Sean now, I'm using male pronouns, and I'm going to be patient with you while you try to get used to those things." Being patient with people is probably the hardest part of the social transition. Getting used to my new name is pretty easy, but pronouns are so subconscious that people really have to be focused on what you're saying to change them. Extended family would say, "I'm going to screw up your pronouns, your name." Once I had physically transitioned, I would tell them, "I haven't seen you in a year. You're going to see me, and you're not going to make a mistake because I don't look anything like I used to look. It's going to be really hard for you to call me 'she' looking the way I do now." So the social transition was probably the second hardest part.

I would say the physical transition was the easiest part because there is nothing to do except wait. Once you get on your hormones and start

your surgeries, then that's kind of the end of it. Of course, the opera-
tions are frustrating, especially if you can't afford them. However,
I made the sacrifice to work in a job for a year where I was discriminated against daily. I tell people we all make sacrifices and we all pay
a price. And it's not necessarily a monetary one. For me though, in the
end it worked out really well. Now I say I don't work there anymore,
they paid for my surgery, and we move forward. The rewarding part is
when you finally see the changes you want to see in yourself physically.
Then you can just start living life, as you feel inclined to do so. I will say
now having done most of my physical transition, I watch other people
setting their goals – their first shot of testosterone or their first surgery –
and I miss having my next goal. At the same time though, it's just good
to be where I am. I would consider myself post-transition now.

Right now, living my life means going to the University of Saskatchewan this fall. I want to pursue a psychology degree. Eventually, I would
love to do a PhD in psychology, but we'll see how realistic that goal is.
I've already done a workshop with the gender therapist, and I hope
to be able to do an internship with her. If you're interested in working
with gender and sexuality, then she's on board because we need more
people in Saskatchewan working in this area. Ideally, I want to work
with queer youth or just queer people in general for a career path. Over
the next few years, I want to find different ways to maintain an identity
in the queer community. When I walk into a building now, people read
me as a guy. It's hard being trans and identifying as a straight male in
the queer community. I'm trying to find different ways to keep myself
involved with the community while keeping my identity. It's probably
the hardest thing that I have to do right now. To the general public, I'm
just a guy that's attracted to women. Obviously, the relationship I have
with women isn't typically heterosexual. It's never going to be. I mean
I'm a trans person, so there's always a little bit of queer there. I use the
term queer very loosely, just kind of encompassing everybody because
I want to be part of that community. I like having my anonymity sometimes, but at the same time I feel very at home with the queer community. I am very comfortable being me.

2 Gender Beautiful: Living in the Fullness of One's Affirmed Gender Identity and True Gender Self

Gender is an ecological creation constructed by the knowing self and sociocultural influences, a beautiful puzzle that can be made and remade, and a construction linking the desire to be one's self-affirmed gendered self to living in the world. It is a complex construction that incorporates biopsychosocial, cultural, and temporal elements:

> A person's gender is no more and no less than a creative individual achievement, and yet it can only develop through social exchange. It is informed by biology, culture, society, and the times in which we live. But it is not clear in what proportions these elements contribute, or whether all these ingredients are totally necessary. (Menvielle, 2011, p. xi)

However it is created, an affirmed gender identity as male, female, or another gender subjectivity is an integral component of our integrity as human beings. People are beginning to acknowledge that growing into gender is an intricate ecological process and construction influenced by history, social expectations, acculturation, geography, and politics as well as by individual reaction and resistance to any or all of these influences. Immersed in this process, the individual thinks gender, engages gender, and confronts the dissonance experienced when birth sex/assigned gender and affirmed gender are asynchronous. This dissonance, which places good comprehensive health and happiness at stake, is a product of genderism that refuses an individual's nonalignment with the male/female binary. Genderism is an ontological assault on trans and gender-nonconforming individuals and their creative expression of being gendered in the world.

Still the gender landscape is changing, with gender being increasingly conceived as something spectral or multidimensional that cannot be contained by the male/female binary. This revision of what gender can be challenges us to rethink what it means to be gender affirmed and gender healthy. Just like a nonconforming sexual identity, a nonconforming gender identity is not point-blank pathological. If there is gender dysphoria, "a strong and persistent ... discomfort and distress with one's birth sex, gender, and anatomical body" (Grossman & D'Augelli, 2007, p. 528), then it is an unwanted way of existing inextricably linked to genderist systems and structures permeating health care, education, and other institutions. It is consequential to the hegemony of a heteropatriarchal, genderist sociocultural framework that has historically prioritized the male and subjugated the female, leaving no in-between space or place for gender variation and expression. This shrinks gender possibility and its construction for individuals for whom the standard male or female categories are not the right fit. These individuals become gender outlaws and cultural captives. Their lives are profoundly affected by genderism and transphobia, which limit gender to male or female categories affiliated with one's birth sex/assigned gender, expect cultural assimilation within the limits of the male/female binary, and tend to result in symbolic and physical violence towards anyone who transgresses traditional gender norms.

It is important to an individual's integrity, understood as respect for one's subjectivities, that one has the right and freedom to construct an evolving and authentic gender self. Gender identity is not a disorder; ultimately, it is an outward expression of what the mind knows and the heart feels. It seems these days there is a gender-identity explosion, at least in Canadian and other Western contexts, whereby possibilities seem limitless within a politics of visibility and hope. In this milieu, it is vital that comprehensive health-care workers, teachers, social workers, guidance counsellors, psychologists, and other caring professionals exercise collective responsibility to help children and youth in processes of social and self-affirmation of their gender identities. The individual and social development of children and youth as gender beings cannot be defined by, or confined to, the gender expectations typically associated with birth sex. The surrendering of gender to conformity is genderism, which impedes self-affirmation and the accompanying social synchronicity needed so these children and youth can biopsychosocially construct their gender identities with adequate social supports. The backing of parents, other caregivers, and other significant adults is crucial here. While these adults have no control over a child's developing gender identification, they do have some control over a child's gender health. Caring adults need to remember that the child is not the problem; the world is the problem because it expects hegemonic male or female gender conformity from the child. They need to see growing into gender identity as a process ameliorated by using gender-affirming biopsychosocial models of development. The success of the process is measured by the degree to which a child is a happy, healthy, and hopeful individual who is gender aware and gender comfortable. When a child reaches this point, he or she is gender beautiful. The child deserves this success, in keeping with the right and the freedom to sustain a true gender identity through experiencing it as congruent with a lived gender reality.

In contemporary times, gender identity is a phenomenon often deliberated in medical and other sociocultural spheres. As new knowledge about and understanding of gender identity emerge, it is increasingly accepted that the parameters of gender exceed birth sex/assigned gender (Byne et al., 2012; Ehrensaft, 2011). Indeed two-sex/two-gender normativity is scrutinized and contested more and more as trans and gender-nonconforming individuals confront the social and cultural disapprobation that accompanies taking gender possibilities beyond the limits of the entrenched male/female binary. Currently, an emergent trans liberation movement is challenging us to rethink and revise gender as an intricate and complex sociocultural construct. Baird (2007) succinctly characterizes this movement: "Assertiveness is replacing shame and secrecy. Questions are being asked, answers demanded" (p. 139). In the progressive tradition of the black civil rights movement, women's liberation, gay liberation, and other transgressive and transformative movements that have variously contested marginalization and disenfranchisement, the trans liberation movement is contesting gender limits and exclusions embodied and embedded in medical and other institutional responses that assault trans being, integrity, and accommodation. Of course, this movement has much to address in the intersection of gender and sexuality. For example, as the trans narratives included in this book as InterTexts suggest, trans youths' experiences of homophobia and sexism, in derogatory words and actions, may supersede their experiences of transphobia and genderism, or be conflated with them, as they mediate life in schools and communities.

Schulman (2013) attests that a trans liberation movement is taking shape and gaining momentum. She says a new generation of politically astute transgender activists has emerged who are "Web savvy, [with] boundless confidence and social networks that extend online and off" (p. 1). These activists transgress gay culture by moving the focus from sexual orientation and loving others to gender identity and affirming their gender-nonconforming selves. As Schulman points out, these cultural workers expand LGBT to LGBTQIA (lesbian, gay, bisexual, transgender/Two-Spirit, queer/questioning, intersex, ally/asexual) in an effort to make room for more sexual and gender positionalities. However, by now it should be clear: no acronym is inclusive enough or sufficient in the SGM language games. No doubt naming will continue to be contested terrain as we learn more about the complexities of sexual and gender differences, subjectivities, and positionalities.

Exemplifying new moves in transgender activism, We*Happy*Trans*, a website (http://wehappytrans.com) created by Jen Richards, provides a social networking space where transpeople can share narratives and videos of positive experiences using seven guiding questions constructed to prompt affirmative responses. These questions ask respondents to discuss (1) naming as part of trans identity formation, (2) who their supporters are in the transition process, (3) the joy and satisfaction that mark the trans identification process or its anticipation, (4) their passions, (5) their trans role models, (6) their personal roles as change agents, and (7) their uniqueness as human beings. As a rich resource for trans knowledge building, the website provides trans and cisgender (or non-trans) individuals with an opportunity to engage in trans community education about the complexity of trans identities, the diversity of trans experiences, and the ways that trans persons grow into resilience. Reflecting on her own experience of being accepted, supported, and happy in the transition process, Richards wants We*Happy*Trans* to transmit a cultural politics and pedagogy of hope for the spectral community of transpeople. To that end, her website is providing counterpedagogy to the negative messaging that she encountered during her own journey. Describing herself as a mostly happy person who did not identify as transgender as a child, Richards found herself invisible in these narratives, "most of which were usually sensationalized, often absolute and, unfortunately, tragic" (We*Happy*Trans*, 2013, para. 6). She provides this synopsis of the narratives:

> The trans people I first read about knew from the youngest ages that they were in the wrong body. They were often significantly dysphoric, depressed, and closeted, saw their trans status as an untenable psychiatric

condition and accepted diagnoses of mental illness, or at least had to pretend that was the case in order to obtain basic medical support. And their need to transition was typically met with scorn, derision, judgment and abandonment. They lost their families, their friends and their jobs. Given the path they faced, there was a sense in the rhetoric I first found that transition was only an option for those who had no choice. For many, the decision was, literally, between transition or suicide. (WeHappyTrans*, 2013, para. 7)

By no means is Richards dismissive of these stories mired in struggles and suffering. She knows they represent reality for many transpeople and are the foundation for informing future progress. Indeed caring professionals might take these stories as impetus to engage in a politics of affirmation that help trans children and youth to grow into gender and become a new generation of trans adults not mired in a politics of resentment that forecloses possibilities for true happiness and health. What Richards maintains is the value of positive communication: sharing encouraging stories assists transition by opening up the space for transgender, which ought to be "a realm of active inquiry, play and creative expression" (para. 10). She believes that sharing trans stories of acceptance and successes in life and work is crucial in the quest for full trans citizenship. Richards concludes, "[W]e're not going to move forward until the rest of the world also sees us as active, adjusted, successful participants in our communities. I don't want to wait to see happy trans lives depicted in the media, so I'm doing it myself. That's what this series [of hopeful stories] intends" (para. 13).

Trans by Any Other Name: The Intricacies of Naming Gendered Subjects

The complexities of dealing with gender-identity formation are caught up in a politics of difference that begins with the complexities of naming gender when one's assigned gender (aligned with biological or birth sex) lacks synchronicity with lived gender roles and expressions. Naming gender varies like gender identity itself, with current descriptors including gender nonconforming, gender creative, gender variant, genderqueer, transgender, and trans spectrum (Ehrensaft, 2011; Marx, 2011; Pepper, 2012). Some like the name "gender creative" because it acknowledges the agency of the child in self-affirmation of gender identity; others dislike "gender nonconforming" and "gender variant" because they sound clinical, suggesting aberrance; still others prefer genderqueer because it locates gender as a fluid and spectral social construct. In contemporary times, naming is still much deliberated and no one name seems sufficient to be a universal term that replaces other names at this point.

Deliberations about naming trans and gender-nonconforming subjects demonstrate the intricacies of grappling with gender identification. While the language used to name and describe gender identity and its expression is still emergent and limited, Schindel (2008) provides typical working definitions of today's commonly used broad terms: gender identity is "a person's understanding, definition, or experience of their own gender, regardless of biological sex" (p. 61), while gender expression is "the way a person expresses his or her gender through gestures, movement, dress, and grooming" (p. 61). Similarly, Brill and Pepper (2008) define gender identity as the internalization of a profound sense of being male, female, both, or neither, which can be different from one's biological sex, used to assign a gender at birth based on physical anatomy. They describe gender expression as the externalization of one's gender that may or may not align with cultural norms and expectations for presentation and performance. In light of these complexities innervating gender identity and expression, Rainbow Health Ontario (2012) indicates an important reality: gender identification is a journey. This means that the gender-independent child may become cisgendered (non-trans), lesbian, gay, or bisexual; or they might remain gender fluid into adulthood; or they may be a trans person who socially (in terms of role and perhaps a change in name, pronoun use, dress, and appearance) and/or medically (in terms of hormone treatments and possibly surgeries) transitions to his/her/hir new affirmed gender; or they may take on another gender identity.

In grappling with this process of gender identification, the complexity in naming, as Stryker (2008) notes, acknowledges that trans language is under construction as deliberations about terminology continue. Shelley (2008) defines trans as an umbrella term that implies a (usually non-existent) unity in difference among its diverse constituents, with his list including transgender, transsexual, intersex, gender-liminal, and Two-Spirit people. Transgender people mediate living to varying degrees outside the male/female binary. Transsexual people mediate living with a mis-sexed body. Intersex people mediate living with genital ambiguity or other sex characteristics that foreclose categorization as being distinctly biologically male or female. Gender-liminal people mediate living with gender ambiguity. Two-Spirit people are Aboriginals who mediate living within the usual cultural understanding, albeit one caught up in colonialism, of the gift of bodies containing male and female spirits (Driskill, Finley, Gilley, & Morgensen, 2011; Driskill, Justice, Mirandi, & Tatonetti, 2011). Cisgender people are non-transgender people whose gender identity matches their assigned birth sex (Teich & Green, 2012). In queer culture and, to some extent, the larger culture, transgender is often used as an umbrella term to include (1) those whose self-affirmed gender identity is different from the sex they were assigned at birth based on physiological anatomy, and (2) those whose gender nonconformity is based on appearance, behaviours, and mannerisms that do not align with socially constructed expectations (Lambda Legal, 2012). As individuals whose gender represents a move away from birth sex or assigned gender, transgender people are those who transgress their culture's understanding and containment of gender. In sum, transgender is *"the movement across a socially imposed boundary away from an unchosen starting place"* (Stryker, 2008, p. 1, italics in original).

Beyond these names with sociocultural meanings, there is medically framed terminology. For example, in psychiatry, "gender variance" (GV) is an overarching term that includes all individuals who show "any degree of cross-gender identification or nonconformity in gender role" (Byne et al., 2012, p. 762). Transsexuals are "adults who meet diagnostic criteria for GID [or gender identity disorder, which was listed in the American Psychiatric Association's *Diagnostic and Statistical Manual of Mental Disorders* from 1980 to 2013] and have employed hormonal and/or surgical treatments in the process of transitioning gender or who plan to do so" (Byne et al., 2012, p. 762). Transgender includes all individuals with cross-gender identification regardless of whether hormonal or surgical treatment have been employed or are planned for the future. Increasingly deliberated and institutionalized in medicine as well as culture and society, transgender is a "collective term to incorporate all and any variance from imagined gender norms" (Valentine, 2007, p. 14). Valentine (2007) traces the location of transgender as an overtly politicized spectral or umbrella term to such early moves as trans-rights activist and cultural worker Leslie Feinberg's call for a transgender liberation movement in 1992. He relates that, since the early 1990s, the institutionalization of transgender – and of sexuality and gender more broadly – has happened via public policy, media (re) presentations, disciplinary deliberations (notably in psychiatry), and grass-roots activism. As Valentine (2007) sees it, today transgender is much more than "an index of marginality" (p. 14) since it is now a social and analytic category and a cultural location where understandings of gender and sexuality as historical, political, and distinct (but connected) categories are arbitrated. Central to comprehending gender and sexuality in contemporary trans-identity politics, theorizing, and activism is the notion that transgender identity is distinct from homosexuality. While this viewpoint is pervasive in academe, as Valentine (2007) argues, "its employment in institutionalized contexts cannot account for the experiences of the most vulnerable gender variant people" (p. 14), who may not know the term "transgender" or who may resist its use. Thus in imagining transgender, Valentine asks us to consider what the concept explains, how it is deployed, how it is altered in intersections with power relationships like race and class, and, ultimately, who it includes and excludes. In doing this, he wants to open up transgender to possibility while exploring ways that the concept is both diffuse and limited in theoretical, political, and ethical contexts.

In general, terms like "transgender" and "trans" and newer terms like "genderqueer" lack mainstream currency. For transpeople, there is also the politics of language use. For example, although transgender is a common and familiar way to name someone whose affirmed gender is at odds with his/her/hir assigned gender, there are those who resist the term because it reifies norms that set gender limits. However, a focus on language, its limits, and its precariousness is a natural dynamic in the emergence of a social movement. Feinberg (1996) maintained that the trans liberation movement ought to be about gender border crossing and the right of people to characterize their gender identities as part of defining the self in intersections with other power relationships like race, class, and nationality. For Feinberg (1996), "the gradations of sex and gender self-definition are limitless" (p. 102). From this perspective, the desire to name in new ways is part of a process of making sense that counters a history that has refused to name or has misnamed certain gender identities either out of ignorance or with untoward intentions. In the process, stereotypes and exclusions are kept intact, defiling non-normative ways of being and acting in the world. Feinberg (1996) speaks to the issue of naming from a personal perspective: "The question 'Is that a boy or a girl?' hounded me throughout my childhood. The answer didn't matter much. The very fact that strangers *had* to ask the question already marked me as a gender outlaw" (p. 4, italics in original). Dealing with this history from the politics of trans location, the desire for new language can be seen as organic and visceral, as an outcome of struggle. "Living struggles accelerate changes in language ... [Language] is forged collectively, in the fiery heat of struggle" (Feinberg, 1996, p. ix). She believes that using language should be a thoughtful act that respects peoples' struggles and wounds. Moreover, she asserts, "[C]hosen language needs to be defended" (p. ix). Still Feinberg is concerned that a focus on language can detract from a focus on people. She speaks to this in relation to deliberations over the use of pronouns by transpeople:

> I don't have a personal stake in whether the trans liberation movement results in a new third pronoun, or gender-neutral pronouns, like the ones, such as *ze* (she/he) and *hir* (her/his) ... It is not the words in and of themselves that are important to me – it's our lives. (Feinberg, 1996, p. x)

Still, as Teich and Green (2012) relate, pronoun usage is an issue for some transpeople, and even though it may be difficult to remember and use nontraditional pronouns, it is important to respect their wishes by using pronouns they use in self-description. In his study, Valentine (2007) noted that most transgender participants used the standard gendered pronouns. However, some used the plural pronouns *they* and *them* as singular references or used *ze* and *s/he* instead of *he* and *she* and used *hir* instead of *his*, *him*, or *her*. He relates that the wider community often finds such usage challenging and unexpected, with the trans pronouns being difficult to pronounce. Thus naming using pronouns is one more facet of the complexity of trans language deliberations.

Like Feinberg, Stanley (2011) asserts, "Gender self-determination ... acknowledges that gender identification is always formed in relation to other forms of power and thus the words we use to identify others and ourselves are culturally, generationally, and geographically situated" (p. 5). Still, like Feinberg, he also believes that gender should be unbounded by language, with transgender and gender-nonconforming individuals adding to "the 'riddle' of gender" and the complexity of gender variation (Stanley, 2011, p. 5). For Stanley, gender identification is political and processual; it is a project of self-determination and self-affirmation, with an eye to social and cultural recognition and accommodation. It is about creating space for gender to be and emerge as an entity separate from sexual identity but inextricably linked to it. In terms of answering the question "Is that a boy or a girl?" – the question that Feinberg and other transpeople have been perennially pestered to answer – Stanley speaks to the realities and consequences of providing an answer that transgresses the either/or boy/girl binary:

> Trans/gender-non-conforming and queer people, along with many others, are born into webs of surveillance. The gendering scan of other children at an early age ("Are you a boy or a girl?") places many in the panopticon ... For those who do trespass the gender binary or heteronormativity, physical violence, isolation, detention, or parental disappointment become some of the first punishments. As has been well documented, many trans and queer youth are routinely harassed at school and kicked out of home at young ages, while others leave in hopes of escaping the mental and physical violence that they experience at schools and in their houses. (Stanley, 2011, p. 7)

Leaving home, whether by ejection or choice, usually compounds difficulties for trans/queer youth. As Stanley relates, some survive in the informal economy, turning to sex work, drug dealing, and other dangerous survival-mode behaviours. He also notes that trans youth have trouble accessing shelters; moreover, group and foster homes can be unsafe for them. The dire consequence, Stanley (2011), points out, is some become lost, "spend[ing] their youth shuttling between the anonymity of the streets and the hyper-surveillance of the juvenile justice system ... Picked up – locked up – placed in a home – escape – survive – picked up again. The cycle builds a cage" (p. 7). Nihilism marks the lives of these youth. For them, the idea that life can get better seems like nothing more than a bad, if not cruel, joke.

Compounding the plight of trans/queer youth, Toronto's Youth-Gender Action Project (Y-GAP) (2009a) provides this stark reminder of the challenges they face in mediating access to service provision and/or the transition process:

> There are few accessible services and few competent providers to support the healthcare needs of trans youth. Receiving quality care often entails travel or lengthy waiting times for services. Because they anticipate poor treatment, some youth are reluctant to use or avoid accessing services altogether ... [When trans youth do access services, they] commonly omit material from their life histories they believe does not fit with the expected professional narrative, as they fear it may render them ineligible for, or delay, treatment. Ironically, these omissions reify stereotypes professionals may hold. (pp. 1–2)

As Sean and Vincent indicate in their InterTexts, the culture of Canadian health care for trans youth has deleterious effects on their visibility, self-acceptance, self-esteem, and health and wellness. For example, Y-GAP (2009a) calls attention to the fact that trans youth face such everyday obstacles as dealing with name and gender on trans-insensitive intake forms provided by trans-ignorant reception-ists and service providers who lack experience with this underserved population. Moreover, service providers lack awareness of new bio-psychosocial treatment models that start where youth are and affirm gender identity instead of diagnosing it as a mental disorder to be fixed. In this pervasive scenario, trans youth often feel that they have to be the educators. "This takes significant emotional energy and time, but is often necessary to get service that is informed and responsive to their needs" (Y-GAP, 2009a, p. 2). What this means is trans youth face yet another stressor that they have to deal with on their difficult gender-identification journey. As Y-GAP points out, this accentuates the need to create trans-inclusive social and clinical services where youth can bring a significant supportive adult to an appointment, if they wish.

Gender Variance and the Diagnosis and Treatment Modality Divide

Gender-nonconforming children have experienced greater social visibility in recent years, which has been accompanied by intense deliberations among scholars, clinicians, trans-spectrum health-care professionals, trans-movement advocates, and others regarding diag-nosis and treatment modalities as children grow and develop during what is increasingly understood as an intricate biological, psychologi-cal, social, and cultural process. While the number of minor children and youth with gender dysphoria is low, with growing social recog-nition and legal support there is an increase in the number seeking resources and professional care at gender clinics, which is ultimately important for those individuals who persist in affirming a gender iden-tity incongruous with their assigned gender/natal sex and who need intervention and assistance with transitioning to their affirmed gender (Drescher & Byne, 2012; Minter, 2012; Rainbow Health Ontario, 2012). Rainbow Health Ontario (2012) provides this succinct synopsis of the long-standing disease model used to pathologize these children, noting the catch-22 of continuing to diagnose variance in gender-independent adolescents:

Since 1980, many gender independent children have been diagnosed with *Gender Identity Disorder in Children*. This diagnosis is highly controversial and has been criticized for pathologizing sexual and gender diversity, reinforcing sexist [and genderist] stereotypes, and casting a broad social problem as an individual pathology. This diagnosis ... [is] *Gender Dysphoria in Children* in the ... fifth version (2013) of the Diagnostic and Statistical Manual [of Mental Disorders] (DSM-5), a publication by the American Psychiatric Association used to classify mental disorders. Although this diagnosis is controversial, it is also used to provide access to important medical gender transition care for gender independent adolescents. (p. 2)

Scharrón-del Río et al. (2014) say this change in the DSM-5 is a result of extended academic deliberations and advocacy. The American Psychiatric Association (APA) (2013) acknowledges that diagnostic terms have two faces: on the one hand, they can "facilitate clinical care and access to insurance coverage that supports mental health"; on the other hand, they "can also have a stigmatizing effect" (p. 1). With regard to the latter, it has been imperative to reframe how gender dysphoria is diagnosed and treated so the focus moves away from core gender identity as the root cause towards the systemic and structural causes of harm to transpeople (Ehrensaft, 2012; Haraldsen, Ehrbar, Gorton, & Menvielle, 2010; Hill & Menvielle, 2009). Importantly, in changing the diagnosis to gender dysphoria, the APA (2013) indicates that "gender nonconformity is not in itself a mental disorder" (p. 1). Rather, the diagnosis of gender dysphoria specifies "the presence of clinically significant distress associated with the condition" (p. 1) and consequential impaired functioning in social and other contexts. Thus the term "gender dysphoria" puts the focus on symptoms and behaviours in an effort to remove the tainting notion of disorder from diagnosis and treatment processes. Still Scharrón-del Río et al. (2014) suggest there is a need to be cautious. While the DSM-5 does focus on client discontent and distress linked to societal expectations, there is also what they call "the persisting focus on the *incongruence* between the person's assigned gender and his or her experienced gender identity as a marker of pathology" (Scharrón-del Río et al., 2014, p. 41, italics in original). They maintain we should be careful, concluding that highlighting incongruence in introducing diagnostic criteria in the DSM-5 "can be seen as a backdoor to continue to pathologize [gender] identity" (p. 41).

As Scharrón-del Río et al. (2014) also relate, the enduring debate culminating in a change in diagnosis from gender identity disorder (GID) to gender dysphoria (GD) in the DSM-5 has significantly revealed that psychiatry remains in a quandary when it comes to setting standards and determining approaches to gender variance. The discipline has to consider whether the phenomenon is symptomatic of other problems, or a response to poignant life circumstances, or a revelation of the repressed true gender self (Edwards-Leeper & Spack, 2012; Ehrensaft, 2012; Rettew, 2012; Stein, 2012). Indeed listing the diagnosis for gender variance as gender dysphoria in the DSM-5, thus replacing GID, requires further deliberations regarding (1) what constitutes a psychopathological gender-variant condition versus a natural variation of gender identity and expression, and (2) what having any diagnosis means in terms of reinscribing the gender binary, even with the acknowledgment of more gender spaces between male and female (Drescher & Byne, 2012). Rettew (2012) maintains that the move to a new diagnostic category, gender dysphoria, involves making the distinction between a disorder and a characteristic or trait, which is most difficult because gender identity is an intricate and emerging construction.

Scharrón-del Río et al. (2014) note that two conflicting therapeutic modalities, both requiring further scientific investigation, are currently used in clinical practice. Surveying the literature, they compare what they call the corrective treatment approach (exemplified in this chapter by the developmental, biopsychosocial model used by Kenneth J. Zucker, who heads up the Gender Identity Service in the Child, Youth, and Family Program at the Centre for Addiction and Mental Health in Toronto) with what they call the supportive/affirming treatment approach (exemplified in this chapter by Diane Ehrensaft's model of relational true gender self therapy):

> The scientific and clinical literature can be divided into *corrective* and *supportive/affirming* treatment approaches to working with GV/GD children. The supportive/affirming treatments tend to focus on supporting children's gender role expression (in whatever form), building strengths and resilience in the child, facilitating parental understanding of the child, addressing environmental factors that contribute to child invalidation, and routinely assessing the degree of GD persistence ... The corrective approaches tend to promote normative gender behaviors through the use of behavioral methods, and incorporating supports focusing on the family's collaboration in promoting the child's assigned gender-role behaviors, in order to reduce stigma and ostracism accompanying transgender identity. (Scharrón-del Río et al., 2014, pp. 43–4, italics in original)

While there is a move to use a case-by-case approach in treatment that considers a child's age, life contexts and circumstances, biological predispositions, and intensity of gender dysphoria, Scharrón-del Río et al. (2014) relate that the two opposing approaches remain largely intact as the pervasive choices in treatment despite the "the multiple shades of gray between our socially constructed binary categories" (p. 51). They go on to say that unresolved debates over the psychopathology of gender variance and appropriate treatment modalities leave gender-nonconforming schoolchildren caught in the crossfire as they try to navigate life in school contexts where the gender binary and traditional gender norms remain the status quo. This reality is recognized and countered in increasing moves in educational policymaking to protect these students from genderist and transphobic discrimination and bullying in schools (Drescher & Byne, 2012; Minter, 2012). Nevertheless, when gender variance is addressed, there is still a pervasive tendency to deal with gender identity using strategies suitable for dealing with sexual orientation and heteronormativity. Even when school psychologists want to advocate for and appropriately support gender-nonconforming children, Scharrón-del Río et al. (2014), like Luecke (2011), note these practitioners can be hampered by a prevalent mindset and professional literature that often conflate gender nonconformity with a homosexual orientation. This conflation reflects the stance taken by both psychiatrist Charles W. Socarides and clinical psychologist Joseph Nicolosi, leading advocates of reparative therapy, who contended that homosexuality was a product of gender deficit (Grace, 2008b; Zucker, 2006). As an orthodox therapeutic intervention inextricably linked to religious (Christian) conservatism, reparative therapy is a highly contentious practice (Grace, 2008b). In fact, there has been much ado about this pseudoscientific invention. Zucker (2006), positioning its advocates as political and ideological rightists and its opponents as leftist social constructionists, concludes, "The rhetoric about reparative therapy has far exceeded any empirical evidence about its effectiveness and efficacy, or lack thereof, and has largely focused on ethics and sexual politics" (p. 5). This leads him to question why mental health associations have come out en masse against reparative therapy. Still there are many existing qualitative research accounts by individuals damaged by reparative therapy, which should prompt every therapist, including Zucker, to consider the issue of harm and its ramifications (Grace, 2008b). Returning to the matter of treating gender variance, there is, of course, more to deal with than the conflation of sexual orientation and gender identity as a legacy of reparative therapy. Even when the professional literature focuses on gender-nonconforming children, gender identity, and possible treatment modalities, expert opinion is varied and sometimes contradictory regarding what constitutes optimal clinical interventions (Scharrón-del Río et al., 2014).

The Real Issue

For those who subscribed to the disease model in treating the APA-sanctioned diagnosis of GID, the purported goal of psychotherapy was "to optimize the psychological adjustment and wellbeing of the child" (Byne et al., 2012, p. 763). Perplexingly though, there has never been agreement among clinicians regarding how to achieve this goal, with some clinicians believing that minimizing gender-nonconforming presentation so GID did not persist in adolescence was an acceptable therapeutic goal (Byne et al., 2012). However, at the end of the day, it is not about diagnosing or treating gender independence in order to curtail it. As Lambda Legal (2012) asserts, for transpeople it really ought to be about making available such psychological and medical supports as individual and family counselling, hormone therapy, and surgery so individuals are affirmed and supported in the transitioning process. This constitutes ethical treatment. Nevertheless, the catch-22 for transpeople will continue to be accepting the diagnosis of a mental disorder, currently gender dysphoria in the DSM-5, so they can access the mainstream standardized medical services needed to become whole, healthy, and happy.

In the case of trans youth, service providers need to realize that the real issue may not be gender dysphoria – the dissonance between assigned and affirmed gender – but body dysphoria and the need to transition: "Trans boys and girls are usually quite certain about and content with their gender – it's their bodies they need to bring in alignment with their gender" (Central Toronto Youth Services [CTYS], 2008, p. 6). In this regard, making room to accept, support, and accommodate trans youth becomes even more crucial with the onset of puberty, when the development of secondary sexual characteristics like breast buds in transgender boys and facial hair in transgender girls betray affirmed gender. The development of secondary sexual characteristics is traumatic because the changing appearance of the body is one more signifier of asynchronicity with the true gender self. With these physical changes, health and safety issues for transgender youth are compounded. Trans youth can experience puberty as a period of challenge and crisis when stressors can lead to risk taking and an array of negative outcomes. Sometimes the mental and emotional upheaval can be more than transgender youth can bear. For nihilistic transgender persons, suicide may seem like the only way out of their gender-identity dilemma:

> [They] might want to bury the true self alongside their own dead body, choosing death over a false life that forecloses any chance for being authentic. As transgender children confront the dreaded body changes of puberty that they fear will strike down any potential to grow up as their true gender self, they may find themselves trapped in the fantasy that death is the only solution. (Ehrensaft, 2011, p. 152)

As Byne et al. (2012) relate, Ehrensaft, intent on saving lives, believes in letting gender identity follow its natural developmental trajectory without having a therapeutic target regarding gender-identity outcome. The goal here is to affirm, support, and help the child to deal with social risks using an integrated model involving the child, the primary caregivers, and community-based intervention. When a child's gender identity is not only self-affirmed but also affirmed by primary caregivers and mental health professionals, Ehrensaft opts to use gender-creative medical treatment that involves early social transitioning to the affirmed gender, "with the option of endocrine treatment to suspend puberty in order to suppress the development of unwanted secondary sex characteristics if the cross-gendered identification persists into puberty" (Byne et al., 2012, p. 763). Prior to beginning this treatment, a team of health-care professionals including paediatric endocrinologists and mental health professionals conduct an assessment to (1) gauge physical and mental health, (2) evaluate the degree and consistency of gender identification, and (3) determine the level of family support (Rainbow Health Ontario, 2012). The use of hormone blockers (gonadotropin-releasing hormone analogues) to suppress puberty is crucial for questioning and transgender children (Ehrensaft, 2011). Their use provides the child time to deal with matters of gender identity using medical intervention that does not alter natal gender. Casper (1991) relates that hormone blockers, which have been used to treat precocious puberty in children since 1981, stop the development of secondary sexual characteristics. He adds that ceasing treatment using hormone blockers reverses this cessation of puberty. Research indicates several advantages to puberty suppression (De Vries & Cohen-Kettenis, 2012; Drescher & Byne, 2012; Menvielle, 2012): (1) It is a minimal risk intervention that provides breathing space for both children and parents (or other primary caregivers) to explore gender identity and decide next steps, including a possible gender reassignment trajectory, without the added stress triggered by the development of secondary sex characteristics in children. (2) It can contribute to positive comprehensive health for youth, with a reduction in emotional problems and depression coupled with an improvement in overall functioning.

After the age of 10, children who persist with self-affirmed genders mediate gender dysphoria in relation to living in genderist social environments, anticipating or experiencing puberty, and falling in love and dealing with sexual orientation as well as gender identity (Steensma, Biemond, de Boer, & Cohen-Kettenis, 2011). When transgender youth want their bodies to grow and develop to complement their affirmed genders, medical treatment using cross-sex hormones (estrogen for transgender girls and testosterone for transgender boys) enables these youth to develop desired secondary sexual characteristics. Although Ehrensaft (2011) supports this treatment for youth ready to transition from assigned gender to affirmed gender, she acknowledges that the use of cross-sex hormones is "not without side effects or untoward outcomes" (p. 147). With regard to surgical interventions, especially genital surgery, transgender youth usually have to wait until they reach the age of majority. Ehrensaft suggests that this may be hardest for transgender youth who have been living their lives in their affirmed gender since early childhood. She explains:

> Adolescence is a time when living with ambiguity or nuance is a challenge, not only but especially when it comes to a teen's sexual self. In offering hormones to adjust secondary sex characteristics but leaving genitalia intact, this is exactly what we are asking of pubescent and postpubescent transgender teens – to live with nuance and ambiguity and accept their genitalia as they are. (Ehrensaft, 2011, p. 165)

This scenario requires medical professionals to consider a question that goes to the heart of medical ethics and the maxim to do no harm: When does the denial of desired medical interventions equate with medical mistreatment of transgender youth, especially those who have persisted, lived, and prospered in their affirmed identity for a significant period of time?

Diane Ehrensaft's Model of Relational True Gender Self Therapy

Diagnosing gender-independent children with gender dysphoria instead of GID is just one change challenging, but not eradicating, the disease model. However, as mentioned earlier, there is a move to replace this model with ethically grounded, identity-affirming treatment modalities that focus on listening to children as they mediate the process of gender identification and helping parents to support their child's growing into gender. This move locates genderism as a systemic stressor that can cause gender dysphoria in gender-independent children. Thus there is much to learn about gender as a sociocultural construct and the nature of gender fluidity and ambiguity, as well as about gender identity and the intricacies of its mindful construction and malleability. What researchers are realizing is biological change, including the physiology of transitioning, is accompanied by an anthropological shift in what it means to be, become, belong, act, and fit in terms of navigating culture in one's affirmed gender (Ehrensaft, 2013). It takes a team of gender-sensitive significant adults like parents and caring professionals to enable this intricate process. Even when a child's gender history indicates a "consistent, insistent, and persistent" (Ehrensaft, 2013, p. 26) gender identity, there are no guarantees about the gender future of the child, as Ehrensaft acknowledges.

Proponents of affirmative treatment models point out that children experiencing gender dysphoria are not the problem; the problem is a systemic one caught up in societal stigmatization and cultural disapproval. In the face of genderism, the gender-nonconforming child's usual response is to present a false gender self, which is the fake public face that a child displays to a world that expects normative gender identities and matching expressions. Ehrensaft (2011) relates two scenarios in which a child may present a false gender self: (1) a child may consciously assume a false gender self as an expedient adaptation to a hetero-patriarchal, genderist situation, or (2) a child may portray a false gender self as an assimilative response to rigid gender policing in genderist spaces. Neither scenario is healthy since the child does not want to adapt. What the child really wants is to be what the mind knows and the heart feels. In this regard, Ehrensaft (2011) relates that the journey to find the true gender self involves the interplay of genetic gender (chromosomal inheritance), physical gender (primary and secondary sexual characteristics), and, most importantly, "'brain gender'" (inner sense of the true gender self) (p. 35). The gender-nonconforming child has to mediate the asynchronicity of these gender categories. This is a creative process that leads Ehrensaft (2011) to conclude, "Gender is born, yet gender is also made" (p. 36).

Although it is unknown how many transgender children there are, they compose a very small subset of gender-variant children, of whom the majority are simply gender-nonconforming (Brill & Pepper, 2008). The gender-variant or gender-creative child – a child who is gender-nonconforming and who may be transgender, gender fluid, or otherwise gender identified – intuitively knows that gender occupies a vast space beyond the male/female binary where there are many options for gender being and expression. Still gender creativity is not about choosing; rather, it is about constructing the true gender self. An advocate for affirmative treatment models, Ehrensaft (2011) locates true gender identity within a dynamic developmental process: "Once we are born, the true gender self is most definitely shaped and channeled through our experiences in life, but its center always remains our own personal possession, driven from within rather than without" (p. 79). From this perspective, gender creativity is not variance from gender norms, which orthodox psychotherapists construe as pathology. Instead gender creativity is the basis for gender health. Ehrensaft (2011) concludes that it "comes to save the day by working actively to circumvent the false gender self as well as privately keep the true gender self alive when it is not safe to let it come out" (p. 94). In sum, it is about accepting the messiness of gender within a politics of gender location that affirms gender possibilities.

Ehrensaft (2011) presents her model of relational True Gender Self Therapy in her book *Gender Born, Gender Made*. In an immediate and personal way, reading her book sparked warm memories of gender play from my childhood. I loved putting on my mother's fur coat and smelling the French cologne that reminded me of her love for fashion and fine things. I also loved wearing her stilettos, which were arranged in a neat row in her closet. My sister and I would head for that closet when we were home alone. We would shape bath towels into a beehive hairstyle so we could pretend we were Diana Ross and the Supremes. I loved watching these pop icons on the *Ed Sullivan Show*. Their outfits were exquisite and their moves as they performed captured a femininity that I loved to emulate. However, it was my mother, my grandmothers, and my aunts who most influenced me. These strong women were the caring adults that I wanted to become. I wanted to be smart, loving, and talented just like they were. My identity today is still caught up in their identities, and the girl play of my youth became my way to be comfortable and content on my developmental journey to being, becoming, and belonging as a gay man with a feminine core. When I identified as a girl, I was strong and self-assured, happy and healthy, comfortable and content. It brought peace to the gay boy inside me as I replaced the symbolic violence of being called a "sissy" with the vibrant image of the happy gay man I desired to be.

In a real way, this was the emerging me engaging in a process of discovering my true gender self, the central construct in Ehrensaft's (2011) treatment modality. Positioning British paediatrician and psychoanalyst D.W. Winnicott as a key influence in developing her treatment protocol, Ehrensaft (2013) has adapted his concepts of the true self, false self, and individual creativity to her work with gender-nonconforming and trans-spectrum children and youth. For Ehrensaft (2013), the true gender self is our owning of our self-asserted and affirmed gender in our mind and heart; the false gender self is our adaptive gender presentation in the face of genderism and transphobia; gender creativity is "weaving together body, mind, psyche, socialization, and culture to create an authentic gender self" (p. 12). Ehrensaft (2013) states that True Gender Self Therapy is about building "'gender resilience'" (p. 13) as a key goal and developing a psychological toolkit, with the therapist helping in its construction so the child is affirmed and protected from transphobia and genderism.

Certainly, Ehrensaft's affirmative treatment modality has its critics. For example, when describing her clinical approach as celebratory of a child's gender nonconformity and positioning her therapeutic approach as an outlier among conventional treatment modalities, Reiner and Reiner (2012) state, "Utilizing inventive terminology, the author provides almost poetic discussions with ethereal references to somewhat nebulous constructs" (p. 438). They argue her therapeutic model fails to focus on risks of therapeutic intervention and on wider theoretical and empirical developments affecting treatment modalities. They contend true gender self therapy raises concerns about perspective and bias because it overly relies on Winnicott's theorizing without providing sufficient evidence to warrant it. Beyond this critique, what Reiner and Reiner fail to focus on, and what is innovative and important about Ehrensaft's (2011) model for gender-creative therapy is the way it complicates gender beyond conventional binary understandings of male and female. True Gender Self Therapy has this basic tenet: "gender is a weaving together of nature, nurture, and culture" (Ehrensaft, 2011,

p. 209). It conceptualizes growing into gender as an unfixed, evolution-ary, ecological, and lifelong process. In light of the complexities marking the gender-identification journey, Ehrensaft (2011) provides this under-standing of gender as an intricate construction: "Gender is not dictated by our chromosomes, hormone receptors, or genitalia but by our own internal sense of self, a self that will be influenced by biology, by rear-ing, and by culture" (p. 34). From this perspective, she has developed a model of relational true gender self therapy that parents and caring professionals can use to help gender-creative children. This model can help them "untangle gender and learn to identify each child's unique gender web as they listen to the children and help them to be the most authentic people they can be in their gender identity and expression" (Ehrensaft, 2011, p. 10). What Ehrensaft calls the gender web is a multi-dimensional gender space with intricate pathways. She describes how the gender web works:

> This web will have to take into account any particular child's assigned gender, that which appears on the birth certificate; the child's gender expressions – those feelings, behaviors, activities, and attitudes that communicate to both self and other one's presentation of self as either male, female, or other; and the child's core gender identity – the inner sense of self as male, female, or other. (Ehrensaft, 2011, p. 4)

Ehrensaft's conceptualization of the gender web recognizes that the gender assigned at birth, as distinguished by birth sex and categoriza-tion within the male/female binary, is not necessarily a lifetime given. While assigned gender is reinforced by gender policing of identity and expression, she asserts it is self-affirmed gender as true gender identity that needs be recognized, respected, supported, and accom-modated as the gender-independent child grows into gender. For parents, foster parents, and other caring adults, it involves (1) start-ing with the child where the child is, (2) overcoming ignorance and denial of the child's gender reality, (3) seeing the emergence of the child's unique gender self as a gender evolution, and (4) transgressing their own acculturation to gender normativity so they can work with the child to achieve gender comfortability and health. For the child, this process involves questioning and being gender curious and cre-ative. In sum, the gender-creative child navigates the gender web to achieve a self-determined, self-affirmed gender identity that replaces an asynchronous gender identity determined and assigned by adults at birth. This is the process of establishing a true gender identity. It is enabled by gender-affirming psychotherapeutic interventions that focus on gender health and reject the long-standing pathologizing of gender creativity as gender identity disorder. This does not dismiss the possibility of disordered gender. Ehrensaft (2011) explains that in new approaches to gender development focused on gender health, clinical psychologists "will be challenged to differentiate disordered gender from nonconforming gender, providing kind and empathetic care from a trained mental health professional for the former and simply making room for support and acceptance of the latter" (p. 39). In this regard, Ehrensaft (2011) calls on these professionals to act ethically as they consider two basic questions: "'What is gender health?' and 'How can we support our gender-nonconforming children?'" (p. 76). Here one ought to consider the ways that the male/female binary can be unwittingly reinscribed even when using affirmative gender-identity treatment modalities. For example, Stein (2012) asserts that following a treatment flow chart from puberty suppression to gender reassignment surgery is in keeping with either a male or a female prototype/stereotype. This limits what it might mean to be gender healthy, as it appears to hold on to the male/female binary as an entity as much as it affirms an individual's gender identity.

Ehrensaft's model, aimed at helping the gender-nonconforming child to self-affirm an authentic gender identity as a basis for gender health, is based on caring adults advocating for and listening to the child, who is seen as an agent in the process. This helps the child to "spin his or her unique gender web," which involves "the developmental unfolding, the psychological experiences, the needed supports, the relationship between the child and the family, and the social milieu of the gender-creative child" (Ehrensaft, 2011, p. 13). To use this model, Ehrensaft insists that gender-creative therapists have to be community activists and cultural workers who advocate for transgender and gender-nonconforming children and youth. This means working with parents, other caregivers, other caring professionals, and community members to promote gender webbing and awareness and to ensure gender safety. Family doctors, paediatricians, mental health service providers, early childhood educators, schoolteachers, school administrators, social workers, and child-welfare service providers are among caring professionals who need to build the knowledge and competency needed to assist gender-creative children (Rainbow Health Ontario, 2012).

Kenneth J. Zucker's Developmental, Biopsychosocial Model Used in Treating Children Diagnosed with Gender Identity Disorder

In reviewing the developmental, biopsychosocial treatment modality constructed to treat gender identity disorder since the mid-1970s at the Gender Identity Service in the Child, Youth, and Family Program at the Centre for Addiction and Mental Health in Toronto, Kenneth J. Zucker and his colleagues relate that the process has regularly begun with a referral initiated by a parent or health-care professional (Zucker, Wood, Singh, & Bradley, 2012). These referrals prompted use of an assessment protocol based on a question set aligned with the DSM-IV-TR diagnosis of gender identity disorder when the 2000 version of the *Diagnostic and Statistical Manual of Mental Disorders* was the standard. The assessment protocol also included questions about the child's socioemotional development that could include foci on other DSM diagnoses, the child's comprehensive (including physical and mental) health, and the family's mental health history. This last line of questioning problematically raised the spectre of parental fault up front as a reason for the nonconforming turn in a child's gender-identity development. The traditional psycho-logic that there is something wrong with the child because there is something wrong with the parents or the dynamics of their relationship tends to increase stress and worry for parents, especially those who do not want their child to feel abnormal (Hill & Menvielle, 2009). It leaves parents vulnerable and open to subjugation in a relationship where the clinician has the power to position the child as damaged, with the parents becoming collateral damage. As Johnson, Sikorski, Savage, and Woitaszewski (2014) conclude, the psychopathologizing of gender identity raises two major concerns for parents: the first is worrying that their child's gender nonconformity is due to something they did, and the second is wondering what clinical recourse, if any, is best for their child.

In keeping with a corrective treatment approach, the Toronto clinic's assessment starts with a quest to determine gender identity disorder or another psychopathology. Of course, there is a central question here: "What is abnormal – that which is merely atypical or that which is maladaptive?" (Reiner & Reiner, 2012, p. 435). The answer is crucial because parents who have reached a limit dealing with the persistence of their child in naming and expressing gender nonconformity might use an assessment's confirmation of GID as impetus to seek a "cure," foreclosing the possibility of supporting their child during the process of growing into a self-affirmed gender identity. Problematically, the Toronto clinic's approach keeps the focus on the child and corrective treatment of gender abnormality instead of truly emphasizing the impact of ecological factors, such as the everyday environments where a child is confronted by systems and structures unfriendly to gender variance. Still Zucker et al. (2012) purport that gender-identity development is a complex "multifactorial model that takes into account biological factors, psychosocial factors, social cognition, associated psychopathology, and psychodynamic mechanisms" (p. 375). Of grave concern, this last component focuses, in part, on the "transfer of unresolved conflict and trauma-related experiences from parent to child" (p. 380) such that gender dysphoria is viewed as symptomatic of family dysfunction. In many ways, the multifactorial nature of the model, coupled with clinicians using a case-by-case approach in treating gender-nonconforming children, should open up possibilities for understanding intricacies of gender identity. However, the strong thread of psychopathology suturing this therapeutic modality paradoxically leaves the model reductionistic. What is deeply problematic is the goal of using treatment to have a gender-nonconforming child "feel more comfortable in their own skin" (p. 383), which, in the Toronto's clinic lexicon, is a euphemism for squashing a child's true gender self in order to maintain the false identity of the assigned gender matching the birth sex. When parents patently desire this goal, Zucker et al. (2012) state that the therapeutic approach is developed around it. This involves focusing on two main issues: "a) the potential role of parental factors in the genesis and maintenance of GID, and b) naturalistic interventions" (p. 388), which involve parents in setting limits to nonconforming gender expression. Here parents seem to compose the main engine driving the therapeutic approach, which raises questions about the role of psychotherapists as experts in the treatment process. This can be construed as a nod to the reality that there is no empirically fail-safe way to proceed with treatment anyway. Zucker et al. (2012) do say they do not impose their treatment approach on uncertain parents, leaving specific decisions about interventions to later in the therapeutic process. Still the treatment modality has considerable currency. And yet it remains troublesome, with Wallace and Russell (2013) critiquing it for its apparent inattention to improving the parent-child attachment relationship as well as for not specifically attending to the shame that gender-nonconforming children may experience, notably in relation to social exclusion.

Paradoxically in relation to their focus on the child and correcting abnormality, Zucker et al. (2012) primarily focus on factors outside the child's psyche when they list benefits of their treatment modality. As they see it, reducing gender dysphoria can improve family social dynamics and comfortability as well as the child's social environment and relationships. Less emphasized however is how treatment affects the child, especially the child who persists in affirming a true gender identity not synchronized with birth sex and assigned gender. If the gender variance is "corrected," what does feeling more comfortable in one's skin mean for this child? What if their treatment modality damages a child whose happiness, health, and hope about life emanates from being true to a self-affirmed gender identity? What about parents who feel that fixing gender identity to align with birth sex is a necessary intervention to prevent homosexuality? What about reaching those parents weighed down by such systemic millstones as their own homophobia, stereotypical worries about HIV/AIDS, or conservative Christian worries about their child going to hell?

Writing with Cohen-Kettenis in 2008 about persistence in gender variation before GID's removal from the DSM-5, Zucker acknowledged there is significant theoretical and clinical discord regarding diagnosis and treatment of gender variance (Zucker & Cohen-Kettenis, 2008). This article (included in a handbook of sexual and gender identity disorders) problematically suggested that GID persistence could be a consequence of the contemporary politics of sex and gender, which includes the notion that gender is a social construct, or a consequence of referral bias associated with clinical evaluation followed by therapeutic intervention during childhood. The first suggestion should lead therapists to consider how a contemporary politics of sex and gender bent on variation and inclusion is a necessary response to the systemic confinement of gender within the myopia of the male/female binary. The second suggestion is tantamount to an assault on affirmative treatment modalities, patently casting as suspect the ethics of therapists who use them. The handbook article also misidentifies stigmatization and discrimination as individual risk factors when, ecologically, they are systemic and structural factors that make life difficult for gender-nonconforming and trans individuals as they navigate the larger culture and society.

At the end of the day, treatment of the child or parents should not be a trigger that leads a gender-nonconforming child to live stealthily and mask true gender identity with a gender facade. Zucker et al. (2012)

do acknowledge this possibility: "We are mindful of this concern (the development of the false self in the Winnicottian sense) and emphasize that this is not a good outcome – the goal is to help the child work through their gender dysphoric feelings" (p. 390). They also state, "If, for example, children with GID who persist in their desire to be of the other gender showed a better psychosocial adjustment and adaptation than children with GID who desist (e.g., become gay or lesbian or heterosexual without gender dysphoria), then one could, quite reasonably, question the prevention of transsexualism as a legitimate treatment goal" (p. 392). They note the importance of considering this when treating adolescents with GID since, as they relate, "there is much less evidence that GID can remit in adolescents than in children" (p. 392). Thus when an adolescent demonstrates persistent gender-identity differentiation on a pathway to transsexualism, Zucker et al. (2012) suggest a therapeutic approach "that supports this pathway on the grounds that it will lead to a better psychosocial adaptation and quality of life" (p. 392). Here it appears these clinicians would use a gentler, more affirmative therapeutic approach with adolescents than with children, which is inequitable and unfortunate.

Zucker et al. (2012) contend that many children grappling with gender identity are psychiatrically vulnerable, which they maintain needs to be investigated "in relation to the stressors associated with an atypical gender identity … [but more particularly in relation to] risk factors, including biological and psychosocial parameters within their families" (p. 394). They raise the ethical challenge of studying gender identity in children in terms of the importance of natural history and the influence of contexts, relating that "one would have to conduct a randomized psychosocial trial in which, for half the children, some type of intervention was attempted to alter the child's gender identity" (p. 375). Importantly, they do acknowledge this could do immeasurable harm to the children involved. Thus Zucker and his colleagues are aware that the kind of study needed to determine whether gender identity is mutable or immutable is unethical, which leaves the issues of the nature and aetiology of gender identity unresolved, if not unresolvable (Schwartz, 2012). Drescher and Byne (2012) concur that it would be unethical for researchers to conduct a randomized, controlled trial, even though it is a research method commonly and effectively used to gather empirical evidence. This makes it difficult to study gender-identity formation in children.

In the end, the treatment model expounded by Zucker et al. (2012) speaks to the necessity of conducting research to understand gender-identity formation better. Interrogating its eclecticism and inattentiveness to the aetiology of gender identity, and questioning its utility in treating children, Reiner and Reiner (2012) assert the Toronto clinic's treatment modality is "based on a somewhat loosely coherent 'developmental, biopsychosocial model informed by a variety of theoretical and empirical advances'" (p. 435). Similarly, in examining the utility of the Toronto clinic's biopsychosocial model for understanding the complexities of gender-identity development, Fausto-Sterling (2012) asserts that the elements in their model are "curiously unlinked and static" (p. 402). Moreover, she considers these elements as a universal feature of gender-identity development in all children and not just a template for making sense of gender identity disorder.

Differences and Common Ground in the Fray of
Treatment Modalities: Zucker vs. Ehrensaft

Describing Zucker and the Toronto clinic as part of a kinship of "agnostics" (p. 400), Fausto-Sterling (2012) notes their developmental, biopsychosocial treatment model for gender identity disorder (1) uses multi-element analyses while situating pathology, including possible co-morbidity, as a key aspect of gender-identity variance; (2) asserts gender identity is generally a fixed trait for most individuals within a binary in which instances of gender nonconformity represent instability; (3) suggests gender identity disorder may be parent-induced, with biopsychosocial factors constituting mindful parental responses to nonconforming gender identity and expression; (4) uses a case-by-case approach to treatment; and (5) despite multifactorial analyses refuses to focus on causality because of what they consider to be a lack of empirical evidence. Positioning Ehrensaft within a kinship of "naturalists" (p. 400), Fausto-Sterling (2012) notes her True Gender Self Therapy model (1) suggests that gender identity has an innateness to it; (2) proposes gender can be created and affirmed beyond the limits of birth sex/assigned gender; (3) positions gender as a web, not a binary; (4) considers gender-nonconforming children healthy children from healthy families, with no presumption of pathology; (5) perceives stress and anxiety as likely products of systemic and structural influences or of parental unreadiness and not of gender nonconformity; (6) treats children to accept and self-affirm gender identity while learning to navigate a genderist world; and (7) helps families develop social networks where safe interactions and social learning about gender nonconformity build supports and strategies for everyday living.

Despite apparent differences between the two treatment modalities, Fausto-Sterling (2012) maintains there is common ground between agnostics and naturalists: "They both see biology including genes and hormones as a scaffolding on which the psyche is built. They both agree that there are probably several kinds of gender variance" (p. 400). Both clinical camps also fail to theorize the aetiology of gender identity as perhaps a product of the body's systems, leaving the concept and its formation as a matter of the mind that is "strangely disembodied and outside of the world" (p. 403). With the failure to consider aetiological factors, what remains is "the controversy over gender dysphoria as a developmental psychopathology itself" (Reiner & Reiner, 2012, p. 446). Suggesting that gender identity is inherently complex, Fausto-Sterling (2012) concludes, "Not a thing, gender identity is a pattern in time. In any one individual, it is shaped by the preceding dynamics and becomes the basis of future identity formations" (p. 405). Thus she suggests that gender identity is not static. It is dynamic and capable of reconfiguration. Indeed, she argues that providing families with "a deeper conceptualization of gender identity formation in childhood may well be the best therapy of all" (pp. 407–8). In the end, there is much to learn about what gender identity is and how it emerges in an individual. This leaves a vital question that Fausto-Sterling (2012) proposes: "How, clinically and experimentally, do we make it operational?" (p. 406).

All in the Gender-Creative Family

As mother Kim Pearson (2012), executive director and co-founder of TransYouth Family Allies, recounts it, her transition of the heart began on the day her depressed 14-year-old daughter (assigned gender) asserted his gender identity as her newly confident and content son (affirmed gender). However, as her son "began to walk in truth" (p. xiii), she as his mother simultaneously walked a genderist gauntlet, enduring criticism and even censure in family and institutional contexts:

> It is difficult to explain the sense of isolation parents raising a gender nonconforming child often experience. Many endure the disapproving gaze or comments of strangers in the grocery store. Family members may criticize their parenting skills and occasionally they are reported to social service agencies for alleged abuse of their children. Then there is the particular struggle of the parents that didn't see any signs of gender

nonconformity in their young children. They are taken totally off guard when their children assert their cross-gender identity and it's quite a struggle to make sense of this situation. (pp. xiii–xiv)

As Pearson indicates, parents struggle to build understanding and come to terms with the gender realities of their children. She relates that many parents immersed in this process and bent on loving and accepting their children in their self-affirmed genders become child advocates, educators, and protectors. In their research on mothers of gender-nonconforming children, Johnson et al. (2014) noted these mothers proved to be strong advocates, protecting their children and providing resources, educating and garnering support from family members, educating their child's school, fighting for changes in exclusionary school policies and legislation, starting support groups for similar families, and writing resources for other parents. When parents form peer support groups and navigate the realities of life with gender-nonconforming or transgender children, they grow as knowledgeable parents who engage in a collective process in which hope and inspiration frame educating others and other actions (Hill & Menvielle, 2009; Pepper, 2012). This process helps parents as they run a trans gauntlet, having to figure out what to do. Still they can take comfort in an empirical fact: gender variance/gender dysphoria are not linked to a particular parenting style (Scharrón-del Río et al., 2014). Hopefully, at least one thing is clear to parents: they need to support their children across gender differences. The Trans PULSE Project (2012), a community-based research project that included a focus on 84 trans youth who had at least started the social-transitioning process to their affirmed gender and had disclosed to their parents, found that parental support of a youth's identity and expression was directly related to the youth's assessment of better personal health (including mental health) and well-being. When parental support was stronger, trans youth were healthier, which included decreased instances of suicide ideation and attempts. Moreover, they had better self-esteem and were more satisfied with their lives. Consequently, the project concluded, "it is parents and caregivers themselves who provide the foundation for their children's health and well-being with their support. Therefore, policymakers and service providers need to ensure effective services are available directly for parents and caregivers of trans youth" (Trans PULSE Project, 2012, pp. 3–4). Of course, not every parent is a good parent, and trans youth can experience misery and violence at the hands of unaccepting and non-supportive parents. As the Trans PULSE Project (2012) indicates, negative parental responses "may be the root cause of many adverse health and well-being outcomes" (p. 4). Here one needs to rely on teachers, youth workers, and other caring professionals to be among those significant adults who act *in loco parentis* to meet the needs of trans youth who lack parental support. In fact they have an ethical responsibility to make life better *now* for the trans youth they serve in their practices.

Still it is parents who ought to be the most significant support for their gender-independent child. Since gender dysphoria tends to present itself at two key points in a child's life – starting school and entering adolescence – parental support is very important because more intense bullying and victimization experiences are likely (Menvielle, 2012; Scharrón-del Río et al., 2014). Parents need to be part of their child's process of growing into gender, even if it is incrementally at first as they grow into acceptance and find resources and their own support system. Parents of gender-variant children need to have social supports and to be educated about gender variance and gender dysphoria so they can build the knowledge and confidence needed to help their child at home and in community settings (Riley, Sitharthan, Clemson, & Diamond, 2011). While families with gender-nonconforming children often experience social ostracism, they do better with the support of peer groups and health-care professionals, and their children do better with family and other supports (Scharrón-del Río et al., 2014). When parents grow strong in the process of helping their child to grow into gender, it is the basis for their child to be strong also and just be. Parents need to listen to their child, offer protection and support, and enable the child to self-determine and self-affirm their gender identity. In this regard, gender-variant children feel the need to be heard, accepted, supported, and affirmed as agents with the capacity to live their lives in their own way in their own time (Riley et al., 2011). Parents have to be open to gender creativity in their child and in themselves. They need to advocate for their children against the grain of genderism in schools, medical centres, other institutional settings, and communities. This advocacy work locates parents as cultural workers and change agents who learn, share their knowledge, and infuse it into actions abetting gender creativity. It also locates them as good parents who love, nurture, and support their gender-creative child.

In addition to parental support, transgender youth want schools to affirm their gender creativity as they socially transition in a peer-intensive environment. Krieger (2011) relates that these youth will test the waters of acceptance and accommodation by confiding in close friends, dressing more androgynously, and building community with other queer and queer-positive students. Transgender youth will likely experience varying degrees of success because ignorance about trans-gender students is the norm in most school districts (Brill & Pepper, 2008). To assist youth processes of growing into gender, it is vital that school personnel take responsibility for engaging in gender diversity and sensitivity training that is trans* inclusive, with the asterisk repre-senting the array of trans-spectrum identities (Marx, 2011). Marx (2011) recommends providing all school staff members, including school administrators, teachers, support staff, and school health-care provid-ers, with professional development on trans* issues and transphobic harassment and bullying so a school's response is cohesive and school-wide. Here professional development needs to represent gender iden-tity and trans* as complex constructions in cultural intersections and in interactions with other relationships of power, including race and Indigeneity (Marx, 2011). For example, it is important the caring pro-fessionals interrogate how the *en vogue* descriptor "Two Spirit" lacks room to represent the spectral nature of Indigenous sexualities and genders. Here readers need to understand that "Two Spirit" is a con-tentious term requiring interrogation of the ways both colonialism and Indigenous cultural perspectives inhabit and alter its possible mean-ings beyond some simplistic understanding of a corporal embodiment of both a male spirit and a female spirit (Driskill, Finley, et al., 2011; Driskill, Justice, et al., 2011).

When gender-nonconforming children experience school as a gen-derist and thus trans-hostile space that negatively influences their comprehensive health, parents and other significant adults are left to worry about the physical and emotional safety of their children as they navigate life in schools where cultural gender norms rule (Luecke, 2011). For transgender children, every day is filled with triggers that dismiss or defile the desire to develop and belong as human beings with self-affirmed nonconforming gender identities. For example, starting a health unit on puberty can be gut-wrenching, with some chil-dren unable to sleep, or wetting the bed, or wanting to die as responses (Luecke, 2011). This is because the onset of puberty signifies the loss of the authentic gender self for these children. Interestingly, wetting the bed in response to worries of puberty's assault on the transgender body is also a response to holding in urine because using the washroom can be a dangerous place for transgender students (Luecke, 2011). In both cases the incessant mental stress is profound. From the perspective of such trauma, it is vital that parents and their transgender child meet with the school administrator, guidance counsellor, or the teacher adviser of the school's gay-straight alliance club, if one exists (Krieger, 2011). As Brill and Pepper (2008) suggest, parents ought to gauge the empathy of these professionals and their willingness to accommodate their transgender child's need for a secure and supportive learning environment. Such issues as accessing a single-occupancy bathroom and accommodations for changing and showering for physical education classes and sports need to be addressed. It is important for parents to ask how the school has or will prepare teachers and students to deal with transgender students so they can experience schooling in safe and respectful ways. To ensure their child's needs are accommodated and that a school culture of safety and support is created and sustained, Brill and Pepper (2008) recommend that parents ask what policies the school has in place to protect transgender students against gender discrimination. They should also ask questions about the school's philosophy and disposition towards students across differences, including gender differences.

Parents have a right to expect school personnel to act ethically, without bias, so every child experiences a caring school environment where bullying is not tolerated. The end goal is to transgress any resistance to find ways to support the transgender child, who has the right to learn in a safe, secure, and accommodating school environment. If school personnel are unhelpful, then parents should seek support from community groups who support and advocate for transpeople. They should also approach school-district personnel and the teachers' association for assistance. In dealing with their transgender child's transitioning process, which is demanding and even traumatic in so many ways, parents need to create a social support system to help them help their child at home, in school, in extended family, and in the community. Krieger (2011) urges parents to keep an open mind and engage in open communication so they can support their child. He suggests, "Listen, ask questions, be flexible, be patient" (p. 64). Central Toronto Youth Services (CTYS) (2008) emphasizes listening in its resource guide for parents of trans youth so parents may learn about their child's fears associated with transitioning as well as what their child needs to be accommodated and comfortable in family life.

Parents' positive commitment and actions nurture gender health as they help their child to be and belong. Mark's discussion of his mother's support in his InterText affirms this. Of course, other parents' negative reactions can interfere with all this good work. Thus the parents of a gender-creative child have a right to expect that the school administration will respond when other parents act unethically. The actions of those parents whose behaviour is driven by ignorance and fear can be detrimental to the gender health and overall well-being of a transgender child. Brill and Pepper (2008) provide this synopsis:

> Other parents can be very afraid of transgender children if they haven't had any education in gender variance. Their anxiety about the unknown can cause them to act in a primal way. This commonly manifests as demanding that the transgender child not use the bathroom of their affirmed gender, forbidding play dates, and even insisting that their own child publicly shun the transgender child. Some parents ask for their child to be transferred to another class, and some even choose to remove their child from the school. In some instances, parents have created a smear campaign against the child's family by talking to as many parents and community members as possible in an inflammatory manner. (p. 181)

These fearful and anxious parents ought to realize and question their consequential inhumanity in targeting vulnerable transgender children and their families. Through their behaviour, they are teaching their children to be transphobes who engage in symbolic violence or worse. Moreover, they are teaching transgender children that they are little monsters who shouldn't be allowed to even go to the bathroom in peace. As these unnurturing parents engage in genderist surveillance, transgender children have yet another reminder that school is a panopticon. Brill and Pepper (2008) see such problems with gender identity as a systemic issue: "When a child emerges as gender-variant, the problem lies not with the child nor with its parenting, but with a social system that places rigid limits on gender expression" (p. 12). Here race/ ethnicity, religion, class, and culture all play a part in constructing purportedly normal gender roles, which can be problematic on many levels. For example, transgirls have to navigate both genderist and sexist worlds where many desire and choose to emulate stereotypical understandings of femininity and beauty so they perform and appear more "girly" in their affirmed gender (Luecke, 2011; Schwartz, 2012; White Holman & Goldberg, 2006). This can create the stress of being not just a girl but a certain kind of culturally desirable girl.

Situating gender as an outcome of innate core identity and the influence of sociocultural norms, Brill and Pepper (2008) are emphatic on this point: if parents have a gender-variant child, they need to realize this reality is not a consequence of something they did or didn't do. Situating a child's gender identity as a core part of being, these researchers are clear on what parents *can* do: they can provide support so the child's self-esteem and happiness remain intact in the complex process of growing into a gender identity. Brill and Pepper (2008) declare that parents' acceptance and positive responses, along with good parenting strategies and a caring home environment, are the greatest influences on a transgender child's well-being. They relate that parents may need to tune into what their child is saying and start offering support early in their child's life since children aged 2 to 4 may start articulating the incongruity they sense between their gender identity and anatomical sex. These researchers indicate that the next time frame in which a child's transgender identity may emerge is when the child is 9 to 14 years old (prepuberty to early puberty). If the child is transgender, this can be a time of great turmoil as hormonal and physical changes towards maturation provide roadblocks on the way to desired or affirmed gender. Brill and Pepper (2008) relate that a transgender child experiencing the trauma of these changes may try to tell parents or may exhibit such negative outcomes as withdrawal, acting out, depression, or self-mutilation. The third time frame when a child's transgender identity may emerge is late adolescence, when gender identity becomes clear as part of the holistic development experience to that point. At whatever time a child discloses a transgender identity to parents, Brill and Pepper (2008) say it is important to listen, engage in open-ended, two-way communication with the child, and learn from the child and from competent, open-minded caring professionals who do not conflate being transgender with being gay and who acknowledge there is no recipe or timeline for transitioning. The bottom line, as they see it, is for parents to see gender identity and expression as an evolving process that takes both time and a support system for their child and for themselves. During adolescence, these positive, supportive actions can help a transgender youth to be resilient and gender healthy. Brill and Pepper (2008) encourage parents (1) to get educated on transgender issues so they can support their child throughout the natural process of gender-identity development, make decisions about privacy versus necessary disclosure, and deal with any cultural backlash; (2) to meet other families with gender-nonconforming children; and (3) if they have other children, to help them so they can learn to adapt to their changing family and accept their transgender sibling. The ultimate goal, as Brill and Pepper (2008) affirm, is true acceptance, which "is reached when you have a positive outlook for the future of your child and fear no longer dominates that view. When you imagine your child as an adult, happy and well loved, you know you have reached parental empowerment" (p. 59).

In the case where a transgender or gender-nonconforming child has siblings, Ehrensaft (2011) cautions parents to monitor family dynamics so they can deal with scenarios where their other children tease, share family matters inappropriately, or otherwise hurt their transgender or gender-nonconforming sibling. To help siblings, she suggests that parents assess the cause of negative behaviour, which is often related to the anxieties, discomfort, and confusion that collectively burden siblings. She also stresses the importance of dealing with the anxieties and fears a transgender or gender-nonconforming child may have that his or her gender journey is harming siblings. As parents intervene to address these difficulties, Ehrensaft (2011) emphasizes the importance of promoting gender freedom so all family members can live in and express their gender identities. She concludes that constructing the gender-creative family involves seven Ts:

> The *transgender* child who *transgresses* binary gender norms may face *transphobia* and psychological *trauma* within the family while leading the way to the family's *transcendence* of that transphobia by creating a *transformation* in the family's thinking, feelings, and actions as the child *transitions* from the gender assigned at birth to his or her authentic and affirmed gender identity. (p. 187, italics in original)

Within this dynamic, Ehrensaft (2011) further elucidates the role of parents as they support their child's ongoing and fluid process of gender-identity formation not only at home, but also with extended family, parents of the child's peers, friends, teachers, family doctors, counsellors, and therapists:

> [T]he new role for parents is to oversee the delicate dance and evolving transactions between constitution and environment as they help their children find an authentic gender identity and expression that will in the best of all possible worlds be a good fit for their sons or daughters. (p. 37)

Of course, in the face of the predominance and acceptance of traditional psychotherapeutic models that conflate gender nonconformity with gender identity disorder or gender dysphoria, parents who wish to support their gender-nonconforming children against the grain of hetero-patriarchal, genderist cultural bias and the tendency to blame the parents, especially mothers, for gender nonconformity "may face aspersion, pathological diagnostic labeling, or dire legal consequences – specifically, having their children taken away from them" (Ehrensaft, 2011, p. 49). Parents have to be courageous and find the strength to be assured of their identities as caregivers who are driven to affirm their child's gender identity and be a key support in the child's gender-identification journey. Ehrensaft (2011) asserts that to become gender-creative parents, they have to become facilitators of the child's process of self-affirming his or her gender identity. This means these parents have to become cultural warriors who contest gender norms and demand that health, education, the legal system, and other institutions learn to operate within a more spacious gender-creative mindset. Ehrensaft (2011) calls on gender-creative parents to (1) acknowledge their child's gender-identity location, (2) seek the support of gender-affirming therapists and other caring professionals for their child and for themselves, and (3) build community with other gender-creative parents. Reflecting on her experience working with parents of transgender children in her practice, Ehrensaft (2011) also speaks to the importance of these parents taking the time to process their situation:

> [Parents] had to carve out an inner place where they could let go of the child they held in their mind, to be able to embrace the child who stood before them. Without that space to mourn, parental gender creativity might easily transform into psychic collapse or, alternatively, parental gender mania, where there is a frantic leap into action ("Let's just say yes to the transition and get this going as quickly as possible") that misuses the time that should be spent digesting the situation and discovering new ideas. (p. 113)

As Ehrensaft (2011) concludes, gender-creative parents face the challenge of having "to figure out how to balance the blossoming of their children's true gender self with the natural parental urge, if not obligation, to keep those children as safe as possible in a potentially gender-unfriendly world" (p. 102). It is most important to listen to the children in this process and to tune into their cues regarding their health and happiness. For parents, this is getting it right. It speaks to the importance of family processes – including communication styles, cohesion, and adaptation – and not family structures in good family functioning (Hsieh & Leung, 2009; Sharkey et al., 2008).

These dynamics describe what ought to happen in a transgender or gender-nonconforming child's nuclear family. However, when a child mediating gender-identity issues is in foster care, they may lack the significant adults and other supports needed to work through the process of living in their affirmed gender identity. Ehrensaft (2011) relates that these children worry about disclosing their gender status and being supported and safe. They also worry about who has access to their gender history. With confidentiality and their safety at stake, transgender youth in foster care need to be recognized, respected, and accommodated in the placements and services that are provided to meet their particular needs (Lambda Legal, 2012). Within an ethics of care for trans youth in foster care, there should be no violation of gender identity and no blatant or insidious attempts to coerce transgender youth into gender conformity replicating the male/female binary. As part of the ethical treatment of these youth, Lambda Legal (2012) stresses that caring professionals including youth workers need to be "educated about transgender issues and prepared to work sensitively with these clients" (p. 1). This training begins with the recognition that gender identity is a personal characteristic distinctly different from sexual orientation. As Lambda Legal (2012) indicates, it should include

- building awareness of World Professional Association for Transgender Health (www.wpath.org) protocols for diagnosing and treating transpeople;
- learning how to support transgender youth in expressing their gender identity via naming and pronoun usage, attire, and behaviours;
- learning how to advocate for transgender youth by helping them find knowledgeable and affirming comprehensive healthcare providers as well as legal supports to assist them with such issues as legal name change and changing birth certificates to acknowledge affirmed gender identity;
- learning how to accommodate transgender youth so sensitivity to gender identity guides placement decisions by "taking into account their level of comfort and safety, the degree of privacy afforded, the types of housing available and the recommendations of qualified mental health professionals" (p. 2);

- educating teachers, youth workers, foster parents, and other youth so trans youth are safe and supported as they mediate life in schools;
- learning how to support trans youth so they can mediate the legal, educational, and training aspects of finding employment; and
- building knowledge of the larger trans community so caring professionals can find trans role models and mentors to help transgender youth in foster care create a sense of family and community.

The last point needs to be emphasized. Research indicates that awareness of and connection with a trans-spectrum community, notably for younger pre-transition individuals, may decrease negative outcomes and promote resilience (Testa et al., 2014).

Concluding Perspective: If Gender Became Undone

The gender matrix with its male/female binary embodied and embedded in sexism, genderism, and heterosexism is really the gender mire that strangles possibilities for gender identities and their expressions. In their book *Gender Failure*, Rae Spoon and Ivan E. Coyote each discuss navigating this mire as trans comrades-in-arms making, as Ivan puts it, "a space together to be brave inside of" (Spoon & Coyote, 2014, p. 15) in order to be, become, and belong as transpeople. Spoon provides this understanding of gender failure, positioning gender as something presumed to be fixed and non-negotiable, in keeping with the social fiction of assigned gender as immutable gender:

> My attempts at being a girl failed epically throughout my teenage years, but I had never considered that it was something that I would be allowed to change. I had no way to talk about gender. I wasn't allowed to express how uncomfortable it was for me. To resist would have put me in danger, so I kept any subversive thoughts covert. As a person who couldn't conform to what was expected of me, I thought I was a failure and kept it to myself ... When I retired from gender, it was because I came to the realization that the gender binary was what had been failing me all along. (Spoon & Coyote, 2014, pp. 17–18)

Spoon grew up feeling that gender had to be worn like a uniform. When they – the pronoun that Spoon uses to name and locate their gender-transgressing self – could finally hang gender at the back of the closet, they became gender free to be, become, and belong. Retiring from gender, which Spoon defines as "the refusal to identify myself within the gender binary" (Spoon & Coyote, 2014, p. 249), is their way to say they are fully engaged in a politics of resistance that is really about transforming gender as a social and cultural construct. For Spoon, that has meant letting boy impulses, mannerisms, and ways of being and presenting in the world play outside. It is transgressing the gender binary box to be excited and exhilarated about being all one can be or all one is meant to be in the gender matrix, now constructed as multidimensional, unbounded, and spectral to the point that gender becomes meaningless. Within this contemporary gender matrix, a person exploring gender can't tell the bottom from the top. This means one refuses to let gender define, categorize, limit, or stop oneself from living in the fullness of an affirmed gender identity. Only the individual self-determines and self-affirms gender as a matter of mind and heart that confronts and supersedes biological determinism. As Spoon relates, this does not mean they are not "default gendered as a woman" (Spoon & Coyote, 2014, p. 250) at many times and in many spaces. It does mean they navigate the world by positioning gender as arbitrary and being playful when those around them presume a gender category without ever asking. Spoon strategizes,

> [At times] I need to match my assignment to the sex on my ID, which reads "F." I sometimes tell people that the F stands for "Fuck Gender," but I am quick to let people assign me incorrectly if I need to get on a plane or cash a cheque. In these situations, my Gender Assignment by Convenience rule overrides my internal need to let people know about my retired state. (Spoon & Coyote, 2014, p. 251)

The implication here is one can't escape the hegemony of the gender binary, but one can challenge it and play with it in ways that decentre it. This provocation opens up gender to possibility. The resulting gender porosity flies in the face of sexism, genderism, and heterosexism collectively constituted as negative forces that have historically bound gender and what it means to be a girl or a boy.

Because transgender people transgress the sex/gender binary in their desire to live self-affirmed cross-gender lives, Shelley (2008) locates them among acutely disenfranchised individuals who are subjected to "a daunting array of institutional barriers and (inter)personal repudiations" (p. 3). However, he also locates them as the principal experts regarding their own complex lived and unliveable lives. Shelley (2008) uses the term "trans repudiation" to describe what makes trans lives unliveable. It can include internalized transphobia, interpersonal and institutional phobic reactions, and political and religious forms of trans dismissal. Thus, as Shelley sees it, transphobia is a subset of the more multifaceted trans repudiation. In speaking to experiences of trans repudiation, Shelley holds psychologists and psychiatrists among those responsible for the negation of trans subjects. While some clinicians are trans advocates, those who repudiate transpeople would have them withdraw into the perceived normalcy of the sex/gender binary. Shelley (2008) considers such clinical (mis)management, which is premised on the notion that distress emerging from trans sex/gender dislocation is a form of psychopathology, tantamount to a denial of the trans subject. This premise is grounded in "an uneasy ambivalence towards tampering with the embodied sexed binary, which remains sacrosanct in Western culture" (p. 6). This dis-ease with trans should force people to think more deeply about what it means to be human, whole, real, and alive. Speaking to this, Shelley (2008) maintains,

> [Trans-ness] both valorizes and questions "wholeness" or "integrity" as a goal (belonging to the *right sex*), implying a degree of essentialism and certainty. It also valorizes and questions border-crossing, in-betweenness, fragmentation, or indeterminacy as an attractive, transgressive alternative. Both positions have utopian aspects in theory, but prove to be uncomfortable, even infernal, in the real lives of transpeople. (pp. 11–12, italics in original)

While transpeople as a multivariate population across sex/gender differences may not find unity in difference, Shelley relates that they all struggle for selfhood as they live with paradoxes: First, transpeople are visibly marked or branded as sex/gender outsiders, yet they are often erased from a social world framed by the traditional sex/gender binary. Second, one is allowed to be trans to access medical interventions, yet this permission exists within a larger sociality that perpetrates intense trans repudiation, including transphobia. The upshot though is trans repudiation can be an impetus for trans and allied activism. As Shelley (2008) concludes, "Trans repudiation, whether through utterance, erasure, gaze, spectacle, alienation, phobia, sexual objectification, or violence, requires the solidarity of others to erase it" (p. 212).

In psychiatry, trans repudiation finds expression as gender identity disorder. When GID was first included in the American Psychiatric Association's *Diagnostic and Statistical Manual* in 1980, it provided what Valentine (2007) calls a diagnostic space for gender-variant people. In this space, gender variation, including GID, is considered psycho-pathological. It has been listed as such in versions III through IV-TR of the DSM (Byne et al., 2012). Right into the present, much controversy continues to surround the diagnosis and treatment of GID. This is indi-cated in the recent report of the APA Task Force that considered this matter as well as whether GID should be listed in the DSM-5 (Byne et al., 2012). Now, with GID being delisted as a psychopathology and recast as gender dysphoria (APA, 2013), there is hope that gender inde-pendence may one day be viewed as a normal variation of the human condition (Teich & Green, 2012). The fact that the APA has been delib-erating the matter of gender nonconformity is a pivotal moment in the emergence of the understanding of gender identity. Still the Task Force engaged in deliberations has been in a quandary, as Byne et al. (2012) indicate:

> The Task Force could not reach a consensus regarding the question of whether or not persistent cross-gender identification sufficient to motivate an individual to seek sex reassignment, per se, is a form of psychopathology in the absence of clinically significant distress or impairment due to a self-perceived discrepancy between anatomical signifiers or sex and gender identity ... Similarly, a consensus could not be reached regarding the legitimacy of particular goals of therapy with children diagnosed with GID (e.g., prevention of transgenderism or homosexuality) even when consistent with the religious beliefs or sociocultural values of the parents or primary caregivers. (p. 761)

Despite their quandary, the Task Force ascertained that an adequate, credible literature base did exist to develop recommendations for treat-ment of GID. The Task Force felt it is time for the APA to state its posi-tion "regarding the medical necessity of treatments for GID, the ethical bounds of treatments for minors with GID, and the rights of persons of any age who are gender variant or transgender" (Byne et al., 2012, p. 761). Here the Task Force pointed to the challenge of treating chil-dren, which is deemed more controversial than treating adolescents or adults. Children, as minors, cannot provide informed consent and are essentially at the mercy of primary and other caregivers who control decision making regarding the treatment of gender variance, including GID. In this regard, Spack (2008) declares that the conundrum for parents and health-care professionals is how to help children aged 8 to 10 years who have persisted for five or more years in performing gender independently of natal-sex expectations and dread the onset of puberty. He adds the situation is made worse by the reality that there are few health-care professionals – including mental health professionals, paediatricians, adolescent specialists, and paediatric endocrinologists – who have the knowledge to be competent in helping gender-variant children and youth by providing appropriate medical interventions such as, when warranted, pharmacologic suppression of puberty. Moreover, he says many health-care professionals have been hesitant to treat minor gender-variant children because of gender identity disorder's status as a form of psychopathology. Even worse, as Brill and Pepper (2008) relate, some who do treat transgender and gender-nonconforming children are guided only by personal beliefs and biases rather than research-based clinical evidence. Since decisions made can have long-term consequences, this raises an important ethical question for mental health professionals: Should they listen to children in deciding a course of action in keeping with the fundamental precept of medical ethics to intervene without causing harm? Those who affirm gender creativity believe what children have to say should be a counterweight to expert opinion made nebulous by such mitigating factors as experts' theoretical orientations, religious viewpoints, and beliefs and assumptions "regarding the origins, meanings, and perceived fixity or malleability of gender identity" (Brill & Pepper, 2008, p. 763).

With medicine unclear about gender and its possibilities, we might draw on Butler (2004) to ask, What would gender be like if it became undone? This is the question she asks us to deliberate as she conceptualizes gender as "a kind of doing, an incessant activity performed, in part, without one's knowing and without one's willing, … [and] a practice of improvisation within a scene of constraint" (p. 1). If gender is understood as performative, then growing into gender should be open to possibility. Traditionally however, Butler asserts gender is determined outside the self and socially imposed. A GID diagnosis is an example of this imposition at work to reify gender norms. Butler states that the diagnosis assumes that GID is a form of psychopathology simply because transgender persons want to express themselves or live a gendered life asynchronous with natal-sex expectations. With gender coherency determined by the American Psychiatric Association, she concludes, "This imposes a model of coherent gendered life that demeans the complex ways in which gendered lives are crafted and lived" (Butler, 2004, p. 5). The diagnosis means transgender people live with a paradox: while the diagnosis pathologizes the transgender person, it can also enable access to the medical intervention and financial aid needed to live one's self-affirmed gendered life. For transpeople, liveability has a very high cost.

Of course, upholding traditional gender norms is still the crux of the problem enabling GID to exist. As a matter of ethical treatment of transpeople, Butler (2004) maintains, "The critique of gender norms must be situated within the context of lives as they are lived and must be guided by the question of what maximizes the possibility for a livable life, what minimizes the possibility of unbearable life or, indeed, social or literal death" (p. 8). Butler relates that those who dismiss or defile transpeople seek to maintain a familiar sociality based on intelligible gender restricted to the traditional sex/gender binary and its genderist norms. However, these gender malcontents misunderstand gender:

> To assume that gender always and exclusively means the matrix of the "masculine" and "feminine" is precisely to miss the critical point that the production of that coherent binary is contingent, that it comes at a cost, and that those permutations of gender that do not fit the binary are as much a part of gender as its most normative stance. (Butler, 2004, p. 42)

As Butler sees it, gender cannot be contained. It is fluid, moving, more than two. This realization has weakened the binary foundation on which GID was constructed. It undergirded deliberations regarding the removal of GID from the DSM-5, which is a significant move towards respecting the integrity of transgender people and enabling a liveable transgender life.

InterText 4
Larissa: *My Heritage Is a Big Thing*

For Larissa, finding place is about being a whole person as a lesbian youth who is Two Spirit. And it's about finding ways to belong inside her Aboriginal community and in the larger community. Larissa is emphatic: youth are not problems. She challenges and inspires us to make things better for Two-Spirit youth at Camp fYrefly, which she says must grow as a more welcoming and accommodative space where Aboriginal youth can see themselves and their culture reflected in camp culture. As she sees it, Camp fYrefly needs to reach out to the most vulnerable of the vulnerable, helping them to steel life and live full and happy lives.

I'm from Poundmaker Cree Nation, which is about 45 minutes past Battleford, Saskatchewan going north. I've been a camper at Camp fYrefly twice before, once when I was 16 and once again when I was 18. I'm 21 years old now, and I graduated from high school two years ago. I've been working for the past year, and in September I'm starting my first year of university. I've registered for fine arts classes, but I'm thinking seriously of studying anthropology.

My grandma who has been in the education system for 30 years is my biggest inspiration for actually going to university. She always pushed the importance of education and she loves the arts. I always thought I would be an artist or work in the arts in some way. However, right now I'm drawn to anthropology, which is the study of humans and their behaviours around the world. Anthropology also looks at sexuality and genders and how, in many cultures, there are not just female and male. I am really interested in this.

I first came out as lesbian when I was 15. Coming out for me wasn't such a huge scary thing because I was raised by my uncle and he's gay. He made my lunches. He braided my hair. He took me to school. When he had boyfriends, he introduced me to them. I just thought it was a normal thing. I never knew there was such a word as *gay* and I never knew the words *fag* or *homo*. I just didn't know these words. Then when I started going to school, people would ask, "Oh, is your uncle gay?" And I wondered, "What is this gay thing that people are talking about?" Also, half of my family living up north is really Catholic and they'd ask, "Oh, is it true your uncle's gay? Does he have a boyfriend?" And I'd say, "Yeah, he has a boyfriend." I still didn't know what this gay word meant. I just knew that there was love, so being gay was just love to me.

This year I'm a youth leader. It's great. All the campers, all the youth in my pod group, have said, "Come back next year. You're the best pod leader." The first year I came to Camp fYrefly, I was going to school on the reserve and trying to start a GSA, a gay-straight alliance club. One of my teachers was a really strong ally. I still thank him for so many things that he's done for me. Once he took me to the *Breaking the Silence* conference at the University of Saskatchewan in Saskatoon. That's when I saw the whole thing about Camp fYrefly. It was just out of the corner of my eye. I didn't think too much about it because I thought it wasn't really for me. It didn't seem to be for Aboriginals. When I did go to camp, I struggled with the reality of being the only Aboriginal person there. I remember thinking, "Man, there are not a lot of positive role models out there for me." It was hard for me to find myself as a Two-Spirit person, to know where I fit. That's important because it is what young Aboriginals need. They need a sense of belonging. It's going beyond skin colour to explore where you come from, your heritage. That's a big thing for me. It's important for me to talk about it at camp this year because one third of the campers are Two Spirit.

My second time attending camp, I remember focusing more on how youth leaders interacted with the campers and adult volunteers. I reflected on what I thought a youth leader should be for campers, especially first timers. I applied to be a youth leader this year because I feel I'm in a very good place in my life right now. I can be there for younger campers. When I took a break away from camp, I did some self-work. I took some training to help me be a facilitator, and I've done training so I can work with younger people. This year my friend who is just coming out, and having no end of trouble with his family, wanted to come to camp. He is also an Aboriginal, and he was really nervous. He said, "I would love to go to Camp fYrefly, but would you please come with me? Can you?" For me, that clinched it – I was going to camp. But when he asked his family, his father said, "No, you can't go, because I don't want you coming back gay." However, the youth centre helping this youth took him to the campsite for the first day. When he and his youth worker called home, his dad gave in and said, "Okay, you can start camping there." That meant a lot to me.

What I notice this year is a lot more Two-Spirit Aboriginal youth are coming here. They're feeling more comfortable and I'm really proud of them because they are, in a way, paving the way for others to start feeling more comfortable in their brown queer skin. They're really getting along with everyone. It's really empowering. Still the past few days at camp have been difficult for me because I'm here as a youth leader, and it's about maturing and growing up. Of course, that's going to be a hard thing for anybody. But I also really love this camp. I am trying to be a good role model who is very visible. I really feel that I can connect with younger people who have difficulties. When I meet these youth, it's just a matter of giving them time and getting to know them. It's not just laying out the camp rules for them. You have to remember that you are here for them. I think that is one of my strengths as a youth leader. You have to remember that you're not here for yourself or to portray your own ego. You're here to get to know them and to make sure that they're comfortable and having a good time. I wish that other youth leaders would just understand that while it is important to be a good role model and to get youth organized, it is also important to take the time to get to know the campers and their specific needs. It is important not to see youth as problems. You need to see where they come from and that really does build a better understanding. Of all people, those of us in the LGBTQ community should know how hurtful it is for people to assume things about us and judge us right away. Youth leaders should remember this before they act.

To help Camp fYrefly grow and be a better place for Two-Spirit youth and our culture, I would focus on getting the word out about Camp fYrefly in places like inner-city youth centres. I would also go out to reservations and do presentations. When I was younger and I lived on the reservation, it was really rare to have people come out to our school to speak to us. It would have been good for someone to come and say, "You know there are places for you out there." Just that invitation would help. It's really sad, but when the encouragement is not there, youth on reservations think that this is all they have. They stay stuck in that cycle of the whole colonialism thing. Two-Spirit people who are coming to Camp fYrefly need to reach out in their communities. It's a really big thing in the teachings to give back to your own community, so it's important to go back and spread the word so people know what Two Spirit means. That's what I want to do.

3 Camp fYrefly: fostering, Youth, resilience, energy, fun, leadership, yeah!

It's 27 July 2012. I'm at Camp fYrefly in Edmonton. I'm sitting in on a dance workshop where a group of youth is engaged in an improvisation exercise with their instructors. They are energetic, intense, involved, and animated. I can see and feel their happiness. Watching these youth dance gives me the same peaceful feeling as ocean waves crashing on a beach. This is the way I have always dreamed that schooling could be. The dance is happening in a classroom in a building that was formerly a public school. I envision the spirits of queer youth past also dancing with joy as they look in on this present moment.

It's 4 August 2012. I'm at Camp fYrefly Saskatchewan in Regina. Camp fYrefly is the kind of educational and social world I have long envisioned for youth. I know schools can be terrorizing spaces for sexual and gender minority youth. I still carry the scars of my own experiences throughout junior and senior high school. I know how homophobic bullying can wear a body down. I want this generation of youth to know and experience something better *now*. Some might think that Camp fYrefly is a surreal queer space, even something idealistic. It's not. It's signifies the way that social learning can be. In some ways, as a person and an educator, I hope Camp fYrefly is a depot to deposit hurt and a social and pedagogical space to have hope and possibility returned. Many SGM youth who come to camp bring more baggage than their backpacks can hold. They've experienced too much adversity and trauma as a result of the stressors, risk taking, and negative outcomes that have marked their young lives. The difference at camp is that they can talk openly about the pain and find peers and caring professionals who will listen and help them in diverse and meaningful ways. At camp, SGM youth can learn how to grow into resilience one step at a time. As I tell them: At camp, you can laugh. You can be. You can cry. You can be. You can dance. You can be. You can learn. You can be. You can sing. You can be. You can try. YOU CAN BE.

Growing up, I couldn't even dream of Camp fYrefly. I had no such reference point in the K-8 school or in the community in the Newfoundland fishing village where I grew up. I had no such reference point in the Jesuit high school that I later attended in nearby St John's. I knew how to be sad. I knew how to run. I knew how to make mistakes. I knew how to think about escaping to heaven. I knew how to hide, but I didn't know how to be. The youth who come to Camp fYrefly have an opportunity not only to be but also to become and belong in a queerly safe and caring environment. It looks like the dream I couldn't have is now coming true for others.

In his call for education for uncompromising social transformation, educator and queer activist Robert J. Hill (2010, 2012) says social movements, including SGM social movements, are vital and energetic sites for lifelong learning and social education for youth and adults. Moreover, he asserts that social movement activities profile civic engagement and real-world contexts, influence political action, and create opportunities for social policy development and implementation. This perspective emulates Eduard Christian Lindeman's (1926/1961) notion of social education as critically progressive education recognizing human diversity. Lindeman believed "difference is the base of personal integrity" (p. 36). He challenged learners to acknowledge and value difference by developing an ontological sense of self and others "within the organic unity of particularized selves" (p. 36). As Lindeman saw it, a key goal of the process of social education is to assist learners to build awareness of difference and the larger social context, with this end result: knowing and accommodating difference, which enables freedom as an achievement, replaces fearing difference, which inhibits freedom. Lindeman (1926/1961) maintained that achieving this goal leads to creative living following the sequence of "intelligence for power, power for self-expression, and self-expression in the context of relative freedom" (p. 53). Here Lindeman stressed the importance of making relationships with others an intellectual concern so we can engage in conscious problem solving whereby we juxtapose the interests of self and others when challenges and conflicts arise in life, learning, and work as spheres of activity. He said this provides a basis for intelligent living.

These days education for creative and intelligent living focused on sexual and gender minorities and other vulnerable populations has to include education for citizenship that emphasizes problem solving in relation to rights and freedoms. It should attend to the historical, social, cultural, political, and economic dimensions of citizenship, ultimately seeing learning as encompassing educational and cultural work for social transformation (Allman, 1999; Grace, 2007b, 2012, 2013c). To zero in on sexual and gender minorities, education for citizenship has to expose systems and structures that perpetuate heterosexism, genderism, and attendant homo/bi/transphobia (Grace, 2010). As Hunter and Mallon (2000) relate, "Having to keep sexual identity and affectional preferences a secret creates stress that is a result not of the individual's homosexuality but of society's heterosexism" (p. 230). Similarly, I would argue that it is society's genderism, not an individual's gender identity and expression, that produces stress. Moreover, same-sex sexuality and gender nonconformity do not deter individual development and socialization; it is negative environmental responses including victimization, discrimination, and stigmatization that stunt these processes (Ehrensaft, 2011; Savin-Williams, 2008; Savin-Williams & Ream, 2003).

Informed by such contextualized learning from social movements and social education, Camp fYrefly, the flagship social program for SGM and allied youth developed and offered by the Institute for Sexual Minority Studies and Services (iSMSS), University of Alberta, provides these youth with opportunities to engage in social learning in non-formal (through workshops and other structured educational programming) and informal (through socialization in a four-day residential learning experience) contexts. The camp is set up as an interactive learning space where SGM youth can explore how internal and external conflicts, coupled with the consequential fracturing of the self and the social, affect their everyday lives. At Camp fYrefly, youth learn what it means to be recognized, respected, and accommodated in family, school, and community contexts. They get to experience the camp as a 3-H club, focused on helping them to be happy, healthy, and hopeful. In part, this is an engagement in comprehensive health education: being happy is linked to good mental and emotional health, being healthy also includes good physical and sexual health, and being hopeful is about steeling life and growing into resilience, where being at promise can be a reality. In sum, the Camp fYrefly experience is an example of what Mark (2011) describes as engaged pedagogy and education for citizenship. In this regard, campers critically explore ways to become empowered and to grow as change agents who start with the self and move out into the world. This growth proceeds from a core standpoint: SGM youth are not to blame for the harm done to them by heteronormative and genderist systems and structures. Through fYrefly programming, campers learn about ethical and equitable treatment, rights and freedoms, and justice. They build knowledge of protective policies and supportive practices linked to the recognition, respect, and accommodation of sexual and gender minorities in education, culture, and society. They also learn strategies for surviving and thriving. Such knowledge- and skill-building emanates from understanding ways that sexual and gender minorities have been marginalized and disenfranchised. The sum of this learning provides a basis for creative and intelligent living as campers seek new ways to help themselves and their communities.

Camp fYrefly programming aligns with Hill's (2010, 2012) perspective on social learning as a basis for agency. This perspective reflects Lindeman's (1926/1961) understanding of critically progressive education. It also reflects the idea that lifelong learning should be about learning for all and for all of life. Schuller and Watson (2009) made this idea the central theme of *Learning through Life: Inquiry into the Future for Lifelong Learning*. In this 2009 record of the national inquiry into lifelong learning in the United Kingdom, these researchers came to the sorry conclusion that formal lifelong learning was insufficiently concerned with social education, which they saw in decline in neoliberal times, in which the individual as an economically productive citizen is the primary focus. This inattention to the social is worrisome, especially in relation to those whom mainstream lifelong learning fails. To counter this failure, Hill (2012) suggests that many vulnerable youth and adults turn to social movement activities as spaces for informal and non-formal social learning that sees linking action to the improved well-being of participants as a primary goal. This move away from mainstream lifelong learning and formal education for youth and adults requires a revision of institutionalized lifelong learning in schooling and other formal contexts so it is recast as active learning encompassing educational and cultural work to create an inclusive and multi-textured sociality (Allman, 1999; Grace, 2013c). This would help position contemporary institutionalized lifelong learning as critical action (Grace, 2013c).

At Camp fYrefly, lifelong learning as critical action finds expression in ethical and democratic learning practices that SGM campers take up as counterpedagogy to practices of marginalization and disenfranchisement normalized in everyday schooling. This counterpedagogy embodying dynamics of a social movement towards place engenders commitment to the mobilization and social inclusion of SGM youth as historically omitted learners. Recalling the history of ignorance, fear, silence, symbolic violence (like derogatory name calling), and exclusion that have marked SGM experiences in mainstream lifelong learning and formal education for youth and adults (Hill & Grace, 2009), it is vital that schooling be transformed so SGM learners can engage in ethical and inclusive social education. Indeed lifelong learning should be for all in formal contexts because programs like Camp fYrefly, while impactful, are not ubiquitous. They are short term and localized, with limited capacity and resources. While such programs are an important smaller-scale strategy in facilitating individual development and socialization of vulnerable youth, Sesma et al. (2005) emphasize, "Programs alone cannot offer the kinds of supports, opportunities, and relationships young people need. This work requires a broader strategy in which multiple contexts in young people's lives [including schooling] are strengthened to promote the kinds of factors that sustain and support positive development for all youth" (p. 291). An encompassing strategy to make life better *now* for sexual and gender minorities has several goals: (1) exclusionary policies and practices in education, culture, and society have to be exposed; (2) communication in the intersection of the moral and the political has to be enhanced; and (3) the state of the struggle, the extent of transformation, and the need for further social and cultural action have to be monitored (Grace, 2013b; Grace, Hill, Johnson, & Lewis, 2004).

Camp fYrefly: Creative and Intelligent Experimentation to Help SGM Youth Show Signs of Thriving

Suggesting that preoccupations with theorizing and scholarship may be barriers to acting in real-world contexts where "hands get dirty, hearts lifted up and hearts broken, and most importantly, systems challenged through direct action in solidarity [with peers and mentors]" (p. 10), Hill (2012) calls on academics and other professional educators to engage in activism as a core educational practice. Camp fYrefly is a unique example of how a university can be successfully involved in such activism as community engagement, using research to inform programming for vulnerable SGM youth whom, paradoxically, schools as another formal educational institution have largely failed (Grace & Wells, 2007a). Webb (2011) suggests that such community-based learning can help participants to mediate daily life as they learn about commitment, intention, behaviour, outcomes, and the dynamics at play. At Camp fYrefly, SGM youth learn about the ways cultural and social systems and structures work against them and why this has been their reality from historical and political perspectives. Camp fYrefly operates in the intersection of "lifelong learning, social justice and conceptions of community" to engage campers in meaningful social and cultural learning that can influence their daily lives in the homes, schools, and communities where they live and learn (Webb, 2011, p. 83). Professors, graduate and undergraduate students, and volunteers get their hands dirty by engaging camp participants in research-informed, community-based social learning initiatives that advocate for SGM youth. In the work to mobilize campers to be, become, and belong, academics, institute staff, students, and volunteers take on roles as advocates, actors, and agents for change. This work recognizes that adults matter and can make a significant difference in improving and enhancing the lives of SGM youth. Reflecting the importance of a supportive relationship with an adult as a key finding in research on resilience (Pianta & Walsh, 1998), Brooks (2005) relates, "It is well established that a basic foundation of resilience is the presence of at least one adult (hopefully several) who believes in the worth and goodness of the child, ... a 'charismatic adult,' an adult from whom a child 'gathers strength.' One must never underestimate the power of one person to redirect a child towards a more productive, successful, satisfying life" (p. 305). Thus "[y]outh cannot be the only target of change – adults are implicated as much if not more so in this work" (Sesma et al., 2005, p. 292). Indeed significant adults are crucial to helping SGM youth to steel life and grow into resilience.

In 2004 Kristopher Wells and I co-founded Camp fYrefly as a summer leadership camp for SGM youth and young adults. Camp fYrefly is the largest leadership camp of its kind in Canada, with sites in Alberta and Saskatchewan and plans to expand to Ontario in 2016. Its affiliation with a major research university ensures that the camp operates using research-informed programming and inclusive pedagogical principles to focus on the individual development, socialization, and potential leadership and growth into resilience of SGM participants. The camp has evolved into a four-day, volunteer-driven, residential-style summer leadership retreat where SGM youth can thrive (Grace & Wells, 2007a). SGM youth came up with the camp's name, with the acronym *fYrefly* standing for "fostering Youth, resilience, energy, fun, leadership, yeah!" In researching fireflies, the youth learned that these insects are ubiquitous and produce their own light energy. Building on this metaphor, Camp fYrefly is a counterspace where SGM youth can learn about coming out, coming to terms, and growing into resilience in the face of the adversity and trauma they experience as consequences of heterosexism, sexism, genderism, and homo/bi/transphobia (Grace & Wells, 2007a). Camp fYrefly focuses on building and nurturing SGM youth's leadership potential and personal resilience in order to help them become agents for positive social change in their schools, families, and communities. SGM youth who attend Camp fYrefly come to know this counterspace as an affirming ecology in which they can find the recognition, acceptance, respect, affirmation, friendship, and accommodation that often eludes them in schools and communities (Grace, 2013b).

In a reflection on moving lifelong learning forward that ties neatly into Lindeman's (1926/1961) emphasis on the importance of social learning, Wildemeersch and Salling Olesen (2012) assert that lifelong learning ought to be creative experimentation that revitalizes concern with public matters and public engagement. Camp fYrefly constitutes such a creative experiment in social learning that underscores ethical practice and upholds the political ideals of modernity: democracy, freedom, and social justice. The camp's programming, which emphasizes responsible intervention and outreach, constitutes a political, pedagogical, and ethical practice in Blewitt's (2011) sense:

> [Such programming] has a pedagogic import that is not readily recognized by many educators in the formal education system but is real nonetheless ... [It] focuses on the experience of learning by the [historically excluded] groups or individuals. They deal with change, sensation, intentional and unintentional thinking and the emergence of transitional spaces where new opportunities and capacities can be developed which relate our inner to our outer worlds – to others, to the environment, to the past and to the future. (p. 35)

At camp, SGM and allied youth have opportunities to build the personal, social, spiritual, and environmental assets needed to survive, thrive, and improve their well-being, their social and self-knowledge, and their comprehensive health. Camp directors apply findings from our research on growing into resilience to camp programming to help SGM youth develop senses of self-worth and hope, a sense of belongingness and dependable attachments, and strategies for enhancing safety and security in their everyday lives.

Camp fYrefly is an engagement in educational and cultural work that mobilizes sexual and gender minorities, their families (as they construct them), and their allies to transgress adversity induced by heterosexism, sexism, genderism, and homo/bi/transphobia; to set realistic goals and engage in problem solving as part of surviving, thriving, and acting in life, learning, and work contexts; and to build supportive, collaborative relationships. The framework that guides the development and delivery of the Camp fYrefly program comprises five themes:

- *Creating a Socially Just and Inclusive Community:* As citizens, we all have a social responsibility to foster a sense of community spirit and to take care of one another (Lindeman, 1926/1961). Creating a community that is inclusive, welcoming, and harmonious is crucial to ensure that everyone is connected, included, and accorded respect and dignity regardless of their differences. At Camp fYrefly, we build a community that demonstrates acceptance, accommodation, inclusivity, and respect through engagement with individuals from different ethnocultural backgrounds, faiths, beliefs, abilities, ages, socioeconomic backgrounds, sexualities, and genders. Programming developed around this theme functions to help SGM youth to build awareness and understanding of democratic and inclusive citizenship in innovative ways that address barriers to full participation in our society.
- *Growing into Resilience and Youth Leadership Capacity:* Engaging SGM youth in learning how to make significant contributions to their own lives and to their schools, families, and communities helps build a strong, ethical, and just community for tomorrow (Grace & Wells, 2007a, 2007b). By developing a resilient mindset, SGM youth can make informed and healthy decisions about the issues and challenges that influence their lives and social interactions. Programming developed around this theme focuses on social and cultural learning about human and civil rights, advocacy, media awareness, public speaking, peer-to-peer mentoring, sex and gender stereotyping, healthy living, protective factors, harm reduction, and leadership skill development.
- *Helping Youth to Know Their Rights as a Basis for Empowering Them to Address Bullying, Harassment, and Hate Incidents/Crimes:* Knowing one's rights as persons and citizens comes with concomitant responsibility to advocate for others to advance a socially just society (Grace, 2007a, 2013b). Helping SGM youth to feel supported and empowered to

address discrimination, bullying, harassment, sexual harassment, and hate incidents/hate crimes is key to change processes focused on nurturing the self as well as assisting schools, families, and communities. Programming developed around this theme focuses on personal well-being, social activism, anti-oppression, inclusive cultural work, healthy decision making, safety, and coalition building.

- *Learning through Art, Music, Writing, Visual and Performing Arts, and Games:* The arts have the power to open up both the heart and mind. At camp, SGM youth learn about themselves and others through creative exploration and expression (Grace & Wells, 2007a). This helps them to develop new forms of communication, understanding, and community building. Programming developed around these themes often uses arts-informed pedagogy whereby youth engage in songwriting, improvisation, dance, visual arts, personal journaling, poetry, photography, and learning leadership skills through games.
- *Self and Social Development:* In this complex and rapidly changing world, SGM youth often struggle to find support, purpose, and a sense of space and place. Finding access to non-judgmental information about the issues that affect their lives is critical to social and self-development (CPHO, 2011). Programming developed around this theme focuses on personal development, personal wellness, self- and social-esteem, healthy minds and healthy bodies, spirituality, family (as youth construct it), and overcoming internalized homophobia and transphobia.

Using a by-youth-for-youth approach in camp programming, adult volunteers and youth leaders work in collaboration with a team of artists, dramatists, and community leaders. Camp fYrefly incorporates arts-based pedagogy that helps SGM youth build social and self-understanding and empathy that sees others in their spectral community of queer peers (Grace, 2013b; Grace & Wells, 2007a). They learn to strategize so they can be change agents in their own lives, the complex SGM community, and the larger community. In sum, Camp fYrefly's arts-informed pedagogy focuses on four key areas: individual development, socialization, leadership, and comprehensive health and safety linked to growing into resilience. Ultimately, Camp fYrefly is about saving and sustaining lives. It is a meaningful individual, social, and cultural learning engagement, and it provides a way to know, understand, and engage the queer and larger worlds.

Campers' Voices Carry: Youth Perspectives on Growing into Resilience

While it is essential to situate Camp fYrefly within a theorized understanding of social education, and within research on growing into resilience that can be used in advocating for youth, it is also vital to stay in tune with the perspectives of SGM campers. I learn so much from these youth whose voices carry, reverberating and reminding me of what's important about Camp fYrefly and what needs to be done so the camp continues to evolve as an SGM youth-centred social and cultural learning space. Campers inform adults about what the camp needs to be and, more importantly, who needs to be included in a camp that is intended to work in the intersection of differences.

In the excerpts from interviews with campers conducted as part of my research in recent years funded by the Social Sciences and Humanities Research Council of Canada, there is a rich basis for critical reflection on programming that abets the individual development of SGM youth and their socialization as well as leadership skill building and building assets to support growing into resilience. In sum, these themes are pervasive in the following interview excerpts: (1) Camp fYrefly is a source of supports and an energizer for growing into resilience; (2) the camp focuses on individual development, providing assistance with coming out, coming to terms, building leadership skills, and becoming a change agent; and (3) the camp emphasizes SGM youth socialization and the importance of community and building peer support.

> *Josh:* At camp you get to be out to people who are already out themselves, and you feel open and comfortable. Even if you are not out to the world, you get to be comfortable at Camp fYrefly. You get to be with fun people in a fun facility. You learn about leadership, and you become comfortable with yourself to be a leader. And later on, you may get to become a youth leader so you can give other youth the confidence to be proud of who they are. The expressions and creativity in Camp fYrefly – the dancing, the art, the music – I enjoy all those. I also enjoy learning about healthy and unhealthy relationships and safe sex. And don't forget the food. You get well nourished. Also, if you know you're gay and you're trying to come out, but you're still in the closet to your friends and family, you learn in Camp fYrefly about who to call or where to go to become more comfortable with coming out to your parents face-to-face, if it seems safe.

Liz: So this is just everything I could possibly want in an experience. I really wish I had known about this camp when I was young and was struggling with my sexual issues because I think it could've been very beneficial for me. Back then I was dealing with mental health concerns because I have a lot of those. This would have been such a great resource.

Zach: Camp fYrefly is really cool. I've met a lot of great people, and this might sound weird, but I've never seen an openly transgendered person in my life. I've never known anything about them, but I respect people who are open and now I have a level of perspective.

I'm not going to lie: it has been really uncomfortable for me because I've never been around other gay people before. However, my comfort has increased, and I think if I want to help somebody else, then I need to be comfortable with it. I've learned about a lot of things like zines [cyber-magazines] and gained lots of ideas. It's also having a connection to resources and people that can help you if you really need it.

It's hearing campers' stories, too. I bawled so much last night. And just the friends that I've made – they've made me a stronger person, yeah. For me personally, the camp just gave me a lot of self-confidence about my sexuality. It gave me information that I wasn't connected to in my community. Those are probably the most important things.

Jessica: I just love the atmosphere at camp. Last night I felt in this wonderful mood. You can just feel the magic. You can see that friendships are being created. Campers do talk about having bad experiences, and you get to understand different stories. Before I met Mark, I had never met anyone who was trans before. Hearing his story was like, wow. This experience opens up 10 times more doors. I just love the entire camp experience. I'm learning so much and meeting new people. It's just been mind-boggling. I'm in heaven right now.

I really want to help out with Camp fYrefly in the future because it's such a great program and it has helped me the past couple of years. Camp provides the time for you to come back and reconnect with all those people you met last year so you can find a way to make it through the other 361 days. This year I brought my girlfriend Ashley. I've also been pumping camp up to all my friends, telling them, "Come to fYrefly. It's good. It's fun." One day I would love to be an adult volunteer. I just want to keep helping.

I love that everybody at camp decorates a little box with their name on it and people fill it with happy notes. It provides a lot of really good memories of new friends who are going to be there when it seems like nobody else is. That's what I came away with last year, and I'd really love to know the youth campers are going away with that idea this year. Since last year I've started being more open-minded about everything and I try to give things a shot. Sometimes if I have a problem, like when Ashley and me are fighting, I'll use skills I learned at camp about resolving the conflict instead of just making it worse.

Evan: I think Camp fYrefly is incredible and there should be more structures like it. Camp helps me realize that there is so much more I can achieve. It has given me a safe space where I could feel really comfortable with my orientation and have lots of people to relate to. I have a sense of belonging and community. More than that, though, I have a sense of understanding. I was really lucky because I have very understanding parents, but my parents didn't have any gay friends or colleagues or anything. So although they were very supportive, they didn't understand my perspective totally, which was huge for me.

It was really good to have some awesome, supportive role models at camp because outside of camp I find a lot of the gay community is formed at clubs and gay bars. Bars can involve a lot of alcohol and that can have a negative effect. I think it was good for me to have camp as outreach that was supportive and didn't involve drugs or alcohol.

Erica: I come back to camp every year basically because it's fun. But also because I'm still learning, and I still need that help sometimes. This is the place where I can really be completely who I am. For four days I can remind myself of who I am and what I actually can do because near the end of the summer or during the school year it just starts getting really confusing regarding what I can and need to do. I'm the kind of person that likes to help. Camp fYrefly is about taking time for myself even though I'm helping people here. The friendships are important, most definitely. I'm not a person who does Facebook a whole lot. I'm not a person who does texting. I can't have full conversations texting. At camp I make really good friends. I know that I have a place in their hearts just like they have a place in mine.

Shawn: I never had an outlet to discuss my sexuality openly in a safe space, and Camp fYrefly was the first opportunity that I had to do it. It just poured out of me. It just came out. It's not just about your sexuality and gender. It's also about your self-esteem. At one point during camp at the discussion tables, I sat at the eating disorder table. It was really an opportunity to discuss my own issues with self-esteem and my own body issues in a really safe, non-judgmental environment. I had a camper come up to me after that and he talked about his own issues with eating disorders, body image, and self-esteem. That is a specific moment I have in my mind because he spoke very encouragingly to me. That really helped with my self-esteem and with other issues I was going through as well.

Before Camp fYrefly, I had never really known a sense of queer community. I had never been in a room with more than two other queer people, so I was never sure how to go about coming out. Even though I'm 23 years old and on the older end of the spectrum, I was still struggling with who I was and with accepting this. I was closeted. I wasn't out to my family, and I was struggling with being open with my friends. Camp fYrefly really propelled me into not just accepting myself, but also realizing my potential as a leader and a person who can educate others. It has helped me realize that this is inherent in who I am as well.

I know I came away from my first Camp fYrefly as a much better, stronger person. The second I got home I came out to my mother because I felt confident enough to do it. It was definitely a positive experience. Having all of my fYrefly paraphernalia – my guidebook, my happy notes, my T-shirt – was a great icebreaker. I could say, "Oh, look what I got at camp." And as I am flipping through the guide and talking about the happy notes, it's kind of dawning on her what kind of camp this was. But it was a very positive experience and she reacted very well, which I'm pleased with. I even told her when I came out that you don't have to accept this because I don't expect you to, but it was very positive.

I also felt: How could I not come out after this experience? I was interacting with 13- and 14-year-olds who were completely out, and here I was a 23-year-old and I wasn't out. I thought, this is an opportunity not only to have a giant weight lifted off my shoulders, but it was also an opportunity to be visible and to educate others. That was probably the biggest change. Camp fYrefly was other things, too. It was building your leadership skills, and it was self-esteem building. It's not just about sexuality. It's not just about gender.

Derek: I'm really enjoying my role this year as a youth leader at Camp fYrefly. I wanted to be a youth leader because I've had a great experience at fYrefly as a camper these last couple of years. There are a lot of people that obviously need the support system of the other people at fYrefly, and the camp is a really good thing to have for that reason. I have such a healthy and stable life now, so I want to do what I can to give back and be there for the people who do need a little more. That was my biggest reason for wanting to do this. I want to give back in my capacity as a gay young adult leader.

A big thing with youth is that they'll meet people on websites and they'll have conversations. Sure you can make a bond, but meeting someone face-to-face, having conversations, and spending a lot of time with them is really helpful. The people I've met through Camp fYrefly have been one of my bigger support systems. So I want to engage youth and help them grow. Self-realization during camp is extremely important.

Camp is important, especially for a lot of the youth who have never met a trans person or a Two-Spirit person before. It's an important thing to understand all the queer culture and everyone who is involved in the community. I've definitely seen an increase in the number of trans and Two-Spirit youth who are participating in the Saskatchewan camp. Obviously, there is a lot of history where we are right now. The opening ceremony was Métis-based because we're on Métis land. I thought that was very powerful. Having Adrian Stimson who is a Two-Spirit Blackfoot performance artist here as the artist in residence is also quite powerful.

Ryan2: I thought, "What? You can't be serious! This is like my dream!" It took time for it to actually register that there was really a summer camp in my province for queer youth. I had never heard of something like that before, and it was just so amazing. I had never been in a room before with more than two, maybe three other queer people and I thought, "I'm going to be going to a camp with 50+ people who are all going through the same things I am. It is amazing."

I knew I could get so much out of it, so much. I've learned so much about leadership here. Camp fYrefly has helped me be more comfortable with meeting someone and just being my normal gay self. I'm just so much more comfortable with my sexual identity now that I don't have to put up my facade.

I came back to camp the second year to try to get to know myself better and to know the community better. That's because, aside from Camp fYrefly, I pretty much have no contact with the gay community. I've never lived in Edmonton. I come down here and travel 12 hours all the way back. That's just how it is.

QC: Community is important for support. In an event like Camp fYrefly, kids can come in feeling really isolated at first. Then over the weekend they can start to become whole, and start to feel unified and connected. I think for queer people in general, or the world in general, the trick is leaving behind the idea that we are alone. We need to connect with the idea that we are all a part of something. We need to get away from the alienation. I feel there's so much hatred. So many things go wrong because we feel so separate from each other. I think that sense of isolation and separateness is what causes all of our pain.

I hope campers take away a sense of being loved, a sense that they are not alone, and a sense that if things get so bad in their lives, at least that there is a place, once a summer, that they can return to. It can be their solace. That one thing can foster resiliency in people for a long time.

Helen: I think the biggest thing I have found with the camp is that you realize how many other people there are in the community who are willing to stand behind you and support you. On the day I left camp my first year, my youth leader gave me his email address and said, "If you ever have problems, you can contact me and I can help you find support." That was a huge thing. It feels like going to the Pride Parade for the first time and seeing that many gay people in one place. I think it's overcoming isolation and realizing that you're not alone. It's the knowledge that, at the end of the day, there are people out there who will help you and care for you.

Concluding Perspective: Engaging in Critically Progressive Education

In his reflection on the contributions of Eduard Lindeman to education for social purposes, J. Roby Kidd (1961) characterized the social philosopher as an ambitious educator who affirmed social education as the modus operandi for transformation of a world where "injustice [had] to be fought, and the inhumane [had] to be brought to bay" (p. xiii). Lindeman (1926/1961) believed that social education was the foundation for envisioning and building social democracy. To achieve this end, he asserted that study and action – thinking and doing – had to be in dynamic equilibrium so social education could be organic and whole. Valuing participation as the driving force for social education as an active and non-prescriptive engagement, Lindeman provided this caveat: both democratic and non-democratic forces have the potential to drive social action, which means we always need to analyse social action in terms of its rationale and positive or hazardous consequences. As mentioned earlier, this perspective is a core tenet undergirding

Camp fYrefly's philosophy and programming. When working with sexual and gender minorities, it means recognizing that vulnerable populations aren't the problem in a social democracy. At Camp fYrefly we use everyday examples to remind SGM youth that it is the systems and structures constricting education, health, and culture that oppress them, keeping them invisible and immobile. We talk about priests, politicians, and other purported community leaders whose conservatism in the name of tradition ignores the humanity and integrity of sexual and gender minorities as persons and citizens. However, we also remind them that there are queer mentors and other good people in the world – allies including many politicians and religious leaders – who support them and advocate for them.

At Camp fYrefly, we work to be proactive change agents who use our research to propel the camp into the arena of engaged pedagogy in order to achieve a central goal: to make the world better *now* for SGM youth. At its heart, Camp fYrefly is an engagement in critically progressive social education, which Lindeman (1926/1961) said gives meaning to learning. This engagement focuses on social interaction and learner agency in an emancipatory context and on social learning and education for the public good (Grace, 2007b, 2012, 2013b). In this reflexive process of education, learning is linked to critical action as SGM youth learn to address ignorance and absences in the work to enhance their everyday lives in individual and social contexts. The goal here is to locate lifelong learning as critical action, as a collective endeavour where problem solving and acting in the real world are summative of the contributions of all participants, from camper to youth leader to adult volunteer (Grace, 2013b, 2013c). Here advocacy and agency nurture the social and engender hope and possibility for continuing social advancement. The end goal of Camp fYrefly is to contribute to the development of a social democracy in which there is no inside/outside for sexual and gender minorities, just space and place for all. This is cultural work for social transformation as something real and dynamic.

InterText 5
Mark: *Being the Boy I Am*

Mark is growing into resilience and, as a youth leader at his third Camp fYrefly, he is strong, vibrant, centred, and energetic. He is very comfortable speaking with people about his experience as a trans youth. He has dealt with huge challenges that, with support, he has managed to transgress and has steeled life because he just had to be himself. Mark knows what he needs and what he desires. His mom and his partner are huge supports for him. He wants to use what he has learned so far in his FTM (female-to-male) journey to help other youth.

This is my third Camp fYrefly. I've been to one in Edmonton, one in Saskatoon, and one in Regina. What brought me back is just the atmosphere at camp. It's nice to be part of a majority for once. As an FTM person, I don't have to worry that someone is going to expose me. I am able to walk into a gender-neutral washroom and not be anxious about guys getting uncomfortable or starting something with me. It's the total acceptance at camp that keeps me coming back. So this year I wanted to try something different. I'm here as a youth leader so I can learn more about what goes on to make a successful camp. I've realized certain things that I took for granted as a camper. There is stress you experience as a youth leader responsible for a pod of six to eight campers who have very full daily schedules and places to be throughout the day. You realize why it's so important for campers to be cooperative with their youth leader and the adult volunteer assigned to provide support. I'm learning a lot about team building and the responsibilities of being a leader. I bring my personality and experience to what I do. Sometimes I worry that some of the campers in my pod are too introverted and not talkative. A part of that is my pod has fairly young campers, but I think it's more: they're still worried that they're going to be judged for what they say.

I know as a camper I use to worry about what to say. Sometimes I got asked, "Why don't you want to go swimming or why don't you want to be in a water gun fight?" At first, I'd just say, "Oh, I just don't like getting wet." I wasn't comfortable admitting that I wore a chest binder and couldn't get wet while wearing it. Talking was stressful. If I said, "Oh, I have a doctor's appointment coming up," others would say, "For what?" I'd answer, "Just for a check up." I didn't want to tell anyone that I was going to get my testosterone level checked. However, at my first camp in Edmonton I met an adult volunteer who is a trans man. He was just so comfortable with where he is in life. I was absolutely blown away by that. It was so incredibly empowering to see this strong, powerful, and confident trans man. He had made it through his transition. He was in a successful relationship and had a family. This experience made me more comfortable with the idea that I could do this, too. On certain levels, he and I are the same. We both have had feelings of gender dysphoria. I don't want to say that this makes us the same, but in a way we have a bond. We are a brotherhood because we both understand what it feels like to be in the wrong body and not be seen by the world as we are inside.

Once I realized that no one at camp was going to judge me, I was able to come out of my shell. I'm hopeful that campers in my pod will also come out of their shells and just be comfortable saying what's on their minds. It's hard though because many campers don't live in particularly accepting areas. They're not used to being so open. It's hard for them to say, "I'm here and I'm proud." When you grow up in a small community, it is risky to be out and proud. You could get hurt because everybody knows your business and everybody knows where to find you. It's a very unnerving feeling. You always feel you have to be on guard. At camp I realized I was tired of being terrified. I just decided to say, "To hell with it." And my shell shattered just like that. I started to say, "Yeah, I've got my binder on and it's great." It was so good to talk about things in my life that I was happy about. I guess at some point you just have to say, "I could get hurt crossing the street. I mean there are so many things that could potentially hurt me. Why live in the closet and be miserable?" Sometimes I'm still nervous and afraid that something is going to happen to me but, at the same time, I'm so much happier being out and proud. This is who I am. I can say, "I have a doctor's appointment to get my testosterone level checked because I'm an FTM transsexual and I'm going through a transition." I'm perfectly comfortable saying that to somebody. If they want to know more about it, great! Then I can educate them. If they don't want to learn more, that's their business.

Looking back, I actually came out twice in high school. The first time I came out, I came out as queer, and I was viciously harassed although I was never actually physically harmed. Queer is my sexual orientation. After about a year, I had my second coming out. I started asking people to call me Mark. I began binding my chest and sometimes I would do drag makeup with artificial hair and a beard. Then one day in the cafeteria somebody asked me, "Well, what are you? Are you a transsexual or something?" I just said, "Well, no. I haven't undergone any surgery, so I'm obviously not transsexual, yet. But I do identify as transgendered." I like to call this my coming out of the locker room because I was finally admitting that I'd rather be in the other locker room. When I said this, I was promptly shoved into a locker. A few days later I was assaulted leaving the school and hospitalized for 2 weeks. So at 16 years old I'm terrified that I'm going to be hurt. I moved from Kirkland Lake, Ontario, out west to Fort St John, British Columbia, just to get away from that. I went back into the closet. I stopped binding and just lived my life presenting as a queer woman. I was miserable. Then when I was 18 years old, a friend of mine mentioned that her teacher had been at a conference and heard about Camp fYrefly. She said, "Mark, you should go." She was the president of our GSA, so I felt comfortable coming out to her and her friends from the GSA. They all knew. She told me the deadline for applications was just two days away, so I ran home, printed out the application, and faxed it in after I filled it out. I got accepted and I was ecstatic.

At camp this year I do have a trans-identified camper in my pod. He was at camp last year as well, but he hadn't come out as a trans man. He was presenting as a lesbian. Towards the end of that camp he approached me and said, "You seem so confident in your gender and with your identity in general. Would you like maybe to sit and talk about it?" When we started to chat, he asked, "Well, how do you know that you're a guy?" I answered, "How does anyone know he's a guy? It's what you feel." I told him how I had looked at the women in my life and felt like I didn't have anything in common with them. I said that I didn't identify with women in the media either. However, when I looked at the men in my life – those men who are strong and confident – I knew they were the ones I wanted to be like. I told him this was a big indicator for me. I wanted nothing more than to be like my nonno [grandfather]. I had nothing in common with my nonna [grandmother].

When I saw this camper in my pod this year, I was so excited. As a youth leader, I am now able to help him more. I can be there for him. I can talk to him and share resources he might find useful. I can tell my story about how I have three older sisters who now have a trans brother. I can tell him about the questions I have asked myself: Why am I the only one in my family who is trans? Is it nature or was I nurtured differently? I can share conversations I've had with my older sisters who told me, "Well, we're not trans. Why would you be trans and not us? We were all raised by the same people." I can also talk about being a trans parent because I do have a 19-month-old son. Of course, it's up to the camper to decide what we will talk about. I just want to help him and to know that he's doing okay. I hope he will be able to go home and say, "Here I am. I'm your boy."

I've done a lot of self-education, but I have also had some people along the way who helped me to learn about and understand the trans experience. I was fortunate enough to meet Nina Arsenault who is known as Canada's T-Girl. She is an out and proud MTF transsexual. She is an activist, an actress, a writer, and a model. I went to Toronto to see her perform her monologues. I was lucky enough to get to meet her afterwards. She told me to be strong. She said, "If some people hate you, let them hate you. They're jealous. You know who you are. They don't." I loved how fierce Nina is. She puts herself out there, telling the world, "Here I am." She actually had to do most of her transition in Guadalajara, Mexico, and she took great risks to become a woman. She's a trans pioneer. She's out and proud and I'm out and proud.

However, my mom is my greatest supporter. When I came out to her I was in tears because I was terrified that she was going to kick me out. She was in tears, too. After I told her, I asked, "Mom, are you okay?" She answered, "I'm so happy you finally told me." I was confused by her answer, but as we chatted she told me how she already knew. She's totally there for me now even when she is at work. When I was in the closet, her co-workers knew me as her youngest daughter. Now she makes sure they know me as her son. For example, once when I visited her workplace, a co-worker phoned her to say her daughter was here. When she came up to the front area, she asked, "Where's my daughter?" I was standing right there in front of her. When her co-worker pointed towards me, my mom said, "My son's here, but where's my daughter?" Her co-worker nodded, getting it. My mom is incredibly supportive. Two of my sisters are also supportive. However, my dad and one other sister have not supported me. They believe that being trans is something that can be solved through therapy. Despite being practising Catholics, my nonno and nonna were very supportive before they passed away. I have often wondered if my nonno would have preferred me to be transgendered and attracted to women as opposed to being a woman and attracted to women. However, his motives for supporting me weren't my concern. Since he was my male role model, I really wanted him to support me. My partner is also incredibly supportive of me. She actually didn't know that I was transgendered when we first met. Before we started a relationship, I told her. She said it didn't matter to her. She is heterosexual, but she wears a rainbow belt buckle. If anyone ever asks her if she's queer, she says, "No, but my boyfriend is."

During the next few years, I definitely want to transition further to become a more physical male. I don't necessarily feel like I have to do this. I just really want to do it. I do feel more comfortable when I appear more physically male with a flatter chest, so surgery is definitely in my future. However, certain aspects of the surgery are not covered by the medical services plan in British Columbia, so I'm saving up. It's coming, just not any time soon. My testosterone hormone therapy is going to continue and, hopefully, my voice will drop again. I've got two more drops, I think, to come. Apart from my transition, in my future I would like nothing more than to have a home with my partner and perhaps a bit of the white-picket-fence life. I want to keep volunteering in the queer community. I want to continue to be open to my friends and family. I would like to help other people who are transitioning. I want to educate people about trans identities and gender roles. I'm not an expert, but I do like to read up on these things because it's something that is incredibly important to me. If along the way I can meet more people who have something to teach me, great. If not, I will continue to learn on my own. These days I'm not in high school anymore. I am out in the real world. Granted that means there are more people who can harass me, but it also means there are more people who can support me. I am not going to hide anymore because of past experiences. I can't change what happened in high school, but I can choose not to let it affect me. I can have a good life.

InterText 6
Paul: *Bringing People Out of Silence*

Paul overcame a history of shyness to become very involved in his communities of interest in Surrey and Vancouver. In many ways, he is an entrepreneur, learning on the go and building his capacity as a leader. Paul speaks about Camp fYrefly, Queer Prom in Vancouver, and other inspirations that have helped him in the processes of coming out, steeling life, and growing into resilience. He talks about why he dropped out of school and his self-direction in eventually getting his high school diploma online. For Paul, the Internet has been a learning space and a social space. He has interests in building queer community, youth leadership, and transportation and urban planning. Paul is self-motivated and makes his own way in his own time. He discusses his close relationship with his dad as well as the ups and downs of dealing with immediate and extended family.

I'm 19 now, and I first came to Camp fYrefly three years ago. The camp has inspired a lot of community involvement for me. My sexual orientation – in some ways it is a major part of my identity, but in other ways it's not something I put out there a lot. It's hard to explain. For some people it's all about being gay, whereas I'm involved in so many different other things that it's just one section of my personality. For example, I was always a very shy child. That's still a big factor, but I've overcome my shyness a lot in recent years. I think part of that is I'm a really good listener and observer, so I can bring together different people and build bridges. It's about breaking people out of their silence. I'm good behind the scenes.

I came out to myself – or accepted it – when I was 14. I came out to my parents at 17. When I first came to camp, it was about 6 months after I started regularly going to a queer youth group in Vancouver. Some of the people there knew about Camp fYrefly because they had moved out from Edmonton. I was encouraged by one of my friends to sign up last minute. I was really excited because I had never travelled by myself before, so that was a huge factor for me. That was a major leap forward. It was my first plane ride. I wondered, "Oh my God, how is it going to go?" With that shy factor, it was nice knowing that there were a few people that I knew at camp. The first few days were tough for me, just being around so many people – almost 24/7. It was way too much to handle. But as the days went on I started to build connections with a few different people and be more open with everybody. By the end of it, I felt, "Wow, this is amazing. I'm so inspired. The energy is just completely overwhelming." I went back home, and I was just so excited to be home. I thought, "I love Vancouver! This is so awesome!" I actually arrived back home on the day of the Pride Parade. Camp fYrefly was a lot to take in. That inspiration held through for a couple of months. Then I thought, "Okay. I'm more comfortable with myself now. I've learned all these leadership skills. Now how can I make my community a better place?"

I had dropped out of school in grade 10. Because of that I transferred to an online school, so I was socialized through the community rather than going to school with peers. That had a major influence on me wanting to be involved in the community. Camp fYrefly also inspired me in terms of getting out there and wanting to be in a leadership role. I also found out more about other camps and conferences. I started attending them, which helped me to keep my energy levels up throughout the year. For example, I joined the Surrey Youth Leadership Council. We had a mandate to organize a forum about the future of the community and that was about a nine-month process. Then I wanted to take more things on. I've been passionate about sustainable transportation in my city because I live in the suburb of Surrey and ride the bus. So I helped out for a while with the Vancouver area cycling coalition. I had also been blogging for a while. I just started sharing my opinions and doing a lot of research on my own time. Overall, I've been involved in the queer community, youth leadership, and transportation and urban planning. I do the general youth leadership work in Surrey, whereas I do a lot of my queer work in Vancouver. There is a small queer community in Surrey, but the reason I go to Vancouver is that I just connect well with the people there.

There were a lot of reasons why I dropped out of school. In BC we go into high school in grade 8. Grades 6 and 7 were really great for me. I really enjoyed it. We were a small class and everyone was getting along together. But six months into grade 8, I really started to experience that this is high school and you have cliques here. There was a certain way of the world, or way of the land, and I didn't really get it at all. I would go on my computer and try to figure out how to manoeuver my way through this school, but I wasn't grasping the concepts. I didn't really know how to communicate with these people. Also, I had been told not to hang out with the druggies or the people who drink alcohol, but that was pretty much everyone. I didn't know how to handle that, so I cut myself off a lot. I thought, "If I wasn't going to bother with the social aspect of school, then I'd focus on the educational side." I did that for the first year, but by the second year I didn't know why I was doing half the stuff I was doing. I read a lot online and learned about entrepreneurs who became very successful throwing up their own websites and doing their own innovations. I thought, "People can make a living doing that. I can make a living doing that. Why do I have to go to school to do that?" At a certain point I decided, "I'm not going to school anymore. This is ridiculous. Parents don't get it. They don't know what is happening in the world these days." So I just stopped going. However, I quickly realized that you can't get far in the world without a high school diploma or a bachelor's these days. The only option in my hometown was online, so I pursued that for a while. But it was extremely difficult. I dragged my feet through that whole thing. I only finished 4 courses out of what probably would have been 10 in the traditional school. I would do a bunch of work, stop, and do a bunch a few months later, and stop again. The grades were decent, but nothing spectacular. Ultimately, the way I graduated was that I found a loophole in the system called Independent Directed Study. I really broke it down into what I needed to do to finish school. I just needed to do courses, some PLOs [prescribed learning outcomes], and adapt them to the work I had been doing. I submitted my involvement in Camp fYrefly, activism in transport, all the blogging and writing I had been doing – all these different little projects. I put them together and basically got four or five courses worth of credits and that's how I graduated.

After I dropped out and went to online school, I got a job and worked at McDonald's for a while. The first gay guy I ever met was a co-worker. I was fully out at work and could be myself. After working together for a few months, he asked me to go with him to Queer Prom in Vancouver. We went as friends, not as a couple. Having that experience – having never really left Surrey before – and seeing the gay village in Vancouver and all these other queer kids was just amazing. That built my confidence. Now at 17, I started going to the queer youth group. I finally had a support network.

Self-motivation is the reason I do the things I do. That probably connects to spending so much time alone during my teenage years. I also want to emphasize the importance of being online because I draw on so many of the experiences of people who post online and say, "I've accomplished this. This is my project." I think that's really cool. A lot of sharing happens that way. Once I got more out there in Vancouver, I found friends and developed certain networks, which really helped me. Having a best friend that I can call anytime if there's an issue, or if I need some support, or if I want to just brainstorm – that's just great.

In terms of my parents, I had a long conversation with my dad about a number of issues and just eventually came out saying, "Oh, by the way I don't really like girls." He was really supportive about that. He took a minute to himself and said, "Well as long as you're sure and you're happy and healthy and successful, then that's all that matters." That was really, really nice. I hadn't been close to my dad prior to that. I had been close to my mom, so that was huge. About six months later I did the same thing with my mom except I didn't have the courage to do it verbally. I just wrote her a long letter and being gay was just one of the things. She blew up a bit but, you know, I gave her a couple of weeks and she was more accepting.

Dad respected my choice to tell family members in my own time. He did caution me, "You know you should be careful who you tell. Don't tell your grandma because she'll go around telling everyone. She likes parading around her children and her grandchildren." So I was very cautious. I asked him not to tell my stepmother. I told him I would tell her if and when I wanted her to know. He kept my secret. Just having had that response from him was really important. Telling dad brought us closer. He grew comfortable with me. I remember a few months after I told him he started saying things like, "Oh, there's a cute guy over there." That was good.

Since I am a person who tries to avoid confrontation or getting hurt easily, I was cautious telling family. With relatives, I think not being able to or not wanting to share my whole sexuality experience with them really closed me off in a way beyond just being a regular teenager. I'm still struggling with that sometimes. I can't really draw on any energy from my aunts or my uncles or my grandparents, so it's like I'm a completely different person when I'm around them. That's why I'm usually not around them. I would say the family connection during my teenage years was really cut off. It still is really cut off.

The Asian side of my family is third generation, so they've integrated to become very Canadian. In some ways, they are fairly progressive – all things considered. I've connected with my grandmother recently over some other things, and I felt like I was in a space where I was comfortable revealing the gay part of myself. I wanted to share it with her. She had been pretty devoutly Christian when she was younger, but she took it really well. However, she immediately asked, "Well, what are you doing about AIDS?" We talked. It was a good opportunity to educate her and bring her up to date on what's happening nowadays. It was good to be able to have that mindset rather than thinking, "I'm scared. I don't want to reveal this at all." That's a complete 180 from where I was even a couple of months ago. Still I don't really put being gay out there that much. Maybe that's why I haven't experienced as much negativity as other people who are really out there.

4 Policies to Protect Sexual and Gender Minority Youth in Schooling and Health Care

Propelled by the Canadian Charter of Rights and Freedoms, which became an integral and unique part of the Canadian Constitution when it was patriated from Britain in 1982, the civil rights movement to enhance personhood and citizenship for sexual and gender minorities in Canada has made significant progress. While homosexuality was decriminalized in 1969, for the most part, real incremental progress happened after Section 15 of the Charter came into force in 1985. While the Canadian judicial system and federal and provincial/territorial governments constituted first frontiers in this civil rights movement, today health care and education as social institutions, and schools in particular, collectively constitute a contemporary frontier. Historically, schools have been expected to replicate the status quo in which heteronormativity and genderism are driving cultural forces. There is a dire consequence for sexual and gender minority students: as heterocentric and genderist cultural sites, schools can hurt; as a means of transferring dominant cultural knowledge to the exclusion of SGM knowledges, schooling can hurt. Mara, Paul, and Sam make this point particularly clear in their InterTexts. Indeed, public schooling in Canada, which includes a critical mass of publicly funded Catholic schools in Alberta, Ontario, and Saskatchewan, has been built on a foundation of heteronormative and genderist structures and symbols. This system has historically positioned SGM bodies within a politics of silence, exclusion, and debasement, often deliberately, sometimes by default. However, since schooling is mandated by law for Canadian children and youth, K-12 schools should be expected to be core institutions in promoting well-being, especially for vulnerable populations such as sexual and gender minorities.

State of the Canadian Nation for Sexual and Gender Minority Youth

Three national reports profoundly demonstrate the need for conducting research on SGM youth and their needs and concerns: the transdisciplinary Chief Public Health Officer's 2011 and 2012 annual reports on the state of public health in Canada and the 2011 Egale Canada – the national organization committed to SGM inclusion – report entitled *Every Class in Every School: Final Report on the First National Climate Survey on Homophobia, Biphobia, and Transphobia in Canadian Schools* (Taylor & Peter et al., 2011). I served as one of the external reviewers for the two public-health reports. Within the broad scope of these reports, attention was paid to (1) the comprehensive health of SGM youth and young adults, including lesbian, gay, bisexual, transgender, intersexual, and Two-Spirit Aboriginal individuals; (2) the impacts of sexuality and gender on health; and (3) the importance of comprehensive health education in schools.

The CPHO (2011) report – *Youth and Young Adults: Life in Transition* – draws a disturbing conclusion: while, in general, Canadian youth and young adults compose a healthy and resilient population, SGM individuals are disproportionately represented among those young persons who are not thriving. Moreover, the report indicates that the plight of these youth is further exacerbated if they are also Aboriginal, immigrant, or street-involved youth, or if they are struggling economically or living in rural and northern communities. In sum, the report indicates that these youth are at inordinate risk of experiencing physical and electronic bullying, verbal and sexual harassment, and physical violence in key life spaces including families, schools, and communities. Indeed SGM youth are more likely to feel disconnected proximally (in relation to parents, families, teachers, and other youth) and distally (in relation to neighbourhood and community ecologies). SGM youth are also more likely to ideate about, attempt, or complete suicide. Since they commonly experience threats to their safety and security, SGM youth have difficulties sustaining attendance and feeling accommodated at school. In the face of these stressors and risks, they also experience more comprehensive health problems, which the report states are exacerbated by a lack of adequate and appropriate health and educational policies, health and social services, protective measures, and educational and community programs. Linking health care and education, the report specifies the failure of schools in comprehensive health education, especially mental health and sexual health education. Moreover, the report accentuates the importance of school-based comprehensive health education and interventions, which need to start early and consider the histories, social and cultural attributes, and sexual and gender differences that locate SGM youth as a multivariate population.

In an encompassing consideration of the spectral nature of both sex and gender and their expressions in biopsychosocial and cultural contexts, the CPHO (2012) report – *Influencing Health: The Importance of Sex and Gender* – is clear that this diversity affects the comprehensive health and well-being of individuals. The report describes sex as a multifaceted construct that normally refers to the anatomical (including body features), genetic (including chromosomal differences), and physiological (including hormonal and organ functioning) characteristics that usually situate male and female in binary terms, although many of these biological characteristics are considered to exist on a continuum. The report locates gender as a social and cultural construct that traditionally incorporates the roles, norms, personality traits, behaviours, dispositions, and power relationships associated with differentiating male and female sexes, although it is increasingly acknowledged that there is diversity in gender identities, expressions, and experiences that contests masculine versus feminine as discrete descriptors, indicating the spectral nature of gender. In speaking to the interrelationship between sex and gender, the report points to the reality that "sex neither determines gender, nor gender sex" (p. 35). This complexity of sexual and gender differences creates dilemmas and absences in normative institutional and cultural practices in health care, education, and other core institutions, including the family, law, and religion. Steadfast in operating within heteronormativity and the parameters of the male/female binary, these institutions have traditionally dismissed sexual and gender possibilities. Still, with the recent focus on gender nonconformity, for example, support is emerging as a small but growing number of parents, health-care professionals, researchers, and educators in Canada take an affirmative stance to support children variously labelled creative, independent, fluid, and variant in terms of their gender positionalities (Gulli, 2014). In addition, there is a trend indicating that more provincial/territorial governments and human rights tribunals are making room for the spectrum of gender differences by providing human rights protections and revising bureaucracy to handle documenting of nonconforming gender designations (Gulli, 2014). Is this having a trickle-down effect in schools where gender-nonconforming and trans-spectrum students navigate everyday life? Such an effect appears limited, as Gulli (2014) asserts trans progress in schooling is hampered by the "disconnect between public policy and public opinion in accepting gender variance" (para. 8). She concludes this affects trans students as they run the genderist gauntlet in classrooms and corridors and parents as they figure out what it means to be nurturing and protective of their trans children once they leave the house.

The Chief Public Health Officer's 2012 report on the importance of sex and gender makes a key point: with sex and gender traditionally expected to function within the parameters of heteronormativity and the male/female binary, SGM youth have problems adjusting to boundaries and expectations guiding behaviours and practices in key arenas, including parenting, schooling, and health care (CPHO, 2012). Not adjusting can influence an individual's social acceptability, cultural status, educational performance, employment and career opportunities, economic security, and comprehensive health. Thus, to improve population health, the report accentuates the vital need to consider sex and gender in the development, implementation, and evaluation of comprehensive health research, policymaking, programming, and interventions. In fact, the report states that sex and gender should be considered in all research areas. In its focus on education research, the report stresses the need to study how both sex and gender affect the individual, social, and environmental needs of youth, their learning experiences and outcomes, and the kinds of educational initiatives, interventions, curricula, and instructional strategies needed to create sex- and gender-inclusive schools. The report concludes that transdisciplinary research coupled with exchange and distribution of findings can help professionals in health, education, and other caring professions to build awareness and challenge assumptions as they learn how sex and gender contribute to identities and expressions composing human diversity.

Significantly, in discussing comprehensive health, the 2012 report emphasizes the importance of mental health and its linkage to sexual and gender health, which is a topic discussed in detail in chapter 7: "Addressing mental health with a sex and gender lens requires increasing understanding, providing sex and gender sensitive services, ... and improving capacity of LGBTQ organizations to address stigma and offer support" (CPHO, 2012, p. 3). This is because sexual and gender minorities perpetually mediate internalized and cultural homo/bi/transphobia and consequential intolerance, bigotry, stigmatization, and alienation as significant stressors that can lead to anxiety, depression, and suicide ideation or completion. As the report relates, in general, sexual and gender minorities have difficulty accessing and feeling accommodated in their quest for comprehensive health care, notably mental and sexual health care. Moreover, gender-nonconforming youth and adults make up a particularly ignored group in terms of health care as well as population health research: "To date, little research has examined the physical, mental, and sexual health needs and concerns of transgendered and transsexual youth or adults ... In general, gender minorities have difficulty addressing their trans health needs with health care professionals who are under-prepared and inadequately trained to deal with the comprehensive health needs of this population" (CPHO, 2012, p. 45). In addressing trans health issues as a continuing gap in health care, the report stresses that caring professionals in the mainstream practice of public health need to remember that both sex and gender are on a continuum and that transgender and gender-nonconforming individuals compose a heterogeneous group.

Complementing these two transdisciplinary reports, in 2011 Egale Canada released the results of *Every Class in Every School: Final Report on the First National Climate Survey on Homophobia, Biphobia, and Transphobia in Canadian Schools* (Taylor & Peter et al., 2011). The Egale Canada report importantly recognizes the prevalence of SGM youth in Canadian classrooms, and it provides evidence of significant homophobic and transphobic harassment and bullying – verbal, physical, and sexual – substantiating the vital need to address these stressors in schooling. The report also notes the magnified discrimination that youth experience if they are transgender or gender-nonconforming youth, or youth with multiple subjectivities such as SGM youth of colour and female SGM youth. Of importance, the report indicates that both SGM and non-SGM survey participants expressed their disappointment with school staff for their lack of knowledge and inaction with regard to homo/bi/transphobia. This points to the need for educator in-service and sex- and gender-diversity and sensitivity training. Setting directions for policymaking, the climate survey found that (1) generic safe school policies that do not include anti-homophobia guidelines are ineffective in providing safer climates for SGM youth; (2) having specific anti-homophobia policies reduces incidents of harassment and bullying based on non-heterosexual orientation; and (3) specific anti-homophobia policies, however, do not appear to reduce harassment and bullying based on gender identity, thus signalling a need for schools to develop anti-transphobia policies to advance gender-minority inclusion.

The Egale Canada findings reflect two smaller Canadian studies conducted in the same time frame. In its study, Toronto's Youth-Gender Action Project (Y-GAP, 2009b) found that school, which ought to be a safe and stable environment for trans youth mediating genderism and transphobia, has failed these youth. Y-GAP reports that schools are spaces where trans youth usually experience ignorance of their gender identities, the unresponsiveness of teachers, the lack of mentors, the lack of library and other resources, unchecked harassment and violence, invisibility in the curriculum, and the absence of policies that accommodate their affirmed genders regarding dress, washroom use, locker room use, sports participation, and other gender-based aspects of schooling. Moreover, as Y-GAP (2009b) points out, "[t]rans youth feel discouraged when their own initiatives and efforts to improve the school environment are met with indifference or resistance" (p. 2). This speaks to the need to engage school administrators, teachers, and other school staff in professional development that builds their knowledge of trans youth and the ways that they can support and accommodate them in policymaking and practice as part of the school community. It also speaks to the need to have trans-inclusive gay-straight alliances in schools so gender identity and sexual orientation are both addressed in a collective social environment where recognition, respect, accommodation, safety, and inclusion are guiding values. In keeping with the Out and Proud Affirmation Guidelines developed by the Children's Aid Society of Toronto (2012), these GSAs should be anti-oppressive ecological sites, welcoming trans and gender-nonconforming youth into a positive environment that acknowledges and affirms sexual and gender diversity and other personal differences, enables positive outcomes for them, and makes achieving equity a focus and a modus operandi. In this environment, youth are heard, accepted, supported, treated as persons, safe, and dealt with in a fair and equitable manner.

In their research into homophobic and transphobic harassment fed by heterosexism and genderism in high schools in British Columbia, Haskell and Burtch (2010) dealt with certain contemporary realities: (1) the voices of SGM students have not been sufficiently influential in deliberations to develop and implement anti-bullying policies in schools; (2) stakeholders, including educators and parents, usually take a generic approach in addressing bullying and do not name or tackle homo/bi/transphobic bullying; and (3) many stakeholders presume, often unthinkingly but even when they bother to consider sexuality and gender at all, that all students are heterosexuals with fixed gender identities. Their study found that symbolic violence was more frequent than physical violence, with verbal abuse, avoidance, disenfranchisement, vandalism of personal property, observing homo/bi/transphobic graffiti, and mediating environments insensitive to sexual and gender differences being common experiences. When physical violence did occur, the perpetrators and targets of the violence were usually male. Symbolic violence was often minimized or ignored by school administrators, teachers, and other students because it was not judged to be as serious as physical violence. This is demeaning to SGM students and an assault on their integrity. Wherever these inappropriate responses occur in Canadian schools, they have the potential to exacerbate homo/bi/transphobia when perpetrators see it go unchecked. For some SGM students, their responses when offences against them are ignored include being truant in order to be safe or becoming bullies themselves. More positively though, Haskell and Burtch (2010) also found, inattention or inaction by school administrators and teachers can spur some SGM students to become activists and change agents who work to help other students harassed because of their perceived or actual sexual and gender differences. However, this does not let oblivious or ignorant school administrators and teachers off the hook. Indeed they are the significant adults who need to be caring professionals, even though school administrators and teachers are often ignorant and silent on SGM issues, sometimes homo/bi/transphobic, and unlikely to initiate a safe and caring environment for SGM students and their parents/caregivers in overt ways (Shelton, 2013). For many school administrators and teachers, "managing diversity means ignoring diversity" (Shelton, 2013, p. 79). This means (1) SGM-inclusive curriculum is a pedagogical void; (2) school libraries are SGM-knowledge deserts; (3) educational and cultural SGM websites are something to be blocked as suspect; (4) gay-straight alliances for SGM students constitute dangerous terrain; and (5) homo/bi/transphobic bullying is often categorized as violence to be expected.

As the preceding research documents indicate, there are many dangers and negative outcomes associated with schooling for SGM children and youth. They also indicate the sorry truth of this grave reality. Nevertheless, Russell (2002) asserts, "it is also true that, unlike faith and family life, schools may be the setting most susceptible to change *by and for* marginalized youth" (p. 262, italics in original). In this regard, it is time for schools and school boards to do more for SGM children and youth by developing stand-alone policies for them that are strategically and fully implemented to make life better *now* for this multivariate population (D'Augelli, 2002; Holmes & Cahill, 2004; Russell, 2005). Because schools have a fundamental responsibility to facilitate child and adolescent development, and because, as noted in chapter 7, children and youth are self-identifying at earlier ages regarding their sexual and gender identities, schools have a duty not only to assist children and youth with their development but also to help youth so they can reach the goal of successful transition into young adulthood. However, there are many indicators that schools are failing at this. The Canadian documents discussed earlier report that SGM children and youth (1) still feel unsafe in classrooms, corridors, gyms, and other school spaces; (2) link their victimization to a lack of empowerment and human agency coupled with being blamed for their problems; and (3) feel that teachers do little to intervene. With regard to teachers' inaction, this is not only an abrogation of their ethical, professional responsibility to be there for all students, but it also reduces the notion of the good teacher to a myth, at least for SGM children and youth. After all, students identify teachers "as 'enduring socialising influences'" (Johnson, 2008, p. 386), and "children have quite firm beliefs about the relative power of teachers to 'do something' if a student's wellbeing ... [is] threatened" (p. 393). Furthermore, "[f]rom the students' perspective, intervening to stop bullying ... [is] considered teachers' core business" (p. 394). The issue of homo/bi/transphobic language provides a case in point. As Perrin et al. (2004) relate, "Adult bystanders seldom intervene to halt this blatant prejudice. As these terms infiltrate the vernacular, they lose their sexual meaning to all but their gay and lesbian victims" (p. 365). In sum, teachers' professional inertness around addressing the needs and concerns of SGM children and youth contributes to their alienation and to choosing concealment as a safeguard and survival strategy in the face of pervasive harassment and violence perpetrated against them (Callahan, 2001; Grossman et al., 2009; Trotter, 2009).

Every day many SGM children and youth walk wounded in our schools. Evidence of this for transgender and transsexual students in K-12 schools is duly noted in the Canadian Teachers' Federation's guide for supporting trans students, which takes an affirmative approach to supporting this vulnerable population by clarifying the role and responsibilities of schools (Wells, Roberts, & Allan, 2012). When schools and school boards are not there for SGM youth in their care, they are bystanders that must take the blame for student risk taking and poor health and wellness. To counter their inattention and inaction, they need to engage in SGM-inclusive policymaking and take policy from the page to proactive implementation in curricular, instructional, and extracurricular practices. Drawing on the Canadian Teachers' Federation (CTF) guide for educators, the CPHO (2012) report highlights this need:

> Students should be able to participate in physical education classes and team sports in a safe, inclusive and respectful environment. Participation in sports, locker room access and privacy for changing clothes often create stress for some youth. To address the issue of physical activity for transgender and transsexual youth, the Canadian Teachers' Federation created a guide to assist educators in supporting transgender and transsexual youth who, like their cisgender [or non-transgender] peers, should be able to participate in physical activity classes and recreational and/or competitive sports. Policies and procedures should be inclusive, regardless of gender identity or gender expression, in an environment free of discrimination and harassment. Schools can create this environment by educating staff and coaches, and by working with parents so transgender and transsexual youth are understood and accommodated in schooling. (p. 59)

Of course, SGM students should be able to see themselves and feel accommodated in all their activities and classes across subject areas. Such action would help counter a history of SGM invisibility in non-inclusive schooling (Ginsberg, 1998; Reygan, 2009; Trotter, 2009). As this history shows, it is one thing to address heterosexism, genderism, and homo/bi/transphobia in school corridors and on school grounds where the emphases are on improving school climate and culture. It is another thing to address them in curriculum and instruction such as in physical education classes, which requires collective action on the part of provincial and territorial ministries of education, schools, and school districts.

Schools and school districts need to engage in front-line work to fulfil the requirement to provide individual protections guaranteed in Section 15 of the Canadian Charter of Rights and Freedoms. In this regard, they need to (1) recognize the constitutionally protected rights of children and youth; (2) respect the public nature of education in a social democracy and the obligations that go with accepting public funds, even when schools are faith-based; (3) operate from the premise that schools exist to safeguard all children and youth by engaging in public ethical and inclusive practices; (4) ensure that school administrators, teachers, and other school personnel act professionally by not allowing restrictive private morals to pre-empt the requirement to engage in inclusive and ethical practices in schooling for all children and youth; (5) recognize that it is not a parental right to be prejudicial or exclusionary; and (6) understand that religious and parental rights are not absolute or unencumbered in a democracy where the constitutionally sanctioned human and civil rights of minorities have to be safeguarded and accommodated. This last point reflects the intention of Section 1 of the Charter, which upholds the tenet that institutional rights cannot be held above individual rights and vice versa.

What Good School Trustees Do: The Case of Edmonton Public Schools

Here I want to speak to a specific example of SGM educational inclusion in my home province, noting the work of Edmonton Public Schools (2013), "the first school jurisdiction in both Alberta and the Prairies to develop a comprehensive stand-alone policy and administrative regulation to support sexual and gender minority (LGBTQ) students, staff and families" (para. 1). Tuesday, 8 November 2011 was a significant day in the history of moving civil rights forward for sexual and gender minorities in education in Canada. On that day the Board of Trustees for Edmonton Public Schools unanimously approved the draft policy on sexual orientation and gender identity on first and second considerations. On 29 November 2011, the draft policy was brought forward for third consideration, and it received unanimous final approval. This groundbreaking policy recognizes and affirms the rights of all SGM members – students, staff, and families – of the school community to "be welcomed, respected, accepted and supported in every school" (EPSB, 2013a, para. 1) and free from discrimination, prejudice, and harassment. The policy explicitly states that the "Board will not tolerate harassment, bullying, intimidation, or discrimination on the basis of a person's actual or perceived sexual orientation, gender identity, or gender expression" (EPSB, 2013a, para. 2).

As someone born before homosexuality was decriminalized in Canada in 1969 – thank you, Pierre Elliott Trudeau, for your vision and work to build a just society – I have spent my life waiting for days like this. At the 8 November meeting, I was particularly moved by remarks made by youth from Edmonton Public Schools. These youth spoke with eloquence, courage, strength, and passion regarding why they needed this stand-alone, SGM-inclusive policy to protect and assist them. I am grateful that I was present to hear them share their stories from the heart in profoundly meaningful ways. These youth long to be safe and accommodated in their schools. In the spirit of Paulo Freire (1998, 2004), they are activists and cultural workers who are changing the world.

During that meeting, I made the following public remarks. While my words are not as powerful as the words of the youth who spoke, I offer them in solidarity with the youth in the work to make life in schools better *now* for SGM youth:

I am Director of the Institute for Sexual Minority Studies and Services in the Faculty of Education, University of Alberta. This year I served as one of the external reviewers for the 2011 Report on the State of Public Health in Canada, which was recently tabled in the House of Commons. I was delighted to contribute to research focused on sexual and gender minority (SGM) youth as a vulnerable population. This report, which is entitled *Youth and Young Adults – Life in Transition*, relates that SGM youth are regularly subjected to discrimination, stigmatization, or harassment as a consequence of their subjugated social status. The likely consequences are increased levels of stress and a higher risk of mental-health problems. The report provides an alarming synopsis of the acute vulnerability of SGM youth who are at inordinate risk of being victimized. It includes these key points:

- SGM youth are often disparaged by bullies who spread rumours or lies in vile conversations at school or through text messaging or the Internet.
- SGM youth "are disproportionately represented among the street-involved youth population as a result of a prior history of victimization" (CPHO, 2011, p. 60).
- SGM youth are also more likely to have health issues due to substance abuse, and they also tend to engage in risky sexual behaviours at younger ages.

In the face of these problems, the Chief Public Health Officer's (2011) report states that school boards and schools in Canada have much work to do to provide programs and services that meet the educational, health, social, and cultural needs of SGM youth. Currently, as the report highlights, there is "a lack of appropriate education, services, protective measures, and policies" (p. 32), which places SGM youth at risk of physical-health and mental-health issues. Today Edmonton Public School Board has an opportunity to approve a Sexual Orientation and Gender Identity policy so life can get better *now* for SGM youth in the district's schools. By implementing this policy, the school board can create a climate and provide the resources and supports necessary to accommodate SGM students.

In conclusion, respecting and accommodating SGM students is an important part of the call for educators to engage in a public ethical practice. In the year 2000, Alberta Education and its partners described this engagement as being there for every student (Alberta's Education Partners, 2000). By voting for the policy today you are sending a clear message that SGM students matter. Edmonton Public Schools can be a place where SGM students thrive instead of being sick and fearful. Therefore vote for this policy and be there for every SGM student attending school in this district.

Now that history has been made, the real work has begun to create respectful and accommodating environments for sexual and gender minorities in Edmonton Public Schools. The effectiveness of the new policy will be gauged by the degree to which it is implemented through developing resources and supports and delivering programs and services that have the goal of making schools truly safe, caring, and inclusive spaces for those stigmatized because their sexual and gender identities fall outside heteronormative, genderist limits. This work can be strengthened by focusing on good communication with community groups and by encouraging them to be actively involved in SGM-inclusive policy implementation (Cagle, 2007; Henning-Stout, James, & Macintosh, 2000).

On its website, Edmonton Public Schools details its stand-alone *Sexual Orientation and Gender Identity* policy (EPSB, 2013a). In this policy statement, the school board has expressed its commitment to creating safe and accommodating SGM-inclusive schools where sexual and gender minorities have full access to SGM-specific and larger school supports, services, and protections. Policy tenets are linked to the right to learn in a safe environment where individuals are protected against discrimination, as guaranteed by the Canadian Charter of Rights and Freedoms, the Alberta Human Rights Act, and the Alberta School Act. The school board emphasizes the right of sexual and gender minorities to fair and equitable treatment, confidentiality, self-identification and determination, and freedom of conscience, expression, and association. The school board states that sexual and gender minorities have unencumbered access to remedies in the face of discrimination and maltreatment. Among its stated commitments, the school board pledges to educate interest groups to (1) build understanding of sexual and gender minorities and their positionalities; (2) deal with homo/bi/transphobic behaviours and language; and (3) develop, implement, and evaluate inclusive educational strategies, professional development opportunities, and administrative guidelines to accommodate sexual and gender minorities and their families. Here the role of the principal in accommodating SGM students and their families is duly and specifically noted. Importantly, the school board requires principals to (1) support students' requests to establish gay-straight alliances (GSAs) as supportive clubs in their schools and (2) ensure that school staff do not refer students to reparative therapy, which presumes sexual orientation or gender nonconformity are "curable" forms of pathology (see chapter 7). In keeping with the call of the Chief Public Health Officer to accommodate SGM students in physical education and school sports, EPSB (2013b) policy contains the following directive:

> All schools shall proactively review their student athletic policies to ensure they are inclusive of sexual and gender minority students. Transgender and transsexual students shall not be asked or required to have physical education outside of assigned class time, and shall, subject to safety considerations, be permitted to participate in any gender-segregated activities in accordance with their consistently asserted gender identity, if they so choose. (Regulation F, Gender Identity and Gender Expression)

The school board also provides for similar accommodation regarding restroom accessibility and a dress code enabling expression of a student's self-affirmed gender identity. Problematically though, the school board includes the following statement regarding conflict management in relation to gender-segregated activities:

> The principal shall be the final determiner of disputes that may arise with regard to a transgender or transsexual student's participation in educational or athletic activities. The principal shall ensure that the resolution of any conflict ensures reasonable accommodation and inclusiveness. (EPSB, 2013b, Regulation F, Gender Identity and Gender Expression)

While the school board fully expects a school administrator to engage in a public ethical practice that is SGM-inclusive, it will need to monitor what this "final determiner" does to ensure that conservative principals, whether for religious or other reasons, do not conflate private morals with public ethics in administering public schools.

Taking SGM Inclusivity into Professional
Ethical Practices in Caring Professions

This book constitutes a journey into the intersection of education and health care in exploring ways to make life better *now* for SGM children and youth. These institutions have had a chequered history of recognizing, respecting, and accommodating this vulnerable population. Taken together, these institutions ought to compose a dynamic and interactive dyad that fortifies SGM children and youth within an ethic of care. Indeed SGM youth benefit when these institutions work synergistically, exercising caring professionalism and good communication as core elements of a daily modus operandi.

What should best practices for caring professionals in these institutions look like? Previously, I have discussed what school administrators might do (Grace, 2007a, pp. 33–6). The guidelines that I developed are quoted at length in an abridged version here:

- Work every day to see, speak to, and interact with every student and teacher across ... [SGM] differences.
- Set a caring tone and use an ethic of respect to accommodate ... [SGM] differences in your school.
- Use language that is inclusive and sensitive around issues of ... [SGM] differences.
- Educate yourself about the realities of sex, sexual, and gender differences, and different constructions of family. As a corollary, learn about heterosexism, sexism, [genderism, and homo/bi/transphobia] ...
- Educate yourself about the history of Canadian and provincial/territorial laws and legislation that have abetted sexual [and gender] minorities in efforts to achieve the rights and privileges of citizenship ...
- Learn about the social and cultural realities of living as a member of a sexual [or gender] minority in Canada ...
- Assist your teachers to engage in similar education and learning, and provide them with opportunities for professional development so they can build knowledge of sexual [and gender] minorities and learn about age-appropriate ways to address ... [SGM] issues and concerns ...
- Build a resource base in your school that will provide you with material to help you mediate conflict with those within and outside the school who resist ... [SGM] inclusion. The resource

base will also be useful to teachers who want to engage in pedagogical and co-curricular practices inclusive of sexual [and gender] minorities ...

- Check with your teachers' association and school district to see what educational policies have been developed to assist and support you and your teachers in educational and cultural work to create a school that respects and accommodates sexual and gender minorities. If such policies are not in place, then advocate for and work to have policies inclusive of sexual [and gender] minorities developed and implemented. Remember, policy enables protection.
- If you are an administrator in a Catholic school, then check with your diocese to see if they have pastoral guidelines for working with ... [SGM] youth ...
- If you are an administrator in a Catholic school district that has a policy recommending reparative therapy as a possible treatment for unhappy sexual minority youth, then educate yourself about the dangers of reparative therapy as stated by the Canadian Medical Association and an array of mainstream national and international mental-health associations ... As well, read critiques of Courage, a Catholic apostolate that promotes sexual-reorientation therapy in religious and psychotherapeutic forms ...
- Intervene in your school by supporting students who want to initiate a ... Gay-Straight Alliance Club. Help them find a teacher-facilitator and provide them with advice around safety and security issues ...
- Intervene to enable ... [SGM] teachers to have their needs met in relation to their welfare and work, and their personal safety and professional security. Learn about teachers' association initiatives and sections of collective agreements that provide them with individual protections in keeping with the Charter.

Best Practices for Caring Professionals in Health and Social Care

As indicated by the preceding list of best practices that school administrators can use to help SGM children and youth to adapt and develop positive identities, interventions need to be ecological, focusing on children and youth, significant adults in their lives, and their everyday lived environments. In this light, the following best practices are recommended for caring professionals working with SGM youth in health care and social contexts:

- To engage in holistic intervention and prevention practices with SGM youth, caring professionals need to be educated to
  - build cultural awareness and professional competence around sex, sexual, and gender differences;
  - understand the intricacies of SGM identity development and its effects on physical, mental, and sexual health while realizing that many SGM youth are healthy, happy, and adjusting well to their differences;
  - understand that SGM youth may also have difficulties associated with race, class, and other differences as well as family and money problems;
  - avoid making assumptions about SGM youth;
  - minimize negative messaging and challenge derogatory language and stereotypes regarding SGM differences;
  - provide access to comprehensive sexual health education and knowledge and legitimize safer and alternative sexual practices for SGM youth to enhance their sexual and mental health;
  - utilize harm reduction strategies;
  - provide access to free educational and sexual health resources to help educate about, and minimize exposure to, risk-related behaviours and practices;
  - be able to provide referrals to SGM peer support groups in school and community contexts as vehicles to assist youth socialization and counter isolation and alienation;
  - recognize the increased probability of suicide ideation and attempts among SGM youth in general;
  - develop effective and encompassing ecological interventions that account for personal, familial, cultural, social, and systemic issues in the lives of SGM youth; and
  - build a repertoire of ways to help SGM youth deal with conflict, peer and other relationships, risky sexual behaviours, and depression as part of a holistic contextualized response to adversity, which these youth can experience as both a personal problem or a problem constructed and assigned in a heteronormative, genderist social context (Callahan, 2001; Dysart-Gale, 2010; Ginsburg et al., 2002; Hunter & Mallon, 2000; Sanders & Kroll, 2000; Scourfield et al., 2008; Trotter, 2009).
- Caring professionals have to address issues of naming and labelling since words and phrases traditionally used to describe SGM persons can carry the weight of a long history of heterosexism, sexism, genderism, and homo/bi/transphobia. As well, new words

and phrases emerge and old words and phrases can acquire new meanings tied to social, cultural, and political changes abetting the human and civil rights of SGM citizens. Names and labels reflect particular social and cultural world views and, as they are learned and exchanged in different institutional and social environments, it is important to gauge their meanings, their use in different contexts, and their historical or present significance (Angell, 2000). With this in mind, caring professionals need to use language that is culturally sensitive and affirming when working with SGM youth so they can feel safe and understood (Sanders & Kroll, 2000).

- To engage in affirming interactions and interventions, caring professionals need to develop a respectful and accommodating therapeutic and educational mindset that
  - does not presume that all youth fit into heteronormative categories of sex, sexuality, and gender;
  - views SGM youth positively with respect to their care;
  - provides clinically safe, welcoming, and affirming environments;
  - continually evaluates programs and services to ensure they are inclusive of the needs and concerns of SGM youth; and
  - views SGM differences as clinically relevant and enriching and not as negating and detracting from humanity (Dysart-Gale, 2010; Sanders & Kroll, 2000).

  When an open and caring milieu exists where practitioners have a positive attitude towards SGM youth identities and provide clinically and culturally competent care, SGM youth are more likely to be honest and accurate when providing medical histories, including histories of sexual activity (Dysart-Gale, 2010).

- Caring professionals need to realize that some of their younger clients are SGM youth at various stages of identity development. When these youth present, caring professionals ought to employ intervention strategies that are (1) empirically, theoretically, and ethically informed; (2) contextually and culturally relevant and age-appropriate; and (3) linked to good use of specific resources. Caring professionals should focus not only on reducing risks and maladjustment but also on emphasizing continuity and greater independence via processes of positive adaptation that help this particular population of youth as well as their parents or guardians and other caregivers to build capacities and competence (D'Augelli, 2002; Luthar & Zelazo, 2003). Enhancing a sense of school and family connectedness are two such positive factors that promote positive adaptation (Saewyc, Wang, Chittenden, Murphy, & The McCreary Centre Society, 2006).

- With respect to SGM youth, caring professionals need to realize that processes of positive adaptation whereby these youth build capacities and competence are not linear moves from vulnerability to resilience. Once resilient, youth can experience setbacks during adolescence when they are likely to worry, be fearful, and develop internalizing symptoms that impede SGM identity development (D'Augelli, 2002; Luthar & Zelazo, 2003).

- Caring professionals can assist parents or guardians by educating them about SGM identities and differences, connecting them to community resources and supports (community resource centres, crisis centres, hotlines, and support groups like PFLAG Canada for parents and gay-straight alliance clubs for youth in schools), and clarifying the link between a stable, supportive, and accommodating home ecology and positive and resilient SGM identity development (Bringaze & White, 2001; D'Augelli, 2002; Forman & Kalafat, 1998; Perrin et al., 2004; Rak & Patterson, 1996). Here caring professionals have an obligation to enhance the relationship between parents/guardians and the child by counselling parents or guardians to help them to dispel myths, pinpoint concerns, and create a loving home ecology that accepts and accommodates the child's sex, sexual, or gender differences and provides a support base for counteracting stigma in school and other life spaces (Perrin et al., 2004).

- Caring professionals need to recognize that gender nonconformity is a less common issue in their practice than sexual orientation, but it should be seriously addressed when it arises since gender-variant youth are often victims of bullying and violence who also experience social isolation and cultural dissonance, leading to physical, emotional, and mental health problems (Marksamer, 2011; Perrin et al., 2004).

- Caring professionals should advise SGM youth to be cautious about disclosing to parents, helping them to consider what the consequences might be, to get information and advice from PFLAG Canada, and to find out about community resources that could help them and their families deal with disclosure and its impact. When disclosure is not prudent, caring professionals should help SGM youth to develop alternative social supports and a peer network, hone independent living skills, and find alternative, supportive living arrangements (D'Augelli, 2002; Hunter & Mallon, 2000; Perrin et al., 2004; Wilber, Ryan, & Marksamer, 2006).

- In order to help SGM youth counter negative messaging associated with heteronormativity, heterocentrism, genderism, and homo/bi/transphobia so they can develop positive SGM identity mindsets, caring professionals should not have unresolved issues. If they are religious, they should put ethical care and the requirement to do no harm before faith-based biases. They should be comfortable regarding their own sexual and gender identities and able to confer with SGM colleagues who can provide insights into SGM identities and related issues and challenges (Bringaze & White, 2001; Ginsburg et al., 2002).

- In order to protect SGM youth from homo/bi/transphobic responses and practices in schools, medical facilities, homes, and group homes, caring professionals should be advocates for SGM youth experiencing adversity in these social ecologies, providing education and supportive care as they take the lead in addressing the harassment and abuse that SGM youth encounter every day (Callahan, 2001; Chen-Hayes, 2001; Dysart-Gale, 2010; Flicker et al., 2010; Henning-Stout et al., 2000; Hirsch, Carlson, & Crowl, 2010; Hunter & Mallon, 2000).

In sum, these best practices are about being there for every SGM youth as they grow and develop, question and come to terms, steel life, and seek respect and accommodation as persons and citizens of Canada. In light of Section 15 of the Canadian Charter of Rights and Freedoms, this respect and accommodation are expectations in keeping with protection against discrimination based on sex, sexual, and gender differences. These best practices have particular application to health-care professionals but can be appropriated to guide the ethical practices of other caring professionals. It is imperative that caring professionals have such guidelines aimed at meeting their obligations to assist and support SGM youth. As Callahan (2001) concludes, when caring professionals fail to accommodate SGM youth, they are "narrowing their worlds and are ethically and legally shirking their responsibilities to students" (p. 9).

Concluding Perspective: A Queer Rant, an OUTburst

It's time for an OUTburst. Queer rage is valid and justified, so this is my queer rant: when they work with SGM youth, caring professionals have a responsibility to help them counter a turbulent queer history, make a better present, and create a hopeful and possible future. This work is about

- empowering and integrating SGM youth, placing foci on consciousness raising and engendering participation and on accommodation rather than assimilation;
- helping them to be, become, and belong in SGM and larger communities;
- helping them focus on the need to know, what to know, and how to know it;
- helping them to emerge from adversity and trauma as self-directed change agents, which involves emphases on acting and not standing by, creating sustainable lives, attending to matters of context, disposition, and relationship, and assisting individual development and socialization; and
- helping SGM youth to transgress stressors, risks, and negative outcomes by building assets that help enact positive outcomes.

This is helping these youth to steel life, grow into resilience, and be at promise.

The social, cultural, and political work involved here requires a deliberate and deliberative pedagogy so SGM youth can learn to move beyond oppression, limitations, unhappiness, and unhealthiness. This pedagogy locates steeling life and growing into resilience as dynamic and integrated processes of excavating stressors and risks, with an eye to building assets and revealing signs of thriving. It is about engaging youth on the margins, helping them to deal with anger, helping them to build life and social skills, and helping them to build confidence as they grow personally and socially. In sum, this engaged pedagogy is about living and livelihood, making life better *now*, and strategizing to help SGM youth realize future possibilities in individual and social contexts. Guided by a politics of hope and possibility, this pedagogy has a clear goal: to help SGM youth to be happy and healthy individuals with the personal integrity that comes from having identities recognized, respected, and accommodated in the quest for full citizenship. Thus situated, these youth can be hopeful change agents in their own lives and, when they are ready, in the communities where they mediate living, with all its challenges and complexities.

PART 2

From At Risk to At Promise

It should be our goal to help SGM youth to steel life so they can build assets, grow into resilience, and be youth at promise. While the Canadian reality is that many SGM youth are still at risk, there are many other youth who not only survive but also thrive. These youth are at promise; that is, they have abilities and capacities that translate into the potential to be agents of change in their own lives, in the lives of their peers, and in their families, schools, and the other social spaces they navigate every day. In part 2, co-authored with Kristopher Wells, we focus on both populations. We know many SGM youth are still hurting as they deal with life in an array of contexts. Their journeys from adversity to access, affirmation, and accommodation remain an ongoing struggle that is increasingly a collective one, with incremental moves forward. Fortunately though, we also know there is a trend indicating many SGM youth are doing better. To help this trend continue, caring professionals need to work in the intersection of research, policy, and practice so SGM youth are helped in meaningful ways that affirm their being and belonging in the world.

Part 2 further elucidates what it means for SGM youth to steel life and grow into resilience. This theme is evident in chapters 5 and 6, which represent our early research on SGM youth whom we approached to tell their exemplary stories, which we initially learned about in the media or through meeting them in iSMSS programming. The story of Marc Hall's challenge to his Catholic high school to include him as a gay student demonstrates the divide that still persists between institutional church rights and individual rights in relation to sexuality and gender in Canadian schooling. Chapter 6 continues to explore SGM youth as change agents as it explores the initiatives of three youth activists in different Canadian locations. These discussions of challenges and dangers that SGM youth face constitute a segue to chapter 7, which discusses the vital need to focus on the comprehensive health, including the mental health and sexual health, of SGM youth in schooling and health care. Here the importance of a social-solutions approach involving families and caregivers is emphasized. A diversity of exemplary initiatives is also highlighted for those seeking to use solutions-based approaches in their own work with SGM youth. Chapter 8 continues the discussion on recognizing and accommodating SGM youth as it focuses on the specific example of gay-straight alliances in Canadian schools, which are a more recent and growing phenomenon in this country. The GSA chapter provides a particular example of a social and educational support that can abet socialization and good health for SGM youth. As in part 1, InterTexts are interspersed among the chapters in part 2, providing coverage of themes, issues, and concerns that enhance discussions as the chapters unfold.

InterText 7
John: *Learning to Own Gay*

John is a gay youth who has struggled with reconciling his gay identity with other identities that he considers core to the person he is. In his coming-out process, he began to steel life and resist the gay stereotypes that he felt pressured to live out. At university he learned to be comfortable with being gay. He was very involved in student politics and served on the students' council as an openly gay vice president academic. John has strength and resilience, which enable him to mediate the differing social contexts of university and family living. He is the first camper at Camp fYrefly to transition from camper to youth leader to adult volunteer. John owns gay and he is helping other youth to own their sexual and gender minority identities.

Talking about me, and the kind of person I am, is difficult. I'm complex. For me, the fact that I am gay tends to be the fifth or sixth element in my identity. I am really a rural, small-town Albertan, which is a big part of who I am. I am a huge science geek who loves physics. I am a nerd and very proud to be one. I love student politics and the challenges of working and building consensus with people who have different points of view. And I am a gay male. It is one of those things that I really struggled with as I started coming out. It was really challenging for me for the first couple of years. I had to deal with all the stress of taking on the gay label as well as owning and making a gay identity a primary part of me. There also seemed to be so much pressure to live up to the stereotypes about being gay. I really didn't learn to own gay until I lived in residence while attending university. It took some time. In conversations with friends there, I would casually mention that I had a boyfriend. However, I never really identified with the rainbow symbol and I'm not pierced at all. Still my friends say they only had to spend five minutes with me to know I was gay. I guess I set off gaydar all over the place, but it's not something I do consciously.

In my coming-out process, I had two major supports: one was a supportive university residence environment and the other was Camp fYrefly. I came to university in Edmonton from a small town of 1,400 people where I was raised Roman Catholic. During my first year, I got a laptop, which was the first time I had my own private personal computer. When I was online looking at porn, it was gay porn. But I never thought of myself as gay until my second year at university – never at all. For me, there had been such conditioning and separation in my life that I didn't even know what gay was until grade 12. I grew up with no exposure to gay life and no way to make sense of the feelings and drives I had had since grade 7 or 8. Then, in second-year university, I attended a campus dance. I saw my best friend dancing with his girlfriend. I was just so torn up, so completely and utterly upset, but I did not know why. I started crying when another friend asked me, "John, who is he dancing with?" Then she asked, "Are you jealous of him or are you jealous of his girlfriend?" That question started to put words to it, and I bawled for about six hours. I asked for another one of my residence friends who, back in December, had told me about her cousin's coming-out story while we were studying for finals. We all went back to my room and I started talking. From that point I started coming out to people on my floor in residence. Luckily, I never once encountered a negative reaction. About a month later, I ran and was elected as a floor coordinator in my residence tower for the following year. And two weeks later I stumbled across Camp fYrefly on the Internet. My mind exploded because there it was at the University of Alberta. This was my home. The people who ran it were in Education, literally blocks from where I sleep every night. I sent them this huge application package. I wrote answers to questions that spilled on to the back of every sheet, telling them, "I want to be there. I want to do this." When I got accepted to go to Camp fYrefly, it was so exhilarating. I spent several months looking forward to it. At this point I was just coming out, just starting to explore what it means to be attracted to males. For me, it was now undeniable: I was attracted to males and not females.

My first year at Camp fYrefly, I started crying within a half hour of arrival. When I got to the pickup zone for the camp, I sat there with my duffel bag. My heart was going a mile a minute. I wondered what to expect and what would happen. Then this woman who later told me she was a PFLAG mom pulled up in a van and jumped out. She came to the kerb and said, "Hi! Are you the queer kid I came here to pick up?" I went pale. I thought, "What the hell is going on?" I was just completely blown away by being called queer. When I got to camp, I kept hearing the words *gay*, *lesbian*, and *trans*. It was complete sensory overload since these words were ones that had been taboo for me. Before camp, saying them would mean looking over my shoulder. And now I saw people owning and controlling these words. It was such a transformative experience. That first year played such a role in helping me to be able to own gay. When I started floor coordinator training just three weeks after camp, I started coming out in my residence. I realized I had an opportunity to be a role model. When we had a lecture about inclusive language and what it means to people, I outed myself as an example of how inclusive language or the lack of it can impact floor mates dealing with their sexuality.

I still hadn't told my family. At that time, thanks to scholarships, I was financially independent. I didn't have to rely on them or worry about them for my material survival. So my biggest concern in telling family members was how to be gentle with my mom. Ultimately, I knew that my family loved me. My parents always told us that they loved us unconditionally. I am the oldest of five children, and I knew that it would be very hard for them. I also knew that they would eventually come around. I took it very gradually with them, giving them the space they needed. Even now though, we don't talk about it unless I force them. For example, my sister is 21 and she's engaged. She's been dating her fiancé for about three years, which is right around the time I first came out to my family. I told my mom that I expected her to treat my partner and me like she treated my sister and her boyfriend. My family is at a place now where they realize I am gay, that it is not just a phase, and that it is for life. They realize that I expect them to be okay with it one day. They're not there yet. They're at tolerance, not acceptance.

I think the biggest family issue for me right now has to do with my youngest siblings, who are five and six years old. There was an incident that happened last Christmas that frustrates me. My five-year-old brother came downstairs while I was writing an email to my boyfriend. He climbed up on my knee and asked, "What are you doing John?" I told him, "I'm emailing Luke," and he asked, "Who's Luke?" I said, "Go talk to your mother." My mom had said that she doesn't want my youngest siblings to know that I am gay until they are old enough for her to be able to explain what that means. However, this is really code for the fact that she doesn't want them to know until she can tell them, "We love your brother, but being gay is evil, sinful, and bad." I believe that by telling them now, they would not have that prejudice. I know

I am asking a lot of them. My parents are very devout Catholics who don't know how to deal with my sexuality.

Still my parents made me resilient. My grandpa is also a key figure when I look back to figure out why I am strong. We have lived in the same yard as my grandpa since I was in grade 2, and my grandparents on my mother's side played a huge role in my growing up. I know that grandpa was always very strong. He always said, "All you've got is your word and your honour. You have to be honest, and have integrity, and be truthful." So when the bolt-out-of-the-blue that I'm attracted to males hit me in second-year university, I realized, "This is who I am and this is who I've always been." Since I had been told all my life to be me and to stand up for myself, I knew I had to stand up for my gay self. You know, I graduated from high school with a 98.5 per cent average, and I finished an honours physics degree with first-class standing. My intelligence is something that no one has ever doubted or questioned, and I take tremendous strength from this part of me. I use these reserves to deal with different aspects of being gay. I can take a stand on the gay hill and I don't have to turn tail and run the instant adversity shows up. Now I can let gay be. I can get beyond dilemmas like what to do when I'm standing in line at the 7-Eleven and a cute guy walks in the door: Should I look at him for a few seconds or should I shamefully look away? I look. Otherwise, it would mean that I couldn't look at the half of the world that is male, that I would have to stifle joy. Being gay shouldn't mean always watching your behaviour. That's why you need to own gay so what you've feared becomes part of the person you are. Then instead of holding back, you express yourself. You look at guys who are attractive and interesting. You speak out and you speak up. You interact. Owning gay means you can freely be yourself. Part of me wants to feel resentment that there were 19 years of my life where I didn't have that mobility. I didn't have that freedom and space, but I cannot waste my time looking back. I need to acknowledge the fact that I'm here now. I need to value the freedom I didn't know earlier.

I've been coming to Camp fYrefly for four years. I know what camp is about. The first year I was extremely selfish in that I came to camp to absorb and take a huge basket of resources away. My second year was much the same. I needed things. For the last 2 years though, I've been a youth leader. Now it's about coming to camp and trying to create that supportive culture and that space and atmosphere for someone else. When one of the youth in my pod this year told me that her first day at camp was terrifying, it made me remember the first day of my first year at camp when I found it shocking that everyone was being so open. She's coming into the camp climate for the first time. Now that we've had some pod time to chat and share, she's starting to laugh out loud. She's interacting with people and making friends. She's connecting. She's getting to know queer youth from all across Canada. For me, that opportunity to see others grow and gain strength is an extremely rewarding experience. As a youth leader, I get to help create that environment for them. It's about helping queer youth to move forward hopefully sooner and in a healthier way than I did myself. Camp fYrefly has been a good place for me to take things when I needed them, and now it's a good place to give back.

5 The Marc Hall Prom Predicament: Queer Individual Rights v. Institutional Church Rights in Canadian Public Education*

WITH KRISTOPHER WELLS

John's InterText about suppressing gayness and navigating Catholic family life is typical of stories that many Catholic youth tell as they try to cope with their sexual and gender minority (SGM) differences. While John lacked parental acceptance, another Catholic youth, Marc Hall, had supportive parents. However, Catholic schooling proved to be his nemesis. In 2002 Marc Hall found himself an accidental advocate for gay individual rights in Catholic schools just because he was a high school senior who wanted to attend his prom with his boyfriend. Although his case against Durham Catholic District School Board never made its way to the Supreme Court of Canada, it did rekindle long-standing deliberations regarding the constitutionally protected right of the Catholic Church to have separate schools versus the individual rights of students who attend them. In keeping with the Canadian Charter of Rights and Freedoms, institutional rights cannot supersede individual rights, and vice versa. However, the normative act of attending a school prom, albeit with a same-gender partner, provided one more blatant example of the difficulties of delineating parameters to rights and freedoms in Canada. Marc persevered and the prom predicament became his immersion in steeling life. He successfully used the legal system as his last recourse in his quest to attend his prom. A wonderful subtext in this story is the fact that Marc had unwavering parental support, which enabled him to mediate the challenges of an exclusionary Catholic politics. These politics are bent on protecting theocracy,

* Reproduced with permission from the *Canadian Journal of Education* (28(3), 2005, pp. 237–70), http://www.csse-scee.ca/CJE/Articles/FullText/CJE28-3/CJE28-3-gracewells.pdf.

which is disconnected from Canadian democracy as the nation attends to matters of human and civil rights for sexual and gender minorities. Theocrats who create a binary of institutional religious rights versus individual rights to inclusive education forget that many SGM individuals see themselves as whole persons working to reconcile their sexuality and spirituality. Another important subtext in Marc's story is that youth are persons and citizens in this country, with rights and responsibilities just like those over the age of majority. It is also important to mention that the Ontario English Catholic Teachers' Association and Catholics for Free Choice, both living out the notion of Catholic social action at a grass-roots level, were part of the Coalition in Support of Marc Hall and intervened in support of Marc in his court case.

Marc Hall's Prom Request and the Privatization and Politicization of Queer

In writing this account of the people and events surrounding Marc Hall's request to attend the prom at his Catholic high school with his boyfriend, we proceed not only inspired by Marc's courageous undertaking but also motivated by our own histories of schooling as marginalized gay Canadian youth. We cannot escape the politics of our own locations, which are shaped by such influences as history, culture, ideologies, and communities of exclusion (Giroux, 1992). Thus we begin with narrative vignettes of our pasts that provide some explanation but never any apology for our collective passion.

André: I attended the same Catholic school from primary through junior high. That school was in a small community where everyone I knew was Catholic and where life focused around a small church that had a granite grotto dedicated to Our Lady of Lourdes as its backdrop. As a young boy, I was given some comfort by the Catholic religion, but it was always mixed with guilt and fear about being a bad boy, a sinner, and someone who might go to hell.

   I spent high school in an all-boys' Jesuit school that the principal-priest continuously referred to as a Roman Catholic public school. It was there that I had my first crushes on certain male teachers and other students. It was also there that I remember repeatedly experiencing or witnessing overt and subtle expressions (in word and in action) of heterosexism, sexism, and homophobia. Many students called me a faggot; some mentally and physically abused me. However, sometimes it was a teacher who became the problem. For example, stamped indelibly in my memory is the response of that principal-priest – my grade 11 religion teacher – who, when one of my friends asked him about homosexuality during a religion class, abruptly responded, "There's just no place to put it!" Apart from the inappropriateness of his response, I never forgot the homophobic sentiment in his retort. His words silenced me. I felt ashamed.

Silence and shame about my gayness are indelible parts of my history. While they have had enduring effects on my life, I have learned to live wholly as a gay person intellectually, emotionally, sexually, and so on. For me, the legacy of Catholic schooling is a wedge between sexuality and religion, which I see as two incompatible forces in my life. My peace now comes from people who respect my gayness and who do not reduce my physical expression of love for another man to an act of grave depravity.

Kris: My experience of schooling was not marred by religious ideology, practices, or interference. However, like André, both growing up queer and going to school were marked by invisibility and silences. In retrospect, I do not remember much about my public school experience. In order to survive, I learned that it was best to simply turn off all my emotions and feelings. I dealt with my "difference" by becoming an average student who always tried to blend in rather than stand out from the crowd.

As a queer youth, religion was always something outside my lifeworld. It was just another kind of oppression, an oppression that I avoided. I didn't need religious people telling me that I was deviant, immoral, or disordered. I got enough of those messages in school hallways and in my classes every day.

Today I have tremendous respect and admiration for the many queer youth whose courage and convictions drive them to demand their human and civil rights. Instead of the invisibility and silences that marked my experiences of schooling, many making up today's queer student body are vocal, visible, and proud. They are making their schools key sites in their struggles for social justice and cultural recognition and respect.

The story about Marc Hall's request for his principal's permission to take his boyfriend Jean-Paul Dumond to his Catholic high school prom is ultimately part of the larger narrative of what we perceive to be the Catholic Church's institutional efforts to privatize queer – to keep it hidden, invisible, silent, unannounced – in religion, education, and culture. In privatizing queer, the Catholic Church aligns its actions to its particular exclusionary beliefs about queer without regard for broader public laws and legislation that are in keeping with Section

15 of the Canadian Charter of Rights and Freedoms. This section has always provided protection against discrimination on the ground of sexual orientation, which was first confirmed by the Supreme Court of Canada in *Egan v. Canada* in 1995 (R. Douglas Elliott, personal communication, 23 November 2005). Since then Canadian teachers' federations and associations have amended their codes of professional conduct and statements of teachers' rights and responsibilities to include sexual orientation as a character of person to be protected against discrimination in keeping with the law of the land (Canadian Teachers' Federation & Elementary Teachers' Federation of Ontario [CTF & ETFO], 2002).

Despite this remarkable change, we maintain that the Catholic Church continues to privatize queer by defining and setting parameters to it in institutional terms that segregate being religious from being sexual in ways which limit queer acceptability, access, and accommodation. For those who succumb to it, this privatization is about policing the queer body; that is, it is about "silencing oneself, self-censorship, and self-consciousness in mind and body" (Frankham, 2001, p. 465). These self-guarded reactions represent complicity in maintaining the hegemony of heterosexism as a cultural technology that systematically privileges heterosexuality, assumes that everyone is (or ought to be) heterosexual, and values heterosexuality while reducing homosexuality to deviance and intrinsic evil (Friend, 1998; Grace et al., 2004). By using heterosexism as a never innocent cultural technology to assert its authority, the Catholic Church engenders institutional perspectives and practices that deliberately frame meanings, identities, values, and codes of behaviour (norms and standards) in heteronormative terms (Grace & Benson, 2000; Simon, 1992). In this light, heterosexism is the precursor to homophobia, which is an ignorance- and fear-based manifestation of symbolic and/or physical violence in relation to a homosexual positionality as an undesirable identity and expression. As Friend (1998) remarks, "Homophobia ensures that violating the rule of heterosexuality has consequences" (p. 142).

Institutional churches have been among the most invasive cultural forces making certain that there are consequences for living queer. They "historically have taught and often still teach children [and youth] that homosexuality is wrong and undesirable and that gays and lesbians are 'bad' – unless perhaps they are ashamed of what they desire and repress their feelings" (MacDougall, 2000, p. 98). Marc Hall's prom predicament provides an opportunity to reflect critically on this pedagogy of negation and on what the institutional Catholic Church and those who safeguard it do to youth whom they demean or dismiss and fail to protect (Silin, 1992). In the legal hearing resulting from this predicament, the Catholic Church attempted to achieve its apparent goal of keeping queer privatized by using its constitutional right to make decisions with respect to denominational education in order to stake a claim to power over the individual in public space. As a gay Catholic youth, Marc Hall resisted this privatization. Indeed in events leading up to the granting of an interlocutory injunction enabling him to take his boyfriend to the prom, Marc continuously made being, desiring, and acting queer personal and political. His resistance created a dilemma that resulted in a lawsuit against his principal and the Catholic school board after they denied his request. The heart of the dilemma is captured in this question: Does the school board's decision align with institutional church rights regarding the provision of denominational education as guaranteed in Section 93 of the Constitution Act, 1867, or does it violate Marc's individual human rights as protected under Section 15 of the Canadian Charter of Rights and Freedoms (Elliott & Paris, 2002; MacKinnon, 2002)? The Canadian judicial system still has to make a decision regarding this matter of institutional versus individual rights. The 10 May 2002 decision granting the interlocutory injunction so Marc could attend his prom did not address this more substantive issue. In 2015 this issue remains unaddressed.

As the prom story unfolded, church-supporting interest groups and the Coalition in Support of Marc Hall all staked claims in deliberations over Marc's individual rights versus the Catholic Church's institutional rights. The coalition consisted of interveners including the Canadian Auto Workers Union, the Ontario English Catholic Teachers' Association, Catholics for Free Choice, and Egale (Equality for Gays and Lesbians Everywhere) Canada, the last being the national queer organization engaged in cultural work and political action to support the spectral community of those marginalized because of sex, sexual, and gender differences. Thus, Marc's story is also a story of the politicization of his prom predicament. To reflect the contextual, relational, and dispositional complexities of this story, we employed two research methods. First, we engaged extensively in document analysis. This included a chronological analysis of reports and commentaries, press releases, and newsletters from various news groups and organizations. We reviewed open letters written by those with vested interests in the prom predicament, including the Catholic bishop for the Durham region of Ontario, various politicians, and Egale Canada. We also examined legal records, including the legal factum prepared by the lawyers representing the Coalition in Support of Marc Hall and the court record prepared by Justice Robert MacKinnon in granting the interlocutory injunction. As well, we surveyed material from two key websites: the Marc Hall website called Have Your Voice Heard (Ryan, Hood, & Hall, n.d.) and the Durham Catholic District School Board website (DCDSB, n.d.). Second, having built our knowledge and understanding of interest groups and events shaping the prom predicament, we conducted a two-hour, open-ended interview and held follow-up discussions with Marc, who helped us build a deeper understanding of how he mediated the whole politicized process and how it affected him. The interview took place on 3 October 2002, nearly five months after his prom had taken place.

Drawing on these sources, we begin with a chronology and analysis of events and interest groups shaping, and politicizing, Marc's prom predicament. We incorporate a critique of Catholicized education and what we perceive as the Catholic Church's efforts to privatize queer by defining and setting parameters to it in institutional terms that segregate being religious from being sexual. We discuss how we construe this privatization as a failure of the Catholic Church to treat queer Catholics, especially vulnerable queer Catholic youth, with dignity and integrity as the church sets untenable limits to queer acceptability, access, and accommodation. We examine case law regarding individual rights that has been affected by Section 15 and Section 1 of the Canadian Charter of Rights and Freedoms. Given that Marc's lawsuit was dropped, leaving the issue unsettled, we conclude with a queer perspective on the importance of upholding the Charter in the name of democratic principles.

It's My Prom, Too! The Unfolding of the Marc Hall Prom Predicament

Marc Takes a Stand: Choosing Resistance, Being Resilient

The stories of queer youth as at-risk individuals are well documented in narratives about confusion, depression, substance abuse, alienation, truancy, quitting school, gay bashing, running away, and suicide (Epstein, O'Flynn, & Telford, 2001; Friend, 1998; Grace & Wells, 2001; Herdt, 1995; Human Rights Watch, 2001; Quinlivan & Town, 1999; Ryan & Futterman, 1998). When youth are labelled as both queer and at risk, this can "doubly pathologize" them, accentuating their alienation and difference (Quinlivan & Town, 1999, p. 512). Increasingly though, stories of at-risk youth are being transgressed by stories of queer youth as advocates, social activists, cultural workers, and survivors (Friend, 1998; Grace & Wells, 2004; Weis & Fine, 2001). These stories of resilience locate queer youth as thrivers who mediate "a paradoxical mix of empowerment and conflict" as they contest "sanctioned silences and institutionalized invisibility" (Friend, 1998, pp. 138–9). Marc Hall epitomizes these thrivers. He contested the status quo and transgressed the limits to individual freedom put in his way, especially by the institutional Catholic Church as an exclusionary cultural formation. His story captures his struggle to be, become, and belong through a series of chosen, calculated, and uneasy acts of resistance that protected, rearticulated, and laid claim to gay personal and cultural identities and life experiences. These acts of resistance can be understood as transgressive performances and acts of resilience (Bottrell, 2007; Hall, 2007). They reflect key tenets of queer theory. These tenets include interrogating the hetero-regulated construction of normality that has traditionally placed queer on the margins of "normal"; deconstructing the culture- and power-laden categories of sexuality, gender, and desire; and contesting the heterosexual/homosexual binary as an exclusionary organizing principle (Dilley, 1999; Grace & Hill, 2004). The Marc Hall prom predicament provides a rich opportunity to engage these tenets as we research and theorize "why/how/when lives are homosexualized, 'queered' outside the norm" (Dilley, 1999, p. 469). Moreover, as a story of resilience, Marc's narrative helps us to understand how we might fulfil the political and pedagogical task of queer theory: to question presumptions, assumptions, dispositions, and perspectives, especially those that are not generally questioned (Dilley, 1999). As we do so, we ought to remember that it "is not a question of 'who is queer,' but 'how is queer'; not so much 'why are they queer,' but 'why are we saying they are queer?'" (Dilley, 1999, p. 459, italics in original). Deliberating such questions is vital to making sense of Marc's story of resistance and resilience.

When the prom predicament erupted, Marc was 17 years old and a grade 12 student at Monsignor John Pereyma Catholic Secondary School in Oshawa, Ontario. He had recently declared his gay sexual orientation to his parents, friends, and his high school. Marc had attended Pereyma since grade 9, and he had also attended Catholic schools as an elementary and junior high student. At the end of his grade 11 school year, Marc approached his English teacher, with whom he had an excellent rapport, asking her to speak to his principal, Mike Powers, about an issue he sensed might be problematic: Marc wanted to attend his Catholic high school prom with his boyfriend Jean-Paul. With no response forthcoming from the principal after his English teacher spoke with him, Marc approached Mr Powers directly early in his grade 12 year to request permission. With the principal seemingly avoiding him, Marc remained persistent. Finally, on 25 February 2002, Mr Powers refused Marc permission, maintaining that interacting with a same-sex partner at the prom would constitute a form of sexual activity that contravened the teachings of the Catholic Church (MacKinnon, 2002). Although the Catholic Church maintains that homosexuals should not be subjected to unjust discrimination, its catechism nevertheless explicitly states, "Basing itself on Sacred Scripture, which presents homosexual acts as acts of grave depravity, tradition has always declared that 'homosexual acts are intrinsically disordered.' ... Under no circumstances can they be approved" (Canadian Conference of Catholic Bishops [CCCB], 1994, para. 2357, p. 480). During our interview with him, Marc provided this recollection of what he perceived as the Catholic Church's unjust discrimination towards him:

> When I started school in grade 12 and more and more people were talking about the prom, I approached Mr Powers and asked to speak to him because he hadn't gotten back to me. I'd see him in the halls and tell him that I had to talk to him about something. I did this three or four times before he responded. One day I was sitting in my English class, and he buzzed me down to the office. After I walked into his office, he told me that he had been thinking about my request for several months. He said that he talked to our pastor about it as well as the school board. Basically, Mr Powers said that I couldn't bring JP [Jean-Paul] to the prom because it was against school policy and the Catholic teachings. I sat there in shock. While I had expected the worst, I still felt betrayed. I had learned in religion class to love thy neighbor and to treat everyone the way that you want to be treated. It felt like my pastor, the school board, and Mr Powers were all contradicting those teachings. That's when I got really upset. I started crying. He kept saying, "I'm sorry! I'm sorry!" I got up and left the room.

In reality Marc was just another casualty of what has become known as the 1986 "Halloween Letter," in which the Catholic Church privatized queer in institutional terms by emphatically denying queer Catholics the individual right to live as whole persons in the fullness of their sexuality. In this infamous (at least to many of us who are queer) *Letter to the*

Bishops of the Catholic Church on the Pastoral Care of Homosexual Persons,
the Congregation for the Doctrine of the Faith (CDF) (1986) made the
Catholic position on homosexuality explicit. Describing homosexuality as a phenomenon, these Catholic gatekeepers described "the homosexual condition or tendency ... as being 'intrinsically disordered,' and
able in no case to be approved of" (Dignity Canada Dignité [DCD], n.d.,
p. 1). Having located the "homosexual condition" (p. 1) as an "objective disorder" (p. 2), they asserted, "Although the particular inclination of the homosexual person is not a sin, it is a more or less strong
tendency ordered toward an intrinsic moral evil" (p. 1). The CDF said
that acting on the inclination was sinful, requiring a "conversion from
evil" (p. 5). Placing the institutional church above civil law and legislation, they emphatically stated, "It is true that ... [the church's] position cannot be revised by pressure from civil legislation or the trend
of the moment" (p. 4). Apparently, it cannot be revised by theological research either. For example, philosopher and professor of religion
Cornel West (1996) concludes from his research that "Jesus is not only
silent on the issue [of homosexuality], but he goes about engaging in
forms of touch and intimate relation, not sexual that we know of, but
in intimate relation in the best sense of sensual" (p. 365). Moreover, he
asserts that the condemnation of homosexual acts is based on "thin and
impoverished conceptions of the gospel" (p. 365). As well, Father Daniel A. Helminiak (2000), a theologian and Roman Catholic priest who
has ministered to lesbian, gay, and bisexual Catholics since 1977, concludes from his research, "The Bible supplies no real basis for the condemnation of homosexuality" (p. 19). Believing that a choice between
religion and sexuality is a choice between God and human wholeness,
Helminiak (2000) maintains that to deny or be afraid of one's sexuality
is to "short-circuit human spontaneity in a whole array of expressions –
creativity, motivation, passion, commitment, heroic achievement" (p. 26).

The Halloween Letter, which we maintain represents symbolic
excommunication of queer persons who choose to live full spiritual *and*
sexual lives, continues to be the Catholic word on homosexuality and,
as such, influences the Catholic educational approach to it. For example,
in November 2004, the education commission of the Ontario Conference of Catholic Bishops released *Pastoral Guidelines to Assist Students
of Same-Sex Orientation*, a document intended to help school chaplains,
guidance counsellors, principals, and teachers to address the "pastoral challenge" of counselling and caring for lesbian and gay students
(Swan, 2004, p. 4). Bishop Paul-André Durocher, who headed the team

of authors that drew up the guidelines, made it clear that the document was aligned with the catechism of the Catholic Church and the October 1986 letter from the CDF (Swan, 2004). In other words, the pastoral guidelines repeated the Catholic stance that homosexuals are called to chastity, which, as Durocher put it, "will involve for them celibacy also" (Swan, 2004, p. 4). The guidelines represent part of an effort by Ontario's Catholic bishops to counter anti-gay bigotry and bullying in their schools. They align with the earlier culturally deficient approach of the Ontario Catholic Family Life Educators Network, which has usually limited its consideration of homosexuality to the context of anti–sexual harassment education (see, for example, Pódgorski, 2001).

The Prom Predicament Continues to Unfold

After his meeting with Mr Powers, Marc was very upset. When he got home, he told his parents about the devastating meeting with the principal. Deeply concerned, Audy and Emily Hall requested a meeting with Mr Powers with Marc present. During that meeting, which occurred the following week, Marc read a letter he had drafted to the principal. Marc told us about the origin of the letter:

> When Mr Powers said no to me the first time, and I knew that he was going to have a meeting with my parents and me, that's when I wrote it. I read it to him in front of my parents.

In this excerpt from the letter, Marc demonstrated his determination and resilience in the face of what he perceived as unequal individual treatment as a result of his gay sexual orientation.

> I just want to be treated like a normal human being, because guess what ... that is what I am. I mean, look at me, I'm not here to cause trouble. I have an 82% average, a lot of friends, and a great family ... Don't you see that I'm not fighting for this just because it's my prom? It's my whole life and the lives of other gay people. I'm fighting for what so many people don't understand. I'm trying to speed up the process of equality because I am sick of being treated like someone absent of feeling and emotion. I have been waiting for my prom since grade 9. Prom, to some people, is an important step in someone's life. It makes you realize that you're actually finishing high school and that this event is one of the last times you and your friends will all be together. So maybe

I'll take things to the next level [to court], but it's better than not caring about anything ... Not only is what you are doing morally unjust, but you are also violating the laws of the *Ontario Human Rights Act*. Hopefully we can resolve this issue peacefully and before it escalates into a legal hearing. (Ryan et al., n.d., pp. 1–2)

Despite the letter and Marc's fervour, no progress was made at this meeting. In his conversation with us, Marc reflected, conveying his sense of sadness and loss:

After I read the speech I felt that what I wrote didn't mean anything to him. My mom thought that if she and my dad agreed that I could go with JP, then it would be okay. But Mr Powers still said no, saying it was against the Catholic teachings. I just sat there and started crying again. He just said, "I'm sorry." Those were basically the two meetings – very, very emotional.

In refusing to change his mind, Mr Powers essentially discriminated against Marc because he was gay. Moreover, he took *in loco parentis* to the extreme, overriding parental authority by ignoring Marc's parents' desire to have their son and Jean-Paul attend the prom together. The Halls have been loving and accepting parents. Their support for their gay son has grown through Marc's coming out and their coming to terms with his gayness. Marc recounts the emotional process that took its toll on all of them:

I actually remember the exact date that I came out to my parents – May 23, 2001. I actually remember the situation. My mom was downstairs watching *Wheel of Fortune* in the living room. I was upstairs in my room telling myself that I had to tell her. I went downstairs twice intending to do it, but each time I chickened out. Finally, the third time, I told her. I started off babbling about how people get older and have different sexual attractions, but when I came to the point of telling her I was gay I froze. My mom looked at me and said, "I think I know what you are trying to say. Are you trying to tell me that you like boys?" I said, "Yes." She said, "I kind of thought so." And then the whole crying thing began.

A few days later she told my father. He continued to talk to me, asking little things like "How was your day?" A few weeks later he and I went to the cemetery where my brother is buried. My dad started talking to my brother Marcel's grave, saying how I was still the same person that I always was, and how he and my mom were going to take care of me. My dad said he would be behind me 100 per cent. Ever since then we've been really close. My mom and I have always been close.

My parents' point of view is that God created me the way I am, and they love all of me no matter what. The Catholic teachings say to love everybody basically. My parents' view never changed. My dad has said countless times that because the Catholic school board made this decision doesn't mean that it is right. He also believes in a God who loves everyone. My dad says that he doesn't pray to the school board, he doesn't pray to the priest, he prays to God. My parents never rejected me, and supported me right from the beginning. If I never had their support I probably wouldn't have done anything.

Strong parental support like this is usually a key reason why queer youth like Marc thrive and are so resilient (Friend, 1998). Indeed many parents do not react so well when a child announces they are queer (Grace & Wells, 2001; MacDougall, 2000). Some appear as traumatized by this announcement as they might be if they had been told that their child had a terminal illness. They experience a profound sense of loss and grief inextricably linked to cultural homophobia and interwoven with heteronormative thoughts, such as there will be no grandchildren. More compassionately, they may worry that their child might become a victim of violence. However, Marc's parents were able to put their love for their child first and move beyond any trauma to nurture their queer child. Throughout the prom predicament, Marc's parents remained supportive despite the barrage of media attention and other difficulties emanating from the politicization of Marc's request.

All Marc wanted was to attend his prom with his boyfriend. However, in hegemonic terms, his wish amounted to a transgression of the prom as a heteronormalized rite of passage and a hyper-heterosexualized cultural technology.

> In secondary schools, the "prom" ... provides a space where, however uncomfortably, students are expected to interact, producing themselves as feminine and masculine in iconically heterosexual and exaggerated ways. The heterosexualization of this process is often unremarked, and young people are seen generally within a developmental discourse of "normal" gender development. (Epstein et al., 2001, p. 152)

As a hyper-heterosexualized cultural event, the school prom has not only functioned to replicate norms of the masculine, the feminine, and the heterosexual pairing of male and female, but it has also operated to mark and police heterosexuality as the desired and assumed expression of sexuality. The heterosexual/homosexual binary assists this regulation as it "function[s] to reinforce certain practices through signalling the disadvantages and dysfunctionality of other practices" (Frankham, 2001, p. 457). The Catholic prom – framed within the precepts and myths of biblical patriarchy and religious tradition, which are cultural technologies of control – is perhaps the ultimate expression of hyper-heterosexualized policing, even as it disdains any form of sexual expression by youth expected to be chaste and non-sexual. This is interesting if not hypocritical. After all, the Catholic religion, which is as an apparatus of controlled knowledge, a political force, and "a superb instrument of power for itself, [is] entirely woven through with elements that are imaginary, erotic, effective, corporal, sensual, and so on" (Foucault in a 1978 taped discussion, quoted in Carrette, 1999, p. 107). Within Catholic ideology, heteronormative knowledge has been safe, protected, unquestioned, and exclusionary knowledge that is ensconced "within hegemonic regimes of truth in relation to gender and sexuality" (Epstein & Sears, 1999, p. 2). In fact the Catholic Church as a regulative institution has policed gender and sexuality (Epstein & Johnson, 1998; Grace & Benson, 2000). Catholic schools are conduits for this policing. Thus across sex, sexual, and gender differences, "everyone lives, daily, a relation to the heterosexual norm both within and outside the school" (Epstein & Johnson, 1994, p. 221).

The Politicization of Marc's Prom Predicament

In the aftermath of Marc's two distressing and unsuccessful meetings with his principal Mr Powers, a website called Have Your Voice Heard was set up in response to his prom predicament. The home page featured a picture of Marc with Lance Ryan and Cassy Hood, two of his close friends who created the website, where they set up a message board and posted the letter that Marc had written to his principal. On the home page the three stated that the purpose of the website was to assist in the fight against the segregation of gay students in the schools of the Durham region and elsewhere (Ryan et al., n.d.). In a website editorial entitled "Prejudice in Catholic Schools," Hood asserted that the principal's refusal to permit Marc to attend the prom with Jean-Paul was an act of discrimination and harassment. She categorically admonished educational leaders: "Discrimination from peers is a large enough burden to homosexuals, but this kind of harassment coming from principals, teachers, and school boards is abominable. There is no excuse. It's illegal, immoral, and unfair" (Ryan et al., n.d., p. 1).

What followed next was a complex set of events. Through the involvement of diverse interest groups in the prom predicament, Marc experienced a politicization of his youth, his sexuality, and his individual right to participate in school activities. In a real sense, his activism was not planned but provoked. It was provoked not only by a Catholic Church and school that he felt had failed him, but also by supporters who saw this citizen student as a youth with a cause advanced by Section 15 (1) of the Canadian Charter of Rights and Freedoms. This section, which came into force in 1985, states,

> Every individual is equal before and under the law and has the right to the equal protection and equal benefit of the law without discrimination and, in particular, without discrimination based on race, national or ethnic origin, colour, religion, sex, age or mental or physical disability. (Department of Justice Canada [DJC], 2003, p. 4)

While in the spirit of the Charter this equality provision has always provided protection against discrimination on the analogous ground of sexual orientation, it took a decade before this was actually confirmed in *Egan v. Canada* (Lahey, 1999; MacDougall, 2000).

The politicization of the prom predicament was truly set in motion during the March break that came a few days after Marc and his parents met with Mr Powers. As Marc told us, news of his situation and the subsequent establishment of the website spread quickly.

> During the March break more and more people got to see the website. In Windsor, Ontario, a guy named Chris Cecile who hosts a weekly radio show called *Queer Radio* saw the website. I think he's the one who got the whole thing rolling using email. That's when other radio stations and newspapers started to call me. After the March break, I got ambushed by TV cameras outside my school. That happened for a while. I did all my interviews during lunch break.
>
> Another person that really stands out is George Smitherman. He's a gay MPP [Member of Provincial Parliament] from Toronto. He contacted me through the website email. We got together and started formulating plans to pressure the school board. He organized the press conferences at Queen's Park [home to the Ontario provincial legislature] and various rallies. He's been there from the beginning, and he's become a family friend.

The media coverage that escalated in the wake of this grass-roots activism included national attention in a news story covering Marc's prom predicament that aired on the 18 March 2002 edition of *CTV National News*. Although the extent of the exposure was quite helpful in terms of the politicization process, it was much less helpful to Marc on a personal level because it left him even more visible and, consequently, more vulnerable to violence and retaliatory dangers (D'Augelli, 1998). Marc shared his experience of the threats and violence that came with openly taking a stand:

> After the media interviews started at school, some students didn't like the idea of JP going to the prom with me. That's when a lot of name-calling like "faggot" and "queer" started. The homophobia increased. For example, they shoved this piece of paper in my friend's locker. It was a really good drawing, but very morbid. It was an old cross and it had cobwebs and spiders and goblins and stuff on it. On the side of the cross someone wrote, "Die Marc, Die!" On top of the drawing were the words, "We're all out to kill Marc Hall!"
>
> When the website first started, 95 per cent of the responses were supportive. As the whole thing continued though, more and more hate mail came. I also started getting letters and other mail at my school. Most of it was pretty supportive, but there was some negative stuff. One card had a picture of a penis, and it said, "Marc Hall sucks cock!" I just threw it out. I realized that if I took a stand like this, there would be some negative feedback.
>
> The worst thing though was feeling unsafe. There was one point in which I was a little nervous. A police officer came to my house and told us that he received information that a group of guys had said they planned to ambush my family and me. My parents and I were all edgy after that. My dad put a piece of wood in the patio door for extra protection in case they broke the lock. That happened a few weeks after the whole media thing blew up.

The Prom Predicament Escalates

In a 19 March 2002 press release, Grant A. Andrews, Director of Education for the Durham Catholic District School Board, stated the school board's position regarding Mr Powers's decision:

> This action is consistent with the views and values of the Durham Catholic District School Board. As a Catholic School Board, we are charged with upholding the values of the Church. The Church does not

condemn an individual for his or her sexual orientation. However, the behaviours associated with a homosexual life style are not consistent with Church teachings and our values as a Catholic School system. We are constitutionally entitled to administer our schools in a manner consistent with the teachings of the Church. (Gay & Lesbian Educators of British Columbia [GALE-BC], 2002, p. 4)

This statement preceded the 25 March 2002 school board meeting at which Marc, his parents, and numerous supporters were present. Despite their presence, Mary Ann Martin, the board chair, said the prom issue was not on the agenda due to insufficient notice, so no one would be heard regarding the matter. Mike Shields, president of Local 222 of the Canadian Auto Workers Union, Canada's biggest union local and a strong advocate for gay rights, had attended this meeting as part of the Coalition in Support of Marc Hall. When Martin made her announcement, Shields angrily interjected, which resulted in police being called to escort him from the property (365Gay.com, 2002, p. 1).

Subsequently, school-board trustees acknowledged that even if proper protocol had been followed and supporters had been allowed to speak to the prom issue, they would not have changed their minds because they considered allowing Marc to attend his prom with his boyfriend tantamount to condoning homosexual behaviour (CBC News, 2002a). Thus the school board's decision was predetermined and fixed, bounded as it was by Catholic theocratic moral knowledge: "When a certain knowledge opens up the way in advance, the decision is already made, it might as well be said there is none to make; irresponsibly, and in good conscience, one simply applies or implements a program" (Derrida, as quoted in Biesta, 2003, p. 144). This is what the school-board trustees did. It is what the principal had already done. It is what the regional bishop, despite feigning distance from the decision making, would subsequently do.

In a 4 April 2002 open letter to Dalton McGuinty, a Catholic and then Leader of the Ontario Liberal Party and the Official Opposition, Anthony G. Meagher, Auxiliary Bishop of Toronto for the Northern and Durham regions, reiterated the school-board trustees' position. Appearing oblivious in the letter to his ultimate authority and responsibility as bishop of the Durham region, he maintained, "The decision is obviously not mine to make in this issue" (Meagher, 2002, p. 1). What would he have said if the school principal had decided to let Marc attend the prom with Jean-Paul? The bishop did acknowledge a need for those in authority to be wary in light of the high suicide rate among gay teenagers. And he did go on to say that no student in a Catholic school should ever "be made to feel excluded or ostracized at any school event because of his or her sexual orientation" (p. 1). However, the bishop unequivocally stated, "There is no doubt in my mind that if permission by a principal in our Catholic school system is given for any 17-year-old boy to take another male as his 'date' for the prom this will be a clear and positive approval not just of the boy's 'orientation,' but of his adopting a homosexual lifestyle" (p. 1). Elsewhere in the letter, the bishop asserted that Marc was being manipulated. He also distinguished Marc as "the boy" and Jean-Paul as "the 21-year-old man" (p. 2). With his distinctions, his choice of words and italicizations, and his subtext positioning gay men as paedophiles, the bishop reinscribed heterosexism, blatant homophobia, and the pathologization of queer as Catholic cultural technologies scourging queer. He also reinscribed the prom so it epitomizes what Weis and Fine (2001) describe as a heteronormalizing and thus exclusionary social and cultural practice. Moreover, the bishop's Catholicized rhetoric demonstrated that he is certainly not tolerant in the Freirean sense in which tolerance is viewed as a virtue vital to the political and pedagogical tasks culminating in inclusive education. Freire (1998) asserts, "I cannot see how one might be democratic without experiencing tolerance, coexistence with the different, as a fundamental principle" (p. 42). If the bishop had been living out the notion of Freirean tolerance, then he would have enabled and supported Marc to attend the prom, not as a favour or courtesy, but as a right of the citizen student in a society that prohibits discrimination. Moreover, he would have honoured and encouraged others to honour Marc's difference as a character of person that makes him whole and complete.

At a subsequent school-board hearing on 8 April 2002, the prom predicament was on the agenda and several individuals and groups made presentations. Prior to this hearing Marc, Cassy, and Lance had posted comments on their website. Rage and resilience permeated their words: "We're trying to prove to them [the school board] how much more organized and sophisticated we are! If they try to blow us off this time, let's watch the roof fall down on them!" (Ryan et al., n.d., notice board, p. 1). At the hearing George Smitherman suggested the prom issue touched on values undergirding our identity as a nation (Fisher, 2002). However, his comments and those of other supportive parties were made in vain. The Durham Catholic District School Board confirmed the principal's decision, denying Marc permission to attend his prom with Jean-Paul. Suggesting that taking a date to the prom is a form of romantic relationship, Mary Ann Martin, the school-board chair, read from an already prepared statement:

> The principal's decision and our decision to support the principal is [sic] consistent with the instruction of the Church to accept Marc with respect, compassion, and sensitivity. Just as the Church urges such an approach, it also draws a line. Like the Church, we accept and support Marc, but we also accept and respect the line that the Church has drawn. Marc wants us to help him cross this line at this Catholic school function. This we will not do. (Andrews, 2002, p. 1)

Hearing this decision, Marc cried. Still he maintained, "I believe in justice and that God loves me for who I am" (CBC News, 2002b, para. 6). He exclaimed, "They [the trustees] promote equality except in some cases. They take Jesus's rule [– do unto others as you would have them do unto you –] and bend it a little bit for their liking" (CBC Toronto, 2002, p. 1). The school board's decision served only to make Marc more resistant and resilient, intensifying his desire to attend his prom with his boyfriend. He left the hearing ready to have his lawyer take his case to court to ask a judge to reverse the school board's decision (CBC Toronto, 2002). At this point, Marc was ready to actualize his desire as performance and to engage in acts of resistance that would make his queer being, acting, becoming, and belonging visible. On a micro level, he simply wanted the "right to an everyday [experience] not organized by violence, exclusion, medicalization, criminalization, and erasure" (Britzman, 1995, p. 152). However, on a macro level, Marc's acts of resistance would mean much more. As Britzman (1995) asserts,

> Gay and lesbian demands for civil rights call into question the stability and fundamentalist ground of categories like masculinity, femininity, sexuality, citizenship, nation, culture, literacy, consent, legality, [religiosity,] and so forth; categories that are quite central to the ways in which education organizes knowledge of bodies and bodies of knowledge. (p. 152)

To the Courts: Marc's Prom Predicament and the Legal Hearing Seeking an Interlocutory Injunction

On 6 May 2002, a two-day legal hearing began in Whitby, Ontario (CBC News, 2002c). Justice Robert MacKinnon of the Ontario Court of Justice heard the case between plaintiff George Smitherman, in his capacity as litigation guardian of Marc Hall, and defendants Michael Powers and the Durham Catholic District School Board. David L. Corbett was the lead lawyer for the plaintiff; Peter D. Lauwers was the lawyer for the defendants. Through the hearing, Marc sought an interlocutory injunction restraining his principal and the school board from preventing his attendance with his boyfriend at his Catholic high school prom. However, this was Marc's immediate interest, as Justice MacKinnon (2002) noted:

> [T]he substantive thrust of his claims for trial, as pleaded, are for trial court declarations that his *Charter* rights have been violated. Included among the matters in issue for an eventual trial, if pursued, will be the question of whether the School Board's decision falls within its power to make decisions with respect to denominational matters and thus are protected under Section 93 (1) of the *Constitution Act, 1867* and whether the Board's decision violates individual human rights protected under the *Canadian Charter of Rights and Freedoms*, including the right to be free from discrimination on the basis of sexual orientation and age. (para. 13)

In opening the case, David L. Corbett responded to the school board's assertion that those who don't like Catholic values are free to leave the school and the Catholic Church. He argued that, by accepting public funds, Catholic schools also accept a mandate to provide an education to every student in their care (Egale Canada, 2002). He also argued that the school board, in taking the position of respecting homosexuals while condemning homosexual conduct, made a distinction that had already been rejected by the Supreme Court of Canada in its ruling in *Trinity Western University v. British Columbia College of Teachers* in 2001. In that ruling, while the Supreme Court supported TWU's constitutional right to offer a "full program [to] reflect ... [its fundamentalist] Christian worldview" (Supreme Court Judgments, 2001, para. 1), it made the distinction between the broader right to hold discriminatory beliefs and the more limited right to act upon those beliefs. However, in her dissenting decision in the case, the Honourable Madame Justice L'Heureux-Dubé found that it was reasonable to conclude that without adequate exposure to diversity in teacher-training programs, there would be an "unacceptable pedagogical cost" to students (Supreme Court Judgments, 2001, para. 12). Her conclusion amounts to an important caution: if a public educational practice is to be ethical, then it had better be about educating *all* students, including queer students. This point ought to be made clear, starting in teacher education. Unfortunately, in preparing pre-service teachers to take up their professional responsibilities, teacher-education programs have generally failed to provide them with any significant focus on sex, sexual, and gender differences (Kissen, 2002). In keeping with Section 15 (1) of the Charter, it would seem imperative that "lgbt issues *are* inextricably interwoven into the basic concerns of preservice education" (Kissen, 2002, p. 4, italics added).

In representing the principal and the Durham Catholic District School Board, Peter D. Lauwers argued that Catholic schools are beyond Charter reach because of the constitutional protection guaranteed in Section 93 of the Constitution Act, 1867 (Egale Canada, 2002). He submitted that the plaintiff's motion should be dismissed on that ground (MacKinnon, 2002). Unfortunately, as he presented his case, Lauwers, in keeping with the Catholic Church's disdain of acting queer on seemingly any level, spoke condescendingly about Marc: "He's an example we cannot approve. He's a bad example from a Catholic perspective and what he wants to do is not consistent with the teachings of the church" (CP, 2002, para. 2). Lauwers added that, in keeping with Catholic educational values, Marc could be disciplined or expelled if he kissed, held hands, or danced with his boyfriend at the prom (CBC News, 2002d). Lauwers suggested the judge had to examine the mandate of Catholic schools, emphasizing, "We're about indoctrination, plain and simple" (CP, 2002, para. 10). However, this perspective attempting to justify the actions of the principal and the school board did not "frame inclusiveness as a moral career for all participants" in education (Friend, 1998, p. 158). Indeed it was used to suggest that those with vested interests in Catholicized education were exempt from such moral behaviour and responsibility.

In his judgment made just a few hours before Marc's prom on 10 May 2002, Justice Robert MacKinnon granted an interlocutory injunction. It provided an immediate order allowing Marc to attend his Catholic high school prom with his boyfriend (Siu, 2002a). The principal and the school board had previously agreed not to cancel the prom if the injunction was granted (MacKinnon, 2002). In this poignant excerpt from the judgment, Justice MacKinnon speaks to protecting rights and promoting inclusion as fundamental Canadian values:

> In my view, the clear purpose of Section 15 is to value human dignity
> in a free society where difference is respected and equality is valued.
> The praiseworthy object of Section 15 of the *Charter* is to prevent

discrimination and promote a society in which all are secure in the knowledge that they are recognized as human beings equally deserving of concern, respect and consideration ... The record before me is rife with the effects of historic and continuing discrimination against gays. The evidence in this record clearly demonstrates the impact of stigmatization on gay men in terms of denial of self, personal rejection, discrimination and exposure to violence ... It is one of the distinguishing strengths of Canada as a nation that we value tolerance and respect for others. All of us have fundamental rights including expression, association, and religion ... We, as individuals and as institutions, must acknowledge the duties that accompany our rights. Mr. Hall has a duty to accord to others who do not share his orientation the respect that they, with their religious values and beliefs, are due. Conversely, for the reasons I have given, the Principal and the Board have a duty to accord to Mr. Hall the respect that he is due as he attends the prom with his date, his classmates and their dates. (MacKinnon, 2002)

Following the issuing of the interlocutory injunction enabling Marc to attend his prom with Jean-Paul, Marc's mom, Emily Hall, said, "I am so very proud of him. He has opened the doors for other gay students" (Siu, 2002b, p. 2). During his interview Marc recounted the emotional events of that momentous decision day:

I remember every moment of that day. The judgment was to be made before five o'clock because that's when the prom started. I expected a phone call at any time. My tux was ready. We were all sitting in my kitchen. It was about 2 o'clock when we got the phone call. I got up and gripped the phone, and I thought, "Please, please let me win!" I answered the phone, and David Corbett said, "Marc, you're going to the prom!" I started jumping up and down and screaming. Everybody in the kitchen started cheering. Once I got off the phone, my mom phoned all my relatives in New Brunswick saying, "We won! We won!" It was amazing. It was crazy, and it was quite a rush after the decision was made.

Shortly after the decision, dressed in tuxedos that had been laid out just in case the justice's decision was good news, Marc and Jean-Paul attended the prom. Marc recounted the unusual scenario and the politicization process that never stopped.

We had our champagne and then the limo came. When JP and I walked outside, people were clapping as we got into the limo. The first thing we did was go down to CAW [Canadian Auto Workers] Local 222 where we had this big, huge media event. We did the media event, but JP and I just wanted to go to the prom and be left alone.

As we were driving to the prom, there was a helicopter from Roger's Television following the limo. As we got to the gateway [of the place where the prom was held], there were cameras and reporters everywhere. Thankfully they weren't allowed inside. Finally, we were at the prom. Students were shouting, "You won!" The principal sat in his chair with his arms crossed, just slouching and staring at everybody. There were some teachers who congratulated me. Most of the students there said that they were really happy that I fought to take JP. They kept saying how happy they were that I was there.

The dinner was good, except we had rubber chicken and gross stuffing. JP and I danced together and slow danced, just like any other normal couple. We kissed just like any normal couple. The prom was worth fighting for, definitely!

Finally attending his prom with Jean-Paul is a testament to Marc's resilience. In the midst of a very public and deeply emotional predicament, both he and Jean-Paul struggled to maintain their relationship. Through the tumult and strain Marc remained courageous, proud, vocal, visible, resistant, and resilient, as he raged hard against the institutional forces of a church determined to keep queer privatized.

On 16 January 2004, R. Douglas Elliott, the lawyer continuing to represent the Coalition in Support of Marc Hall, a key intervener in the impending lawsuit, emailed us, providing this update. Regarding the interlocutory injunction, he wrote,

No appeal was taken from that order. However, an injunction is an interim step in a lawsuit. The lawsuit, in which Marc challenges the right of the [Durham Catholic District] School Board to discriminate in these circumstances, is still proceeding. The Board is concerned that unless they have a full trial of that underlying issue [institutional church rights versus queer individual rights], future cases will be resolved by injunctions and always in favour of the student. (R. Douglas Elliott, personal communication, 16 January 2004)

In further email correspondence on 14 December 2004, Elliott relates,

The trial was supposed to proceed in October 2004, but lawyers from both parties agreed to seek an adjournment, which was granted by Justice

[Brian] Shaughnessy in Whitby on September 30, 2004. His Honour agreed to adjourn the trial (with no further adjournments) to October 11, 2005, on the basis that the Supreme Court of Canada's decision in the same-sex marriage reference will assist the trial court in Marc Hall's case. (R. Douglas Elliott, personal communication, 14 December 2004)

Sadly, Marc Hall dropped his court case on 28 June 2005. There were three key reasons. First, David L. Corbett, who had been representing Marc on a pro bono basis, could no longer act for Marc because he had been appointed as a judge of the Ontario Superior Court of Justice (R. Douglas Elliott, personal communication, 13 August 2005). Second, while lawyer Andrew Pinto assumed Marc's case file, continuing the case became cost prohibitive, with the Coalition in Support of Marc Hall unable to raise the money needed to continue. Third, Marc, now a 21-year-old university student, decided that he just wanted to continue with his post-secondary studies and get on with his life (CP, 2005). Subsequently, there was a hearing before the Regional Senior Justice. R. Douglas Elliott recounted the outcome:

> The parties agreed on the basic outline of an order that would be made by the Court dismissing the action. To its credit, the Board did not insist on its costs, as it was entitled to do. The Board requested as part of the dismissal that the original injunction be officially dissolved ... The Court refused that request, so the original order stands. However, doubtless any similar future injunction request will be made more difficult by virtue of this subsequent history. Since the dismissal itself was on consent, there can be no appeal by the Board. The case is over. (personal communication, 13 August 2005)

Unfortunately, as Elliott implied and Justice Shaughnessy related in granting Marc leave to drop the Superior Court case, the interlocutory injunction granted in 2002 does not carry the same weight as would a legal decision arrived at after a trial (CP, 2005). Still we can hope that one day another student will win a similar court case so school doors will be kept open for every queer student, including Pete, for whom Marc became a gay youth hero. Marc recounts Pete's affirmation:

> One day I was sitting in my room doing homework, and I got a phone call from this guy named Pete. He was 14 years old, and he called me to tell me that I was his hero. He wanted to know how to come out to his parents.

I told him about my parents. A few weeks later he called again to tell me that he had come out to his mother and that she was supportive of him. I told him I was really proud. I said that coming out is a really hard thing to do, but you really have to be true to yourself.

Looking back, the most important things that I've learned are to be true to your self and to be honest. The Catholic school board said that if I went to the prom with a girl, and one of my other girlfriends brought JP, we would each have a female date and we could still see each other at the prom. To me, that's a form of lying and not being who I am. Catholics teach you that you should be honest. If I went to the prom with a girl, then that would be dishonest. So just be true to yourself and stand up and be who you are. No one deserves to be oppressed.

In the Name of Democratic Principles: A Concluding Perspective

Catholic schooling is marked by perpetual power plays inextricably linked to cultural technologies like heterosexism and tradition and by codes of obedience demanding acculturation to Catholicized ways of being, acting, and expressing oneself in the world. It is bent on regulation, which Gore (1998) defines as "controlling by rule, subject to restrictions, invoking a rule, including sanction, reward, punishment" (p. 243). The principal's rejection of Marc Hall's request to attend his prom with his boyfriend provided an expression of this regulation and an example indicating that Catholic schooling has produced "its own 'regime of pedagogy,' a set of power-knowledge relations, of discourses and practices, which constrains the most radical of educational agendas" (Gore, 1998, p. 232). Inclusive education that incorporates queer (as a spectrum of sex, sexual, and gender identities and differences) and queerness (as queer desire, action, and expression) exemplifies such a radical agenda. Catholicity undermines this agenda as it works to privatize queer and pathologize queerness. The simple fact that homosexuality is such a contested topic in Catholic schooling (and indeed in many other conservative quarters in culture) demonstrates how sexual ideology has supplanted democratic principles in the public discourse around queer space and place in education and culture (McKay, 1998).

And yet democratic principles are what the institutional Catholic Church relies on to maintain its right to provide its Catholicized version of denominational education. MacDougall (2000) offers this perspective to explain why maintaining the right to denominational education is so important to institutional churches:

Institutions that once had a more direct role in determining the standards of society now attempt to retain such a role through influencing educational policy. Religions thus fight hard to control and retain public funding for their own schools because of the propagandistic role the schools play. Religions, all of them proselytizing to some degree, ... expend a great deal of energy to preserve or extend their hold on the school system. (p. 104)

From a Catholic perspective, clergy, school-district management, school principals, and school-board members use denominational education as a vehicle to impose and maintain Catholic tradition. Although this is their right under Section 93 of the *Canadian Constitution*, they might remember that this section was initially included to protect minority religious rights, including the right of Catholics to have their own schools in Ontario, at the time of Confederation (R. Douglas Elliott, personal communication, 23 November 2005). In the wake of that history, questions remain: How far can the Catholic Church go before Canadians say stop in the name of democratic principles that protect individual rights? Can an institutional church be allowed to claim its constitutional right to be absolute, enabling it to use the cloak of denominationalism to justify actions like interfering with Marc Hall's individual right to be free from discrimination based on his gay sexual orientation? Considering that Catholic schools are publicly funded, are not their actions "state actions subject to *Charter* scrutiny" (MacDougall, 2000, p. 104)? In the Marc Hall legal hearing, those with responsibility for Catholic education in Durham District claimed they were exempt from such scrutiny. In making this claim they refused to move outside the parameters of their moral ideology to consider ways that it might be oppressive. As well, they failed to answer a question central to ethical public practice in education: In what ways does the institutional Catholic Church disable inclusive education when it translates its "moral disapproval of homosexuality into a rationale and justification for infringing on the rights of homosexuals" (McKay, 1998, p. 162)?

Burdened as churches are by what they perceive as the weight of individual rights guaranteed by Section 15 (1) of the Charter, one might expect institutional churches to turn more to the courts to assist them in their efforts to control what happens in schools. No doubt they will rely on the continuing existence of a judicial culture that has long supported them. Historically, the courts in Canada have sustained a pervasive conservative Christian disposition that discriminates on the basis of sexual orientation (MacDougall, 2000). Indeed, focusing more on institutional church concerns with morality than state concerns with ethics and equality, "[t]he judiciary has internalized much of 'traditional' religious dogma in this area and has tended to give precedence to conservative religious interests over the interests of equality of sexual orientation, especially when young people are involved" (MacDougall, 2000, pp. 99–100). Thankfully, to the benefit of democracy, justice, and ethical educational and cultural practices, this judicial culture has been changing slowly, surely, and in crucial ways. For example, one of the three most important Canadian Supreme Court decisions, as ranked by Peter W. Hogg when he was Dean of Osgoode Hall Law School at York University, Toronto, is the decision in *Vriend v. Alberta* that confirmed equality rights for lesbian and gay citizens of Canada (Saunders, 2002, cited in Grace, 2005c). Delwin Vriend, an openly gay educator at King's College (now King's University College, a Christian college in Edmonton, Alberta), had been dismissed in 1991 on the pretext that his sexual orientation violated that institution's religious policy. The Supreme Court of Canada handed down its long-awaited decision in *Vriend v. Alberta* on 2 April 1998. The court's ruling was in keeping with equality provisions in Section 15 (1) of the federal Charter, in which sexual orientation, as a protected category of person, is considered analogous to other personal characteristics listed there. Moreover, the *Vriend* decision made it clear that Section 15 (1) of the Charter prohibits legislative omission of sexual orientation (Lahey, 1999).

Although the final outcome in the *Vriend* case is remarkable, there is still need to exercise caution in trusting the judicial system to do the right thing. Comments made by Justice McClung conflating homosexuality with sodomy in the earlier Court of Appeal decision in Alberta favouring King's College ought not to be forgotten. Replicating biblically incited conservative religious objections to homosexuality, his reasoning exemplifies the tradition in the courts of "bow[ing] to 'religious and familial forbiddence'" (MacDougall, 2000, p. 109). Justice McClung's ruling stands as "an example of the jurisprudence that supports or condones the cleansing of youth by keeping homosexuality and homosexuals away" (MacDougall, 2000, p. 111). It cautions us to be wary of justices, bishops, or others with authority who might try to elude the Charter. Fortunately, the Supreme Court of Canada is now exerting the kind of ethical leadership focused on the inclusion and integrity of citizens that sends a clear message to all in positions of power. This transformative leadership was demonstrated in its 9 December 2004 *Reference re Same-Sex Marriage*. In this reference, the

Supreme Court of Canada (2004) adhered to a most fundamental principle of Canadian constitutional interpretation that maintains, "[O]ur Constitution is a living tree which, by way of progressive interpretation, accommodates and addresses the realities of modern life" (p. 710). The court held that proposed federal legislation extending the right to civil marriage to same-sex couples was consistent with, and indeed flowed from, the guarantees of equality rights as protected by Section 15 (1) of the Charter. It also held that the guarantee of freedom of religion under Section 2 (a) of the Charter was broad enough to protect religious officials from being compelled by the State to perform same-sex marriage contrary to their religious beliefs. What might have been most pertinent to the resolution of issues in the Marc Hall case is this section from the Supreme Court reference:

> [T]he mere recognition of the equality rights of one group cannot, in itself, constitute a violation of the s. 15 (1) rights of another. The promotion of *Charter* rights and values enriches our society as a whole and the furtherance of those rights cannot undermine the very principles the *Charter* was meant to foster ... Although the right to same-sex marriage conferred by the proposed legislation may potentially conflict with the right to freedom of religion if ... [Bill C-38] becomes law [which it did on 20 July 2005], conflicts of rights do not imply conflict with the *Charter*; rather, the resolution of such conflicts generally occurs within the ambit of the *Charter* itself by way of internal balancing and delineation. It has not been demonstrated in this reference that impermissible conflicts – conflicts incapable of resolution under s. 2 (a) – will arise. (Supreme Court of Canada, 2004, pp. 719, 700–1)

With regard to this last point, the Supreme Court of Canada (2004) maintains that the "collision between rights must be approached on the contextual facts of actual conflicts" (pp. 720–1) and that the potential for such a collision does not necessarily imply unconstitutionality. Had the trial in the Marc Hall case proceeded, the onus would have been on the lawyer representing the Catholic school board to demonstrate the factual existence of impermissible conflicts resulting from a high school student taking a same-sex partner to a prom. Such a finding would then imply that the right to religious freedom enshrined in Section 2 (a) of the Charter is not expansive enough to accommodate Marc Hall's individual rights as a gay citizen. From this perspective, the school board's lawyer would then probably have argued that a true conflict of rights exists. However, in the resolution of any conflict pitting institutional rights against individual rights, the Supreme Court must proceed "on the basis that the *Charter* does not create a hierarchy of rights" (Supreme Court of Canada [SCC], 2004, p. 720). If the conflict between rights cannot be reconciled, then, as the *Reference re Same-Sex Marriage* notes, the court would follow the precedent set in *Ross v. New Brunswick School District No. 15* in 1996 and "find a limit on religious freedom and go onto balance the interests at stake under s. 1 of the *Charter*" (p. 720). However, if the lawyer representing Marc Hall had identified unjustifiable limits that religious freedom placed on the gay youth's individual rights (DJC, 2003), then the argument could be made that the Catholic school board had violated Section 15 (1) of the Charter. Because the Charter exists and has the power to protect and expand human rights (DJC, 2003), such untenable limits would be deemed unacceptable, suggesting that, in the realm of individual rights, religion and schooling are separable and Catholic tradition cannot prevail over the Charter. In keeping with Section 1 of the Charter, however, any limits placed on religious freedom would have to be justified in Canada's democratic society in order to be acceptable (DJC, 2003).

Canada has come a long way since 22 December 1967, when then Justice Minister Pierre Elliott Trudeau proposed amendments to the *Criminal Code* that resulted in the decriminalization of homosexuality. As Trudeau spearheaded this law reform and moved Canada away from state control of individual freedoms like those embodied and embedded in sexuality, he made the poignant and memorable assertion, "The State has no business in the bedrooms of the nation" (Goldie, 2001a, p. 18). The amendments passed in 1969. During the Marc Hall legal hearing, Justice MacKinnon (2002) reminded us, "The separation of church and state is a fundamental principle of our Canadian democracy and our constitutional law" (para. 31). If we uphold this democratic principle in relation to schooling, then schools should carry out their public duties in accordance with strictly secular and non-sectarian democratic principles representative of the inclusive cultural democracy that the Canadian Charter of Rights and Freedoms protects. In this light, perhaps it is time to add a corollary to Pierre Elliott Trudeau's poignant statement and say, "Institutional churches have no business in the classrooms of the nation." Although Trudeau's statement was intended to protect the private sexual lives of individuals from public institutional (state) scrutiny, this corollary is different. It is intended to protect the sexual lives of individuals in public spaces like schools from the kind of Catholic institutionalized religious scrutiny embodied in the privatization of queer. Ultimately, the sexual lives of Canadians need to be protected in public *and* private spaces so queer and other persons can be, become, and belong fully and holistically as the Charter espouses. With the Marc Hall case dropped, this goal remains to be achieved.

Acknowledgments

We would like to thank Marc Hall and R. Douglas Elliott for being incredibly accessible and informative as we conducted research for this case. R. Douglas Elliott is a prominent constitutional lawyer and advocate for sexual minority rights and freedoms. His high-profile Supreme Court of Canada cases include *Vriend v. Alberta*, which, most significantly, granted equality rights to sexual minority Canadians, and *Trinity Western University v. British Columbia College of Teachers*, which focused on the broader right of Trinity Western to hold discriminatory beliefs versus the more limited right to act upon those beliefs.

InterText 8
Sam: *It's Like Piranhas, Man*

Sam had supportive teachers in grade 5 and that helped him to be courageous to deal with his experiences of homophobia and confront his classmates. It may have been the moment when the seeds for his resilience were sown. He had been pushed to the limit and he decided to do something about it. He found the voice that eludes so many queer kids. Usual and understandable responses include hiding away, being silent, or skipping school. In that pivotal moment, Sam stood up for himself and, as young as he was, he started to steel life. He continues to do so and deals with situations himself, which is a real asset. For Sam, family has been a gift, offering him unconditional acceptance when he came out in junior high school. While Sam puts true effort into mediating everyday life, being strong, and making good choices, he recognizes that he is who he is because of his family.

I actually came out when I was in grade 7. It was all thanks to the loving support of a really amazing family. And I guess, to my own credit to a degree, because of the gifts I have been given when I was born into the world. I can remember being bullied starting in kindergarten. I was teased and pushed around a lot. Even kids in grade 7 or grade 8 – kids who should know better – pushed around the kids in kindergarten and called us fags. That was really traumatizing for me. I remember going home and saying to my mom, "Am I gay?" With everyone calling me gay, I had to ask the question. She just looked at me and said, "You know, I really don't know, kiddo. You're the only person that's going to know that." It didn't exactly please me that I didn't have my answer, but it was actually the healthiest thing she could have said to me. The teasing didn't stop in my primary and elementary schools. It was brutal. It made me extremely angry. I felt upset, confused, and unaccepted. I had all these girlfriends who supported me, which was great, but I obviously had some gay tendencies and people picked up on them. It just got worse and worse. I remember one day in music class when one of the kids had been riling me up. He kept going and going. Finally, I just got so angry that I took one of the xylophone mallets and whipped it at his head. For a fairly calm, kind, and gentle person like me to be pushed to that extreme – and at such a young age as well – it was completing unnerving. Even though it was just a xylophone mallet, it's what it represented. Homophobia was having a terrible effect on me.

Fortunately, the next school year I was lucky. I was placed into a grade 5/6 split with really wonderful teachers that tried their best. The kids were still cruel, but the teachers supported me. It came to the point though where I went up and talked to one of the teachers and said, "It's like piranhas, man. I cannot be fed to them like this, you know. What are we going to do?" So after school one day, the teacher kept the entire class, sat me in front of them, and let me speak. I just basically looked at them all and said, "I don't understand what it is about me that you all find so offensive. I don't understand what it is that makes you treat me this way. It has a huge effect on me. I don't know if you guys realize it, but I just want to be your friend. Just have some compassion." I probably said this in less astute words at the time – you know, you're in grade 5. But I did get up in front of the class and just spoke to them like human beings. I held them accountable. It was better after that to the point where I didn't get hassled.

For me, the first stage of the coming-out process was denial. I remember just saying to myself, "I'm straight. I'm straight. I'm straight." I got myself a girlfriend and I kissed her and everything. Even at my young age, it just lacked something. Of course, if you're having a relationship at that age, it's going to be lacking regardless. Anyway, I dated a girl, we kind of broke up, and I started coming to terms with my feelings. Instead of always saying, "I'm straight," I started to say, "Well, I'm bi." It was easier to say. It seemed like a kind of middle ground. Then finally one day I said, "Okay, fuck it. I'm gay." You know, you reach that point, so I ended up coming out. The first person I came out to was a girl in my seventh-grade class. I just figured I needed to tell someone that I was gay. I remember she looked real spooked. It was surprising because she was pretty liberal. She didn't have a negative reaction, but you could tell she was uncomfortable. She said, "Why would you tell me that?" I remember being a little disheartened. I think I ended up coming out to all my grade 7 class after that because it would only get around anyway. I think I told my class before I told my parents. There wasn't a lot of support. As a gay youth, I don't really know how to describe the loneliness or the isolation that you feel.

In order to find some resources, I turned to the Internet. I read gay fiction online to explore who I was and to find out what's what. I remember there was this story that I loved, so I emailed the author. I wrote to him and I gave him my feedback. I said, "I love your story. It's beautiful." What I hadn't realized at the time is that when you click a direct link it goes from Outlook Express. The author actually emailed me back with links to other stories that he recommended. My dad received the email, which he sat on for about a week. He wanted to talk to me, but he didn't want to scare me. He was just thinking about the best way to go about it, which I love him for. Finally, he brought me right to the computer and said, "Read this." I read it and my life has never fallen so quickly. It was absolute shock – your whole body tingling, going cold. It was extreme displacement like you've been ripped out of your body and you're just disconnected. I looked at dad and said, "I was just curious." He said, "You know, it's okay." At this point you're not even thinking rationally, the scare is so big. He went on, "It's okay if you are, if you need to talk about it." I said, "No, I'm *just* curious. I'm just curious." It's all I could say, so he just said, "Okay. If you ever need to talk, you know, it's alright." He let me go and then, five minutes after the shock wore off, I went back and said, "Actually, I'm gay." So that's how I ended up coming out to my first family member. What is funny is that after I told my dad, I couldn't have boys sleep over, but I could have girls stay at my house. Really my parents went about it the way you would raise anyone else. My parents looked at their kid and raised me the way they raised their other kids. They just tried to give me that extra support as far as the gay part of the situation went. My parents are my rock and my safety net. They are my resources. If I didn't have them around to remind me who I really am and to believe in me when I can't, then I would have lost faith a long time ago and given up.

School was another matter. The system is flawed and it's a struggle for sexual minorities. Having said that, I always did what I could to improve my situation as I went through school. In grade 9, I wanted to start a GSA. Maybe I got some confidence and experience to do this because I read all of those stories online, avidly and ferociously. I knew what GSAs were. There were stories about them, even if they were fiction. About the first week of school, I approached the vice principal and I said, "How do you go about starting a club?" He looked at me and said, "Well, you have to write a letter to the faculty." Then he said, "Well, what kind of club is it?" And I said, "It's a GSA that I want to start." He looked at me and asked, "What's a GSA?" I said, "It's a gay-straight alliance." He replied, "Oh." He was polite, but you could tell it shocked him a bit. He asked a few more questions and told me to write a letter to the faculty. I put quite a lot of effort into writing that letter. I brought it back to him and asked him to present it at the next staff meeting. He said, "Sure." I was really lucky. My school had an artsy feel. Teachers were doers and everyone had a busy schedule. Still at the meeting when the vice principal asked for a volunteer to be teacher supervisor for the GSA, three or four teachers put up their hands. Afterwards when I approached one of the teachers and asked her myself, she said, "Yes."

We went through the usual stuff getting the GSA off the ground. Some students would rip down the posters we put up. Once a kid filled up condoms with ranch dressing and threw them at us, calling us fags. It was a bit rough starting up but, to be quite honest, the GSA was generally well received. As for the teachers, before we had a GSA I think they weren't aware that homophobia was a big issue. Once we had a GSA, the teachers listened to us and stepped up to the plate. It wasn't perfect – and maybe it will never be – but we did see an improvement, which was heartening. I always felt safe regardless of being gay. There were points, of course, when I felt scared, but I could handle it because I'm well adjusted and confident. For example, instead of going to a teacher, I addressed the issue with the kid who threw the condoms, although not in the best way. He was a kid with a bad rep. When he interacted with people on a daily basis, he was very belligerent, ignorant, rude, and unkind. After he threw the condoms, I just took him by the shoulders and put him against a locker. I looked at him and said, "What do you think you're doing?" He looked at me, and he pushed right back. It did come to a physical altercation. At the time I was proud of myself for it, but not so much now. Someone that is having so much trouble has a larger issue. Still, regardless of how I did it, I held him accountable.

They say that the road to hell is paved with good intentions. I didn't understand that when I was young, but I understand it better now. Just because you have the ability or feel the need to protect someone or to do something for him or her, that doesn't mean you are necessarily helping that person. I think that when teachers step in too quickly, they complicate the issue. There is an interaction going on between two youth and they completely shut it down, sometimes reprimanding one or both students. Teachers should focus more on providing students with the tools they need so they can do it for themselves and survive. While there are times when teachers need to step in and give students a bit of help, as a general rule, we need them to give young people the tools. I respected my teachers more when they said, "What do you want to do?" That helped me to be accountable for my words and actions. People who don't learn to be accountable can get really unhealthy.

Beyond my teachers and family, the Avenue Community Centre in Saskatoon has been a real asset for me. My mom took me there when I was 13. It was called the Gay and Lesbian Health Centre back then. Mom had found this pamphlet and showed it to me. She asked me, "What do you think?" It was a pamphlet for Out and Proud Youth, which was a youth group for older kids, probably 17 through to their early 20s. My mom is a warrior, and she'll do what's right regardless. So she took me down there and told them, "My son needs this, but I can't leave him here unless he's safe." It was all worked out with respect all around. I was left behind on a Friday night to hang out with the big kids and they all treated me well. It was totally what I needed. For me, the biggest part about attending the youth group was realizing that I was not alone. It's all so new, so overwhelming in the beginning. And then you find this camaraderie – people who get you from your point of view. You have a lot of common interests and there's that spark.

At this point in my life, I feel like I've come through a slow evolution. Being involved in the gay community and being gay myself has really opened my eyes to this. I know sexual minority rights are part of a larger issue. What I'd say to any young person is that you can fight separately – gays can fight for gays, blacks can fight for blacks, and so on – but really, when it comes down to it, humans have to fight for humans. We need more coalitions because hate is hate. In life what it comes down to is that the most important thing is love. That's what my dad has always taught me: love conquers all.

6 Gay and Bisexual Male Youth as Educator-Activists and Cultural Workers: The Queer Critical Praxis of Three Canadian High School Students[*]

WITH KRISTOPHER WELLS

Education is a thoroughly political process that is essential to cultural action for social transformation (Allman, 1999). These days as SGM (sexual and gender minority) or LGBTQ (lesbian, gay, bisexual, trans-identified, and queer) students act to free themselves from the silence, exclusion, and symbolic and physical violence that heterosexism, genderism, and homo/bi/transphobia provoke in schools, they seek transformation of historically disenfranchising cultural practices and social relations. To achieve this goal, they are learning and teaching others how to interrogate language and omissions in educational policy and practice that amount to proscription of ways of knowing, being, acting, and relating as SGM persons. They are also working to find ways to challenge and change the heteronormative status quo in schools and transgress the victimization wrought by heterosexism, genderism, and homo/bi/transphobia so that SGM students can enjoy basic protections (like freedom from discrimination on the grounds of sexual orientation or gender identity) and privileges (like having a gay-straight alliance club in a school for SGM and allied students or attending a prom with a same-sex partner) (Grace & Wells, 2005; Wells, 2006). Given that heterosexism, genderism, and homo/bi/transphobia are so culturally ingrained that they are residual and lingering in public spaces, this political and pedagogical work focused on greater accommodation and respect is taxing. It continues even when some struggles for SGM inclusion are won and schools become more just and equitable places. This ongoing and extensive work involves public dialogue,

* Reproduced with permission from the *International Journal of Inclusive Education* (13(1), 2009, pp. 23–44), http://www.tandfonline.com/doi/full/10.1080/13603110701254121.

educational activism, and cultural work focused on problematizing queer-exclusive educational policies and practices, enhancing communication in the intersection of the moral and the political, and monitoring the state of the struggle, the extent of transformation, and the need for further social and cultural action (Allman, 1999; Grace & Benson, 2000; Grace et al., 2004). This production is an engagement in queer critical praxis (Grace & Hill, 2004). Taking a position applicable to SGM youth, a diverse population, Cronin and McNinch (2004) consider it an effort to make a better world, which they describe as "a more caring and understanding world in which Canadian gay and lesbian youth can grow up with the same expectations of all young people, not feeling ashamed of who they find themselves to be, and being fully respected as human beings" (p. ix). Anonymous Queers (1999) add to such an ontological perspective:

> Being queer ... is about the freedom to be public, to just be who we are. It means everyday fighting oppression, homophobia, racism, misogyny, the bigotry of religious hypocrites and our own self-hatred ... It's about being on the margins, defining ourselves; it's about gender-fuck and secrets, what's beneath the belt and deep inside the heart. (p. 588)

While Freire (1998) calls on every teacher to be a cultural worker for social change, few teachers and other educational players have taken up this task on behalf of SGM students (Grace & Wells, 2004; Kissen, 2002; Lipkin, 2004). In the face of this indifference and inaction, some students with courage and conviction take up the task themselves (Grace & Wells, 2005, 2007c). Not only do they become cultural workers who struggle to change unjust and unethical policies and practices in schools, but they also become educator-activists who teach peers, teachers, school administrators, and others with interests and degrees of power in education about a queer critical praxis that brings ethics and the political ideals of modernity – democracy, freedom, and social justice – to bear on educational policy and practice in the name of equity and justice for all SGM students, a multivariate population, across diverse identities and subjectivities. In this chapter, we consider how three of these students – Ryan from Edmonton, Alberta; Jeremy from Sault Ste. Marie, Ontario; and Bruce from Port Coquitlam, British Columbia – engaged in this educator activism and cultural work. As their biographical ethnographies indicate, each young man struggled in his high school to profile the desires and needs of all students across sex, sexual, and gender differences. Their queer critical praxis involved communicating and strategizing about actions to advance SGM inclusion. All are now high school graduates, and all signed a consent form stating they wished to use their own names in their accounts in this research. We chose to focus specifically on these three young men mindful that, historically, male homosexuality has been an incessant object of ridicule, with homophobes often targeting gay males out of their ignorance and fear of difference (Fone, 2000). Indeed the rash of gay male youth suicides in Canada and the United States over the last few years indicates that we have not moved beyond this history and still deal with its devastating consequences (Grace, 2013b).

In our research, in addition to "SGM," we use both "gay" and "queer" as descriptors. We offer the following contextual and theoretical explanation for their concomitant use. First, in the context of our study, the research participants used both "gay" and "queer" as descriptors in their stories of self and experience. In fact, "gay" was quite prevalent as a term in our conversations. Goldie (2001b) relates, "gay" remains a more specific term to refer to male homosexuality. On a similar note, as Fone (2000) remarks in his history of homophobia, for most homosexuals "the primacy of 'gay' has yet to be seriously challenged" (p. 411). Second, from a theoretical perspective, we find utility in using both terms, although we are cognizant that they have limitations. "Gay" is a limited descriptor because it does not readily speak to the array of differences occupying sex, sexual, and gender spectra. Nevertheless, "gay" has a historical link to engagement and action that rejects victimization and involves risk taking. Gay liberation emerged in the late 1960s as a lived expression of a cultural politics of optimism disposed to the belief that a better world was possible for those on the periphery of heteronormativity (Marwick, 1998). This historical movement can be positioned as an example of a grass-roots critical social engagement. It aligns neatly with the intention of critical praxis, which is to struggle against the forces of social conservatism that, in this case, have limited hope and possibility for non-heterosexual persons and citizens. In his discussion of the history of gay liberation in Canada, Warner (2002) describes the tenor of gay liberation's critical praxis: "Resistance and astonishing perseverance, textured with the exuberance of outlaw sexuality" mark this struggle (p. 7).

Queer has contemporary currency in academe, where its use is considered de rigueur. In this political culture, queer is about redeploying, twisting, and challenging the stable, intact, and unitary categories that have historically marked essentialized notions of lesbian and gay

(Butler, 1993). Here the value of queer lies in its inclusive and incorporating nature that knows no bounds. From this perspective, queer is emerging and expansive, transgressive and transformative, resistant and resilient. Queer says it matters while still asking, "What does it matter?" In the everyday world outside academe and queer theorizing, queer has some currency as a street term. Queers, usually younger and ready to challenge heteronormativity, have reclaimed queer as a way to name and know the spectrum of sexual and gender differences as part of a politics of resistance. Nevertheless, "queer" is a much less pervasive term in popular culture and everyday life, where "gay" remains the more common descriptor. Queer is limited in a social change context because, in its focus on the fluidity of sex, sexual, and gender differences, it refuses even some partial closure of identities, which is necessary to lay a basis for social action that would engender cultural transformation. Kirsch (2000) argues in a US context,

> Beyond small theatrical [grass-roots] endeavors such as Queer Nation and Sex Panic, the arguments around Queer theory are firmly rooted within the halls of theoretical treatises where political movements and social action have traditionally taken a back seat to the explication of theory. (pp. 33)

To move the queer project forward as a social and political engagement, we need to acknowledge sex, sexual, and gender identity markers and the voices of SGM persons, at least in particular times and spaces. Still, we have to be careful in any process of partial closure in marking identity because we do not want to "doom ourselves to repeating the terms of our identities, to keeping 'the space of the possible' small and contained" (Talburt, 2000, p. 10). This creates a quandary for queer in academe and beyond. As Honeychurch (1996) notes, an uneasy cultural politics has shrouded the use of the term in contemporary academic research as history meets the present. Yet, he points out, "queer," a harsh term that recalls a historically harsh existence, is finding quarter:

> While it is perhaps even more difficult to disentangle the word queer from its pejorative history and the denunciative mythologies that surround it, the term is being reclaimed by those long despoiled by its derogating accusations – individuals and communities now more vigorous in an insistence on ending both narrow categorizations and repressions based on sexual diversity. (p. 342)

It would appear though that queer was intended to be in some dynamic equilibrium with social activism and cultural work for change. In her groundbreaking essay on the genesis of queer theory, de Lauretis (1991) asked a question that queer theorists have not grappled with sufficiently: "[How] can our queerness act as an agency of social change, and our theory construct another discursive horizon, another way of living the racial and the sexual?" (pp. x–xi). In answering this question today, one could build on de Lauretis's (1991) understanding that queer sexuality "acts as an agency of social process whose mode of functioning is both interactive and yet resistant, claiming at once equality and difference, demanding political representation while insisting on its material and historical specificity" (p. iii). Queer may be messy, but, as de Lauretis emphasizes, it has intention bent on action.

Studying How Sexual and Gender Minority Students Are Doing It for Themselves

To construct the biographical ethnographies of the three research participants in this study, we began by exploring materials including correspondence, pamphlets, newsletters, and website materials that they had prepared for use in their educational activism and cultural work. This provided us with some insights into their involvement in queer critical praxis. We then conducted two-hour, open-ended interviews with Ryan, Jeremy, and Bruce, which enabled us to examine the contextual, relational, and dispositional complexities of three facets of their work for cultural change and social transformation: the impetus that drove their praxis, their ensuing educational activism and cultural work, and the supports that enabled them to keep going. To help us gauge impetus at the beginning of the interview, each research participant engaged questions that explored his experiences of being ridiculed and targeted in high school, and how he dealt with the omissions, exclusions, and violence that variously mark and mar experiences of being, acting, and relating queer. Ryan, Jeremy, and Bruce also grappled with questions that dealt with the throes of coming out – that is, naming one's sex, sexual, or gender differences – and coming to terms in their family, peer, and community contexts. Hearing their stories about the hurts and troubles they experienced, we then wanted to know what enabled them to steel life and choose visibility and voice, which led to a discussion of the supports in each young man's life. We asked them questions about what bolstered them and what made them resilient as they engaged in queer critical praxis on an ongoing basis. In the last part of the interview we asked them questions about their work as educator-activists and cultural workers. This enabled us to learn about how they communicated and strategically acted to achieve their goals focused on SGM inclusion.

The open-ended interviews were recorded and transcribed. The data analysis involved a dialogical process of constructing meaning that included both the researchers and the research participants in the selection and interpretation of data (Lather & Smithies, 1997). Efforts were made throughout this process to keep the personal/experiential in dynamic relationship with the cultural. Research participants reviewed the transcribed manuscripts, which involved them in an iterative process in which their edits, interpretations, and feedback were taken into account in a writing and editing process. The transcripts were revised as dialogic texts in which the researchers and the research participants build an accurate account through open conversation (Fine, Weis, Centrie, & Roberts, 2000). During this process we held follow-up discussions with each research participant. In sum, this interactive research process helped us to build a deeper understanding of the research participants' queer critical praxis and the place and meaning that impetus, supports, and educational activism and cultural work have in it. It enabled us to write the research participants' vignettes as engaging, authentic, evocative, and reflexive co-constructed narratives in which experience and reflection were in dynamic equilibrium (Ellis & Berger, 2003; Tedlock, 2000). These constructed vignettes constituted a kind of found narrative in which the integrity of the research participants' words and positions was maintained. Collectively, the vignettes provide a textured account of how Ryan, Jeremy, and Bruce constructed their versions of multifaceted queer critical praxis. This account follows.

Impetus: The Plight of Heterosexism and Homo/Bi/Transphobia

Historically, Canadian schools have been hostile and unsafe spaces for those othered by sex, sexual, and gender differences (Grace & Wells, 2005; Schneider, 1997). However, since the early 1990s there have been incremental moves to deal with the terrible reality that schools are danger zones for SGM students. Indeed many teachers' federations and associations as well as some school boards in Canada have had success in introducing anti-homophobia programs, developing and implementing policies and curricula dealing with same-sex orientation, and providing some attention to developing and delivering workshops for teachers on sexual and gender diversity (CTF, 2005; CTF & ETFO, 2002; Grace & Wells, 2004). This success is noteworthy in mainstream education, where socially conservative religious and secular groups fight, fortunately unsuccessfully in many cases, to keep schools heterosexually pure (Grace & Wells, 2005). Their anti-queer agenda, grounded in a politics of ignorance and alarm that intensifies public anxieties, helps ensure an unfortunate cultural reality in education: "[H]omophobic remarks and harassment, ostracism, vulnerability, and fear about coming out remain features of Canada's schools" (Warner, 2002, p. 340). This climate of negation exists despite the fact that in 1995, in *Egan v. Canada*, the Supreme Court of Canada explicitly and unanimously agreed that sexual orientation is a protected category analogous to other personal characteristics listed in Section 15 (1) of the Canadian Charter of Rights and Freedoms (MacDougall, 2000). It also exists despite the fact that, in the 1998 decision in *Vriend v. Alberta,* the Supreme Court of Canada confirmed equality rights for lesbian and gay Canadians (MacDougall, 2000). These judgments reflect the view of the Supreme Court of Canada that "our Constitution is a living tree which, by way of progressive interpretation, accommodates and addresses the realities of modern life" (SCC, 2004, p. 700).

With school culture and the larger Canadian culture lagging behind legislation in this inclusive approach, it is no wonder that more and more students feel the need to realize these legal protections in their everyday schooling and lives through their own efforts to fight heterosexism, genderism, and homo/bi/transphobia in classrooms, corridors, and communities. In tandem with teachers' federations and associations and school boards, students have been engaged in educational and cultural work such as organizing gay-straight student alliance clubs in schools (Wells, 2006). Indeed what we are now witnessing is a phenomenon that places the education system at the forefront of gay liberation (Warner, 2002). Today's schools are a primary battleground where SGM minorities "must be the agents of their own liberation" (Fone, 2000, p. 371) as they work to contest a melding of conservative morals and politics that dismisses or defiles homo/bi/transsexuality as a composite assault on social purity and "an offense against the [traditional] family and social expectations about [sexuality and] gender" (Fone, 2000, p. 385). With sexual and gender differences thus cast as constituting a social evil, homo/bi/transphobia "remains, perhaps the last acceptable prejudice" (Fone, 2000, p. 3). The Surrey

Teachers' Association (STA) of the British Columbia Teachers' Federation locates homo/bi/transphobia in an educational context: "Schools remain one of the last bastions of tolerated hatred toward glbt [gay, lesbian, bisexual, and trans-identified] people" (STA, 2000, p. 2).

To be sure, schooling has historically been about preserving the status quo and tradition, which, in regard to sex, sexuality, and gender, means assuming the exclusive morality of heterosexuality and the limited ontology of two biological sexes as cultural imperatives. However, such assumptions place contemporary schooling at odds with disciplines like law and psychology that hold broader and more inclusive views regarding the parameters and protection of sex, sexual, and gender differences. In their study of the secondary schooling experiences of lesbian, gay, and bisexual youth, Ellis and High (2004) conclude that the pedagogies and social and cultural practices of schooling need to get in sync with cultural changes around sexuality that have emerged in recent decades. Specifically, they call for a positive positioning of sexuality as a socially performed facet of identity and culture. Gender should also be viewed this way (Ehrensaft, 2011). Advancing these viewpoints constitutes a vital part of being there for SGM students and meeting their needs. It helps in the struggle against heterosexism, genderism, and homo/bi/transphobia, dehumanizing forces that damage SGM students when they are left unexposed and unchecked in schools and communities. The vignettes in which Jeremy, Bruce, and Ryan recount their encounters with homophobia attest to this:

Jeremy: At school I was attacked a couple of times in the hallway. Once I was walking down the hallway and a guy jumped on me and pretended to fuck me. It was a big joke for him and his friends. After throwing him off me, I collapsed. I couldn't believe that I had been violated in such a sexual way in front of the school. Worst of all were the days after when I had to deal with my parents. I skipped classes for two days and people were wondering what was going on. I also had to deal with the students going around and saying that I was going to take him to court. I had to deal with total strangers coming up to me and saying, "What are you doing to my friend? How come you are taking him to court?" These people didn't even recognize that I was the victim. I was not the one at fault.

Bruce: Not only was there verbal abuse in my school, but there was also physical violence. The violence was there before and after I came out. It just seemed like a constant. One time this group of boys surrounded me outside my school and they grabbed me by my hair and smacked my head on the kerb. Another time in grade 11 I was in a park after school with a gay friend and another group of guys came along. My friend and I weren't dating or anything. We were just sitting in the park talking and they came up to us and beat us up. These are the things you expect to happen to you when you're gay. Of course, I was always afraid of being physically hurt, but I guess I just decided that I wouldn't let it bother me emotionally. I prepared myself. I decided I wouldn't let it affect me in terms of making me feel bad about myself or who I was. I have to be myself.

Ryan: My boyfriend and I like to hold hands, but at the same time we are always looking over our shoulders, especially because my boyfriend is deaf and he won't hear them coming. People do and say things. It's not pleasant. For example, last weekend we had just come off a bus and we were holding hands. Some guy came up to us and said, "What the fuck are you two guys doing?" I just stood there. It was the first time that anyone had ever said anything like that to me. I was more shocked than angry.

As these narratives indicate, Jeremy, Bruce, and Ryan have variously experienced discrimination, harassment, and violence, both symbolic (such as verbal abuse) and actual (such as physical assault). These manifestations of homophobia have been profound in their social lives and cultural learning. They have indelibly marked their schools and communities as uncivil and unsafe spaces for them. The dangers and damage that come with local visibility in schools and communities are symptomatic of widespread heterosexism, genderism, and homo/bi/transphobia in Canadian culture and society (Janoff, 2005). D'Augelli (1998) relates that SGM youth are also frequently victimized as part of a backlash against the larger visibility of SGM persons in the media and other sociocultural venues. As an example of this extensive hostility, in 2003 the Hate and Bias Crimes Initiative of the Edmonton Police Service reported a surge in hate-related activities against the SGM community. Overall for that year, the Edmonton Police Service recounted that the SGM community had reported the highest number of hate-related crimes and incidents of all the city's minority groups (Camp & Huggins, 2004).

The dire nature of such reporting prompted a 2007 study, commissioned by the Alberta Hate and Bias Crime and Incidents Committee. The study indicated, "GLBT communities were significantly more likely to experience physical and verbal hate against them ... They were also more likely to use telephone help lines for assistance in reporting hate and bias crimes. The bisexual segment of this community is significantly less likely to report crimes due to fear and reprisal" (Stewart, 2007, p. 14). In terms of overall reporting by all target populations, Stewart (2007) provided this synopsis of findings from the Alberta Hate Crime Survey:

[A]lmost 70% of the respondents indicated that members of their community would rarely (0–25%) report hate/bias crimes. Most respondents (83%) said that the biggest barrier to reporting hate/bias crimes is the fear that reporting will not result in help or action and that victimization will not be taken seriously. Even greater numbers believe that police would fail to classify it as a hate crime at the scene, offenders would not be charged, the Crown would fail to prosecute under hate crime legislation, and the judge would not likely convict. (p. 20)

Importantly, the report emphasized that schools and police services needed to do more to combat bullying as a primary expression of hate and bias since 50 per cent of hate crimes in Alberta occur in elementary and secondary schools, with teachers sadly among those targeting young victims (aged 13–20 years old). The report reiterated that the greater visibility of sexual and gender minorities in Canadian culture and society is a likely trigger here, as demonstrated by the increase in hate crimes based on sexual orientation during the period leading up to the passage of Bill C-38, An Act Respecting Certain Aspects of Legal Capacity for Marriage for Civil Purposes, which legalized same-sex marriage in Canada in 2005.

In 2008 in Edmonton, 14.8 per cent of hate crimes were motivated by sexual orientation (Statistics Canada, 2010). The Alberta Hate Crime Report 2008 highlighted, "In light of the extremely low reporting rate, and the disproportionately high rate of violence in hate crimes directed at gays and lesbians, a principal focus of any hate crime strategy should be upon the gay/lesbian communities" (Pruegger, 2009, p. 45). In part, this is recognition of the reality that hate crimes motivated by sexual orientation tend to target persons, not property, with the majority being violent crimes involving assault. However, in stating the obvious from an SGM perspective, any hate crime strategy has to focus on the larger, multivariate population of sexual and gender minorities, including trans-spectrum and other vulnerable subgroups, whose constituents are also victims of hate crimes. It also has to focus on youth in general since, as the Alberta Hate Crime Report 2008 indicates for 2006, youth aged 12 to 17 in cities like Edmonton and Calgary composed the majority of those accused as perpetrators of the 892 police-reported hate crimes in Canada (Pruegger, 2009). Of course, any hate crime strategy is hampered by the reality that there is no common national definition of a hate crime. To work towards a definition, the Alberta Hate Crime Report 2008 lists key characteristics of a hate crime: (1) it is motivated by hate, bias, or prejudice because of race/ethnicity, religion, sexual orientation, gender identity, or other individual characteristics; and (2) it is criminal behaviour "motivated by hate, not vulnerability," as the Canadian Association of Chiefs of Police defines it (Pruegger, 2009, p. 8).

The upward trend in police-reported hate crimes in Canada continues. As Statistics Canada (2010) relates, Canadian police services reported 1,036 hate crimes in 2008, which represented a 35 per cent increase from 2007. In 2013, the Edmonton Police Service reviewed 111 files and classified 18 as hate incidents and 50 as hate crimes (Edmonton Police Service contact, personal correspondence, 13 March 2014). Statistics Canada (2010) defines police-reported hate crimes as "criminal incidents that, upon investigation by police, are determined to have been motivated by hate towards an identifiable group" (p. 4). During 2008, hate crimes motivated by sexual orientation more than doubled to 16 per cent of police-reported hate crimes. They were the most violent criminal incidents, as compared to other targeted and vulnerable populations. Of hate crimes against sexual and gender minorities, 75 per cent were violent in nature and 85 per cent of the victims were male. As dire in nature as these statistics are, there is a caveat: the statics represent only police-reported hate crimes, with victim-reported hate crimes remaining underreported, as also noted by Stewart (2007). In addition, the numbers of police-reported hate crimes are influenced by whether police services have hate crime units or specialized initiatives to address hate crimes. For example, Toronto Police Service (n.d.) has a public awareness campaign called Report Homophobic Violence, Period (RHVP), which is intended to help counter negative perceptions that SGM youth have about police officer responses when they report a homophobic or transphobic hate crime. As the police service notes, many SGM youth tend to steer clear of police officers because they fear being ignored or re-victimized by them.

Supports: A Focus on the Value of Family in Coming Out and Coming to Terms

For SGM youth, coming out and becoming resilient appear to be matters of both degree and approach that are tied to family relations, class, geography, religion, and a complexity of other contexts. For example,

Ryan's coming out as a white urban middle-class youth who had a younger gay brother appeared to involve less strife than Jeremy's coming out as an Indo-Canadian youth living in a small Canadian city where he experienced racial slurs, homophobic taunts, and physical threats. Still today's SGM youth are coming out at younger ages in their families, schools, and communities (CPHO, 2011; D'Augelli, 1998; Grace & Wells, 2001). They tend to have a greater sense of self-awareness and greater knowledge about their sex, sexual, and gender differences than previous generations (Savin-Williams, 2005). This has enabled many SGM youth to lead more fully integrated lives as they successfully learn to come to terms with their marginalized identities (Ryan & Futterman, 1998). These resilient youth have moved beyond seeing themselves as sexual or gender misfits (Ehrensaft, 2011; Russell, 2005). They now focus on how their schools perpetuate their marginalization and exclusion by leaving heterosexism, genderism, and homo/bi/transphobia unchallenged. Nevertheless, coming out and coming to terms "at younger ages also means greater stress, more negative social pressure, and greater need for support" (Ryan & Futterman, 1998, p. 10). This support is of paramount importance in helping SGM youth to combat feelings and experiences of difference, alienation, and isolation (Wells & Tsutsumi, 2005). It can take such forms as positive representations, family and community acceptance, positive peer and school relationships, SGM support networks, and access to a variety of coping strategies (Fenaughty & Harré, 2003). These supports, which Fenaughty and Harré (2003) call resiliency factors, can enable higher levels of self-esteem and an increased sense of belonging. Of the resiliency factors that can sustain SGM youth, Fenaughty and Harré (2003) suggest, "Positive social acceptance may be the most influential" (p. 16). For Jeremy, Ryan, and Bruce, family acceptance was the pivotal support enabling them to evolve socially and engage in cultural action for social transformation. Each young man valued family support as he spoke about the challenges and successes in the personal process of coming out and coming to terms. The vignettes that follow capture the tentative nature of this process. Jeremy's vignette also captures his emergence as a social activist engaged in a process of resistance tied to growing into resilience. As Jeremy demonstrates in this vignette, his resilience blossomed with family support:

I came out to myself as bisexual in grade 11. I've continued to identify as bisexual, but I don't really want to label myself anymore. I like the word queer because it seems to be more of an umbrella term for anyone in the gay community that doesn't want to fall under gay, lesbian, bisexual, transgender, or questioning categories.

Soon after I came out to myself, I came out to my parents. One evening I was watching television with some of my gay friends. My mom kind of picked up on something different. She asked me to come upstairs and she said, "Listen Jeremy. Are you gay or something?" I said, "No mom, I'm actually bisexual." She said, "Oh, OK." She went out for a little while. When she came back she told me, "That's good, I'm proud of you." The next morning she wanted to make T-shirts that said something like "I'm a proud mom of a proud gay son." I was excited that she was so great with it. My stepdad was also very supportive. He had already been working with the gay community. He works in social work, so he had been advocating for gay rights for a long time, especially when it came to adoption and foster care.

Jeremy had the acceptance and support of a family with a tradition of involvement in social advocacy, which would enable his educational activism and cultural work. Yet Jeremy had to mediate the difficult intersection of race and sexual orientation (Kumashiro, 2001). During his interview with us, Jeremy discussed how his essentialized racial and bisexual/queer identities oppressed him in his community and drove his advocacy work:

Being born and growing up in Canada I didn't really see myself as Pakistani like my mom or Indian like my biological father. I saw myself as a Canadian, but at the same time I have experienced racism. When I came to terms with my sexuality, then along came homophobia. In a sense homophobia was easier for me to deal with because I had already experienced racial discrimination based on misconceptions and a lack of education.

When I entered high school in Sault Ste. Marie, there was very little cultural diversity. I stood out like a huge sore thumb. You could tell I was brown. Everybody saw it. They'd yell, "Hey, brown boy!" Or I'd get called "nigger." Or they'd say, "Hey nigger, fuck off and go back to your own country." It was a huge shock. I had never ever in my life been called a nigger. I was a Canadian! There was a lot of buried hatred in that community when it came to cultural diversity and a lot of belief in stereotypes.

It seemed like every time that I was at one of the worst spots in my life, something would happen like a racial slur or a homophobic remark. That's when it would hit home. I'd be really shocked and part of me would be feeling, "Crap, not another thing to deal with." But then another part of me would say, "I can deal with this. I can make a change and prove to these people that I'm more than their stereotypes. I'm more than that queer faggot brown boy." Thinking that would lift me up in a way that I could delve into my work and prove – mainly to myself – that I could be better than the names that they called me.

I wouldn't have done it at all without my family, the people I come home to everyday. We had all sat down and talked about it. When I started the Break the Silence campaign to create an environment that welcomed sexual diversity and advocated tolerance in my high school, we were never quite sure where it would take us. We felt that this could go in a million and one directions. In a worst-case scenario, our house could be vandalized. Or nothing would happen. Or it could affect my brother and me. Or it could also affect my parents' jobs living in such a small community. Taking all the risks into consideration, our family's history [of commitment to activism], and our personal beliefs, we all decided that it was important to just go with the activism. My mom and stepdad were fully supportive, and quite willing to help out in any way, shape, or form.

In the next vignette Ryan speaks to his own process of coming out and coming to terms in his school and family as primary social spaces in his life. His preoccupation with an insider (jock) versus outsider (gay youth) binary in his urban high school is indicative of the shaping presence of the closet and the pressure to cast off any suspicion of gayness, even by engaging in or being complicit with homophobic acts (Sedgwick, 1990, 1993). It is also indicative of society's presumption of what Rich (1980) characterized as "compulsory heterosexuality." Ryan's reflection exemplifies the way that heteronormativity routinely scripts identity roles. Indeed Ryan's privileged identity as an athlete enabled him to remain above suspicion in his school. Nevertheless, Ryan endured enormous pressure, self-isolation, and the fear of his gayness betraying him as he attempted to maintain a heterosexual facade:

In grade 9 I was the athlete of the year in my school. I always fit in on the jock side, but after the game was over and you went to hang out with your teammates it wasn't the same. I always felt different and kind of strange. It was stressful.

I found that people who play sports joke about being gay a lot more than others. I tended to joke the most, which is funny because no one really suspected that I was gay. I talked about girls just as much as they did. Because I was a jock, I guess I was above suspicion.

There's definitely pressure to be straight. Everyone assumes you are. They asked me over and over, "Why don't you have a girlfriend?" I started to get that a lot in grade 12. That just made it harder to make friends or to get really close to anyone because you know that as soon as they start to find out about your life they can figure it out pretty easily. No one ever made fun of me though because I don't act like it or show it in any way that I can tell. Yet the easiest way to tell that I'm gay is to watch my eyes. When I see a couple walking by, I don't look at the girl. Other than that I don't think it's too obvious.

"Naming one's sexuality to family and friends is felt by many young people to be one of the most challenging aspects of coming out" (Epstein, O'Flynn, & Telford, 2003, p. 127). Sexual minority youth hope that this act of disclosure will help them to build supports so they can become secure people who belong. The following vignette shows that Ryan's mom and dad accepted him after he disclosed being gay to them, even though it meant they had to come to terms with having a second gay son. However, for Ryan's dad the acceptance seemed confined to his family. While he owned his own business where Ryan worked part-time, he had not dealt with heterosexism or homophobia in the workplace. This placed Ryan in an awkward and hurtful position where he felt he had to protect his dad while exposing himself to the anti-queer rhetoric of his dad's employees:

I came out to my parents the night before my calculus final. It was also the day of my parents' twenty-fifth wedding anniversary. I had just gone on my first date with a boy a few days before and I was typing an email to him on my computer. My mom was standing behind me reading the email over my shoulder, so she pretty much just caught me. She said she was going to go wake up my father.

They sat down with me and said that they were proud of me. They said that they could only imagine how hard it must have been to go that long without telling anyone. I guess I had it easier. My brother is gay, too. He came out a year before me. When my brother came out, the first thing my parents did was go to a psychiatrist. All three of them went. They didn't tell me because they thought I was straight and wouldn't take it very well. So it came as a big shock when I came out. Now they have two gay sons. It was hard. I felt like I was their last hope to carry on the family name.

I know that my dad won't talk about it much. He won't tell anyone, especially at work. I also don't want anyone he works with to know because I work for him and they gay bash pretty bad. Sitting in the lunchroom some days makes you feel sick. Here they are making fun of being gay and I'm thinking, "I'm gay – look around!" They just don't seem to see it. A lot of them have said that gay people should be dragged into the street and shot. Where does that come from? Why would anyone say something like that? They're all talk, but it still hurts.

Despite it all, since coming out I finally feel like a whole person. There is no better feeling. I wake up in the morning and I have direction in my life. Having a boyfriend is great. For once, I'm not alone. I have someone to talk to and spend time with. I just feel so much better about life.

Coming out is a lifelong process that involves consideration of individual comfort, safety, vulnerability, and perceived levels of support and acceptance. In his vignette, Bruce situates coming out as a complex process that involves more than just the disclosure of sexual identity. The coming-out experience also involves coming to terms for both the discloser and the family member or friend. When coming out and coming to terms move beyond one's circle of close interaction and response, as it does in school for example, strangers are also involved in a difficult transition:

I came out to my family before my friends actually, which seems to be contrary to what a lot of people my age do. I told my grandmother first. My mother was fine with it. She's got gay friends, so she really had no problem. She already has another son, so I guess she doesn't have to worry about the grandmother thing. However, my biological dad took it kind of hard. I'm his only son. He spent about three hours on the porch shaking his head while I was sitting in the living room going, "Oh, no!" We're still working on my being out. It takes a while. It's a process I guess. It's kind of hard for him.

I'm very cautious about who I am close to. My close friends were fine with it. My best friend was mad that I didn't tell her sooner! However, it wasn't so easy with other students at school. Teenagers are teenagers, and they had the reactions that I expected in school. I guess I got what every gay kid gets: name calling and that sort of thing. I didn't let it get me down. I had my family and close network of friends who supported me.

The vignettes of Bruce, Ryan, and Jeremy all demonstrate that coming out and coming to terms are contextual, relational, and situated processes that can involve both positive and negative experiences. When SGM youth are coming out and coming to terms, they usually deal with feelings of inferiority and letting their loved ones down. Many, like

Ryan and Bruce, who spoke about their parents' loss of perceived heterosexual benefits such as grandchildren, are dealing with internalized homophobia and the residue of compulsory heterosexuality. All three young men are mediating the real or perceived impacts that their revelations have had on their families, friends, and others in their schools and communities. And in the midst of this concern for others, they are trying to find ways to survive and be resilient despite challenges and absences that make it hard to move forward. Still, when the impetus and the supports are clear and present to help them be strong, they can direct their energies towards their ultimate goal: to become educator-activists and cultural workers for social transformation.

Choosing Paths of Resistance and Resilience as Educator-Activists and Cultural Workers

For many SGM youth, coming out and coming to terms mean exposure to a vicious circle of psychosocial responses that may include negative self-esteem, feelings of depression and isolation, drug and alcohol abuse, disruptive school behaviour, increased sexual activity, and decreased academic performance (Blackburn, 2004; Friend, 1993, 1998; McCreary Centre Society, 1999; Peterkin & Risdon, 2003; Ryan & Futterman, 1998). Often these responses intensify senses of alienation and loneliness that can help explain why suicide rates for SGM youth are two to three times higher than for their heterosexual peers (CPHO, 2011; Morrison & L'Heureux, 2001; Remafedi, 1994).

Although Jeremy, Ryan, and Bruce had their battles with negative feelings and experiences, all refused to succumb to the helplessness and hopelessness of this vicious circle or to be part of the troubling statistics. Instead they opted to steel life. Moreover, they rejected roles as victims waiting for the next hard knock, choosing instead paths of resistance and resilience in which they responded to anti-queer malice with educational activism and cultural work to transform their schools into more inclusive entities. They proceeded knowing their work would be filled with challenges and risks as they faced the institutional and social stigmatization and the actual and symbolic violence that usually accompany queer life in schools. D'Augelli (1998) relates that this systemic discrimination and violence are rampant because schools often lack specific policies and procedures to protect SGM youth, who are placed in a position of double jeopardy because they are young and marginalized as a result of their sex, sexual, and gender differences. In the face of this jeopardy, Jeremy, Bruce, and Ryan learned to be socially vigilant, constantly assessing and monitoring their school and community environments for any signs of danger. Despite the risks, all chose to be public about their differences. This helped them to integrate their private and public identities in healthy ways (D'Augelli, 1998). Moreover, it led them to paths of resistance and resilience as educator-activists and cultural workers. For example, Bruce expanded a gay-straight alliance club in his school as a safe and dynamic "countercultural" space where energies and actions could be directed towards liberation based on sex, sexual, and gender differences. Theodore Roszak, who coined the term "counterculture" in relation to youth resistance in the late 1960s, defined it as "the effort to discover new types of community, new family patterns, new sexual mores, new kinds of livelihood, new aesthetic forms, [and] new personal identities on the far side of power politics" (as quoted in Marwick, 1998, p. 11). From the politics of their particular sexual-identity locations in these new countercultural spaces, Jeremy, Bruce, and Ryan contested the limits of who is included and excluded in constituting what Gaskell (2001) calls the *public* in Canadian public schools. In doing so, they provided one specific answer to Fine and Bertram's (1999) question: "Where are the corners in which class, race, language, gender, sexuality and (dis)abilities can be reclaimed, reconstituted and taken back?" (p. 158).

In light of increasing sexual minority student moves to bring the private and the public together by engaging in queer critical praxis in schools, it is time that educational researchers and practitioners moved beyond "at-risk" models and the "psychopathological effects of same-sex sexual orientation on adolescents' lives" to examine the resiliency factors and the "unique strengths that characterize the lives of sexual minority adolescents" (Russell & Joyner, 2001, p. 1280; Russell, 2005; Talburt, 2004). It is also time they moved beyond a male/female binary to accommodate those whose gender identity confronts such simplistic dualistic classification. Such moves could help in refocusing inclusive education for SGM youth in terms that nurture their capacities and abilities as change agents, informal educators, and cultural workers in their schools and communities. It could also help in determining the kinds of resources and supports needed to enable SGM and allied youth to overcome the difficulties of mediating a heteronormative sociality in which ignorance, fear, and the possibility of violence often make it difficult to muster individuals for collective work to counter heterosexism and homo/bi/transphobia.

In the following vignettes, Ryan, Jeremy, and Bruce describe their resistance work and demonstrate their resilience as they engaged in queer critical praxis to liberate themselves and their SGM peers in their schools and communities. Their political and pedagogical strategies for resistance nurtured an unofficial lived curriculum that supported the meaningful inclusion of SGM students in the social fabric and learning culture of public schools. Their stories capture key aspects of their inclusive politics and pedagogy that incorporated "possibilities for interruption" (Weis & Fine, 2001, p. 521). Ryan discusses how he disrupted the public space of schools as a high school graduate:

> When I was in high school, there was no way that I would have gone to my counsellor to get information about being gay. There wasn't even a poster to suggest that I could talk openly about it. But if I had seen a gay-positive poster or something outside the counsellor's door, then I might have had the courage to go in.
>
> Still, it shouldn't just be the guidance counsellor that you can go to. Really it's every teacher's responsibility. Thinking back on how anxious I was, it would be a good idea to give students bookmarks that list all kinds of support groups, including gay youth groups. If a teacher hands them out, then every student will have a whole list. If you have a question or a problem, then you can use the list.
>
> Now that I'm out, I go back into schools and let them know about the sources of support that are available. Even though I've graduated and I volunteer with the [local SGM] youth group, I'm still uncomfortable when I go into a school. I think, "Oh crap! Now I'm in for it! I have to go into this office and basically announce I'm gay and say here are some pamphlets."
>
> I sure was nervous the first time. I went to this large high school and it was extremely busy there. The counsellor hardly had 30 seconds to speak with me, but he was nice. I walked into his office and gave him the material. He looked at it and said, "Thanks a lot. I see that this is an important subject, and it's good that we have these things for kids." He added that he would put some flyers up on the bulletin boards that they had. I suggested that the one outside his office would be a good place to start. I hope it does some good. If it helps one person, then it's worth it!

Like Ryan, Jeremy is a grass-roots cultural worker. In his school, he put both his body and identity on the line as a bisexual/queer person who is also a student of colour. He brought his personal experiences into the public space of the school as part of his politics of voice and visibility. He encountered the ignorance, avoidance, fear, and self-concern of his principal and guidance counsellor, and he endured their inaction. He captured the teachable moment to have a pedagogical encounter with his peers when his family studies teacher gave him the opportunity to make a class presentation:

> I realized that in starting a queer positive-space campaign I had an opportunity to do something with my life. Being in my last year of high school, I knew that if something bad did happen to me, I was better able to defend myself in both the emotional and physical sense.
>
> When I did try to start the positive-space campaign, the principal wouldn't even talk to me about it. On a regular basis I would leave notes in his mailbox saying, "Let's start a gay-straight student alliance. Let's do something." When I came to talk to him, he was always too busy or had to be going somewhere else. I always got booted in the opposite direction. I got the impression that the administration's support for [SGM] youth is confined to just making sure we aren't dead. They sure didn't protect me from being attacked.
>
> I even tried talking to my school counsellor. At first she was very supportive and told me to do some research and bring her all the information. When I did bring it to her, she didn't do anything. For example, I proposed an equality day where the student council would buy a gay-pride flag, an anti-racism flag, and a Canadian flag, and all the students would sign them as a pledge for respect, diversity, and freedom. It never got done. I think she was afraid for her job or that she might compromise her role in the community and her status if she got involved. I just wish she had been forthright with me and said, "Listen Jeremy, I can't do this, so find another avenue."
>
> In my last year in high school I did a family studies report on homosexuality and the family. My teacher asked me to present it in class. She said it was an issue that she couldn't cover because she had no experience with it. After the presentation, I was amazed at the types of questions people asked me: "What do gay people believe in?" "How do gay people have sex?" "Do gay people fall in love?" They couldn't even picture the most basic things. When I talked about my life, they were shocked that I didn't do one-night stands. They were literally surprised that I didn't have a gay friend named Jack, a platonic girlfriend named Karen, and a woman named Grace living next to me just like the *Will and Grace* sitcom. They were shocked to realize that I was just as normal as they were.
>
> In working with my positive-space idea, I had tried talking to the principal, the counsellor, and the school district superintendent. All

rejected me. At that stage of the game, I started a petition and wrote a letter to the Ontario Minister of Education. I also prepared a press release. I felt this was the only avenue available to me. The local media did cover the story, but nothing was ever really resolved. I think the principal was happy that I finally graduated and moved away to go to university.

Ryan, Jeremy, and Bruce have all been involved in educative "space work" (Fine, Weis, Centrie, & Roberts, 2000, p. 132). In describing his involvement, Bruce highlights the importance of his school's gay-straight student alliance club not only as an important space for personal, political, and pedagogical resistance, but also as a vital space for recuperation, where SGM youth can build community and solidarity and find support (Barry, 2000; Wells, 2006). As a safe and shared space, the GSA "may release [students'] imaginations enough to project changes for themselves ... [as they face] the obstacles or injustices ... as common concerns, not only to be resisted and escaped from but also to be transformed and somehow overcome" (Greene, 2000, p. 295). This educational and cultural work requires a sustained set of commitments to counter heterosexism, genderism, and homo/bi/transphobia. It takes significant time, localized effort, and consciousness-raising strategies. In doing this work, students in GSA clubs, as demonstrated further in chapter 8, take up roles as challengers who take on initiatives themselves and "therefore, without knowing or even noticing it, begin to create that public space ... where freedom can appear" (Greene, 2000, p. 297). As Bruce's vignette demonstrates, he is a challenger and a change agent.

When the idea to start a GSA came up four years ago in our school, the principal said that it was too controversial and that he didn't want to have this kind of thing in his school. The student who originally started the GSA worked with his foster dad to show the principal statements about inclusion in the school-board policy that provided the grounds to support the idea of a GSA. The principal reluctantly agreed to let the group meet.

In the first year or two, the GSA was mostly a small discussion group. We met in this little room across the hall from the main office. It had tinted windows with a pride sticker. We would just sit there and eat our lunches while we talked about homework. Sometimes we'd just listen to music.

Over time the GSA became more focused on bringing anti-homophobia education into the school. We started moving beyond being just a discussion group and went out into the school. We made posters and put them up around the building. They were ripped down continuously, but we'd just have poster parties and put up more. We also painted pride rainbows on the walls with sayings like "Love knows no gender!" Then we started talking to the administration and staff about their roles in stopping homophobia. We talked about going into staff meetings and doing staff education. Supportive teachers would ask me what kinds of things they could do to make their classrooms safer. I noticed that these teachers would start to do things like saying partner instead of husband or wife in their classes, and it would grow into a discussion with the students.

In my opinion, every single teacher ought to integrate things into their teaching such as using inclusive language. That would help combat homophobia. I think that there needs to be a unilateral and concrete public show of support from all the teachers and the administration for students who are gay or who get labelled that way. School administrators are certainly a key group in the kind of education that I'm talking about. For example, I think that a principal should always be communicating with the teachers about their roles in relation to every student. I also think the principal should actively support a group like a GSA club.

Besides teaching the teachers, we also started formulating lesson plans for doing anti-homophobia workshops in classes. This past year we focused on having a gay-pride day in our school. We talked about how exciting and groundbreaking it would be to have one. We set the date for May 22, 2002. When I went to that very same principal who had been so reluctant to start the GSA and told him that the GSA wanted to have the first ever pride day in a Canadian high school, he said, "Let's do it!" I worked very closely with him to plan the day. He even gave pride-flag stickers to every teacher to put on their classroom door to symbolize the importance of the day. It's really great how he came around. I think the kind of education that the GSA brought to the school really helped.

In planning the pride day, I thought it would be good to organize the day in conjunction with other student clubs. Maybe this would show all the students that we were working toward the same goal – inclusion. So the GSA invited the school's Christian club to help plan the day. I went and spoke to them and gave them this speech about how important it would be if they joined us and publicly expressed their support. To my amazement they agreed. I brought the news to the principal and told him, "This is the most important announcement you are ever going to read!" The announcement said, "Today at lunch there will be a joint meeting of the Gay-Straight Student Alliance Club and the Christian Club." I bought eight pizzas and we made posters. We decided that we would run this day together and show the school that we were all against homophobia.

We held a school assembly at the pride day and we had Roz Shakespeare, Canada's first openly trans police officer, as our keynote speaker. I also got

GLASS [Gay, Lesbian, and Supportive Singers], the world's first [SGM and allied] youth choir, to sing at the assembly. It was really great. They [Roz and the choir] are groundbreaking and the pride day was groundbreaking. To my surprise, all of the students were courteous and supportive. There were no negative comments.

In his work with the GSA and the school's first Pride Day, Bruce interrupted heteronormative and genderist public space with representations that portrayed SGM individuals as contributing members of society who transgress the parameters of historical "hierarchies, stereotypes, or installments" (Britzman, 1997, p. 184). Bruce and his peers were steadfast, especially during the genesis of the GSA when the continuous ripping down of their posters signified the contestation of their club as a counter-public space within the public space of the school. Contestation of the GSA was to be expected. After all, "the treatment of difference in schooling is never static and is highly politically charged because it references 'our' assumptions about what children [and youth] should learn in common, as citizens" (Gaskell, 2001, p. 20). Nevertheless, Bruce and his peers chose a path of resistance and resilience to claim a space for their liberation, a space where their "individual dreams, collective work and critical thought are ... reimagined" (Fine & Bertram, 1999, p. 158).

In creating this liberatory space, Bruce noted how important it was that his principal "came around." School principals are key figures with power to influence the quality of SGM life in schools; they can enable or deter queer inclusion. Bruce's principal, John Simpson, proved to be an enabler. In a keynote presentation at the seventh annual Breaking the Silence Conference in Saskatoon, Saskatchewan, Simpson (2004) talked about his own educative process in coming to terms with the fact that there were SGM youth in his school. He frankly admitted that he was afraid of the consequences of supporting a GSA in his school, which was occupied by more than 1,700 students and 100 teachers. Still, he had worked to have students engage an ethic of mutual respect as he focused on reducing racial tensions in his school, where numerous languages were spoken. He had spearheaded a two-week festival called Building Bridges to celebrate diversity in the school and to promote student safety and a sense of belonging. As part of his commitment to anti-oppression education, Simpson knew that SGM students had to feel safe and belong, too. There had to be consequences for homo/bi/transphobic behaviour that sent students and parents the message that

SGM students were recognized and accommodated in his school. His gay assistant principal and the SGM students in the GSA became an important source of support in his own education on queer issues and concerns. In accepting his responsibility for the SGM students in his school, the principal provided support to a teacher sponsor for the GSA and deliberated with students regarding how the GSA might function to benefit them. He added to his own learning by contacting other principals who had initiated or supported GSAs in their schools. He was concerned with the GSA's form and function since he knew that SGM students, struggling with their identities and feelings, needed a safe and supportive space that was more than just a social space to meet and chat. He also knew that his teachers needed to be educated and supported as they dealt with the reality of a GSA in their school. Early on, when all the posters advertising the first meeting of the GSA had been taken down, he also realized that support staff needed to be educated and assisted as they dealt with the new reality, too. A caretaker had removed the posters because she felt they went against her religious beliefs. Public fallout from starting up the GSA only included one letter to the editor in a local newspaper and two calls from concerned parents. Simpson met with both parents and argued that the GSA provided a venue to promote the safety of SGM students in his school.

Simpson related that the GSA really thrived under Bruce's leadership. However, he emphasized that the remaining challenge is sustainability. When committed and involved students like Bruce graduate, there can be a void to fill. Thus there is a need for teacher sponsors to include an emphasis on building leadership skills as part of the work of the GSA. Such training is necessary in the continuing work to educate interest groups, build awareness, break down stereotypes, and include SGM content in the curriculum. It is in keeping with efforts to inform and insist on SGM-supportive policy development.

Concluding Perspective: It's All in the Trying

In carrying out their activist education and cultural work, Ryan, Jeremy, and Bruce worked in the intersection of the personal, political, and pedagogical to transform the public domain of schooling into a dynamic site where SGM students can participate fully, equitably, and meaningfully. In doing so, they became queer critical change agents who used innovative resistance strategies to interrupt the heteronormative, genderist social climate and heterosexualizing culture of schools.

They engaged in counter-public pedagogy to contest the exclusionary norms and marginalized subject positions that shape SGM youth's experiences of life in schools. As they followed their paths of resistance and resilience, Ryan, Jeremy, and Bruce engaged in queer critical praxis to disrupt the heteronormative status quo in an effort to find accommodation and respect for SGM peers across sex, sexual, and gender differences. This contestation of public space, whether through initiatives to create GSAs and positive-space campaigns or attempts to share SGM resources, challenges Canadian public schools to promote the idea of public in keeping with the inclusivity protected by the Canadian Charter of Rights and Freedoms. This political and pedagogical project aims to accommodate across differences, and it recognizes that "public educational space is fractured, and the fracturing is constitutionally guaranteed" (Gaskell, 2001, p. 33).

GSAs, SGM positive-space campaigns, and sharing SGM resources provide examples of fracturing space in public schools to engender visibility and place; GSAs exemplify what Fraser (1993) calls "subaltern counterpublics." These fractured spaces or counterpublics are not necessarily designed to be oppositional or combative. In many cases they become key sites for recuperation and resistance that afford time and space for sharing experiences, reflecting, consciousness raising, and action planning, which enables praxis. Fraser (1993) postulates that these counterpublics "signal that they are parallel discursive areas where members of subordinated social groups invent and circulate counter discourses, so as to formulate oppositional interpretations of their identities, interests, and needs" (p. 14). They represent necessary spaces of "withdrawal and regroupment" and "bases and training grounds for agitational activities directed towards wider publics" (p. 15). In these subaltern spaces students learn to name, act, reflect, and take further action based upon their everyday readings of the word and the world around them (Freire, 1998). From the perspective of queer critical praxis, this educative and cultural work resignifies and intensifies the historical work of gay liberation in contemporary times. In their engagement with this praxis, Ryan, Jeremy, and Bruce enacted a politics and pedagogy of hope and possibility as they built knowledge and participated in cultural action for social transformation. They employed what Butler (2002) describes as an ethics of capacity that seeks to create even the most transient space where revolutionary voices can be heard, if only for a brief time. As Ryan, Jeremy, and Bruce avow, it's all in the trying:

Ryan: The world doesn't change on its own. You kind of have to give it a kick. What other choice do you have but try? You're either going to go crazy or do something that's not so good.

Jeremy: Try. Try, in any way, shape, or form. Try to make a difference. It's the best thing that you can do. If it doesn't work one way, try another. If starting a youth group doesn't work, try something else. If you can't do a positive-space project, try a poster campaign. Educate yourself and know what you are doing.

Bruce: I view what I do as a professional obligation to ensure that I am not a second-class citizen in my own country. I just think that I am doing what's necessary for me and for other Canadians who don't fit in. I think that the most powerful thing that we can ever do in facing homophobia is for gay and straight people to hold hands and say that homophobia is wrong. We have to try together.

InterText 9
Jon: *Born to Be, Deserving to Be Happy in My Own Skin*

At 18, Jon has experienced more trauma than many of his peers. His life has been filled with turmoil interwoven in experiences of being adopted, being dislocated from his Aboriginal heritage, and coming to terms with his sexual identity as a gay youth. After a long period of being unhealthy and unhappy, Jon is much happier now. He is steeling life and growing into resilience with wisdom, courage, and a touching gentleness.

I'm going to tell you the truth now. I've probably felt safer at Camp fYrefly than anywhere else in the world. I feel safer than in my home, or with my friends in rehab. It's probably the safest place I've ever been. I can truly be myself here. I can express myself. I can be myself. This has honestly been a life-changing experience. It's just so supportive. There are no cliques. There's no bias. There's no judgment. It's just a really comfortable environment. The older adult volunteers and youth leaders support each other, and everyone listens and interacts. They don't shut you out. It's so welcoming. It's the most welcoming experience that I've probably ever had.

I've been through a lot of things in my life that were tough things to go through, but they make you stronger and they make you appreciate everything you have. Through my experiences with addiction, I've come to appreciate almost every little thing in life. The process took a while. When I first realized I was gay, it was a big realization. It was huge. It was life changing, and it was such a defining moment in my life. The word "gay" describes me as a person. I'm happy and I'm flamboyant. I like men, I really do. I like men a lot. That's how I identify because that's who I was born to be. I'm not straight. I'm not bisexual. I'm not queer. I'm gay. I feel really comfortable saying that.

It was mostly rehab that helped me be truly happy with a lot of things. That's where I began to work out my issues, and when you start to work out your issues, or your pain, and let it out, then it starts to heal, right? It's like when you get a cut on your arm and at first it really stings and it bleeds a lot. But then it starts to kind of heal and do its own little thing. However, if you don't treat it with anything, it'll get infected and get worse and worse and worse. That's what happened to me. I got cut up a few times, and I didn't do anything about it. And it just got worse. I never dealt with it. So there were definitely some low moments in my life.

I didn't really tell them at rehab that I was gay. I mean my own family didn't believe me, so how could I tell everyone else? The family I have now adopted me. They're white, not that there's anything wrong with that. They're also Roman Catholic, but I don't really follow that faith – obviously, right? I don't really follow any religion, not that I don't believe in it. I love the concepts taught by religions, like treat others the way you would want to be treated. I also don't have a strong relationship with my culture. The place I grew up was totally white bred [with Aboriginal children raised as white children], and I don't know many Aboriginals per se. I haven't really explored it very much. I don't have a great cultural background within Native culture – not that I don't want to. I would love to explore it one day because their philosophies, as I have heard, are very beautiful. I would love to explore it one day, just not at this time in my life. I have to concentrate on a few other things right now, but definitely I would love to explore that.

I was about 16 when I came out of the closet. That didn't work, so it knocked the steam out of me a little bit. I wasn't comfortable with who I was and I kind of hated myself for that. When I came out to my parents, they didn't believe me. That really set me back a bit because it felt like a rejection of myself, of who I was. I told them, and they didn't believe me! They said I was full of shit and told me, "You're trying to get attention Jon. It's a phase." It was kind of a rejection of me because here I am giving myself to them, letting them know who I am, and they didn't take it. And I thought, if my parents can't accept me, how can other people accept me? How can I accept myself now?

For a while it was awkward for me to be who I was, and for a while I wasn't who I was and didn't know who I was. I was bouncing all over the place. I was bisexual. I was straight. I was gay. What was I? It was a very uncomfortable time in my life. I really didn't know who I was. It was being lost for a long time – until just this year. That's when I started getting really comfortable with it. And I am comfortable with it now. I'm really happy. I'm probably happier now in my life and in my own skin than I ever have been in the last 18 years. I would definitely encourage being yourself and identifying as whatever you are because when you are who you are, you are the happiest.

Well, my childhood was really good up until about age 10 when the sexual abuse happened. This guy essentially took away my innocence, you know? After that moment in time I was never the same. I wasn't that happy little Jon. I was somebody else. He took away that innocence and it still hurts to this day – quite a lot actually.

Oh yeah, I skipped a part. It was when I was 12, and this was another knock down. I got into an argument with my mother. I had never really thought of it this way, but she brought it to my attention. It was another life-changing moment for me. We were fighting and she got mad at me and said, "Jon, did you know that people think of Native people as lazy?" And my whole world dropped for a second. It just stopped and it just clicked in like "Wow!" That was when I found out that I was definitely different from other people. Like I said, it was a very white-bred community, and it's like you're going to be different for your whole life. You know, it almost branded me as a person. My mom branded me as being this lazy Native guy – her son, her own son as this lazy kid. That was a bomb, and my sexuality was another big bomb. So I was a gay guy, I was a Native, and I had low self-esteem. I hated myself. That's when I found my nice little friend alcohol as a coping mechanism. I didn't really talk to anyone about it, about my sexual abuse or any of my issues. I was on a streak going downhill from there. The heavy drinking really started when I was 16, along with the manipulating, lying, and stealing from my parents. It was a rebellion that was totally destroying everything. I lost a lot of passion just for life in general. I was very suicidal. I didn't like myself and I was in a dark place.

Then in rehab I was in a counselling session with a really intuitive session leader. This is rehab and you're in a room with 12 straight guys and they're all horny because they've been there for three or four months. And they're talking about women, just natural at that point, cause they like women, right? I kind of tried to join in the conversation and I sounded really awkward because I just don't talk about women like that. He totally picked that up right away. He's a counsellor and he knows what he's doing. So he called me into his room and he asked, "Are you gay?" You could totally read it on my face, and I said, "Yeah." And he said, "That's ok, you know that? That's ok." And I still didn't think it was ok, and I still didn't really believe him. But then he made me do this exercise, and I still remember it. It was hard to do at first because I really didn't like myself for a lot of things like for being gay and different and being an Aboriginal. I didn't like that about myself. I blamed myself for the whole sexual abuse incident, blamed myself for being an addict and hurting my family. I blamed myself for a lot of things so I really didn't like myself. I hated myself. I had no internal strength at all. He made me look into a small little mirror, and he says, "Jon, I want you to look in that mirror and say to yourself that you deserve happiness over and over again. Say Jon, you deserve happiness." And for a while I really couldn't do it – to actually say that to myself – and when I did I started crying because it was so emotionally hard to do because I really didn't believe it. But then I just started to realize that I really did deserve it. Everyone deserves happiness. It still gets me to this day. It chokes me up. Everyone deserves happiness, and you shouldn't deprive yourself of that because everybody is beautiful in their own way. So that really helped me out, just to show that if you believe in yourself or if you are happy with yourself, then you can find the strength for anything. You can.

It was good that I went to rehab, definitely. That's where I began to work out my issues, and when you start to work out your issues, or your pain, and let it out, then it starts to heal, right? I learned to keep away from the negativity, keep to the positive, keep hope, and try to be happy.

7 The Comprehensive Health of Sexual and Gender Minority Youth

WITH KRISTOPHER WELLS

As interview excerpts and the InterTexts in this book reinforce, sexual and gender minority youth experience stressors and engage in risk taking that affect their comprehensive health, including their mental and sexual health. Drawing from research, policy, and practice arenas, including research conducted at the Institute for Sexual Minority Studies and Services (iSMSS), University of Alberta, we focus on the comprehensive health of SGM youth in this chapter, highlighting their mental health and ways it is linked to their sexual health. We identify diverse health problems of SGM youth and how they might be addressed so SGM youth become happier and healthier individuals who make good choices and take care of themselves. Ultimately, we write this chapter to inform institutional policymaking and its implementation in inclusive and accommodative programs and practices in multiple social and cultural environments including homes, schools, health-care facilities, in-care settings, and local communities. From this perspective, we survey exemplary community-based intervention and outreach programming that caring professionals can draw on to help SGM youth deal with stressors and risks as they transgress life traumas and grow as more resilient individuals. Such model programs can enable SGM youth to transgress adversity induced by heterosexism, sexism, genderism, and homo/bi/transphobia; to deal with consequential mental and emotional trauma; to grow into self-respect and self-confidence as healthy, functioning persons; to set realistic goals and engage in problem solving as part of surviving, thriving, and acting in their personal and communal lives; and to build supportive, collaborative relationships (Goldstein & Brooks, 2005a, 2005b; Grace, 2013b; Grace & Wells, 2007a, 2007c).

Stories: Youth Are Hurting

Why is a focus on the comprehensive health – including the sexual and mental health – of SGM youth crucial? There are diverse reasons. Certainly, the publicized spate of gay male youth suicides in Canada and the United States during the past few years, which is one testament to the reality that homo/bi/transphobic bullies and heterosexist, sexist, and genderist systems continue to wreak havoc on vulnerable SGM youth, provides a profound reason to focus on their health and safety (Grace, 2013b). Research conducted at iSMSS also provides poignant reasons, as indicated, for example, in Colby's story that follows and in Jon's story, "Born to Be, Deserving to Be Happy," included in the InterTexts. These narratives provide two compelling stories that constitute impact statements from these youth, who have both struggled with mental health issues linked to the stressors and risk taking that have marked their lives. In his account, Colby speaks to the impact that his deteriorating mental health had on his comprehensive health:

I lived in Saskatchewan with my mom and stepdad from the time I was 5 until I was 12. My stepdad physically, emotionally, and verbally abused me. It wasn't until I was 12 that my mom told my grandma, and so I came to live with my dad in Alberta and we went through court procedures. It was a very stressful time when I first moved to live with my dad. I was going into grade 6. The assumption of the kids in the school was he is gay because he's very neat, he keeps his appearance up, and he's very into fashion. He likes to hang around more with girls than guys, and he's not into football or anything like that.

My coping mechanisms were isolation and not eating a lot. Then, as the years progressed, it was still presumed that I'm gay. I was called several degrading names like "fag." In grade 9 I dated my first girlfriend, but there was still something inside of me that drew me to guys. There was just more of an attraction. I like to look more at guys. I had a desire to be with a guy. So I was dating this girl and I was still going through very severe anorexia. At the end of my grade 9 year I was so thin that my stomach was sunken in. I was fairly emaciated because I was still using that as a coping mechanism for most of the people in the school and my community picturing me and placing me in a category that I was not in yet. I had not come out. So my way was to starve myself and to be very focused on my looks. Then during the summer my girlfriend had to move to Ontario. That was a rough time. I was depressed because I thought I was fat. I would self-injure, so it was not good. I ended up having to be hospitalized for four months in the eating disorder ward. Being on that ward gave me the opportunity to think.

That was grade 10 and I was 16. So I was discharged and I went back home. Before I left I was already presumed gay, so I had that going against me. Now I had been away for four months and nobody knew where I was, so I had that going against me, too. I lost all my friends because I was anorexic. I was depressed. When I wanted to talk to them they would say, "Yeah, come talk to us. Come tell us what's wrong." But as soon as I would start, they would say, "That's too much information. We don't want to know anything." It was very confusing and very aggravating.

And so when I got back it was about a month of having no friends and getting dirty looks. I had one group of very straight boys who were making fun of me because it had gotten out that I had come to Edmonton for treatment of anorexia. I was sitting eating lunch and they threw an orange at me. So that happened. I had stuff thrown at me. I also had remarks thrown at me like "you're fat." So my way of dealing with that was to say, "Okay. I have no friends. I don't think I'm ever going to get out of here. I think I'm gay." And my only solution was I'm going to kill myself. So I tried twice and both were unsuccessful. That angered my dad and stepmom even further because they could not fathom why I would do that. I explained to the counsellor that I have no friends, no life, and I'm going through a living hell pretty much. The counsellor said, "We need to get you out of your community." But because I wasn't stable enough with my eating disorder, because I still wasn't taking recovery seriously, and because I was still cutting, my parents said, "No." So I kept going through it for another month until May came along. Then I drank a mixture of pool cleaner and algae remover. I went downstairs and began coughing violently. I ran upstairs and I told my dad, "You need to take me to the emergency room now." And he said, "Why?" I was still coughing. I couldn't catch my breath and I coughed out, "I don't have time to explain. Take me to the emergency room, now." And so he did. I remember when we got there because on the way I was still coughing and couldn't catch my breath. I thought, "This is it. I've done it. I'm going out tonight." But when I got there they stripped me and put me in the shower. I was pulling the cord for the nurse and when she came in I begged her saying, "Please do not let me die." And that was the night I realized that I don't want to commit suicide. I don't want to go out that way.

SGM Youth: A Vulnerable Population

Despite more than a decade of significant changes in Canadian law, legislation, and social institutional policies, SGM youth – especially those under the age of majority in schools, the health-care system, community settings, and other sociocultural spaces – face a stark reality: they remain a vulnerable population subjected to sustained symbolic violence (such as stereotyping and anti-SGM name calling and graffiti), physical violence (such as bullying, including assault and battery), marginalization, and disenfranchisement that entrench mistrust, alienation, nihilism (a sense of helplessness and hopelessness), and susceptibility to life-eroding or life-ending behaviours including suicide ideation and attempts or completions (Grace, 2007a, 2009a; Grace et al., 2010; Grace & Wells, 2001, 2007a, 2007b, 2007c; Public Health Agency of Canada [PHAC], 2006; Taylor & Peter et al., 2011). In the face of the harrowing reality of these cultural markers of being in an exclusionary world, these youth confront many difficulties, including self-doubt and lost developmental opportunities, as they deal with heterocentrism, genderism, hostility, and the intricacies of sexual- and gender-identity development proximally (in relation to parents, family, teachers, and other youth) and distally (in relation to neighbourhood and community ecologies) (D'Augelli, 1998; Grossman et al., 2009; Herrenkohl et al., 1994). As a particular population affected by heterosexism, sexism, genderism, and homo/bi/transphobia, many SGM youth experience adversity and dysfunction in their everyday lives. For example, a US survey of 156,145 high school students, normally 14 to 17 years old, conducted between 2001 and 2009 found that sexual minority and questioning youth were more likely than other students to engage in risky sexual behaviours as they explored their sexual identities (The Lancet, 2011). Such surveys belie the perception in public health that youth in general are healthy, which has historically resulted in inattention to the health of adolescents and young adults and in lost opportunities for preventing disease and harm in these populations, in which, for example, non-lethal mental disorders compose a common and significant disease burden (Gore et al., 2011).

However, the health of vulnerable youth populations is an issue for some caring professionals. Currently, there is a growing concern with determining and tracking SGM-specific stressors, risk behaviours, assets, treatment interventions and processes, and outcomes in work to gauge the status and improve the physical, emotional, mental, and sexual health and well-being of SGM youth as citizens who have rights and deserve protections (Weber & Poster, 2010). There is also a recognized need to educate and connect caring professionals working in education, social work, psychology, and health, including mental and sexual health, so they can work collaboratively in the interest of helping SGM youth engage in holistic and healthy development. In the health domain, for example, patients' sexual orientations and sexual behaviours are recognized as significant predictors of physical and mental health issues among vulnerable youth (The Lancet, 2011). Thus the intention in educating caring professionals to be aware and sensitive is twofold: (1) to address the lack of knowledge clinicians and other caring professionals have about SGM youth health issues and (2) to address the unequal health status of SGM youth associated with social factors (like family, school, and street violence) and medical factors (like lack of youth knowledge of sexually transmitted infections and clinician misunderstanding, bias, and even homo/bi/transphobia) (Dysart-Gale, 2010; Grace, 2008a; Hatzenbuehler, 2011; Hirsch et al., 2010; Weber & Poster, 2010). For example, to treat transgender children and youth ethically, family therapists need to become advocates for this population and their families as they build deep knowledge of (1) treatment modalities; (2) community resources, including peer support groups and Internet resources; (3) legal changes; and (4) findings and trends in contemporary research (Bernal & Coolhart, 2012; White Holman & Goldberg, 2006). Family therapists can be trans-welcoming in their practices, demonstrating trans awareness and sensitivity by having inclusive statements in brochures and having trans identity questions on intake forms (White Holman & Goldberg, 2006). With no universal and empirically supported treatment modality for gender dysphoria, family therapists need to discuss their therapeutic approach and whether it is based on research or clinical experience (Bernal & Coolhart, 2012).

Similarly, in relation to educating school psychologists as caring professionals and allies in the education domain, McCabe (2014) asserts that these practitioners have an ethical obligation to advocate for SGM students, ensuring they are equitably accommodated in ways that respect their rights and integrity as persons. In order to become advocates and allies, school psychologists need to incorporate principles of social justice, taking the following steps: (1) examining how problems are not caused by sexual and gender identity statuses but by systemic stressors like heteronormativity and homonegativity; (2) engaging in self-examination of their biases and preconceptions caught up in homo/bi/transphobia and homonegativity, which tend to be nuanced in intersections with racial/ethnic and other identities; (3) striving to understanding oppression, normativity, and marginalization, which includes learning to combat pervasive heterosexism and genderism; (4) deconstructing heterosexual privilege as a ubiquitous norm, which includes learning to use personal privilege as a counter-force to support youth; and (5) strategizing ways that advocates and allies can help vulnerable youth to grow into resilience (McCabe, 2014; Scharrón-del Río et al., 2014; Shelton, 2013). In sum, practitioners as gay-affirmative treatment providers consider the impacts that communities, the larger society, and their systems and structures have on clients. Moreover, they investigate the ways they may be personally complicit (as a matter of disposition) in exacerbating problems rather than enabling positive treatment.

There is increasing acknowledgment that the needs and concerns of sexual and gender minorities are neglected in professional and larger cultural contexts. For example, a recent US trend analysis of medical publications about SGM persons (1950–2007) reveals that this multivariate and culturally complex population has been largely invisible in or, in some cases, excluded from studies, with medical professionals also failing to recognize their health-care needs in practice (Snyder, 2011). For example, in relation to mental health, the trend analysis indicates that only 1.92 per cent of papers from this 57-year period addressed mood disorders and suicide; only 0.65 per cent addressed health services and needs assessment; and only 0.36 per cent addressed eating disorders and body image issues. Problematically, and contravening post-1973 stances by Canadian and US psychiatric and psychological associations, 5.31 per cent of the papers addressed homosexuality as deviant, depraved, or pathological behaviour, while 2.33 per cent addressed "treating" or "curing" homosexuality. Also, the trend analysis demonstrates that most of the publications regarding the 15 leading causes of death in the United States did not consider a patient's sexual orientation, and the few that did linked common causes of mortality to suicide and homicide. This void in research parallels the hollowness of health-care provision for SGM persons, who often experience fears and difficulties in terms of access and accommodation. The trend analysis associates these fears and difficulties with barriers, including stigmatization and bias on the part of health-care providers and the dire need for training and development about SGM health needs and concerns.

Also focusing on the bigger picture, a recent review of suicide and suicide risks in the diverse US SGM population indicates that while this population, and notably its youth component, is at an elevated risk for suicide, there has been insufficient research regarding the problem of suicidal behaviour in this group and whether public health policies, prevention strategies, and targeted interventions are needed and effective (Haas et al., 2010). The review also indicates that, in general, there is no authoritative or reliable way to establish rates of completed suicide in the SGM population, although global research indicates links between SGM status and elevated rates of suicide ideation and attempts as well as links between mental disorders and suicide attempts of SGM persons. While mental disorders are the leading risk factor, the report points to other explanatory factors, including the social stigma, prejudice, and discrimination that sexual and gender minorities experience in individual and institutional contexts. At the individual level, this can include rejection by family and friends, harassment, bullying, and physical violence. At the institutional level, this can include being subjected to inequitable laws and public policies that fail to include and protect.

As a growing body of research indicates, SGM youth often experience schooling and government, legal, and medical services as fragmentary and insufficient to address the risk taking and negative outcomes that are associated with adversity and the trauma induced by stressors, including heterosexism, sexism, genderism, and homo/bi/transphobia and their multiple enacted expressions (Bowleg et al., 2003). These youth are dealing with minority-specific stress associated with heterocentric and genderist stigmatization and consciousness of it, hiding their SGM identity, lack of SGM group identity, internalized homonegativity (or internalized negative societal attitudes), discrimination, and other negative responses in their family, school, and work environments. Consequently, SGM youth are subject to mental health problems such as major depression, generalized anxiety disorder, posttraumatic stress disorder, conduct disorder, and nicotine dependence (Dysart-Gale, 2010; Hatzenbuehler, 2011; Berghe, Dewaele, Cox, & Vincke, 2010). Even SGM youth who are high achievers in sports, academics, and extracurricular activities may have mental health issues because they are overcompensating for hiding sexual or gender differences: "Although ... [their] endeavors are generally regarded as positive, when they interfere with traditional adolescent functioning (i.e., dating, socializing with peers, and typical adolescent rebellion) they become maladaptive means for coping with a stressful life situation" (Hunter & Mallon, 2000, p. 233). Other risks and effects of trauma associated with living with adversity include low self-esteem; truancy; poor academic achievement; quitting school; running away; homelessness; developing alcohol and drug addictions; being disposed to other self-injurious behaviours like teen pregnancy, cutting, and eating disorders; contracting sexually transmitted infections and HIV; developing inflexible attitudes about appropriate sexual and gender behaviours, which are excessively self-monitored; and being 3 to 10 times more likely to engage in suicide ideation, attempts, and completions (Chesir-Teran, 2003; D'Augelli, 2002; Friend, 1998; Ginsberg, 1998; Grossman & D'Augelli, 2007; Hatzenbuehler, 2011; Henning-Stout et al., 2000; Liebenberg & Ungar, 2009; Marshall & Leadbeater, 2008; McDaniel, Purcell, & D'Augelli, 2001; Perrin et al., 2004; Russell, 2002, 2005; Taylor, 2010; Tonkin, Murphy, Lees, Saewyc, & The McCreary Centre Society, 2005; Trotter, 2009). Clearly, it is important to research these stressors and risks to understand how SGM youth gauge or fail to gauge their impact; to investigate how such stressors compromise the physical, mental, and sexual health of these youth; and to learn how to counter their effects in order to help SGM youth develop as competent individuals and social persons with improved health and wellness (Forman & Kalafat, 1998; Russell, 2005; Trotter, 2009).

SGM Youth as a Multivariate Population

It is important to recognize that, as a multivariate population, SGM youth constitute a complex demographic with characteristics reflecting a wide spectrum of sex, sexual, and gender differences. These youth have particular ways of self-identifying and coming to terms with their identities in the face of the various stressors, risks, and available assets that can influence their everyday lives. Health-care and social-service professionals, educators, and others who help them mediate life, learning, and health issues need to know about these dynamics and how they affect the individual development, socialization, and asset-building processes of SGM youth trying to survive, steel life, and hopefully thrive as they navigate daily living. They also need to know who SGM youth are. This learning is a challenge because long-standing cultural taboos around discussing sex, sexual, and gender differences mean that even many caring professionals can be confused about differences among same-gender affiliative orientation (gay or lesbian individuals);

affiliative orientation to both genders (bisexual individuals); gender-identity positionality (such as trans male-to-female and female-to-male individuals); non-definitive biological sex due to chromosomal, hormonal, or environmental conditions (such as intersexual individuals); gender-atypical ways of behaving and living; and same-gender friendships (Dysart-Gale, 2010; Elizur & Ziv, 2001; Sanders & Kroll, 2000). Moreover, their lack of understanding reflects heterocentrism and genderism, which trivialize the diversity of sex, sexual, and gender differences and minimize the affiliative intentions of SGM individuals to be complete persons who experience intimacy and appropriate sexual contact in keeping with their differences (Sanders & Kroll, 2000).

For youth in general, perhaps the major psychosocial task is personal identity formation, including the development of fulfilling sexual and gender identities shaped over time through meaningful expressions and behaviours (Hunter & Mallon, 2000; Sanders & Kroll, 2000). On average in today's culture, where same-gender-attracted individuals are increasingly visible and accepted in media and everyday contexts, sexual minority youth recognize that they have a same-gender affiliative orientation between ages 8 and 10, often considering the attraction to be a natural part of their identity development that leads to self-labelling after about five years (D'Augelli, 2002, 2003, 2006a; Perrin et al., 2004). In their study of gender minority youth, Grossman, D'Augelli, and Frank (2011) found that, on average, survey participants reported a sense of difference from peers around age 8, with FTM (female to male) first self-identifying as transgender around age 15 and MTF (male to female) around age 13. In general, SGM youth are aware of their sexual and gender minority identities, desires, and attractions at younger ages, and are more assertive about self-identifying than youth were even a decade ago (Grossman et al., 2009; Russell, 2002). Consequently, SGM youth are also disclosing to parents, caring professionals, and significant others at increasingly younger ages, commonly now at age 12 or 13, and appear to be more positive about self-identifying (Adams, 2006; D'Augelli, 2002; Sanders & Kroll, 2000). However, both self-identifying and disclosing increase the probability of repeated SGM victimization, as youth become objects of physical, emotional, and sexual harassment or abuse that is often unaddressed (Chen-Hayes, 2001; D'Augelli, 2003, 2006a; Grossman & D'Augelli, 2007).

Despite the trend towards SGM youth self-identifying and disclosing at earlier ages, there are many reasons why these youth might keep identity matters to themselves. They may fear the onslaught of harassment and abuse, especially at home and at school, as well as the possibilities of parental rejection or being ostracized or rejected by friends (D'Augelli, 2002; Holmes & Cahill, 2004; Lock & Steiner, 1999; Travers & Paoletti, 1999). These fears – linked to self-monitoring, isolation, loneliness, uneasy silences, and disconnection from sources of support in different life environments – are significantly associated with increased mental health problems (Cagle, 2007; Callahan, 2001; D'Augelli, 2002; Tharinger & Wells, 2000). In a real sense then, identity development is impeded for SGM youth who do not disclose their sexual or gender differences to others despite being aware of them for a good portion of their lives (D'Augelli, 2003). Gay male youth appear particularly affected since they tend to self-identify at significantly younger ages than lesbian youth, keeping awareness of their same-gender affiliative orientation to themselves and thus delaying integration of their personal identities (D'Augelli, 2006a). In general, SGM youth are more challenged than their heterosexual peers as they attempt to sort out their identities in interactions with families, peers, and communities (D'Augelli, 2006a; Hunter & Mallon, 2000). Research indicates that the susceptibility of SGM youth to mental health problems is affected by their victimization based on their sex, sexual, and gender differences; their rejection and alienation in heterocentric and genderist peer-group contexts; the greater frequency of physical and sexual abuse among SGM youth compared to heterosexual youth; and the psychological conflict induced by trying to mediate individual and social development in the heteronormative environments of family, school, and community (D'Augelli, 2002; Ginsberg, 1998).

For many SGM youth, it is difficult to form a positive identity because the construction is ultimately carried out against the grain of hetero- and gender-normativity and in relation to stigmatized SGM identities and marginalized SGM communities that many youth may find problematic or alienating (Scourfield et al., 2008). Because SGM youth develop their sexual and gender minority identities over time, they usually do not have the opportunities for learning and socialization afforded, for example, racial or ethnic minority youth, whose identities are apparent from birth (Dane, 2005). In Canada, for example, Aboriginal youth can build cultural resilience in individual and community contexts when Aboriginal culture is promoted and sustained, which speaks to the power of whole community to nurture agency (Filbert & Flynn, 2010). These youth can also benefit from connectedness to extended family in Indigenous cultural contexts, which can be an important asset providing them with a network of family members to help them grow into resilience (Brokenleg, 2010). Indeed the emphases on ecology and democratic engagement in Aboriginal philosophies of educating and raising children can inform contemporary models for helping Two-Spirit Indigenous and other SGM youth to grow into resilience as they explore selves, build strengths in community with others, and navigate environments with the guidance of supportive adults (James, 2010). Nevertheless, as Two-Spirit Indigenous youth experience it, identity development can be quite precarious as they attempt to develop healthy individual and group identities amid competing demands from mainstream society (where any difference can be targeted), from SGM culture (where they may experience racism), and from their Indigenous group culture (where they may experience homo/bi/transphobia) (Fieland et al., 2007). Larissa's story, which is included as InterText 4, provides a poignant example of both the challenges these youth face and the supports that steel them.

Stigmas associated with disapproval of being Two Spirit (often understood as having the gifts of the male and female spirits in the same body) and fears of having a Two-Spirit identity publicly exposed have deterred SGM Aboriginal persons from accessing social and health services (Fieland et al., 2007). These complexities and circumstances associated with SGM and other relational characteristics require more research. While SGM individuals commonly experience invisibility, unjust treatment, isolation, marginalization, and disenfranchisement, different groups within the SGM constellation have characteristics, at-risk or at-promise life statuses, contextual influences, relational differences, issues, concerns, and experiential forms of suffering, surviving, and thriving particular to their reference group, which have an impact on processes of identity development as well as on how health and social problems ought to be addressed (Fassinger & Arseneau, 2007; Russell, 2005; Rutter, 1987). For example, gender-variant individuals are inclined to be preoccupied with the dynamics of gender identity and expression that contest traditional gender roles and behaviours (Fassinger & Arseneau, 2007). However, the ever-present tendency to meld SGM differences into some kind of homogeneous non-heteronormative category demonstrates ignorance of gender identity and replicates the long-standing tendency in research on sexual orientation to work within a heterosexual/homosexual binary (Savin-Williams, 2008). This demonstrates the need for researchers to develop dependable, objective methods for conceptualizing and assessing sexual orientation and gender identity earlier in human development, and for recognizing them as complex heterogeneous biological, physiological, psychological, social, and cultural constructs (Balsam, 2003; Savin-Williams, 2008).

SGM Youth as Ecological Actors

As they deal with the intricacies of sexual and gender identities, variations, and expressions, today's SGM youth self-identify in complex and contextualized ways whereby they take on multiple identities that they may see as transitory, fluid, and changing in different social and cultural contexts (Fassinger & Arseneau, 2007; Meyer, 2007). In this process, SGM youth have to transgress traditional understandings of identity and intimacy as they self-identify and come to accept their sexual and gender minority differences (Russell, 2002). The reactions of SGM youth to stressors and traumas associated with identity development are neither uniform nor universal, involving mixed responses that can be self-destructive, self-preserving, or some combination as youth variously deal with feeling proud, feeling uncomfortable, and feeling isolated from both mainstream culture and those parts of gay culture that they reject (Perrin et al., 2004; Scourfield et al., 2008). In processes of identifying and belonging, it is enabling to have the affirmation and support of one or more key individuals such as a caring parent, guardian, clinician, or teacher or of organizations like an SGM youth community support group or a gay-straight alliance club at school (Adams, 2006; Bringaze & White, 2001, D'Augelli, 1994, Hunter & Mallon, 2000). As well, SGM youth often rely on the Internet as an exploratory site and a context for identity development, understanding difference, and building social awareness and supports (Bringaze & White, 2001; Russell, 2002). When their self-identity as a sexual or gender minority individual is strong, SGM youth may be better able to mediate the stressors that can erode positive self-concept, lead to isolation, and consequently result in psychological problems (Meyer, 2007). More studies of these stressors are needed to explore linkages between the prominence and degree of self and social validation of SGM identities and mental health (Meyer, 2007). While the need to manage one's identity and survive in hostile social environments is a key factor in SGM identity development, it is nevertheless necessary to recognize that developmental trajectories are different for individual SGM youth as they variously succumb to stressors and engage in risky behaviours or develop strengths and competencies to adapt and grow into resilience by linking their identities to opportunities for building personal capacity, life skills, and community support systems (Anderson, 1998; D'Augelli, 1994; Hunter & Mallon, 2000; Meyer, 2007; Savin-Williams, 2008). Furthermore, it is necessary to consider SGM identities in relation to other personal identities like racial and ethnocultural identities since integration of various personal identities is seen as necessary for optimal identity development (Alfonso et al., 2006; Meyer, 2007).

Despite the challenges and difficulties induced by heterosexism, sexism, genderism, and homo/bi/transphobia, many SGM persons are healthy, well-adjusted, and contributing individuals, capable of coming to terms with their sexual and gender identities, coping well, avoiding high-risk behaviours, mediating relationships with partners, and raising children (Cagle, 2007; Russell, 2005; Savin-Williams, 2008). Well-adjusted SGM individuals do not internalize heterocentric and genderist perspectives, instead challenging hetero- and gender-normativity and constructing a positive ontological viewpoint that provides coherence for what it means to have a sexual or gender minority identity shaped by particular relational norms and community and cultural constructs (Bringaze & White, 2001; D'Augelli, 1994). SGM youth need such individuals as role models. They need to meet and job-shadow SGM individuals with successful careers, get to know same-gender couples in happy, working relationships as they construct them, and interact with families where same-gender parents are raising healthy and happy children.

Sexual Health Trends for SGM Youth

In terms of sexuality and sexual health, the diverse characteristics and differences of SGM identities are not antecedents predetermining sexual health problems. Indeed, over the last decade, research has increasingly conceptualized sexuality as a healthy, positive, and normative feature of adolescent development (Tolman & McClelland, 2011). A recent review of adolescent sexuality research during this period identifies three emergent domains of sexual-health knowledge building: (1) *sexual behaviour*, which in its plurality emphasizes key aspects of sexual performances; (2) *sexual selfhood*, which represents understandings of sexual subjectivity and individual development, along with conceptions of identity and comprehension of the complexities of gender; and (3) *sexual socialization*, which represents the multiple social contexts in which adolescents participate in experiential learning to mature as sexual individuals within their schools, families, and peer groups (Tolman

& McClelland, 2011). These foci indicate a move away from conceiving adolescent sexuality as a problem-focused, pathologically driven, and risk-based set of negative outcomes. They also indicate a key new trend in empirical research whereby sexuality is considered an integral part of healthy identity development for all adolescents. This trend has engendered research focused on the critical development of healthy sexual dispositions, relationships, and behaviours during adolescence, all of which have impacts across a lifespan (Tolman & McClelland, 2011). This marked shift in researching adolescent sexuality positions sexual-identity development as an emerging and interconnected physiological and psychological process in a youth's life (Tolman & McClelland, 2011).

Unfortunately, there is limited research about the sexuality of SGM adolescents, which is due in large part to continued heterocentric and genderist biases in the preponderance of research on adolescent sexuality in general (Tolman & McClelland, 2011; Saewyc, 2011). What the available research on SGM adolescence does demonstrate is the complexities of identity, behaviour, and attraction as this research moves away from a problematic focus on a monolithic investigation of "homosexual" teens to an expanded analysis of the diversity and heterogeneity of SGM youth as a multivariate group occupying an array of sexual and gender identity categories. This analysis variously positions these youth as sexually active, asexual, questioning their sexual and gender identities, having same-sex or opposite-sex attractions, and possibly engaging in same-sex or opposite-sex sexual behaviour (Tolman & McClelland, 2011). The newer research does not dismiss the importance of earlier research, which provided detailed descriptions of significant health inequities; unsupportive school, peer, and familial environments; and increased developmental stressors that SGM youth experience when compared to their heterosexual peers. In fact, this prior research knowledge has been critical in at least two ways: it has helped to raise awareness among policymakers and health and educational practitioners, and it has encouraged the development of evidence-informed interventions to improve the health, educational outcomes, and personal and emotional well-being of SGM youth (Saewyc, 2011). For example, a number of large studies comparing sexual minority youth to heterosexual peers have focused on healthy versus risky sexual behaviours in relation to condom usage, HIV, sexually transmitted infections, and teen pregnancy (Mustanski, Newcomb, Du Bois, Garcia, & Grov, 2011; Saewyc, Poon, Homma, & Skay, 2008; Saewyc, 2011). Synthesis of this body of research indicates that, when compared to heterosexual adolescents, lesbian, gay, and bisexual youth

- are just as likely or more likely to have had sexual intercourse;
- report higher rates of an earlier sexual debut (before age 13 or 14 on average);
- are more likely to report a higher number of lifetime or recent sexual partners;
- are no more or less likely than heterosexual teens to have had sex under the influence of alcohol or drugs;
- are less likely to use condoms or birth control at last intercourse;
- are more likely to self-report STI history than heterosexual peers who are also sexually active;
- have significantly higher rates of sexual risk behaviours, which include multiple partners, unprotected sexual intercourse, survival sex, and lower rates of condom usage if homeless or street-involved; and
- have higher rates of pregnancy involvement (2 to 10 times) for both males and females (Saewyc, 2011).

In addition to the aforementioned increased risk factors and negative health outcomes, young men who have sex with men (YMSM) are at the greatest risk for HIV infection when compared to all other youth populations (Mustanski, Newcomb, Du Bois, et al., 2011). For example, in the United States, 68 per cent of all new cases of HIV infection documented in 2008 were among young people aged 13 to 24. In this youth cohort, YMSM were one of the major risk groups to show rising rates of HIV infection. There are parallels to these findings in Canada. Alberta Health (2013) has indicated that age-and-gender-specific rates of newly diagnosed HIV cases among 15- to 29-year-olds in the province are alarmingly high. Moreover, consecutive 2010 to 2012 rates, as well as the 2013 annualized rate of HIV for Edmonton, are the highest among the five Alberta zones for which data have been generated. Statistics for these years also indicate that men who have sex with men (MSM) are the predominant at-risk group vulnerable to HIV infection. This aligns with the Public Health Agency of Canada's listing of MSM as the at-risk population most affected by HIV (PHAC, 2012). As PHAC also indicates, youth need to be a key concern since individuals aged 15 to 29 have accounted for 26.5 per cent of all positive HIV test reports since reporting began in 1979 (PHAC, 2010). Given the significant over-representation of HIV in YMSM, there is insufficient research and a lack of interventions targeting HIV prevention in the YMSM population (Mustanski, Newcomb, Du Bois, et al., 2011). There is also a paucity of research examining the negative mental health of YMSM and how it is linked to stigmatization, which can lead to poor emotional and physical health, increased drug and alcohol abuse, suicide attempts, and risky sexual practices. Moreover, very few intervention programs target the multiple biopsychosocial health disparities that YMSM and other SGM youth experience. Here intervention focused on HIV prevention has to convey the multifaceted nature of HIV risk in relation to overall health including mental health (Mustanski, Newcomb, Du Bois, et al., 2011). Likewise, intervention has to consider the factors that promote positive and holistic health outcomes.

Although more research is now being conducted on the physical, mental, and sexual health needs of SGM youth, to date little research has examined the unique needs and concerns of transgender and transsexual youth or adults (Haas et al., 2010; Nemoto, Bodeker, & Iwamoto, 2011). One recent large-scale study, which examined the mental health needs of 392 male-to-female (MTF) and 123 female-to-male (FTM) transgender persons, found that

- low self-esteem was common among all participants, with 60 per cent classified as clinically depressed;
- 28 per cent of respondents reported having been in alcohol or drug treatment programs;
- 59 per cent had been raped or physically forced to have sex;
- 62 per cent reported experiences of gender discrimination;
- 83 per cent reported verbal abuse and victimization; and
- 32 per cent reported attempting suicide (Clements-Nolle, Marx, & Katz, 2006).

In relation to suicide, the study also found that a history of suicide attempts was significantly higher for transgender individuals who were Caucasian, who were under 25 years of age, and who had previously been incarcerated. Attempted suicide was also strongly correlated with depression, low self-esteem, and a history of forced sex, drug and alcohol abuse, and gender-based discrimination. In another large-scale survey of 573 MTF transgender women involved in sex work, 64 per cent reported attempting suicide and 38 per cent reported being raped or sexually assaulted before the age of 18 (Nemoto et al., 2011). These negative experiences were amplified for transgender women of colour, who often face multiple adversities such as racially motivated discrimination; gender-based violence; transphobia; economic inequalities; substance abuse challenges; and higher rates of mental illness, depression, HIV, and sexually transmitted infections (Nemoto et al., 2011). As this and other research demonstrates, experiences of discrimination and alienation from family and peer groups are significantly heightened for transgender and transsexual individuals, including youth (Grossman & D'Augelli, 2006; Taylor & Peter et al., 2011). Another recent study, one of the few studies to examine the psychological resilience of transgender youth, found that the more youth presented as gender nonconforming, the more likely they were to be subjected to parental verbal and physical abuse (Grossman et al., 2011). In this study of 55 transgender youth between the ages of 15 and 21, 31 participants identified as MTF and 24 identified as FTM. Of the FTM youth surveyed, 71 per cent reported verbal abuse from peers, 17 per cent reported past physical abuse, and 0 per cent reported sexual abuse. Of the MTF youth surveyed, 87 per cent reported verbal abuse from peers, 36 per cent reported past physical abuse, and 16 per cent reported sexual abuse. This study identified three key elements of psychological resilience for transgender youth: (1) higher self-esteem; (2) a higher sense of personal mastery; and (3) greater perceived social support – all of which helped to buffer against depression, trauma and mental health symptoms, and internalizing and externalizing problems (Grossman et al., 2011). The study concludes that critical interventions to improve the psychological resilience and positive mental health of transgender youth ought to focus on task-oriented coping strategies to help gender-nonconforming youth address stereotypes, stigma, prejudice, and experiences of discrimination. Based on this preliminary research, the study calls for pilot intervention studies and programs embodying practices that foster greater self-esteem, independence, and a sense of social support, including family and peer acceptance. Moreover, intervention studies and programs should be contextualized and tailored to address racial, ethnic, cultural, socioeconomic, and religious differences among the diverse transgender and transsexual youth population. Given the significant negative health outcomes and the compromised mental health of transgender and transsexual youth, mental health professionals and agencies should also revise their services to provide specialized counselling, suicide assessment training, supportive referrals, and peer-based outreach interventions for gender-questioning and gender-nonconforming youth (Clements-Nolle et al., 2006).

As the emerging body of research on transgender and transsexual youth indicates, continued research and intervention strategies to support these youth should prioritize healthy sexual- and gender-identity development processes over a focus on risk and its management. From this perspective, more research needs to be conducted on positive dimensions of adolescent sexuality and sexual health that move away from risk-based assessments that exclusively emphasize reducing negative health outcomes such as STIs and HIV. While this constructive research focus is applicable to all youth, it is especially important for research on SGM youth, which has traditionally been conducted through the lenses of pathology, risk, and endangered social and self-development. Therefore, future research on SGM youth should focus on sexual and social well-being, non-heterosexual identities and sexual behaviours, same-sex desire, pleasure, intimacy, emotional commitment, and sexual satisfaction as critical aspects of positive sexuality development (Tolman & McClelland, 2011). More study is also needed to enhance knowledge of the specific relationship between mental health and sexual health for the SGM youth population in general, and in particular for its more vulnerable constituents like YMSM, who may be dealing with an array of health disparities and compromised psychological and behavioural outcomes (Mustanski, Newcomb, & Garofalo, 2011). This research should continue to clarify what constitutes both sexual health and mental health, and it should develop better ways to assess problems with greater diagnostic specificity (Mustanski, Newcomb, & Garofalo, 2011).

In the face of the many systemic and institutional barriers to healthy identity development, it is important not to blame SGM individuals, associating their sexual and gender identities and expressions with the inevitability of risk behaviours (Savin-Williams & Ream, 2003). As SGM youth self-identify at younger ages, families, schools, and faith groups can become increasingly important spaces to assist their healthy individual and social development and positive life outcomes (D'Augelli, 2002; Grace, 2005b, 2008b). However, when these social institutions are heterocentric, genderist, and prejudicial, they interfere with the individual and civic development and engagement of SGM youth (Russell, 2002). Since the communicated developmental, social, and environmental expectations for their futures are shaped in heteronormative and genderist terms, SGM youth are left with no viable means to grow into adulthood in healthy, productive ways that respect and accommodate their sex, sexual, and gender differences (Hunter & Mallon, 2000). For these reasons, it is important to focus on key social environments like families, schools, and faith groups where the health of SGM youth has historically been negatively affected by the challenges of mediating identity development and socialization processes against the grain of hetero- and gender-normative cultural expectations (Ungar et al., 2007). Another crucial focus is the health-care system, also a core hetero- and gender-normative institution in which historical discrimination of SGM individuals has occurred. This discrimination has been evident in the refusal or inadequate provision of medical services, which has resulted in the underutilization or avoidance of health care (Fassinger & Arseneau, 2007). In the health arena, it must be recognized that assorted environmental variables affect development and variously influence negative health outcomes. However, these variables can be altered in processes of recognizing, accommodating, and supporting SGM youth to influence positive health outcomes (Luthar, 1993; Rak & Patterson, 1996; Safren & Pantalone, 2006). From this perspective, health-promoting intervention and prevention processes ought to focus on improving systems and engaging in environmental interactions that enhance the capacities of families, schools, and communities to accommodate the needs and desires of SGM youth, allowing them to develop their identities in socially cohesive, caring, participatory, and productive contexts (Bernard, 1992; Bolger & Patterson, 2003; Bowleg et al., 2003; Carbonell et al., 2002; Corcoran & Nichols-Casebolt, 2004; Cowen et al., 1997; Elias et al., 2005; Gager & Elias, 1997; Johnson, 2008). Cagle (2007) emphasizes that facilitating such change "would require work and change at every level of the social environment. There is a great need, for example, to ensure that queer-identified teachers, youth workers, religious leaders, and others who interact with young people feel safe to be who they are on the job, and to promote services that match queer-identified youth with queer adult mentors" (p. 148). These mentors need to (1) understand how youth are located in their worlds, (2) believe youth have value and potential (are at promise), (3) share their own experiences of navigating everyday life, (4) build trust and rapport, and (5) create professional friendships with boundaries while being conscious of power relationships in work primarily focused on meeting the needs of youth (Philip, 2008). Moreover, for mentoring to be effective, Southwick et al. (2007) maintain it must be frequent and of sufficient duration.

The Family Factor

Stories: Focus on the Family

In our culture and society there is a powerful myth: every parent is a good parent. It carries such weight in schooling that we expect teachers to act *in loco parentis*. There is no doubt that many parents and other significant adults who take on the parenting role are healthy, caring, and supportive parents. However, there are also parents who abuse and damage their children by not loving and accommodating their differences, perhaps especially their SGM differences. Similarly, there can be families that cause harm. It is common to hear SGM persons speak about their families of choice, who are effective sources of hope and accommodation. As Sanders and Kroll (2000) explain, "[T]his family [of choice] could, and most often does, include significant members of the family of origin, but sometimes, introducing the notion of a 'parentectomy' or 'siblingectomy' may be necessary when the child suffers under the rigid views, demeaning actions, and erasing behaviours of some biological family members" (p. 441). Thus families of choice can have many configurations.

The stories that follow speak to the unevenness that can mark parental responses and behaviours in the wake of a child's disclosure of sexual or gender differences that do not align with expectations in the family as a hetero- and gender-normative institution. Again, brave, honest, strong, and reflective youth shared these stories.

> *Helen:* I think the only thing that bothers me is when it's family in some way. There is always this idea that family will always accept you, and there's this realization that this is not true within this [queer] community. It's not true that family will always accept you. Typically, I try to make comments around family like, "I have friends who are gay" or "I know gay people. They are normal people." Listening to the rejection is a little hard to take, so I think that's the hardest thing for me.

> *Ryan2:* When I came out to my mom I was 16 and I had just come home from a party at my ex-boyfriend's house. She took it hard. Looking back on it now I can see that she was going through a lot, but some of the things she said when she was dealing with it were kind of hurtful. She said it was like grieving, like she lost a son, because when you have kids you don't expect them to grow up homosexual. You expect them to grow up and go to college and have a wife and give you grandkids. I'm her firstborn son, so she felt like that part of her life was dead. She was grieving for that. But she bought a lot of books on Amazon ...
>
> I never told mom that it hurt me when she said she was grieving, but for a long time I felt a bit of resentment toward her for it. Now, like I said, I can understand what she was going through, and I can forgive her. She loves me now and we're cool.

> *Evan:* Well, I knew I was gay for pretty much most of my life. I kind of came to a realization at a very young age, but there was a lot of homophobia

in my life. So I suppressed that for a very long time to the point where I almost didn't even acknowledge sexuality and I didn't think about it. Then in my mid-teens I started to come to terms with it. I was really nervous about it and it ended up causing a lot of problems and a lot of anxiety because it was something I didn't deal with.

I was closest with my mom and she seemed like she would be the most supportive. I wasn't sure, but that's the general sense I got. So I eventually wrote my mom a note and then she read it. And we had a talk and there was lots of crying.

Erica: I told my mom I had flyers, and I had information from PFLAG [PFLAG Canada is a support and educational group that provides resources to parents, families, friends, and colleagues of SGM persons]. I had that kind of stuff from my GSA. I gave her the option of looking at it. I gave her the flyers and then a couple of days later I found them in the garbage.

Josh: I hid it from my parents, too. When me and my family were watching a movie, during one part my mom saw two guys kissing and she changed the channel. So I thought, "Oh, scary." Right there it just snapped and I thought, "I shouldn't tell her right now." This was last year. After a while she found out that I was dating Derrick because a friend told her. I was going to tell her myself, too. But a friend had told her already. She was all right with it. I wasn't disowned or anything. So I pretty much have a supporting family.

Iona: It became difficult because my parents were pressuring me: "You have to be straight. You have to do this for your family." Eventually I realized that the best way to get along with my parents and family, while living at home, was to just focus on school because it was the only thing that was steady at the time ...

Because I had problems at home, problems with relationships, problems not knowing – just feeling like I don't know who I am – it all just came rushing back, the not knowing, and worse than ever before. I don't know why. It was probably my family and the pressure they were putting on me that made it worse.

And about being brown – obviously, I think that there are definitely gay, brown kids running around very proudly in hiding. I really empathize with kids who are bisexual, gay, or straight, or trans, and visible ethnic minorities with traditional families. If they have traditional families, I think it's that much harder.

Sam2: It's awkward because I told my mom about the trans thing. I was living in Edmonton and then I ran out of money, so I had to move back home. I was all into, you know, trying to pass. But I can't if I live with my mom. There was this one night and I was just so mad that I ended up punching a hole in the wall. She was like, "Why did you do that?" And I had to explain to her that I was so frustrated trying to keep it a secret. She was crying and said, "Why can't you just stay the way you are and be a masculine woman?" And then she never talked about it again. She said she'd kill herself if I did it [transitioned].

I had come out to her as a lesbian when I was about 17. She was pretty good with it, you know? She like knew, right? Then I guess I was 21 or so when I told her about the trans thing. I don't know. It's just I'm really scared. The one thing I'm scared about is my dad, you know, about the trans thing. And, honestly, I'm actually scared for my life. He's like a violent, violent jer— … person. And it's just like, I dunno.

Zach: My cousin and my sister are completely okay with it. My mom is disappointed, but she still loves me. She's just kind of in denial I guess.

Derek: Growing up there were always friends of the family who were gay and who were around enough that I knew them. My mom had a friend and my auntie had a friend, so I knew people who were older and gay. I knew my family would be supportive because they've had these other people in their lives. Even my grandma is fine with it. She still thinks it's a phase, but everyone in my family's been very supportive of it. I think family is very important because that's where you are for the first 15 to 25 years of your life, depending on how supportive they are or the different circumstances that come up. They play an integral role and they are the people that should be loving you unconditionally.

The way that my family works now is that my mom is one of my biggest cheerleaders. She obviously came [to Camp fYrefly] and she did a media presentation with me. She was quite excited to come to camp and to participate in any capacity that she could. She had said, "If there are any volunteer positions open, I would love to come." So she's been very supportive and does more than I could ever have asked. She is on the [LGBTQ centre's] positive-space committee and she does a lot with them. One of the other things that she does, which I think is really cute, is she has this little button on her backpack that she wears everywhere. It says, "I ♥ my gay son." I think it's a nice little touch to show that she's supportive and that she is okay with taking that everywhere. It strikes up a lot of conversations. She'll come home and she'll tell me about them.

Family Matters

The family can provide a significant proximal environment in interventions that can help a child to grow into resilience (Luthar & Zelazo, 2003). However, "[f]or many sexual minority youth, family relationships are compromised" (Russell, 2002, p. 260). This is because the traditional family is a heteronormative institution that expects and encourages sexual and gender typicality and reinforces and validates heterosexual and gender norms. Thus the family has been generally unprepared and unable to socialize SGM youth and provide them with adequate role models and supports to enable their identity development (Hunter & Mallon, 2000). Family responses when a child discloses and contexts such as familial cultural backgrounds influence differences in the individual development trajectories of SGM youth (D'Augelli, 2006b). If SGM youth experience family support, then they are less driven to seek counselling or community supports (D'Augelli, 2006b). If SGM youth fear or experience family rejection, then likely consequences can include impaired identity development, homelessness, and street involvement, where they are at risk of sexual coercion, unsafe sexual practices, drug abuse, and physical, sexual, and mental health problems (Hunter & Mallon, 2000; Perrin et al., 2004).

A youth's ethnocultural environment can serve as an ecological buffer to social adversity (Aisenberg & Herrenkohl, 2008; Arrington & Wilson, 2000). While youth from groups historically marginalized based on race or ethnocultural differences have been able to rely on family to help them deal with stigmatization and victimization based on racial or ethnic identity, SGM youth hesitate to seek family support because they fear the consequences of disclosure and the possible damage to the parent-child relationship in their hetero- and gender-normative and most proximal social ecology (Bolger & Patterson, 2003; D'Augelli, 1998). When SGM youth belong to a racial or ethnic minority, they may have resources and resiliencies developed from dealing with racism and ethnocentrism that can help them deal with heterosexism, genderism, and homo/bi/transphobia; however, disclosing to family or community members can remain a key problem for them (Bowleg et al., 2003). Indeed heterocentrism and genderism are the key systemic and therefore clinical issues to address when working with SGM youth and their families (Butler, 2004; Sanders & Kroll, 2000). For youth of colour, this is exacerbated by frequent experiences of racism in the white SGM community and society at large (Holmes & Cahill, 2004). In this regard,

Hunter and Mallon (2000) indicate that SGM youth of colour have a tricultural experience as they mediate homo/bi/transphobia in their cultural/racial community and racism in white SGM and larger communities. As they intersect, racial identity can be a millstone for gender identity. For example, Singh (2012) relates that transgender youth of colour may experience ostracism by families, more safety issues at school, lack of access to trans-identity education, and a higher risk for substance abuse and HIV/AIDS. These impacts of racial location clearly indicate a need to understand what growing into resilience might mean when one moves from conceptualizing it using a white western lens to conceptualizing it using other ethnocultural lenses, where different community factors, contexts, and values contour what it means to be resilient (Singh, 2012).

When SGM youth express their sexual and gender atypicality in more overt ways, parents may become more aware, which can result in parents asking questions and youth disclosing (D'Augelli, Grossman, & Starks, 2005). However, many parents, driven by a mixture of concern and shame, try to discourage sexual and gender atypicality in their children by telling them to adjust their behaviours, sending them to counselling, restricting their activities, or punishing them (D'Augelli, 1998; D'Augelli et al., 2006). When parents contest sexual and gender atypicality and urge SGM youth to adapt to conventional sexual and gender roles, they engage in a process of controlling their children that is usually a precursor to victimization (D'Augelli et al., 2006). While a cohesive, communicative, and interactive family can assist positive development of at-risk youth, especially at mid-adolescence (Carbonell et al., 2002), the most vulnerable SGM youth generally lack family acceptance and accommodation, with those attempting suicide often reporting that their parents engaged in more verbal and physical abuse (Grossman & D'Augelli, 2007). In fact, the negative impact that family can have on SGM youth is one of three predominant causes of suicidality among SGM youth, in conjunction with isolation and homo/bi/transphobic reactions (Scourfield et al., 2008).

SGM youth are usually torn when it comes to disclosing their identities. Reasons for disclosing include being tired of concealing who they are and the yearning to be honest and to share with parents; reasons for not disclosing include a fear of distressing or disappointing parents and a fear of rejection or verbal and physical abuse, with the latter being considered the main reason (Cramer & Roach, 1988; D'Augelli, 2002; D'Augelli et al., 2005; Hunter & Mallon, 2000). Disclosure can contribute to better mental health as youth acquire resources and supports to inte-grate SGM differences into other facets of their lives; however, disclosure can also erode mental health because it opens up the possibility of retali-ation and increased symptomatology (D'Augelli, 2002). SGM youth may try to conceal a stigmatized identity as best they can to avoid the reper-cussions of disclosure, even though this can exacerbate stress and dys-function (Meyer, 2007). Parents' negative reactions to disclosure, or the fear of them, constitute forms of censure and victimization that impede identity integration, affecting the emotional and mental health and well-being of SGM youth (Bringaze & White, 2001; D'Augelli, 2002, 2003). When SGM youth do disclose or are discovered, especially at younger ages, victimization by parents can potentially be prolonged, with even greater effects on self-esteem, identity development, the extent of inter-nalized homo/bi/transphobia, and the physical, emotional, and men-tal health of SGM youth (D'Augelli, 2002, 2006a; D'Augelli et al., 2005). Parents may have even more difficulties with disclosure and acceptance when a child was not stereotypically "gay" growing up (D'Augelli et al., 2005). Still, increasingly, it appears that aware parents are more accept-ing and supportive (D'Augelli et al., 2005).

Having interactive parents who are good communicators and make an effort to become educated about their child's differences is associ-ated with SGM youth experiencing better emotional and mental health, with less suicide ideation and fewer suicide attempts (Brooks, 2005; D'Augelli, 2003). Indeed good relationships with parents are more significant than good relationships with peers for enhancing mental health (D'Augelli, 2002). In this regard, "[n]urturing resilience should be understood as a vital ingredient in the process of parenting every child, whether that child has been burdened by adversity or not" (Brooks, 2005, p. 298). When families are socially conscious, accept-ing, empathetic, involved, and accommodating, SGM youth have more healthy adjustment as they develop (Brooks, 2005). Because families can undergo metamorphosis, moving away from heterocentrism and genderism and the stress they induce after SGM youth disclose, it is possible for SGM youth to have a home support system that nurtures their emotional and mental health as they deal with the rigours of SGM identity development (Elizur & Ziv, 2001). However, even when par-ents accept SGM youth, they need help and time to adjust and be more supportive and accommodating so youth feel they can belong and develop their identities at home (Bringaze & White, 2001). In general though, families have not had a positive effect on self-definition as SGM youth deal with sexual or gender atypicality as a core part of identity development, which leaves SGM youth to seek support from friendship and community networks rather than disclosing to parents early on in the self-identification process (D'Augelli, 2002, 2003; D'Augelli et al., 2006; Elizur & Ziv, 2001). Moreover, since parents usually lack knowledge about SGM being and belonging that they can transfer, SGM youth need to be educated about their rights and responsibilities as citizens with SGM differences (Russell, 2002).

When SGM youth do disclose to family, they often gauge disposition towards their sexual or gender atypicality by first disclosing to a sibling or their mother, believing that their father is more likely to respond negatively (Cramer & Roach, 1988; Dane, 2005). In general, family reactions cover a spectrum: from limited to open acceptance, refusal or willingness to acknowledge or accept a child's sex, sexual, or gender reality, and hostility involving verbal abuse or physical assault (D'Augelli, 2006b; O'Conor, 1994). For some SGM youth, it is better to tell family members after they have left home to avoid the risks of being thrown out or becoming homeless (Perrin et al., 2004). The risks are greater in homes shaped by traditional family values, as associated with conservative religious and ethnocultural beliefs (Grace, 2005b, 2008b; Perrin et al., 2004). These values feed homo/bi/transphobia, inhibit the process of SGM youth disclosure, and interfere with family acceptance of SGM differences (Cramer & Roach, 1988; D'Augelli, 2006b).

Parents and Risks of Turning to Reparative Therapies

Sexual minority youth often experience conservative religious institutions as detrimental to their individual and spiritual development and socialization. Russell (2002) asserts, "For some youth, faith communities may serve more as barriers to than as facilitators of the development of citizenship" (p. 260). Reparative therapies – also called conversion, ex-gay, or reorientation therapies – can be construed as impediments to citizenship, understood as full membership in society and its institutions, including religious institutions. They are forms of pseudoscientific orthodox psychotherapy that some clinicians and an array of conservative religious ministries rely on to try to eradicate a sexual minority person's desire for an intimate same-gender affiliative relationship (Grace, 2005b, 2008b).

Some parents, particularly of younger adolescents, who choose to believe that their child's same-gender affiliative orientation status is phasal, changeable, and even curable, turn to these orthodox clinicians and the many religious ministries who use these therapies, despite the

American Psychiatric Association's declassification of homosexuality as pathological in 1973 and despite late-1990s proclamations by major Canadian and US health and mental health associations that reparative therapies are ineffective, with the potential to do harm (Cianciotto & Cahill, 2006; Grace, 2008b; Halpert, 2000; Perrin et al., 2004; Spitzer, 2003a, 2003b). Indeed mainstream professional organizations like the American Psychological Association have rejected sexual reorientation therapies as a result of the lack of empirical evidence to justify a mental-illness model of same-gender affiliative behaviour (Grace, 2008b; Serovich et al., 2008). Still orthodox psychotherapists and an array of religious ministries continue to use conservative religious stances to support the practice of these therapies instead of focusing on ways internalized and cultural homophobia influence patient/client disposition and trauma (Grace, 2008b; Serovich et al., 2008). Of particular concern is the fact that religious-based reparative therapies are often conducted without the involvement of a physician or licensed mental-health-care provider (Hein & Matthews, 2010).

No research (including youth-based research) has been conducted on the efficacy of reparative therapies (Blackwell, 2008; Hein & Matthews, 2010). Yet there are approaches to using reparative therapies that target vulnerable children and their anxious parents, exacerbating ethical and practical concerns about these therapies (Cianciotto & Cahill, 2006). Reparative therapies confuse and conflate same-gender affiliative orientation, same-gender friendships, and gender-atypical behaviours, so that suppression of sexual minority behaviour and increasing heterosexual behaviour tend to be equated with a change in sexual orientation (Halpert, 2000). Indeed control of behaviour rather than changes in affection, attachment, or desire is often used to indicate the success of reparative therapies (Hein & Matthews, 2010). However, what is perceived as sexual reorientation may actually be some sort of resolution of a cognitive dissonance dilemma (same-gender affiliative orientation versus anti-gay religious beliefs) (Rind, 2003; Strassberg, 2003; Throckmorton, 2002; Vasey, 2003). Moreover, reparative therapies fail to account for the effects of systemic or institutional homo/bi/transphobia that create stressors, which could lead to choosing some kind of reorientation therapy as a solution. This suggests mental health professionals ought to employ a more ecological approach that examines both the historical and sociocultural underpinnings of homophobia (Halpert, 2000). As well, they need to understand the psychodynamics of internalized homophobia, which is a negative self-concept about sexual minority identity and behaviour that develops as a result of heterocentrism (D'Augelli, 2002; Halpert, 2000; Meyer, 2007; Russell, 2005).

Since the late 1990s, the American Psychological Association has provided protection for vulnerable sexual minority youth whose parents or guardians may coerce them into treatment (Halpert, 2000). Since sexual minority youth mediate the moral and the political to live queer, they may not see conservative family, community, and faith groups as social supports. Perrin et al. (2004) relate, "Whereas other stigmatized youth who are teased because of physical traits, ethnicity, or religion are almost certain to receive support and guidance from family, community, and religious institutions, gay youth can feel isolated and alone with their 'terrible secret'" (p. 365). Some sexual minority youth may submit to sexual reorientation therapy because they fear multiple personal losses, including the losses of family, friends, and faith community (American Psychological Association, 2000). They may seek such therapy because they feel isolated and no longer able to deal with the verbal and physical harassment, discrimination, and violence that constitute homophobic reactions to a minority sexual orientation and identity. When parents or guardians impose any reparative therapy on a minor in the hope of changing the child's sexual orientation, it is reasonable to question whether such imposition is coercive, legally constituting child abuse and neglect because of the possible harmful effects (Haldeman, 2002; Hicks, 2000). Reparative therapists have used dubious techniques including behavioural therapy, electric shock therapy, chemical aversion therapy, and unnecessary medication (including hormone treatment) (Hein & Matthews, 2010; Hicks, 2000). The consequences of such perceived treatments as cures range from feelings of guilt and paranoia to nervous breakdowns, genital self-mutilation, post-traumatic stress disorder, and attempted or completed suicides (Hicks, 2000). Despite this damage, groups like the Catholic Christian ministry called Courage, in keeping with the church's perspective that homosexuality is intrinsically disordered, promote reparative therapies as curatives for same-gender affiliative sexual orientation (Courage, n.d., 2000a, 2000b). Since some Canadian Catholic school districts have used Courage as a resource in outreach to youth with non-heterosexual orientations, it is important to educate parents, other caregivers, and the public about the dangers of reparative therapies to the health and well-being of sexual minorities (Grace, 2005b).

For some time now, researchers have pointed out a number of conceptual and methodological problems with empirical research on reparative therapies (Bancroft, 2003; Byrd, 2003; Grace, 2008b; Worthington,

2003). The fact that research condoning reparative therapies is method-
ologically flawed was poignantly indicated when Robert L. Spitzer –
interestingly a central figure in the 1973 move to delist homosexuality
as pathological in the American Psychiatric Association's *Diagnostic and
Statistical Manual of Mental Disorders* – apologized for his ill-conceived
and ill-conducted 2003 study that was interpreted as support for reparative therapies as a "cure" for homosexuality (Arana, 2012; Carey, 2012).
In an interview with Arana (2012), Spitzer stated, "In retrospect, I have
to admit I think the critiques are largely correct" (p. 9). Spitzer told Arana
he had asked Kenneth Zucker, editor of *Archives of Sexual Behaviour*, the
journal that published his study, to print a retraction, but Zucker had
declined (Arana, 2012). In a notable coincidence, in the same month that
Spitzer apologized, the World Health Organization's Americas Office
issued a position statement condemning reparative therapies, especially
those that target vulnerable youth. The position statement, issued on
the International Day Against Homophobia and Transphobia (17 May
2012), emphasized these points: (1) homosexuality does not need to be
cured since it is not a disorder or a disease; (2) reparative therapies are
not medically indicated and threaten individual health and well-being;
and (3) these therapies are a "violation of the ethical principles of health
care and violate human rights that are protected by international and
regional agreements" (Becker, 2012, p. 1).

Fortunately, reparative therapies are losing their foothold in the
United States, which hopefully will result in their demise elsewhere.
There has been a move towards legislative banning of reparative therapies in some states, including California and New Jersey, which is pitting free speech against conduct in difficult deliberations over banning
(Victor, 2014). Victor (2014) suggests that it might be easier to end reparative therapeutic practices and the promise of practitioners to "cure"
homosexuals by using "existing state laws that forbid businesses and
professionals to engage in deceptive practices" (para. 6). Hopefully, the
end of reparative therapies is imminent.

Working to Support Sexual and Gender
Minority Youth: Exemplary Initiatives

Focusing on the comprehensive health and development of SGM youth
requires strategizing and networking that ground praxis as research-
informed practice in knowledge of these youths' needs, concerns,
challenges, desires, assets, and life goals. In this regard, accessible and
accommodative programming that supports SGM youth has to have an

emphasis on policy development as its precursor. This policymaking locates policy as protection and recognizes the inherent value of SGM youth, pinpoints their needs and concerns in terms of SGM health education (including mental health and sexual health education), and addresses victimization and violence by dealing with heterosexism, sexism, genderism, and homo/bi/transphobia as causes of distress in proximal and distal social environments (D'Augelli, 2002; Grace, 2007a; Grossman et al., 2009; Hatzenbuehler, 2011; Holmes & Cahill, 2004; Meyer, 2007; Sesma et al., 2005; Trotter, 2009). In developing and implementing initiatives to address the needs and concerns of SGM youth, such work must be located within a larger strategy that helps caring professionals and other caregivers build knowledge and understanding so they can develop positive dispositions and behaviours and provide the kinds of relationships, supports, and opportunities that SGM youth need to develop and be healthy (Grace, 2007a; Sesma et al., 2005). Initiatives for the healthy development and safety of SGM youth need to (1) educate caring professionals and caregivers about SGM identities, socialities, and cultures; (2) incorporate diverse theoretically and empirically informed strategies for helping youth build capacities and competence; and (3) include scenarios that respect and accommodate SGM youth (Jessor, Turbin, & Costa, 1998; Masten & Coatsworth, 1998). Here it is important to remember that the positive identity development of SGM youth is a non-linear and complex process that has to juxtapose a focus on vulnerable youth with a focus on addressing systemic issues such as heterocentrism, sexism, genderism, and homo/bi/transphobia, which threaten youth and affect their development (Johnson, 2008; Pianta & Walsh, 1998). In sum, initiatives that address the positive identity development and socialization of SGM youth should emphasize these elements:

- the development of sustained, strength-building relationships with parents or guardians, mentors, and peers that help empower youth;
- the involvement of a wide range of caring professionals and other adults as advocates and change agents; and
- interventions commonly required to abet inclusivity and safety in health-care and youth-care institutions, families, schools, faith spaces, and other everyday locations (Sesma et al., 2005). For example, in the case of gender-variant (GV) youth and their parents or guardians, interventions ought to include these components:
  ○ educational programming for caregivers and caring professionals that is informative about GV identities and the negative consequences of verbal or physical abuse on mental health;

- o psycho-educational programming for GV youth that teaches them that body changes aligned to their gender identities are possible but incremental over time;
- o other programming for GV youth that helps them manage conflict and stress related to gender identity and expression so they can live more fully as GV persons; and
- o training and development for counsellors, social workers, psychologists, and psychiatrists so they can be better caring professionals as they work with youth and their parents and other caregivers to help youth deal with psychological distress and avoid suicide ideation or attempts and other life-threatening behaviours (Grossman & D'Augelli, 2007).

Many SGM youth navigate their childhood and adolescence successfully. When supported by families, caregivers, peers, teachers, and other caring professionals and trusted adults, these youth often manage to avoid negative experiences or going through the motions of merely coping. They are better able to grow into resilience, as signified by a happy, healthy adulthood. However, some SGM youth experience significant discrimination, prejudice, violence, and other life stressors, which compromise their health and mental well-being. To address these difficulties and their degrees of impact, research and evidence-informed intervention strategies must not only address correlates and predictors of risk among SGM youth, but also critically investigate key protective and promotive factors such as supportive relationships (including positive peer, mentor, intimate partner, and family relationships), social contexts (including supportive school environments and educational attainment), and positive attributes (including realistic goal setting now and in the future) (Grace, 2008c). In this regard, Bronfenbrenner's (1979) ecological theory of development has been extensively applied in prevention efforts with vulnerable youth as a conceptual method to address and influence diverse interrelated developmental contexts that simultaneously influence youth identity development and behaviour. This theory can be viewed as involving three increasingly broad systems that directly or indirectly shape or influence youth development: (1) microsystems, which include familial, peer, and romantic relationships; (2) mesosystems, which include mass media culture as well as local neighbourhood, faith community, work, or school environments; and (3) macrosystems, which are broad overarching structures such as governing societal and cultural norms (Mustanski, Newcomb, Du Bois, et al., 2011).

Given these overlapping systems in which youth develop and mediate their various identities, intervention and prevention programs designed to support SGM youth should address key developmental factors and influences on them. These include the following:

- the issue of non-supportive families and their need to engage in skill building;
- relational issues such as a history of child sexual abuse, involvement in sex work, a lack of intergenerational relationships, and the hazards of navigating online communities;
- individual risk behaviours, including sensation-seeking behaviours, alcohol and drug use, depression and anxiety, impulsivity, compulsive sexual behaviour, and internalized homo/bi/transphobia;
- structural deficits such as a lack of SGM-inclusive school-based programs, policies, and comprehensive sexual health education; and
- societal difficulties such as institutionalized discrimination, stigma, and minority stress (Mustanski, Newcomb, Du Bois, et al., 2011).

As a result of these key health-related factors, the following policies, programs, and supports have been identified as useful based on the ways in which they address influences at the microsystem, mesosystem, and macrosystem levels. These examples also provide insights for programming that is comprehensive, innovative, and evidence-informed as it attends to such issues as self-efficacy, peer-to-peer learning as building agency, and building connections and community in SGM and other contexts.

Intervention and Prevention at the Microsystem Level

At the microsystem level, it is important that intervention and prevention emphasize relationship building so SGM youth experience a sense of connectedness and belonging. In this regard, relationships in familial and peer contexts are vital. These relationships can have biological and environmental parameters affecting the individual development and socialization of the SGM child (Corcoran & Nichols-Casebolt, 2004). Earlier, it was noted that the family ought to play an important and positive role in the identity development and socialization processes of SGM youth. However, it was also noted that the family as a hetero- and gender-normative social construction is generally unprepared to do so, exacerbating the vulnerability, dislocation, and isolation of these youth.

Thus, at the microsystem level, it is vital that intervention and outreach programs and strategies advance positive family relationships by helping families mediate family life in ways that enable parents and siblings to understand SGM family members and their differences and needs. The Family Acceptance Project provides a good example (Ryan, 2010).

THE FAMILY ACCEPTANCE PROJECT

(http://familyproject.sfsu.edu/home)

The Family Acceptance Project (FAP), which began in 2002, is a university-affiliated, research-based program designed to study families of SGM youth. This evidence-informed program is meant to strengthen families to help them come to terms with and provide support for their SGM and questioning children. The FAP goals include

- studying parent, caregiver, and family reactions when SGM youth disclose their non-normative identities;
- developing training and resources to support professional work in education, health care, social work, corrections, child welfare, and mental health so caring professionals and other caregivers can develop the skills, knowledge, and expertise to respond effectively to the needs of SGM youth and their families;
- developing resources to strengthen families to support SGM children;
- developing new models of family-related care to support positive health and mental health outcomes for SGM youth; and
- using research findings to inform policymaking and its implementation in inclusive practices in order to build responsive and inclusive systems of care.

As well, at the microsystem level, intervention and prevention strategies that help SGM youth to identify and strengthen key peer-group relationships are also important. Here supportive peer-group contexts such as SGM youth leadership camps, community youth groups, and gay-straight student alliances serve as critical interventions that can play a direct role in healthy identity development and socialization. In these peer-group contexts, emphases on personal, social, and cultural learning can help youth to deal with stressors and risky behaviours that may compromise their physical, mental, and sexual health. Two programs that the Institute for Sexual Minority Studies and Services operates – the SGM Youth Intervention and Outreach Worker program, described later, and Camp fYrefly, discussed in chapter 3 – provide good examples of this community work. In these safe social environments, youth have opportunities to identify and target issues related to depression, anxiety, drug and alcohol use, suicide ideation and attempts, sexually transmitted infections, eating disorders, and other sensation-seeking and impulsive behaviours that can be negative coping mechanisms for dealing with minority stress and related emotional difficulties. Here a focus on minority stress theory is informative, as it investigates the social impact of prejudice and discrimination on mental health issues, abilities to cope with stigma, and implications for policy and practice interventions in mental health service provision (Alessi, 2014). Minority stress theory can help frame LGBT-affirmative treatment modalities for clients, including those who are living with more than one minority identity, such as a racial/ethnic identity (Alessi, 2014).

SEXUAL AND GENDER MINORITY YOUTH INTERVENTION AND OUTREACH WORKER PROGRAM

(http://www.ismss.ualberta.ca)

The SGM Youth Intervention and Outreach Worker (YIOW) program, which was initiated at the University of Alberta in 2008, is a unique evidence-informed, community-based endeavour that allows SGM youth to have a centralized access point for advocacy and support. The YIOW works in both virtual (online) and real environments to connect these youth to supportive agencies and services in order to help them meet their unique social and health needs. In addition to providing individual supports, the YIOW works to address structural and community barriers to ensure that youth services include and respond to SGM youth. The YIOW also attempts to develop practices and training modules for youth-serving agencies that are sensitive to the heterogeneity of the SGM youth communities they serve.

While many youth-serving agencies understand the importance of developing cultural competency to ensure that their services reach and serve the needs of racially and ethnoculturally diverse minority youth,

SGM youth are seldom included and understood as a distinct but multivariate population in need of targeted supports, services, and outreach programs. As a result, these youth often remain invisible, forgotten, and underserved. The YIOW works with local community-based, non-profit, and governmental agencies to help them understand that SGM youth compose a complex group requiring an array of focused and targeted supports and services to help reduce health disparities, decrease risk exposure, and promote healthy development and community engagement.

THE FAMILY RESILIENCE PROJECT

The YIOW program moved into phase 2 – the Family Resilience Project, based on the Family Acceptance Project (Ryan, 2010) – in winter 2012. This project focuses on providing evidence-informed professional supports for SGM children and youth (under 25 years old), families, and community agencies in the Edmonton region. Referrals are accepted from school social workers, counsellors, family therapists, physicians, teachers, caseworkers, and parents. Self-referrals from youth are also accepted.

The program offers the following supports and services: (1) Individual and Family Counselling, which is short-term, solution-focused counselling for SGM children, youth, and their families, as they construct them; (2) PFLAG Support Group, which meets monthly at iSMSS to support, educate, and provide resources to parents, guardians, caregivers, friends, and significant adults in the lives of SGM youth; (3) Trans and Gender Questioning Youth Support Group, a peer-to-peer social/support group for youth that meets monthly at iSMSS; and (4) Professional Development, which consists of evidence-informed presentations and case consultations for staff in agencies in the Edmonton and Area Child and Family Services Authority who would like to build their professional capacity to support the health, mental health, safety, and socialization needs of SGM youth in their caseload.

In sum, the major goals of the Family Resilience Project are to (1) identify and strengthen protective and resilience-based factors for families to support their SGM children; (2) provide research knowledge, advocacy, and professional supports to help improve the health, mental health, educational attainment, safety, and emotional well-being of SGM children and youth; (3) create safe spaces for parents, guardians, caregivers, and youth to network with and learn from supportive peers so all can navigate the coming out and coming-to-terms processes effectively; (4) reduce homelessness and street involvement among SGM youth by helping parents, guardians, and caregivers to provide supportive and nurturing home and in-care environments; (5) inform public policy and community advocacy; and (6) develop new models of care, prevention, and family wellness to decrease risk factors for SGM youth, factors that compromise life opportunities and inhibit positive identity development (Ryan, 2010).

Intervention and Prevention at the Mesosystem Level

At the mesosystem level, the focus is on helping youth to engage in positive integration of their psychological, psychosocial, and cognitive development in media contexts and in the everyday environments of neighbourhoods, faith communities, workplaces, and schools. This includes feeling a sense of connection and belonging to SGM communities as sources of social support and community identity. Immediate social environments are crucial here (Corcoran & Nichols-Casebolt, 2004). SGM community involvement can enable youth to access specialized supports and services designed to address their unique risk factors and, in turn, help them grow into resilience.

These days, traditional understandings of community are changing, especially with the prevalence of the Internet and virtual online communities. In this regard, prevention, intervention, and treatment efforts will increasingly need to involve more effective utilization of emerging online social networks as key sites to promote the healthy individual and social development of SGM youth who may be seeking sexual health information or potential intimate partners online. Accordingly, SGM youth need to build critical media literacy awareness and personal negotiation skills. They also need access to non-judgmental comprehensive sexual health information, such as the policy and programmatic frameworks provided by UNESCO's (2009) guidelines on sexuality education, the Public Health Agency of Canada's (2014a, 2014b) SGM question-and-answer guides for schools, and the *It's All ONE Curriculum* toolkit for educators (Haberland & Rogow, 2011). Such resources can play an important role in helping SGM youth to become informed decision makers on issues that affect their physical, emotional, sexual, and mental health and well-being.

UNESCO – INTERNATIONAL TECHNICAL GUIDANCE ON SEXUALITY EDUCATION: AN EVIDENCE-INFORMED APPROACH FOR SCHOOLS, TEACHERS, AND HEALTH EDUCATORS

(http://unesdoc.unesco.org/images/0018/001832/183281e.pdf)

UNESCO published this two-volume scientific guide in 2009. Volume 1 provides a detailed rationale for comprehensive sexual health education, highlights key international conventions and agreements, and identifies evidence-informed characteristics of effective sexual health programs. Volume 2, a companion guide, focuses on how to incorporate key sexuality education topics and learning objectives into curriculum and programs designed for children and youth ages 5 to 18. These strategies represent benchmarks that can be adapted to local contexts for purposes of relevance, comprehensiveness, and programmatic evaluation. Importantly, these guides challenge inscribed heteronormative assumptions by bringing recognition to SGM realities and moving beyond pathology or a sole focus on abstinence-only education. These comprehensive documents recognize that behavioural interventions to promote positive sexual health outcomes need to occur simultaneously at individual, group, and community levels. This provides impetus to re-conceptualize how sexual health education should be planned, taught, and delivered to youth using a sexual and human rights framework.

PUBLIC HEALTH AGENCY OF CANADA

(http://www.phac-aspc.gc.ca)

In 1994, the Public Health Agency of Canada (PHAC) published the first edition of the *Canadian Guidelines for Sexual Health Education* to provide professionals working in the areas of sexual health education and health promotion with evidence-informed guidelines to develop, implement, and evaluate sexual health programs, policies, and related services and outreach activities. National feedback from these initial guidelines led to a series of revisions and identified the need for companion documents to provide more detailed information, evidence, and resources on specific sexual health issues. Consequently, in 2010 PHAC published the first resources specifically intended to address sexual orientation and gender identity issues in relation to school-aged populations. These documents, which are available in both French and English, are entitled *Questions & Answers: Sexual Orientation in Schools* (PHAC, 2014a) and *Questions & Answers: Gender Identity in Schools* (PHAC, 2014b).

As a series, the objectives of the 2008 edition of the *Canadian Guidelines for Sexual Health Education* (PHAC, 2008) and these two companion documents include

- making certain that comprehensive sexual health education is inclusive of the pressing health, safety, and educational needs of SGM youth;
- ensuring that the lived experiences of SGM youth are included in all facets of broadly based sexual health education;
- equipping educators, administrators, and school board personnel with a more thorough understanding of the realities of SGM youth; and
- including the health and safety needs of SGM youth in the goals and objectives of inclusive and comprehensive sexual health education.

These guidelines and companion documents embody the notion that comprehensive sexual health education must reflect the diverse needs and realities of all individuals in ways that are rights-based, age-appropriate, evidence-informed, culturally sensitive, and inclusive and respectful of sexual and gender minorities. They represent an important acknowledgment that it is the responsibility of all educators and service providers to address homophobia, transphobia, sexism, genderism, and heterosexism in their policies, programs, and services to make life better for SGM youth in their institutional settings and in the communities they serve.

POPULATION COUNCIL – *IT'S ALL ONE CURRICULUM*

(http://www.popcouncil.org)

This two-book toolkit, produced by the Population Council, identifies the key elements necessary for developing a rights-based, participatory, and gender-inclusive curriculum for comprehensive sexuality and HIV education (Haberland & Rogow, 2011). Book 1 highlights evidence-based policy arguments, provides 22 fact sheets, and includes 7 critical content units. Book 2 identifies effective teaching strategies, outlines 54 educational activities, and includes a detailed list of resources for further inquiry. Collectively, these materials are designed for curriculum planners, classroom teachers, and professional and community-based sexual health educators. The instructional methods at the centre of the curriculum are designed to support higher-order thinking, reflection, and evaluation among students. They also work to foster and support student-school connectedness. In sum, these two volumes engender a critical and integrated approach to the learning process by taking into account young people's social contexts, individual circumstances, and health outcomes in a holistic and interconnected approach to comprehensive sexual health education and health promotion. Of particular relevance to SGM youth, this toolkit encourages the critical deconstruction and challenging of gender norms, advances the right to access non-judgmental sexual health information and services, and positions sexual rights and human rights as fundamental to the health and well-being of all youth regardless of their actual or perceived differences. From this perspective, this toolkit provides an excellent model for creating new or evaluating existing sexual health education programs and services.

Intervention and Prevention at the Macrosystem Level

At the macrosystem level, the focus turns to analyses of structural and systemic factors that inhibit the ability of SGM youth to live safe, healthy, and productive lives. Youth are particularly vulnerable to the negative impacts of homo/bi/transphobia, sexism, heterosexism, and genderism and the ways these forces propagate hostile and discriminatory environments where anti-SGM attitudes and practices can compromise healthy identity formation. For SGM youth mediating systemic barriers and institutional negativity, the perception of stigma and the associated fears of rejection, violence, and victimization are critical factors that can lead to negative health outcomes. Thus interventions at the macrosystem level need to address structural and systemic factors and the associated and particular stressors that affect SGM individuals socially and culturally. Here social policymaking and the provision of resources and opportunities are vital (Corcoran & Nichols-Casebolt, 2004). Intervention efforts to reduce the cumulative impact of hostile environments and minority stress have to take broad and comprehensive system-level approaches. Good examples of this work include the Government of Québec's Policy Against Homophobia, the Government of Alberta's homophobic bullying resources, and the Canadian Teachers' Federation's sexual-orientation and gender-identity educational resources.

GOVERNMENT OF QUÉBEC'S POLICY AGAINST HOMOPHOBIA

(http://www.justice.gouv.qc.ca/english/ministere/dossiers/ homophobie/homophobie-a.htm)

This policy, the first of its kind in Canada, identifies the commitment of the Government of Québec to removing systemic barriers and obstacles to enable the full recognition, participation, and social equality of sexual and gender minorities in all areas of Québec society. This comprehensive policy identifies four overarching guidelines and supplementary strategic actions:

- recognizing the realities faced by SGM members of society, which includes challenging stereotypes, misinformation, and prejudice through direct education and research;
- promoting respect for the rights of SGM individuals, which includes addressing systemic barriers to full social recognition and participation by promoting individual rights and helping individuals to exercise those rights;
- promoting well-being, which includes
  - ensuring access to inclusive services through the provision of support for victims of homophobia;

- ○ adapting public services to become more inclusive of the needs of sexual and gender minorities; and
- ○ supporting community-based action to identify and respond to the needs and realities of SGM individuals; and
- guaranteeing a concerted approach by highlighting the commitment of the Government of Québec to lead the fight against homophobia through coordinated action in public institutions and collaboration with local and regional authorities and government partners.

GOVERNMENT OF ALBERTA'S HOMOPHOBIC BULLYING RESOURCES

(http://www.bullyfreealberta.ca/homophobic_bullying.htm)

In 2008, the Government of Alberta became the first provincial or territorial government in Canada to name homophobic bullying as a societal deterrent to the safety and inclusion of SGM youth. The government has provided resources to help make schools and communities safer spaces for SGM and questioning youth as well as for youth from same-gender-parented families who may be targeted for violence and victimization because of their family status. These innovative print and online resources define homophobic bullying as "bullying behaviours that are motivated by prejudice against a person's actual or perceived sexual orientation or gender identity" (Wells, 2008, para. 1). They discuss how to name, respond to, and act to intervene and prevent homophobic bullying from occurring. These resources include a printed fact sheet and detailed online resources for parents, coaches, and teachers. By being proactive in addressing homophobic bullying, the Government of Alberta is taking a significant step in challenging and changing prevailing societal norms that have entrenched institutional and societal discrimination, prejudice, and contempt directed towards SGM persons and their families. Leadership at the provincial level is significant in helping to create a society that values rather than fears diversity and difference.

CANADIAN TEACHERS' FEDERATION

(http://www.ctf-fce.ca/Documents/BGLTTPolicies - English.pdf)

In July 2004, the Canadian Teachers' Federation adopted a Policy on Anti-Homophobia and Anti-Heterosexism. This policy includes a comprehensive vision intended to make school cultures, climates, and curricula "safe, welcoming, inclusive, and affirming for people of all sexual orientations and gender identities" (CTF, 2004, p. 2). The creation of safe and inclusive teaching and learning environments relies on foundational core values that emphasize

- the role of educators as critical agents in creating positive societal change that addresses SGM realities;
- the ways that sexual minority persons are denied affirmation and accommodation when heterosexuality is assumed to be the only sexual orientation in the school environment; and
- the responsibility of the education system to prepare young people "to develop open, pluralistic and democratic societies, free of discrimination or aggression based on sexual orientation and gender identity" (CTF, 2004, p. 2).

The CTF published a series of French- and English-language resources to assist the implementation of this policy:

- *Seeing the Rainbow: Teachers Talk about Bisexual, Gay, Lesbian, Transgender, and Two-Spirited Realities* (CTF & ETFO, 2002);
- *Lessons Learned: A Collection of Stories and Articles about Bisexual, Gay, Lesbian, and Transgender Issues* (CTF, 2005);
- *Gay-Straight Student Alliance Handbook: A Comprehensive Resource for Canadian K-12 Teachers, Administrators, and School Counsellors* (Wells, 2006);
- *Challenging Silence, Challenging Censorship: Inclusive Resources, Strategies, and Policy Directives for Addressing Bisexual, Gay, Lesbian, Trans-Identified, and Two-Spirited Realities in School and Public Libraries* (Schrader & Wells, 2007); and
- *Supporting Transgender and Transsexual Students in K-12 Schools: A Guide for Educators* (Wells et al., 2012).

These CTF resources are critical to efforts to address the pervasive homo/bi/transphobia, sexism, genderism, and heterosexism that continue unabated in Canadian schools (Taylor & Peter et al., 2011). Like other students, SGM and questioning youth, as well as youth from same-gender-parented families, need to experience school connectedness and peer-group belonging. If schools remain hostile and unsafe spaces that leave these youth vulnerable as they grow and develop, then these youth will continue to face significant challenges and their health, well-being, and potential to be full and productive citizens will remain compromised and fragile.

Concluding Perspective: Sexual and Gender Minority Youth Are Not to Blame

This point cannot be made strongly enough: for being who they are and acting in the world, SGM youth are not to blame. Heterosexist, genderist systems and structures are to blame. Homo/bi/transphobes are to blame. Parents and other significant adults who don't get it and thus harm SGM youth are to blame. Educational, health-care, and other institutions that fail to recognize and accommodate SGM youth are to blame. And yet, as we have pointed out in this chapter, microsystems, mesosystems, and macrosystems can work for SGM youth. What we need are caring parents, caregivers, teachers, health-care professionals, and other significant adults with knowledge, understanding, and a desire to help that are translated into accommodative action.

The world is changing slowly, incrementally. However, every time an SGM youth self-harms, or worse, completes suicide, we need to speed up the change process of creating inclusive spaces in family, education, health-care, and social-service contexts where SGM youth can be affirmed as a crucial step in the process of affirming themselves. Here governments and government agencies need to be present and involved as caring institutions that support the work done in these spaces. This is also needed so SGM youth can grow up happy, healthy, and hopeful. This is what SGM youth need to survive and thrive.

InterText 10
David: *Stealth, but Living Trans Full-time*

David is thinking of studying psychology and working with queer youth. He feels that being a visible trans role model can be a support to youth questioning their gender positionality or transitioning. He knows the benefit such mentorship has had in steeling life and helping him to accept himself. David has come to conclusions that enable him to be himself and think about what is possible. He is growing more comfortable with living trans every day, and he wants to educate people about his experiences. Still he is cautious in the heterocentric, genderist world where heterosexual/homosexual and male/female binaries place limits on self-acceptance and possibility. In the queer world though, he is willing to be present and to mentor queer peers.

I'm a trans male who is also gay. In my everyday life, it's who I am, but it's not something that encompasses everything about me. People who know me are aware of it, but I don't go around saying, "Hey, everybody!" I work part-time for an airline. At work, people don't know, although we have conversations about coordinating outfits, so they probably wonder about me. I'm also a student doing a bachelor of arts in psychology, although I'm not super sure where it's all going. Still coming to school in Edmonton and being out on my own for the past year or so has helped me to grow in leaps and bounds. I'm okay with myself. When I share my story with other trans youth, I hope it helps to validate their experiences of being trans. I know I feel really lucky that I found out about trans and accepted myself when I did.

When I came out to my parents, I told them I was trans, but I never told them I was gay explicitly. I never said, "Hey, I'm gay." They know I have a boyfriend. I didn't think it was something I needed to say right out. Don't get me wrong. I like to be active in the queer community. I participate in Gay Pride and other community events. I was part of the gay-straight alliance back at my high school. I think it's important to be involved, but I don't think it's important to disclose certain things about myself. What I think is important is to share my experiences and educate people, and that's generally what I try to do. Some people don't want to ask questions because they don't want to offend you. But I say, "Seriously, ask me anything. If it's something I don't want to answer, I'll tell you." For the most part I'm cool with answering questions because it helps educate people, especially negative people who don't get it. Being out about my sexuality and gender identity and how who I am affects my daily life is something I've talked about when co-leading the trans workshop at Camp fYrefly. I think it's really important for people to know that there are other people going through similar things. I don't think my story or experiences are unique, but I've had other youth tell me that it's helped them a lot to hear me talk. If I can help at least one or two other people, then it might inspire them to help other people. It could lead to a chain reaction.

For me, coming out as a sexual person was really difficult because I've never been attracted to women. As a kid I thought, "I'm a young female who's attracted to boys. That's the way it's supposed to be." So being FTM and being attracted to guys was so weird to me. Still I always felt this connection to gay rights. I remember feeling it was something *so* important when they started to talk about gay marriage in Canada. I remember thinking, "I know this doesn't affect me personally, but it feels like it does." I felt like I should be a part of it. Still it took quite a while for me to realize that I was not living in the right body. I never felt like I was a lesbian, but as an FTM trans person I know I'm a gay man. Yet the two – being gay and being trans – are so separate. I could always date boys. I didn't need to change myself physically to do that. Many people don't get that. They just don't understand the concept of gay trans person. They say, "You went through all the trouble to become a man, and now you're gay." They just don't understand the differences, and they will likely never get me. Now I'm dating another FTM trans person. I never thought I would simply because I have a hard time dealing with it myself sometimes. I didn't know how I could be a support for somebody else. Being trans is a difficult thing, a huge thing. You really can't just set it aside. But it's been good to have someone who understands the kinds of things you're going through. He's further along in his transition than me, and he can answer questions I have based on his experience.

In terms of me being visibly queer, I have a very limited number of rainbow things. I have one wristband that has a small rainbow on it.

When I am in my hometown, I pull it under my sleeve when I go out of the house. That's because I fear for my safety in that small town with 18,000 people and an oil field. It's also a farming kind of town. I had one situation in high school where people were talking about trans. They were saying, "If you were a guy dating someone and you found out that she used to be a man, does that make you gay?" I wanted to comment on the situation, but I knew because of the subject matter they would say, "Well, what are you?" I didn't want to be called out on it. It was a frustrating situation for me because I wanted to say, "You are so not even getting it." It wouldn't be worth it to speak out though because it would just cause trouble for me. It could put me in danger.

I live with my mom and dad and my younger sister. She's three years younger than me, so she's 15 years old. My dad was born in Alberta and my mom is from the Philippines. She moved to Canada when she was about 20 years old. My sister and I were raised Catholic. I never found it to be a negative thing. I'm not Catholic myself, but I am Christian. My mom instilled a lot of morals in us growing up, which was good. She has a lot of traditional Catholic values, especially coming from the Filipino community. It was interesting when I came out. I told my sister first. Then I told friends, feeling out the situation. Mom was upset that I didn't tell her first but, for me, it was a case of it's easier to make new friends than it is to make a new mom. I understood where she was coming from since being trans is something I was going through and I didn't come to her – my mom. But I came out to her last because I wanted to be sure about being trans and that she and my dad would accept me. It was really hard because I had grown up my whole life knowing my parents had expectations for me. And then you realize this thing and you wonder, "Now what?" You're in totally uncharted territory. So when I came out, I wrote letters to my parents. I hadn't intended to write letters. I did try to do it face-to-face when I sat on the couch with my dad while my mom was at work. We sat there for about two and a half movies. I thought, "Okay, I'll tell him," but I couldn't do it. I was coming to Edmonton the next day, so I decided to write letters to them and leave them behind. I'm actually really glad I did because I was able to get everything I wanted to say out without them interrupting me or without me stammering or being super nervous. My dad was pretty chill about it, but my mom was upset. She's really cool about it now, but initially she said, "We should have taken you to a psychiatrist so we could catch it and fix it." I know she had good intentions because a mom wants to take care of her child. My family doctor who is so supportive and awesome referred me to a trans specialist. It took six months to get to see him after the referral, and my mom came with me. She wanted to know, "What did I do? Where did I go wrong?" She's learned so much. We're now able to talk about trans, and the fact that we can talk is a good sign. We never used to be able to talk about it without having a shouting match. Then a while ago when she asked me about something, she spewed off the whole LGBTQ thing. I was really impressed. She's done a lot of research. When I came to camp last year, I initially told her that Camp fYrefly is a youth leadership camp, but I didn't tell her it was for queer youth. I didn't know how she'd react and I figured, "I'm 18. I can go and do it myself." But she researched the camp and told me, "Oh, yeah. I was talking about it with my friend." She was really glad that I could go to camp for people that are going through a coming-out process. She's growing comfortable in leaps and bounds because she's learning about me. Up until last year we didn't even talk about trans because she thought if you ignore it, then it doesn't really exist. My dad never really had any problems with it, but for the most part he just doesn't like to argue with my mom because she just doesn't concede. But so much has changed for the better this past year. I'm starting hormones in two weeks. My family is super supportive now, which is pretty decent since, initially, I was so afraid that they would not be there for me. Dad is still more in the background because my mom is just the one who does everything. She calls me DJ because she thinks it's cute. When I decided on my name, I told her, "I've chosen David. This is what I want." Then I said, "I'll let you choose my middle name." She picked Joseph. It's super Catholic, so I think she's happy with that.

My sister and I are really close and she's always been super open-minded. For her, having a trans brother is no big deal. I'm really glad because so many kids her age, especially in our hometown, are judgmental and close-minded. I'm also really glad that she's being an advocate. She's part of the gay-straight alliance that 6 or 7 of us started at our high school when I was in grade 11. I got involved with the GSA because there wasn't any kind of safe space. We promoted our GSA by saying, "This is a safe space where you can come and talk about whatever things are on your mind and be in the company of people who are going through the same messy stuff as you." We really just tried to promote education. The first time I talked about being transgendered was at a GSA meeting. When I told my story, people were so glad to learn about things that I had gone through and to have a place to share their own experiences. In the beginning though, it was a difficult process even to be allowed to meet. We did have one teacher who had always been really open-minded and supportive. He let us use his classroom to have our meetings. The principal is also a really good guy. He was so supportive and fought for us, even after a few teachers and some parents sent him nasty emails. In order to get our GSA, our request to meet had to be approved by the school board. We had to go and talk to them so we could get permission to gather as a student group. But the thing is if it had been a Bible study group, we wouldn't have had to do any of that. It was just because it was a gay-straight alliance. Once we were allowed to meet, it was a bit difficult to get people to come to the meetings because our town is small. Even if students were straight allies, they didn't want to attend because they might be harassed for seeming to be gay. Now, it's better, with about 20 students attending regularly. Still there were several student and community petitions to shut us down during the first few months. And we often had our posters advertising our meetings ripped down. We called our GSA *Stand Up* and our posters simply stated "Stand Up on Wednesday in Room #." They didn't really have anything gay on them, but students still vandalized them. Our fearless GSA leader kept a stack of posters in her locker, and every single day she would just put them back up. Despite experiences of discrimination in our school and town, the GSA still exists three years later. That's amazing.

I'm at a point in my life now where I'm passing all the time, so I don't know how okay I am with people knowing. It's not something I put out there because it's easier to survive if I don't. In a situation like Camp fYrefly it's totally cool to be out, but in daily life I'm stealth because I'm passing. If I had a more feminine voice, perhaps then it would be something that I would explain more just because more people would ask. Living trans is a challenge. When I first found out about transgender when I was 14, I thought, "This sounds like what I've been thinking about. I've been having similar feelings for quite a while." I looked into it and did a lot of research, but then I thought, "I'm 14 years old. What do I know?" I pushed it back and I was in denial for about two more years. I forced myself to be more feminine, to wear skirts and do the whole makeup thing. I didn't want other people to make fun of me because they always made fun of the girls who weren't as feminine. I didn't want to be called *butch*. Then the summer before grade 10, I shaved my head. It had gotten to the point where I wasn't okay on a daily basis and wearing girls' clothing actually caused me physical pain. It was just such a huge lie. I couldn't deal with it anymore, so I just started coming out to my friends and living trans full-time. Since I came out and started accepting that I am trans, I feel so much better about myself. That's not to say it's easy. When you're a young trans person, there's stigma and there's a lot of biased information out there. If you're not doing it *this way* you're not trans enough, or you're not doing it right. There are many FTM people who are trying to be hyper-masculine, really butch. I did try to wear lumberjack clothes and loose pants. But that wasn't me. Finally, after a struggle I accepted me: "Okay, I'm trans. I'm a boy. That's cool." I'm happier now.

8 Gay-Straight Alliances and the Quest for Recognition and Accommodation in Canadian Schools

WITH KRISTOPHER WELLS

In this chapter we focus on sexual and gender minority youth as a diverse and vulnerable constituency in Canadian schools. This multivariate population is frequently subjected to heterosexism, sexism, genderism, and homo/bi/transphobic bullying that covers the gamut from symbolic violence, including derisive name calling and defamatory graffiti, to physical violence, including assault and battery or worse (Grace, 2007a, 2010; Grace et al., 2010; Grace & Wells, 2001, 2007a, 2007b, 2007c; PHAC, 2006; Taylor & Peter et al., 2011). With regard to this damage, Trotter (2009) relates, "If [teachers as] professionals could help young people to resist stereotypical classifications and tolerate ambiguities around gender and sexuality, harassment and bullying in schools may be greatly reduced" (p. 19). Indeed teachers as gay-straight alliance (GSA) club advisers can advocate for SGM students, educating teacher colleagues and the entire student population as they share knowledge about SGM issues and concerns (McCabe, 2014). In doing so, they can build a foundation to create support systems that help vulnerable SGM youth to grow into resilience through instrumental, social, and cultural skill building and SGM-dedicated teacher and peer mentoring (Reyes & Elias, 2011; Sharkey et al., 2008). This work includes ensuring that GSAs create opportunities for belonging in junior and senior high schools. As David's InterText indicates, SGM youth want GSAs to be safe spaces where they can connect with peers to advocate and educate in order to enhance belongingness. This can have positive effects on achievement and mental health for SGM youth who may experience safer and more SGM-congenial environments, with less physical and verbal anti-SGM victimization and more visible and supportive school personnel (Heck et al., 2014; McCabe, 2014; Scharrón-del Río et al., 2014). In a larger community context, St. John at al. (2014), investigating the social and political contexts of GSAs in Waterloo Region, Ontario, found that GSAs could function regionally to connect youth inside and beyond their schools, creating opportunities for youth to interact with the wider SGM community and building a support system using resources from community agencies, school districts, and the Ontario Ministry of Education. They found this involvement enhanced the capacity and sustainability of GSAs. It may also help to build community resilience within and beyond GSAs as youth access community-based resources to help them adapt and thrive in the face of individual, social, and environmental risks (Aisenberg & Herrenkohl, 2008). When a GSA builds community resilience, this is sociocultural capital that helps the community to mobilize, experience connectedness, garner resources, and adapt with an eye to sustainability (Ungar, 2011). GSAs then grow as communities in Ungar's (2011) sense of community as a group of individuals, with significant degrees of commonality in identities, interests, and culture, who socialize, provide mutual support, share resources, and engage in action to benefit one and all.

These constructions of community and community resilience are not common realities though in Canada, where SGM youth often experience schools as danger zones where school administrators, counsellors, and teachers can neglect them, leaving them to select truancy, quitting school, running away, drug and alcohol abuse, and suicide ideation, attempts, and completions as perceived escapes from trauma (Grace & Wells, 2005, 2009; Liebenberg & Ungar, 2009; Marshall & Leadbeater, 2008; Murphy, 2012; Taylor, 2010; Taylor & Peter et al., 2011; Tonkin et al., 2005). Indeed it is likely that SGM youth have been more wounded by schooling than any other student constituency. Moreover, it may be up to them to make life in schools better *now*. In this regard, GSAs can be a primary social space for youth to engage in social action and cultural work to help achieve this goal. As Wexler et al. (2009) maintain, GSAs can provide SGM youth with a group identity and an affiliation that can be self-empowering and a springboard for framing and engaging in collective action. Still, in relation to building community and self-resilience, these researchers say more studies are required to (1) clarify why SGM youth join or avoid participating in GSAs, (2) comprehend how youth across sexual and gender differences function in GSAs, and (3) understand how involvement in GSAs influences comprehensive health.

Calling on SGM youth to be creative change agents in their schools, queer Canadian storyteller and performance artist Ivan Coyote (2012) proclaims, "I know that school is still a fucked-up place to be queer" (p. 89). In a message to SGM youth, they – the pronoun that Coyote uses to name and locate their gender-transgressing self – declare, "[I]t is up to all of us to make it better, for ourselves, and for others, too. Always remember that working to make schools safer for queer students, or bisexual students, or gender nonconforming students, is not a selfish act. Creating a safe school for yourself will only lead to a safer school for everyone and everyone deserves a safe place to learn in" (Coyote, 2012, p. 88). In an incremental way then, every youth can contribute to the sum of safety in schools for all SGM youth, who may also be dealing with racial, ethnocultural, class, ability, and other differences. As Coyote (2012) remarks, "Bullies are almost always outnumbered by the bullied. We just need to organize" (p. 89). Harnessing the power of the bullied can make life in schools better *now*. The steeling effects of bullying can enable the bullied to become cultural workers and change agents who create safe spaces, raise consciousness, and mobilize the SGM youth collective to hold principals, teachers, and others with vested interests in education accountable. The subtitle to Savage and Miller's (2012) edited book, *It Gets Better*, makes this clear: it gets better by *Coming Out, Overcoming Bullying, and Creating a Life Worth Living*.

In this chapter we look at complexities of schooling for SGM students and explore gay-straight alliance clubs as part of a solutions approach to recognizing, respecting, and accommodating these students so life in schools can be improved for this historically disenfranchised diverse population. We begin by discussing what GSAs are, how they function, and what enables or deters their presence and activities in schools. We reinforce certain points by interspersing youth perspectives from iSMSS research conducted with SGM youth. Next we provide a synopsis of the struggle to establish GSAs in Catholic schools in Ontario, discussing Catholic perspectives and politics at play and analysing the provincial government's response during the months leading up to passing Bill 13, the Accepting Schools Act. We follow this with a focus on homo/bi/transphobia in schools in the larger Canadian context coupled with a discussion of the concomitant need for GSAs as part of making life in schools better *now* for SGM youth. Then we turn to the research literature to synthesize evident trends into research "moments" or phases in the emergence of GSAs in K-12 schools in North America. We conclude by encouraging SGM students to dream and then do it, providing them with pointers for creating effective and sustainable GSAs.

Why Gay-Straight Alliances?

The process of coming out and coming to terms creates an array of challenges for both the individual development and the socialization of SGM youth. Dealing with the complexities of one's own sexual and gender identities and their intersections with other power relationships can mean that SGM youth put socialization on hold until they feel ready (Adams, 2006; DiFulvio, 2011; Reyes & Elias, 2011). Then finding a supportive peer network can take time (Anderson, 1998; D'Augelli, 1998; DiFulvio, 2011). Some SGM youth wait until high school is over to find this network because they witness homo/bi/transphobia as a harsh and intricate antisocial reality that makes schools hostile and unsafe ecologies where hate incidents and other forms of symbolic and physical violence run rampant (Adams, 2006). Adams (2006) details reasons some SGM youth shared regarding their choices to either stay closeted or come out:

> [SGM youth who] did not come out in high school [said it was] because the atmosphere was too conservative, the environment was too heteronormative in its expectations, they were afraid of being judged and gossiped about, or because they were still struggling with their sexual orientation. Those who did come out to others in high school did so even though they reported that they had learned to be cautious about who they came out to, were afraid of being bullied, and, for those in religious schools, were afraid of how the school administration would react to them. (pp. 105–6)

In sum, SGM youth often experience some level of estrangement from school as well as family and other hetero- and gender-normative social systems that are usually unthinking and unprepared when it comes to facilitating the socialization of SGM youth who, as a consequence, "become socialized to hide" (Hunter & Mallon, 2000, p. 232). Since supportive networks develop slowly, SGM students need community peer-to-peer programs, which can serve as sites for social support and social learning about individual and community identities, problem-solving strategies, and ways to deal with victimization, move forward, and grow into resilience (Bernard, 1992; Dane, 2005; D'Augelli, 2002, 2003; Grace, 2009a, 2009b; Grace & Wells, 2007a, 2007b, 2007c). This need for community supports is largely because SGM youth often experience schooling, and indeed family and faith group environments, as disconnected from their realities and largely silent on issues of sexuality and gender identity (Cagle, 2007). As a primary social site intended to assist individual development and socialization, the school should be an easier space than family or faith group for SGM youth to connect and build knowledge and understanding of their sexual and gender identities, or so one might anticipate. Historically, however, schools have replicated a hetero-patriarchal, genderist status quo and allowed homo/bi/transphobia in symbolic forms like bathroom graffiti and verbal slurs and overt forms like bullying and stalking to go unchecked. Moreover, curricular and extracurricular components of schooling have historically presumed that heterosexuality is normative and being biologically male or female is the whole story of gender. Schools have much to unlearn in the process of becoming safer spaces where SGM youth are fully recognized, respected, and accommodated. To make this happen, there must be available and used resources and supports as well as comprehensive policies enacted in programming that reflects SGM-inclusive schooling.

To mediate queer life in schools, SGM youth often deal with profound trauma exceeding the usual drama and growing pains that mark adolescent lives. In discussing defence mechanisms that gay and lesbian youth use as precursors to identifying as a member of a sexual minority, Butler and Astbury (2008) note these youth employ diverse strategies, including compartmentalization (separating same-sex orientation from other facets of their lives), suppression (not dealing with same-sex affiliative needs and desires), compensation (being hopeful about the future by coping with homophobia now), and sublimation (being a high achiever to divert attention away from having a sexual minority identity). For the most part, these coping strategies can contribute to the isolation and invisibility that these youth equate with being safe. However, coping strategies like compartmentalization and suppression rearticulated from a trans perspective are unlikely options for trans-spectrum youth because gender identity is very focused on recognition and accommodation around visibility and expression. Interestingly, there is a trend towards greater visibility and more consistent participation of transgender students in GSAs, which appears associated with reduced absenteeism for this population (Greytak, Kosciw, & Boesen, 2013; Scharrón-del Río et al., 2014). Indeed GSAs may be a more important support and resource for them than for cisgender LGB youth (Scharrón-del Río et al., 2014), with cisgender a descriptor for "[i]dentifying with the gender assigned to you at birth" (Marx, 2011, p. 7). Thus GSAs need to be enhanced as sources of information on trans-spectrum issues for transgender and cisgender students and school staff (Greytak et al., 2013). In advancing trans-spectrum inclusion here, it is important to "recognize how the needs of transgender youth may be both similar to and different from the needs of cisgender peers" (p. 60), which requires consideration of the impacts of gender segregation on participating in physical education, using bathrooms and locker rooms, and formulating culturally gender-normative dress codes (Greytak et al., 2013). From these various perspectives, social connectedness can be particularly important in enabling SGM youth to grow into resilience (DiFulvio, 2011; Gastic & Johnson, 2009). DiFulvio (2011) credits social connectedness with youth having a sense of belonging in terms of friendships and solidarity based on shared experiences and struggles. In this regard, a GSA can provide "a consistent forum," a public sharing and mentoring space, which youth in DiFulvio's study described as "important to their sense of self and sense of safety in the world" (p. 1615).

Peers and even teachers often make presumptions and damage young SGM lives. In this regard, students interviewed at Camp fYrefly sites in Alberta and Saskatchewan shared these stories innervated with their fears and anxieties about being and belonging in school contexts:

Evan: I think it's incredibly important to have nurturing adults that are queer friendly or an ally. I grew up in the Catholic school system, so I faced a lot of homophobia. There were a few teachers that I got really close with – I was a pretty dedicated student – and I would develop good relationships with them. For example, in high school I finally had one teacher that would let us talk about gay rights in social studies. For me, that was huge, and I think it was paramount to my academic success. I think that if I didn't have a resource like that, there is a chance that I would not have done nearly so well and would not have pursued post-secondary.

But earlier on I had this other social studies teacher that I was really close with and she rigged the scheduling so that I would be in her class. We got along great, and I learned really well from her. I remember that we were doing current events and that was when gay marriage was legalized. I remember she said, "Isn't that sick?" And to me that felt like I had hit a wall head first – really heavy and really hard – because that was pretty much like my teacher saying, "Aren't you sick?"

Zach: I don't know – there was just a moment where it clicked. I never knew any gay people or any openly gay people, and I didn't have access to information. I used to go – I'm not going to lie – I used to go on adult websites because I didn't know any gay people, and I didn't really have any friends in the school I went to either.

The school I went to had about 800 people and, generally, the people were really similar. There wasn't much diversity and they would just bug me about every possible thing. They were constantly criticizing me. Yeah, it was just so constant that I just believed everything everybody said. I thought I was just really useless. My self-esteem – I didn't have any.

I didn't like the way I came out at my school because I was actually outed by my best friend. I didn't want anybody to know because it was a really bigoted environment, and they didn't like me and I didn't like them. I had been slowly coming out to people I cared about, but being out in school was just a bad experience. After I came out, I was bullied about my sexuality. I just had a really bad year. I stopped going to school and I got really depressed. It was just a really scary year.

At the place I'm at now, I'm really happy being out. I haven't had any trouble with it, and the people who know – I care about them a lot. I'm more free to be myself, I guess. I think that you should try to branch out. You're going to feel like you're alone in your community, but I think sometimes you have to connect with other communities in order to get help because if I hadn't done that, I don't know.

Josh: I had great friends, but when I was young I was picked on because I was the weird one. They said I'm a fag and called me names. They still use that name sometimes. I was picked on a lot when I was young.

Helen: My worst point was when I was in elementary school. I was picked on – just mercilessly bullied. I had no friends. My nickname was Ellen. It was right around the time when Ellen DeGeneres came out. Since my nickname was Ellen, I must've been a lesbian. Elementary school was brutal. When you're 12 and you're questioning your sexuality, and you're being called a lesbian and that's a "bad" thing – well, that was tough.

That was part of why I left the more traditional education model. For high school, I went to a nontraditional school. There was a group of us who were the kids who had been bullied or teased to the point that we did not want to be in the traditional school system. I grew up in an Edmonton suburb. It's pretty WASP and there's not a lot of acceptance for anything that doesn't fit into that box. Most of the time I would walk down the hallway and I would hear people laughing behind me. Or I'd hear people pointing and whispering at me.

By high school I had kind of learned to deal with it. I had more support and resilience behind me. I had learned how to deal with a lot of those issues, so I was fine by that point.

Shawn: I had a rough experience in junior high, coming out in grade 9. I had told a friend I thought I could trust about how I was feeling about myself in terms of sexuality. For whatever reason, she felt the need to tell everyone else. And you know, word spreads quickly, and it was a Catholic school. I had some support from my peers during that, but I was dealing with a lot of homophobia and harassment. I didn't see any teacher acknowledge what was happening. No teacher came up to me to talk about it or even kind of broach the subject. There were a lot of rumours about me. I didn't feel like I had an outlet for support at all. Queer was invisible, even when people were out. I was in a position of being very fearful of what could happen to me. I was scared to walk home after school. I just didn't know what would happen to me.

Ryan2: At school I faced a lot of bullying, mostly from this one group of kids all through school. They were about the same age as my younger brother and all through elementary school, middle school, and junior high they teased me and my brother – me for being effeminate and my brother for having red hair. The abuse was mainly verbal – a lot of verbal. I was never physically hurt, though they would throw stuff at me like a pencil or candy or whatever. No one ever threw a punch, so I'm really grateful for that. I've never gotten into a fight about it. It was always a lot of verbal abuse.

In high school I came out to maybe five people. Then I made this speech in class. It was all over school, like Ryan just gave a speech about how he chooses to come out and stuff. It was fun. Then I led the Day of Silence in my school. We didn't have a GSA like city kids, or anything really, so I really liked the Day of Silence. I think it was a really great day to honour people who still can't speak out. I made little cards saying what the day was about and why I was participating in it. I made posters and told all the teachers. I had a lot of students that participated, too. It was really great. I did that for three years after I gave my speech.

I graduated in 2008 from high school in a place in northern Alberta about two and a half hours south of the Northwest Territories. It kind of sucked because I didn't have anyone to connect with there. I really felt like the only gay in the village. It was really hard growing up there, but I've dealt with that, and I made it through.

These realities provide more than enough justification for gay-straight alliances so SGM youth and allied peers have a safe space to learn about and validate their differences as they deal with the tide of homo/bi/transphobic bullying in formal schooling. GSAs are school-based clubs that can act as sites for students to (1) build knowledge and understanding of their sexual and gender identities within a process of affirming themselves and others – queer and straight; (2) communicate and socialize in a safe and accommodating environment where they are supported and affirmed by teachers and other students; (3) learn about ways to garner respect and support for the many sexual and gendered ways of being, becoming, belonging, and acting in the world; and (4) emerge as proactive change agents as they connect and collaborate with peers and significant adults. In this regard, GSAs are a "strategy of resilience" for SGM youth (Scourfield et al., 2008, p. 332). Having access to GSAs in schools can accelerate processes of making connections with peers and building a community where youth participants can share, develop social and self-understanding, socialize, and find pertinent supports. In this supportive milieu, youth can speak about oppression-induced trauma and understand the debilitating effects of homo/bi/transphobia, thus enabling socialization in the context of finding a place in SGM communities, understanding community norms and values, and participating in activities that advance their interests (Adams, 2006; Anderson, 1998; Balsam, 2003; Bringaze & White, 2001).

At the personal and peer levels, GSAs provide a social site for SGM youth to unlearn the negative lessons of homo/bi/transphobia and learn new lessons about queer integrity and possible ways of mediating everyday life. GSAs comprise sociocultural ecologies that enable connection, collaboration, and relationship among SGM youth who can (1) bond with empathetic peers and significant adults; (2) have a safe and supportive space to speak out and deal with negative societal and cultural imaging; (3) engage in social activities that build understanding of queer community ethics; (4) build social competencies and problem-solving skill sets; and (5) participate in advocacy initiatives that help the SGM student collective to build a self-affirming and cohesive community of difference about what it means to be, become, belong, and act queer in the world (Adams, 2006; Anderson, 1998; Balsam, 2003; Bernard, 1992; D'Augelli, 1998; Friedman-Nimz et al., 2006; Grossman et al., 2009; Meyer, 2007; Perrin et al., 2004; Taylor & Peter et al., 2011). In sum, GSAs provide "interpersonal support, leadership development, advocacy training, and recreation" (Russell, Horn, Kosciw, & Saewyc,

2010, p. 11). Here two more Camp fYrefly youth who participated in our Institute's research program share their stories of the utility of being actively involved in their GSAs:

> *Erica:* Another thing that really helped was the GSA at my school. We had a really good student leader and he really helped me be who I was. That helped me become the person I am today. I wanted to be in my GSA since I was in grade 9, but I wasn't able to take an active role until the second half of grade 10. Then, throughout grade 10 and 11, I kind of trained to be the next leader. It was a lot of fun. In grade 11, near the end of the year, I was on the committee to plan a GSA Pride Parade float. Then through grade 12 I did try to keep the GSA going.

> *Derek:* I didn't go to my GSA at first, partly because I was probably still questioning myself on how I felt. In my grade 11 year – at about the middle of the school year – I finally started coming out to my friends that I was gay. They were all very accepting, and I had very good experiences with everyone. I think the worst experience I had was some people asking, "Why didn't you tell me first?" So I was pretty lucky in that sense. For the rest of the year things went smoothly.
>
> I think I really became strong when I was in my grade 12 year. That is when I really became comfortable with myself. That was also my first year going to the *Breaking the Silence* [queer community] conference in Saskatoon. During that year I was sort of the leader person for our gay-straight alliance club and I had two wonderful people backing me up the entire year. We went around to all the different high schools in the city and did presentations to their gay-straight alliances. We went to our school board and I hosted a two-day student leadership workshop. We also sat down and came up with a presentation that we could make to the grade 9 wellness classes in our school. We went and asked the teachers if they would be comfortable with us coming and presenting to their classes, and they all said yes. We had one class in the first semester and we did all four of the grade 9 classes in the second semester. The kids were actually really receptive to it. You could tell the difference in them between the start and end of the session.
>
> We had a lot of supportive teachers at our school. We had a number of openly gay teachers, and the principal that we had was an open lesbian as well. That was also very supportive to have. It was a very good thing.

GSAs can be a bellwether of the degree to which schools are safe, caring, and inclusive spaces that attend to sexuality and gender in policy and practice. As Griffin, Lee, Waugh, and Beyer (2004) relate, "Understanding what GSAs do and how their activities are or are not integrated into other efforts to address safety issues is key in understanding the complexities of addressing gender and sexuality in schools" (p. 10). When they act as vibrant and nurturing ecologies, GSAs help fulfil an important social need to belong as SGM students learn lessons in self and group cohesion and protection. This locates GSAs as buffer zones (O'Conor, 1994). Dane (2005) explains, "Feelings of support and commonality provided by one's own in-group can work to buffer the stressful effects of rejection from a more powerful out-group" (p. 24). In addition to this buffering function, GSAs have other roles. They offer counselling and support, provide a safe space with access to safe people, and engage in consciousness raising through education and building awareness within the group and in the school at large (Griffin et al., 2004; Grossman et al., 2009; Scourfield et al., 2008). When they work well, GSAs can positively affect students' feelings of safety and security, their academic performance, and their sense of accomplishment in their schools and communities (Griffin et al., 2004). Indeed GSAs can be a protective factor in the schooling experience that abets positive development of SGM youth: "GSA presence, GSA participation, and perceived GSA effectiveness in promoting school safety in adolescence [is significantly associated] with psychological well-being [and educational attainment] for LGBT young adults" (Toomey, Ryan, Diaz, & Russell, 2011, p. 176).

However, GSAs are no cure-all for homo/bi/transphobia in schools. As Griffin et al. (2004) conclude, "[W]hen the GSA is the sole agent for such activism, it is questionable how much systemic or even personal change can occur or continue. Without participation and leadership of other adults and students, addressing LGBT issues can become marginalized" (p. 19). This emphasizes the need for a collective, school- and community-wide effort to address systemic and structural issues that perpetuate victimization of SGM students in classrooms and corridors. At best, in the larger scheme of things, the GSA meeting room may only provide a temporary safe space. Moreover, as Toomey et al. (2011) report, "[It is likely] that high levels of school victimization eliminate the benefits of GSA participation" (p. 181). Significantly, they add, "[It is also] a disturbing possibility that GSA participants who experience high levels of LGBT school harassment may be at greatest risk for lifetime suicide attempts" (p. 181). To move towards more SGM-inclusive schools, principals and teachers need professional development, schools need functional policies implemented in attendant programming, and all students need to be educated to overcome ignorance, fears, and stereotypes in the work to transgress homo/bi/transphobia and transform schools so they can be SGM-supportive and accommodative spaces. This work for equity starts with school principals, who need to be supportive change agents as a precursor to teachers and students also becoming change agents to alter heteronormative school cultures and transform schools as safe spaces for all (Grace, 2007a).

While some might prefer that GSAs, if they have to exist, function as social sites, by virtue of the critical fact that education is political, GSAs constitute political sites as well. Indeed GSAs can provide a sociopolitical space for SGM students, allied students, and supportive school administrators and teachers engaging in grass-roots activism to resist heterocentrism and genderism in schooling, challenge institutional homo/bi/transphobia, and work to transform schools to be truly inclusive of sexual and gender minorities (Grossman et al., 2009; Russell, 2005). In their study of trans-spectrum youth, Jones and Hillier (2013) found that these youth engaged in activism to counter being abused in school, which suggests they are human and civil rights activists who can steel life, become empowered, and grow into resilience. Schindel (2008) speaks to this work as *"mobilizing education,* with an intended dual meaning: Youth are mobilizing people and resources directly within schools, as well as creating greater impact through their own increased mobility within these increasingly networked spaces" (p. 57, italics in original). From this perspective, GSAs enable SGM youth and their supporters to affiliate in environments where they can address societal conventions and stigmatization regarding sexuality and gender, and where they can build SGM community cohesiveness by understanding and validating one another's emotions and experiences as a starting point for responding to discrimination and coping well (Meyer, 2007; Perrin et al., 2004; Russell, 2002). As participatory and communicative sites, GSAs can be places where SGM youth share ideas with one another and consider ways to interconnect school, family, faith group, workplace, and community in ways that foster further socialization and expand social networks (Cagle, 2007; Hunter & Mallon, 2000). This can help SGM youth to experience greater coherence as they set goals and mediate life across these social spaces (Cagle, 2007). To be more effective though, social networking has to be expanded to position GSAs as school-based youth organizations that operate in the intersection of power relationships, attending to racial, ethnocultural, class, and other differences. During their brief history, GSAs have tended to help SGM youth who are predominantly white, middle class, and suburban (Holmes & Cahill, 2004). In the future, GSAs have to include a broader public because matters of sexual orientation and gender identity are influenced by culture and the diverse subjectivities positioning students. The core work of GSAs will be enhanced by more collaborative work with students and teachers engaged in anti-racism, anti-sexism, and other anti-oppression projects that align with the GSA's anti-homo/bi/transphobia project (McCready, 2004).

GSAs ultimately have to be about changing systems and structures associated with institutional homo/bi/transphobia and countering the surrounding silences and inaction. Locating GSAs as communities of support and advocacy for SGM youth and their allies, Russell (2002) relates, "GSAs provide settings in which the foundation is set for empowerment, activism, and community engagement. Further study of these and other youth-initiated settings will provide ... important insights into the ways that youth are not only learning about their development as citizens, but are actively engaged in citizenship that transforms their lives and the world around them" (p. 262). This education for SGM citizenship requires helping youth to build knowledge and understanding of the sociohistorical context so they can see themselves and their struggles in relation to histories of SGM oppression and resistance, which can help them frame purposes and possibilities for action (Wexler et al., 2009). This turn to SGM social history can inform SGM and allied students in GSAs and the adults who support them as everyone works collectively to change school policies and have SGM-inclusive versions implemented in caring practices that make schools safer and healthier spaces. As Russell (2002) indicates, this political work involving education and activism can be dangerous work. Importantly though, it constitutes an active engagement in enhancing citizenship that is mindful of the Canadian Charter of Rights and Freedoms. Here the aim is to be transgressive and transformative in the work to create truly inclusive education.

Say It, Say GSA: Struggles and Progressive Moves in Ontario

When certain individuals or institutions don't name sexual and gender differences or use commonplace terms like "gay," as limited as this descriptor is, what messages are sent to SGM youth about barriers to their visibility, respect, and accommodation? Some might say that a

GSA by any other name is fine as long as some iteration of it exists. However, different names suggest that some individuals and institutions have a problem with what the name GSA embodies or a problem with making spaces for SGM youth in their midst. A different name for a GSA raises questions about SGM presence and place. A GSA has to serve multiple purposes, acknowledging the diversity of youth who attend as well as the diversity of needs and wants that they bring with them. For example, while a GSA can exist to address homophobic bullying, and while this is important and vital, it also has to consider biphobic and transphobic bullying as well as bullying experienced because a student is perceived to be gay or has SGM parents, relatives, or significant others in their lives. A GSA should acknowledge that many SGM youth are not victims or at risk – although significant numbers still are – and work to help these youth grow and develop individually and socially as persons with attributes, abilities, desires, hopes, goals, and dreams. A GSA ought to be a safe and supportive space where SGM youth can be, become, belong, and behave, as they are. It ought to be a space to question heteronormativity, genderism, and associated stressors and delimitations that can lead youth to engage in risk behaviours. Every youth has potential, and every youth deserves to thrive and be successful.

In some school districts, this is no mean feat. Take this case in point. In a 6 January 2011 interview with *Xtra* magazine regarding the decision of Halton Catholic District School Board (HCDSB) to ban GSAs in its schools, board chair Alice Anne LeMay responded,

> We don't have Nazi groups either ... Gay-straight alliances are banned because they are not within the teachings of the Catholic Church. If a gay student requests a gay-straight alliance, they would be denied ... It's not in accordance with the teachings of the church. If they wanted to have a club outside of school, fine, just not in school. (Houston, 2011a, para. 3)

Paradoxically, the school board made its decision to ban GSAs when it passed a new equity and inclusivity policy on 2 November 2010 (Houston, 2011b). Sadly, in defending this decision advocating exclusion of sexual minority students – gender minority students do not exist in a Catholic ontological context – LeMay compared GSAs to hate groups. Whether or not this was her intention, the comparison implied that when it comes to respecting and accommodating sexual minority students as spiritual *and* sexual beings, lovingness, courage, and tolerance do not really apply to them in Catholic school culture. In future – Bill 13, the Accepting Schools Act notwithstanding – LeMay will hopefully follow the advice provided by the Episcopal Commission for Doctrine of the Canadian Conference of Catholic Bishops (ECD-CCCB) in its guidelines for pastoral ministry to non-heterosexual youth, which were issued in June 2011: "Be aware that your language and attitudes can inadvertently communicate a message that has nothing to do with the Church's authentic teaching" (p. 5). At least this teaching says to love the "sinner."

HCDSB's decision immobilized sexual minority students in their schools, leaving them silent, invisible, and wanting. While Catholics place tremendous importance on reconciliation – it's one of the seven church sacraments – the school board's pronouncement denies these students the possibility of reconciling their sexuality with their spirituality so they can live in the fullness of both. Fortunately, its stance dismissing sexual minority students is not a universal Catholic stance. For example, as part of the Coalition in Support of Marc Hall, Catholics for Free Choice exhibited lovingness, courage, and tolerance when they backed this gay student, who went to court to get an interlocutory injunction that permitted him to take his boyfriend to his high school prom after Durham Catholic District School Board denied him permission (Grace & Wells, 2005). That school board also defended its decision as compliance with Catholic church teachings (Grace & Wells, 2005).

Although a newly installed HCDSB slate of trustees rescinded the November iteration of the policy in January 2011, the subsequent February iteration of the equity and inclusivity policy neither named sexual minority students – words like "gay" and "lesbian" are not part of the Catholic lexicon – nor clearly endorsed the specific establishment of GSAs to support them in its schools (Edwards, 2011; Whitnell, 2011a). Instead HCDSB chose to take a different tack, forming a new broad-based group to be called By Your SIDE Spaces that would emphasize safety, inclusivity, diversity, and equity for students across an array of relational differences, specifically race, origin, ability, and sexual orientation (Brown, 2011; Whitnell, 2011a). Although, on the face of it, the wider purpose of this group is commendable in a country where Section 15 of the Canadian Charter of Rights and Freedoms upholds individual rights across the relational differences that position persons in culture and society, the GSA counter-group belies true inclusion of sexual minorities in Catholic Christianity. While HCDSB retreated from an out-and-out ban on GSAs when it rescinded the November iteration of its equity and inclusivity policy (Brown, 2011), sexual minority students attending Halton Catholic District Schools remained in limbo, a fit analogy since, in Catholic theology, limbo is the fringe of hell to which certain sinners are confined. In HCDSB's limbo, sexual minority students are caught up in the politics of invisibility that Catholic theocracy has employed to leave them nameless and without GSAs.

In April 2011, when gay trustee Paul Marai questioned whether a student could get permission to start a GSA under the revised equity and inclusivity policy and pushed for an answer, HCDSB Education Director Michael Pautler said that the answer would be no under the wording of the policy iteration that trustees had before them at that time (Whitnell, 2011b). Perhaps Marai's perseverance in the name of social action seeking a visible presence and place for sexual minority students had an impact. By the time the equity and inclusivity policy was finally passed in May 2011, it had become possible for all Catholic high schools in Ontario to form something equivalent to but not named a GSA, starting in the 2011–12 school year (Whitnell, 2011c). In a joint letter considered by HCDSB trustees on the night of the final vote, Cardinal (then Archbishop) Thomas Collins, president of the Assembly of Catholic Bishops of Ontario, and Nancy Kirby, president of the Ontario Catholic School Trustees' Association, stated that Catholic faith and educational interest groups would form a provincial committee to work together to develop a framework (including a common name) for the GSA-equivalent groups that would primarily exist to address homophobic bullying (Whitnell, 2011c). Kirby stated that Ontario Catholic Schools would not use the name GSA because it is associated with activism rather than support (Rodan, 2011).

The naming issue was a key reason why Marai voted against the HCDSB policy, which he felt would keep sexual minority youth and GSAs invisible by not naming the students or their group using the common and popularly understood gay vernacular (Whitnell, 2011a, 2011c). It remained a problem caught up in Catholic rejection of terms like "gay" and "lesbian." The ECD-CCCB (2011), which uses the term "same-sex attractions" in its policy on pastoral ministry to youth, provided this basis for rejecting the popular terms:

> The terms "gay" and "lesbian" are not used to define people in the Church's official teachings and documents. Although these terms are common terms in current speech, and many people use them to describe themselves, they do not describe *persons* with the fullness and richness

that the Church recognizes and respects in every man or woman. Instead, "gay" and "lesbian" are often cultural definitions for people and movements that have accepted homosexual acts and behaviours as morally good ... [Therefore, it is important to help sexual minority youth] avoid involvement in a "gay culture" opposed to the Church's teaching, with its often aggressive and immoral lifestyle. (pp. 1, 6, italics in original)

The subtext here is that to be ontologically gay or lesbian is to be incapable of being a normal, moral, and whole Catholic person. Living visibly in the fullness of one's (homo)sexuality is morally wrong in a Catholic Christian context – end of story. Thus there is no possibility of reconciling one's non-heterosexual sexuality with the Catholic version of spirituality. Interestingly, to avoid using terms like "gay" and "lesbian" would itself seem discriminatory in a faith group that claims sexual minorities "must be accepted with respect, compassion, and sensitivity. Every sign of unjust discrimination in their regard should be avoided" (ECD-CCCB, 2011, p. 1). If, as the ECD-CCCB claims, "same-sex attraction constitutes a trial" (p. 3) for many sexual minority persons, then they might examine their complicity in causing such suffering. They should consider the degree to which the church's institutional homophobia and exclusionary doctrine are stressors inducing turmoil and trauma in the lives of gay and lesbian Catholics.

While the Ontario Ministry of Education's Guidelines for Policy Development and Implementation, issued in 2009, required every provincial school board to revise policy to "embed the principles of equity and inclusive education in all its policies and practices" (Egale Canada, 2011, p. 3; OME, 2009), the problem of GSAs in Catholic schools continued. In another case in March 2011, similar to the HCDSB case, a Mississauga high school in the jurisdiction of Dufferin-Peel Catholic District School Board (DPCDSB) also prohibited students from starting a GSA. Premier Dalton McGuinty did state publicly that this decision was not in compliance with the 2009 provincial guidelines, but he failed to declare that there had been a breach of the ministry's code on ethics (Baluja, 2011a). Nevertheless, it seemed clear that the high school's decision, unequivocally supported by DPCDSB, contravened an Ontario Ministry of Education memorandum from October 2009 that required provincial school boards to provide staff support to students who want to start GSAs and to have school councils and student councils support them (Baluja, 2011a, 2011b). DPCDSB's response, like HCDSB's response, was to hide GSAs behind the rhetoric of a broader Catholic community focus on equity and diversity (Baluja, 2011b). This left such student-led groups unnameable and unspeakable. Such Catholicized framing of community has required SGM youth to live invisibly within the limited social space demanded by church theocracy, restricting possibilities for their inclusion, respect, equity, and accommodation in Catholic school culture. Furthermore, this construction of community places limits on the healthy individual development and socialization of SGM youth, eroding their well-being.

During Toronto Gay Pride 2011 festivities, it was announced that the Government of Ontario would move to guarantee that its equity and inclusivity policy was properly implemented so that "support groups for LGBT youth" would exist in public and publicly funded Catholic high schools by September 2011 (Houston, 2011c, para. 5; Rodan, 2011). Still the naming issue remained since Premier McGuinty continued to use the descriptor "an LGBT support group" instead of the term "GSA" (Houston, 2011c, para.5). This may have been part of a politics to placate Catholic district school boards. However, the ECD-CCCB would never use the LGBT acronym either. Nevertheless, Toronto Centre Liberal MPP Glen Murray remarked that in future "schools will take their cues from students, not administration and principals, for decisions on the creation of school clubs focused on gay, lesbian, bisexual and trans issues" (Houston, 2011c, para. 2). That students wanted a role in establishing school clubs is clear in the cultural work and activism of 16-year-old Leanne Iskander. She led the student initiative to establish a GSA in the Mississauga high school. St Joseph's Catholic Secondary School eventually did allow an anti-homophobia club called Open Arms, a name in keeping with the DPCDSB requirement not to use the name GSA or refer to rainbows (Rodan, 2011). Regarding the name, Iskander stated, "They made us call it Open Arms, which is so generic and no one knows what it is … There's no point having the support there if students don't know it's there, so the name is important" (Rodan, 2011, para. 15). Indeed GSA is now a brand name in several thousand North American schools, where the name signifies a welcoming and safe space for youth seeking to socialize, learn, and mobilize to combat heterosexism, sexism, genderism, and homo/bi/transphobia (Cloud, 2005; Gay-Straight Alliance [GSA] Network, 2013; Mercier, 2009).

On 5 June 2012, the Ontario Legislature passed Bill 13, the Accepting Schools Act, by a margin of 65-36 (CP, 2012a). This anti-bullying legislation mandates that students be permitted to establish GSAs in public and publicly funded Catholic schools, which are now compelled to comply with students' requests (Howlett, 2012). Essentially, what the bill has done is to disallow a school principal's subscription to Catholic morality to contravene an engagement in a public ethical practice that requires educators to be there for every student, despite their differences. Shortly after the bill passed, Education Minister Laurel Broten stated, "Today is about saying to Ontario students, 'You can be who you are. You will be safe and accepted at school and the Ontario government supports you in that desire'" (Howlett, 2012, para. 3). Elementary Teachers' Federation of Ontario president Sam Hammond said, "We are pleased that neither a board nor principal may prevent students from using the name 'gay-straight alliance' if they wish to start such a student organization" (ETFO, 2012, p. 1). In supporting the bill, the provincial New Democratic Party had urged the Liberal government to ensure that students could use the word "gay" in naming their SGM-inclusive clubs, which it did (CP, 2012b). Striking the original wording – "organizations with the name gay-straight alliance or another name" (Lewis, 2012a, para. 4) – the government amended the bill so students had the right to name their clubs GSAs even if the school administration objected (Lewis, 2012a). The amendment spoke to the power of language and the human rights of youth as Canadian citizens. During this debate about naming, Broten was clear: "Schools need to be safe places for kids to be themselves – and for some kids, that means being able to name a club a gay-straight alliance. I don't think there's anything radical about allowing students to name a club" (Lewis & Perkel, 2012, para. 5). Thus the amendment became an exercise in social cohesion that put students in public and publicly funded Catholic schools on equal footing in terms of using the name "GSA" (CP, 2012a). This move thwarted the Ontario Catholic school trustees' proposal to use the name "Respecting Differences" clubs, which would have buried any focus on sexual and gender differences within a generic focus on bullying (Lewis, 2012b). Exercising a politics of surveillance and demonstrating the desire to suppress student advocacy, the trustees wanted a staff adviser always present at club meetings, the chaplaincy to be invited to meetings, and a school review of materials for promoting the club (Baluja, 2012).

While acknowledging that some Catholics were disconcerted by the enactment of the bill, Premier Dalton McGuinty was clear: "There are values that transcend any one faith" (Canadian Press [CP], 2012b, para. 5). The safety of students is one of those values and indeed a basic need. Still, in opposing the bill, the Catholic Church – which operates publicly funded schools in Alberta, Ontario, and Saskatchewan – and its supporters, including Ontario's Conservatives, saw Bill 13 as state interference in constitutionally protected (Section 93) religious schooling (Lewis, 2012c). Cardinal Thomas Collins contended that the Liberal government was micromanaging Catholic education by trying to force the GSA "brand" on Catholic schools (Lewis, 2012a, para. 8). Of perhaps greater political significance, Catholic perspectives on Bill 13 demonstrated that different Catholic constituencies held different viewpoints: the church hierarchy and school trustees rejected the bill while students, parents, and teachers tended to support the bill (Hammer & Howlett, 2012). Indeed a document prepared by the Ontario Catholic school trustees and obtained by the *Globe and Mail* indicated that the trustees feared an erosion of support for Catholic education in the face of the loss of support from different Catholic constituencies (Hammer & Howlett, 2012).

Although Catholic school boards in Ontario are now expected to work within the parameters of the Accepting Schools Act, how Catholic schools comply remains an unfolding story. Ontario's Catholic school boards, like the province's public school boards, need to recognize what contemporary interdisciplinary research is indicating: when policies focused on equity and inclusion include recognition and accommodation of SGM students, these students feel safer and more protected, engage in less risk behaviour, witness a reduction in prejudicial attitudes among heterosexual students, and observe school administrators and teachers enforcing policies to make life better for them now (Russell et al., 2010). However, policymaking is not enough; it must be connected to the everyday life of SGM students in schools and expressed in proximal realities, like the presence of acknowledged and visible GSAs (Grace & Wells, 2009; Russell et al., 2010). Currently, and often as a matter of pressure from that societal contingent concerned with making schools more equitable, safe, caring, and inclusive environments for all students, some school boards (notably those operating in publicly funded nondenominational contexts) have been struggling to develop and implement policies and practices that would achieve this for SGM students. However, this trend is neither universal nor a particular consequence of some newfound altruism bent on true inclusion of these vulnerable youth. Instead, it is likely the compound effect of media watching and fear of litigation. The long-standing reality is SGM students compose a diverse and vulnerable population in schools that, historically, have been unsafe and unsupportive spaces for them.

Establishing and supporting GSAs in schools is one critical way to move a project of equity and inclusivity forward in twenty-first-century schooling.

Homo/Bi/Transphobia in Schools and the Need for GSAs in the Larger Canadian Context

While there have been many changes in federal and provincial/territorial legislation and institutional policymaking since the 1998 Supreme Court decision in *Vriend v. Alberta* (which granted equality rights to sexual minority Canadians), Canadian culture and society still lag behind, as evidenced by pervasive heterocentrism, sexism, genderism, and homo/bi/transphobia affecting the everyday lives of SGM persons. As the preceding discussion demonstrates, nowhere is this more problematic than in schools, where, in replicating the heteronormative, genderist status quo, school administrators, counsellors, and teachers have generally ignored the needs and concerns of SGM students, leaving them vulnerable to unrelenting violence and deteriorating health and well-being. This is perhaps most problematic in middle schools or junior high schools, variously including grades 5 to 9 in Canada. SGM students tend to experience these schools as dangerous places where bullying and victimization on the grounds of difference are inimical to SGM inclusion and student safety (Adams, Cahill, & Ackerlind, 2005; Quasha, McCabe, & Ortiz, 2014). In sum, SGM students have perennially experienced discrimination, prejudice, and abuse within Canadian school systems, presumably designed to provide for their care and education (Egale Canada, 2009; Kosciw, Diaz, & Greytak, 2008). In the context of Canadian schools, this is profoundly demonstrated in *Every Class in Every School*, the final report on the first national climate survey on homo/bi/transphobia (Taylor & Peter et al., 2011). The report includes these key findings:

- 68 per cent of trans or gender-minority students, 55 per cent of female sexual-minority students, and 42 per cent of male sexual minority students indicated that they have been verbally harassed about their perceived sexual or gender identities;
- more than one in five sexual- and gender-minority students revealed that they had been physically harassed or assaulted as a result of their sexual orientation;
- 37 per cent of trans students conveyed being physically assaulted or harassed as a result of their gender identity and expression; and

- 64 per cent of sexual- and gender-minority students and 61 per cent of students with sexual- or gender-minority parents declared that they feel unsafe at school.

Cumulatively, these statistics locate schools as dangerous places for SGM students. Thus *Every Class in Every School* leads us to raise an obvious question: How do we make life in schools better *now* for SGM youth? Strikingly, the report points out that it is not through generic safe school policies that neither name systemic sociocultural problems like homo/bi/transphobia nor provide strategies for problem solving that would bring relief to SGM students struggling to mediate the dangers and survive. As well, the report indicates that even when anti-homophobia policies exist, they may help sexual minority students, but they do little to alleviate stressors and risks that make schools perilous places for gender-minority youth, who need anti-transphobia policies that specifically address their needs in relation to gender identity and expression. As the report highlights, while trans or gender-nonconforming youth may compose a small population, they are a much targeted and harassed group in a hetero-patriarchal, genderist society that rigidly polices gender and expectations of a male/female binary that leaves no room for variations in gender identity and expression. This likely explains these report statistics:

- 90 per cent of trans youth frequently heard transphobic comments;
- 78 per cent indicated feeling unsafe in different ways at school; and
- 44 per cent stated they were likely to be truant to avoid feeling unsafe at school.

Importantly, the report notes that educators have also left heterosexual students vulnerable and unsafe in matters related to sexual and gender identities. For example, a significant number of heterosexual students recounted being verbally harassed, with 1 in 12 pointing out it was due to their perceived sexual orientation and 1 in 4 noting it was because of their gender expression.

As I have emphasized in this book, SGM youth and those perceived to be are *not* the problem. Rather, the real problem comprises complex systemic and structural issues permeating life in schools and communities. Blaming the victim is the easy way out for educational, health, and other social institutions that abrogate their responsibility to SGM youth by saying there is little that can be done for them. These same institutions hold youth accountable for their actions, but individual

accountability, especially in the case of youth under the age of majority, has to be premised on institutional accountability grounded in
respecting and accommodating vulnerable youth. Research supports
this perspective: apparently of greater consequence than individual-
level risk factors, unsupportive social environments increase the risk
of SGM youth attempting suicide by 20 per cent (Hatzenbuehler, 2011).
Moreover, research indicates that unsupportive social interactions in
unaccommodating family, school, and other institutional environments
have a profound and direct impact on the socialization and mental
health and well-being of this historically marginalized youth population (Berghe et al., 2010). For example, research on school environments
as replicators of societal prejudice and discrimination demonstrates that
these social spaces are sources of stressors that are stimuli for youth risk
behaviours (Russell et al., 2010). Within negative institutional milieus,
it has been a struggle for SGM students to find space and place, recognition and acknowledgment, respect and accommodation. The earlier
described attempts to keep GSAs out of Catholic schools provide ample
evidence of this.

In recent years, SGM students have been fighting back to challenge
and change hostile classrooms and hallways in Canadian schools
(Grace & Wells, 2009). Many have had a goal of creating GSAs as sites
for recoupment in the face of institutional homo/bi/transphobia and
heteronormativity. Pointing this out, *Every Class in Every School*, over-
viewed in chapter 1, highlights the need to establish and support GSAs
as an important part of strategizing to improve life in schools for SGM
students (Taylor & Peter et al., 2011). Research indicates that GSAs
can have a significant impact on promoting the safety and well-being
of SGM youth in schools (Russell et al., 2010). In *Every Class in Every
School*, GSAs are defined as safe spaces that are predominantly student
initiated; they are "official student clubs with LGBTQ and heterosexual
student membership and typically one or two teachers who serve as
faculty advisors … [whom students] can talk to about LGBTQ matters"
(Taylor & Peter et al., 2011, p. 10). The report states that GSAs provide
protective social spaces for sharing conversations, resources, and supports useful to SGM students as well as students with SGM parents or
guardians. In speaking to the benefits of consistently available and functioning GSAs, *Every Class in Every School* indicates that SGM students
(1) feel safer to be open and visible, (2) feel the school administration is
more supportive, and (3) feel the school climate is more accommodating and less homo/bi/transphobic. These findings fortify the report's
recommendations that "schools strongly support the efforts of students

to start GSAs, or similar LGBTQ-inclusive student-led clubs, and that in schools where students have not come forward, administration should ask teachers to offer to work with students to start such clubs" (Taylor & Peter et al., 2011, p. 21). Schools also need to address the issues of GSA sustainability. GSAs, which depend on committed student leaders, are marked by short leadership cycles, which result in a loss of experience, a probable repetition of projects and problems, and "a loss of organizational capital (goal momentum and institutional memory)" (Kress, 2006, p. 53). This suggests that GSAs could benefit from using a shared leadership model, with more senior members mentoring and involving more junior members in processes of collaborative planning and shared decision making to engage in an annual program of events and activities.

In sum, for many SGM youth, GSAs serve as critical support systems that help them to transition from feeling at risk to a place where they can feel supported so they can grow into resilience and be at promise. In this regard, research on GSAs contributes to an understanding of the processes of SGM youth identity development and the roles that consciousness raising, individual agency, and coalition-building strategies can play in advocating for personal, social, and institutional changes.

The Emergence of GSAs in North America

A Brief History of GSAs

In the late 1970s, prior to the advent of the Internet, US community-based SGM youth organizations first emerged in New York City and Chicago to meet the health, emotional, and social needs of youth for connection, community building, sociality, and solidarity in the face of oppression and disenfranchisement (Russell, 2002). These groups were created largely separate from families, faith communities, and schools, where SGM youth remained invisible in curricular and co-curricular activities that helped to maintain a heteronormative, genderist status quo (Russell, 2002).

School-based SGM youth organizations are a more recent occurrence. In 1984 Dr Virginia Uribe formed the first formal support group for gay and lesbian youth in a high school in Los Angeles, California. Project 10, as it would later be known, was designed not only to support students struggling with their sexual orientation but also to provide school-based workshops to counter pervasive heterosexism and homophobia found within the school system (Valenti & Campbell, 2009). From its conception, the very first "gay-student support group" was about personal, social, and cultural change. The name "gay-straight alliance" or "GSA" was first used for a school-based SGM organization at a small private school in Massachusetts in 1989 (Blumenfeld, 1995; Schindel, 2008). Growth of these groups nationally in the United States was incremental, with less than 100 GSAs, as they came to be called, existing in US secondary schools in 1995 (Savin-Williams, 2008). However, as a testament to the persistence and sociopolitical engagement of SGM youth, numbers grew. By 2000, there were 162 GSAs in Massachusetts alone, with twice as many started by students as by supportive adults (Russell, 2002). Today, building upon Project 10's legacy of support, over 4,000 GSAs are present in about 1 in 10 high schools in the United States (Cloud, 2005). There is also a national GSA Network, which helps to connect GSAs, train student leaders, and advocate for SGM-inclusive school policies, all in a collective effort to build a national GSA movement (GSA Network, 2013).

This upsurge in the numbers and organization of GSAs has been the direct result of the vocal advocacy and strong support provided by the American Civil Liberties Union (ACLU). The ACLU, citing Equal Access and First Amendment laws, has made it a mission to intervene on behalf of any student who has been denied the right to form a GSA, denied attendance with a same-sex date at a graduation prom, or limited in exercising their right to pro-gay free speech (Mercier, 2009; Whittaker, 2009). Unfortunately, no similar powerful legal organization in Canada has been willing to actively and steadfastly champion the rights of SGM youth on a national level. In this absence Egale Canada, which can be construed as Canada's national SGM task force, has expanded its focus to include GSAs by starting the MyGSA website (http://mygsa.ca/) and hosting the first national GSA summit in spring 2013. In sum, the uptake of GSAs in Canada has been much slower and regionally based, which is due in part to differences between possible legal recourse in Canada and persistent legal recourse in the United States (Mercier, 2009). The ACLU has launched many cases supporting a student's right to create a GSA (mostly within conservative US states), and it has been repeatedly successful in these court challenges. Mercier (2009) argues that such litigation through the US legal system has been critical in helping to heighten the visibility of SGM students and their needs and concerns. He relates that opposition to GSAs has paradoxically demonstrated to the public the very purposes of GSAs: to fight ignorance, combat stereotypes, and promote tolerance.

There have been no similar court challenges in Canada. Perhaps the most logical place to address denial of the right to create a GSA in this country would be to appeal to a provincial or territorial human rights commission, citing discrimination based on sexual orientation or gender identity as the basis for the complaint. Although we do not know whether proceeding this way would advance the emergence of GSAs in Canadian schools, it is worth trying, with so many SGM youth waiting to experience safety, respect, and accommodation in their schools. Since we cannot yet rest easily on the laurels of the Canadian Charter of Rights and Freedoms, SGM citizens, including youth, still need the power of individuals and the force of law to move SGM human and civil rights forward.

How GSAs Have Functioned Over Time: A Typology of Roles

In their pioneering research on early-stage GSAs, Griffin et al. (2004) identified a typology of GSAs, using the four major roles that these groups have traditionally played in schools to classify them:

1 *GSAs for counselling and support* place a focus on providing individual support to students who are deemed to be at risk for bullying, discrimination, or self-harm. These groups tend to be counsellor-led and have a low profile within their school.
2 *GSAs that provide safe spaces* are officially sanctioned school-based groups that include heterosexual allies and teacher supporters. These groups focus on fitting into rather than disrupting the mainstream school environment and often take an assimilationist approach by arguing for inclusion and acceptance based upon their commonalities to, rather than differences from, mainstream school culture.
3 *GSAs that raise visibility and awareness* focus on establishing a vocal and visible school-wide presence. These groups, which are student-led and teacher-supported, focus their attention on social, educational, and political activities designed to reveal the heterosexist and heteronormative nature of schooling. The majority of GSA activities focus on raising understanding and building tolerance among the school population.
4 *GSAs that promote educational and social change* tend to focus their efforts on building coalitions with different student groups. They also work actively to liaise with their school administration and parent groups. Activities are focused on cultural change through outreach initiatives such as staff training, inclusive curriculum development, and diversity day or school-wide anti-homophobia

assemblies. These groups tend to operate using an anti-oppression framework in which issues of power and privilege are woven into their educational mandate. Activities and coalition-building strategies are centred on moving beyond notions of tolerance to an appreciation and celebration of the many and varied differences that constitute humanity.

Unlike earlier stage GSAs (1 and 2), which focused on educators providing supports to individual youth, later stage GSAs (3 and 4) represent moves towards youth activism to change the hetero-patriarchal, genderist order of schools. They provide "an opportunity to understand youth engagement in activities that directly challenge or resist hegemonic structures that characterize adolescents' lives – the gender and sexual order of their schools" (Russell et al., 2009, p. 893). In alignment with this perspective, Fetner and Kush (2008) argue, "High schools, which have significant power to organize and regulate student's lives, can be uniquely conducive to activism or can be harsh repressors" (p. 128). They assert that GSAs mark a pivotal moment in SGM history as "young people are stepping forward to claim support for lesbian and gay rights on their own terms" (p. 118). Moreover, GSAs can be viewed as a new and creative form of queer activism that embraces the fluidity and complexity of sexual and gender identities by reaching outward to build coalitions with allies. This challenges old lesbian and gay activist tendencies, which tended to essentialize identities and have a predominantly inward-reaching and isolationist focus. Positioned as a new form of queer social activism, GSAs can help transform the ways in which SGM youth are made intelligible as they challenge the rigidity of the heterosexual/homosexual and male/female binaries and embrace queerness as a composite of fluid sexual and gender identities that comprise diverse ways to be, become, belong, and act in the world. Using this modus operandi, GSAs can challenge a deficit model, relocating queer youth as thriving agents and rejecting the older notion of SGM youth as passive victims in need of safe spaces for their very survival. Here, as GSAs emerge, a new focus is being placed on using them as a critical space for recoupment from the daily onslaught of compulsory heterosexuality and as an inclusive space to develop strategies for resistance to heteronormativity and genderism. In Freire's (2004) terms, contemporary GSAs provide SGM students with opportunities to develop critical literacies for reading the word and the world in ways that denounce conditions of oppression and announce new possibilities for transforming culture and society. As Marshall (2010) concludes, "Through their resistant reading[s], these young people embody and enact an important part of the everyday work of social change" (p. 77).

Research Moments in Researching GSAs

Denzin and Lincoln (2005) have used the notion of moments to periodize the history of qualitative research in North America since the early 1900s. Here we draw on this notion to divide the history – albeit a brief one – of GSA-related research and practice since GSAs first appeared in North American schools during the 1980s. As these school-based youth organizations emerged, distinct research moments also emerged in relation to the study of the development, changing roles, and impacts of GSAs. These moments identify trends and are historically and culturally located. No research moment should be viewed as static; rather, each research moment should be understood as having a fluid and continuing influence on the possible development, roles, and effects of current and future GSAs. As well, each research moment identifies and highlights perspectives and questions that have become increasingly important to the broadening field of SGM youth research and its components, like researching GSAs. These moments are identified as seven distinct phases, summarized in Table 1.

The seven research moments mentioned here reflect trends identified in the emergence of GSAs and research on them. These research moments help enrich our understanding of GSAs as important catalysts for SGM youth identity formation, socialization, and broad-based coalition building. They also enhance our understanding of how SGM youth can grow and develop as proactive agents abetting individual, social, and cultural changes to make life in schools and communities better for them. Each of the seven research moments provides an opportunity to reflect on the beneficial roles that GSAs can play in moves to enhance schooling as a more equitable endeavour that accentuates respect for and accommodation of student differences. The range of foci collectively contained in these research moments demonstrates that GSAs are marked by a wide variety of ends and approaches. Just as school cultures differ, GSA cultures also differ. GSAs provide an array of experiences for their participants. The seven research moments presented here provide an emergent framework for understanding the contributions of GSAs in challenging and changing heteronormative, genderist educational environments so SGM students can have space and place in schooling as an intricate educational, social, and cultural experience.

Table 1. The Seven Moments in GSA-related Research and Practice

First Moment	Establishing School-based Support Groups Researchers explored the need for dedicated educational supports and mental health services for lesbian and gay youth. The focus was placed on youth as at risk for negative psychological, health, and educational outcomes (Unks, 1995; Uribe, 1994).
Second Moment	Ferment and Formation Researchers focused on GSAs established by concerned teachers committed to providing school-based supports to address pressing issues of isolation, alienation, and homophobic bullying (Murphy, 2012). The first official GSA was started in 1989 in Concord, Massachusetts (Blumenfeld, 1995).
Third Moment	The Rise of GSAs and Role Differentiation Researchers began to investigate the differing roles of GSAs and their benefits to SGM students. They also explored the roles of teacher advisers and school administrators (Griffin & Ouellett, 2002; Griffin et al., 2004; Lee, 2002; Miceli, 2005; Perrotti & Westheimer, 2001; Szalacha, 2003; Valenti & Campbell, 2009). GSA guidebooks and websites began to emerge to help youth and teachers change their hostile schools from the inside out (Egale Canada, 2013; GSA Network, 2013; Macgillivray, 2007; Miceli, 2005; Wells, 2006).
Fourth Moment	Early Legal Contestations In the United States, GSAs became part of the so-called culture wars as students asserted their right to be vocal, visible, and protected within their schools. Youth sexuality moved from a private to public concern, with the strong support of the American Civil Liberties Union. GSAs became part of a wave of litigation focused on gay civil rights across the United States, providing a newfound visibility for SGM youth. Researchers explored the legal, legislative, and educational policy frameworks used to support the creation of GSAs (Mayberry, 2006; Mercier, 2009; Whittaker, 2009).
Fifth Moment	GSAs, Heterosexual Allies, and Arising Homonormativity Researchers examined the benefits of GSAs to both SGM and heterosexual students through the creation of spaces that open up and support conversations surrounding diversity and the spectrum of student differences in public schools (Goodenow, Szalacha, & Westheimer, 2006; Walls, Kane, & Wisnesk, 2010). Researchers investigated how GSAs can become safe spaces for youth who are deemed outsiders in their schools. Researchers also began to question how GSAs inadvertently become homonormative spaces, which struggle to include and serve ethnocultural sexual minority youth, Two-Spirit youth, and trans youth (McCready, 2004).
Sixth Moment	GSAs, Youth Activism, and Coalition-building Strategies GSAs are building alliances with other student-oriented social justice groups. These coalition-building strategies are now striving to link together the "isms," including racism, classism, genderism, sexism, and heterosexism. Researchers are examining GSAs as new forms of queer activism focused on youth empowerment. Rather than simply providing safe spaces, GSAs are embracing the complexity of multiple and shifting identities, with a concentrated focus on education for personal and social change (Fetner & Kush, 2008; Russell et al., 2009).

(Continued)

Table 1. *(Continued)*

Seventh Moment	Queering the Future
	Based on the emergence of GSAs and more than a decade's worth of research, several critical questions focused on key themes are expected to become increasingly important to the field of SGM youth research and constituent GSA research. These questions include the following:

- How do students' participation in GSAs affect their relationships with parents, guardians, or caregivers?
- How do GSAs contribute to individual empowerment and a sense of personal agency?
- With GSAs now being created in junior high schools, what impact will long-term participation in a GSA have on student health, safety, identity development, and educational outcomes? (Here longitudinal and control-group studies to compare students attending schools with GSAs to those attending schools without GSAs are needed.)
- What role(s) do GSAs play within faith-based schools? How are issues of sexual orientation and gender identity understood within faith-based contexts? What are the challenges in creating and sustaining GSAs in faith-based schools?
- How might institutional rights and individual rights be mediated so faith-based schools become safer and more accommodating spaces for SGM youth?
- What are the challenges and opportunities for the creation of GSAs in rural, northern, and cross-cultural school-based environments? How do these GSAs respond to localized needs and cultural concerns?
- Are GSAs becoming increasingly homonormative, or do they work to expand rather than limit identity expression? For example, how do GSAs work to embrace trans, Two-Spirit, and ethnocultural-minority youth?
- What roles do adults play in the creation, support, and sustainability of GSAs? What are the risks to and opportunities for these adults?
- How do GSAs contribute to new forms of queer social activism?

Concluding Perspective: Dream and Then Do It

Hosted by the Institute for Sexual Minority Studies and Services, University of Alberta, in partnership with Edmonton Public Schools and the Stollery Charitable Foundation, the first annual Alberta Gay-Straight Alliance Student Conference was held in Edmonton on 17 November 2012. SGM and allied students and significant adults, including some parents, teacher advisers, and school trustees, came from all over the province. Alberta's Deputy Premier Thomas Lukaszuk opened the conference, telling youth, "Just a few short years ago, within the span of your lives, this [conference] would be almost unthinkable" (Gold, 2012, para. 3). Throughout the day, students shared urban, rural, and northern perspectives on what queer life in schools was like for them based on the culture and politics of their locations. They also discussed the further development and growth of GSAs as a dynamic force for social change in Alberta. This aligned with the core goal of the conference: to engage in the political and pedagogical task of establishing GSAs as a human rights movement in which SGM youth and their supporters are vocal and active stakeholders. To achieve this goal, stakeholders needed to create opportunities to change schools from the inside out into more equitable, inclusive, respectful, and safer spaces. This starts with establishing GSAs and honing them as helping and affirming spaces.

In one conference session – entitled GSA 101 – the message to SGM and allied students was to be who you are. The message to teacher advisers and other significant adults was to listen and be there for these youth. During the workshop, the facilitators – Melinda, a retired school counsellor who was adviser-mentor in her school for one of the first GSAs in Alberta, and Anna, a practising teacher who currently advises and mentors the GSA in her school – asked participants to describe what a dream GSA would be like. Suggestions flowed and are summarized here:

- The GSA would be visible, active, and supported just like other school clubs, and it would be part of the school's clubs fair or listing.
- The GSA would have answers to two basic questions: What is a GSA? What does a GSA do?
- The principal would champion the GSA and the school administration would lead by example and not place too many restrictions on the GSA.
- The GSA would have a large membership, including many allies.
- Peers inside the GSA and in the school as a whole would support one another.
- Parents, guardians, and other significant adults would support the GSA.
- Teachers and other staff would be brave, acting to assist students by being caring educators who won't be frozen by their fear of community responses.
- The school environment would reflect the GSA environment.
- The GSA would provide access to SGM adults as speakers and role models.
- The GSA would arrange exchanges with other GSAs to create opportunities for mutual sharing and learning.

- The GSA would have short-term goals like planning a queer movie night and an annual calendar of events that would set out goals for the school year.
- The GSA would educate about homo/bi/transphobic myths and stereotypes.
- The GSA would advocate for inclusive policies and practices that help create a safe and accommodating school for all.
- The GSA would seek a balance between advocacy and socializing to meet the different needs of different students.
- The GSA would put slogans and posters in high-traffic areas, making them big and hanging them high to counter vandalism.
- The GSA would emphasize listening to peers and having others listen to them.

During the closing activity, youth performed the songs they had written and arranged during a songwriting workshop conducted earlier in the day by transgender musician Rae Spoon, the conference's keynote presenter. One group's song contained these poignant lyrics: "Identity's not clear. Together there's no fear." It ended with a resounding chant: "G-S-A all the way." The verses of the song mixed recognition, desire, and possibility into a real yet hopeful expression for change. The performance was about authentic SGM youth voices, their needs, and their dreams. It demonstrated that these students are ready and willing to be active stakeholders in their schooling and their futures. All they need is support within their school communities to help them break the long-standing silence surrounding the presence and place of their SGM identities in schooling. This silence needs to be broken in schools across Canada.

Appendix

Growing into Resilience: An Emergent Research Typology of a Dynamic Process from the 1980s to the Present

This appendix is provided to help readers understand growing into resilience as a concept, construct, process, and outcome. It presents an emergent typology, providing a synopsis of research on resilience from the 1980s to the present. With understandings of resilience still emerging, the appendix provides a synopsis of developing knowledge about stressors, risks, assets, and indicators of thriving. It uses an ecological framework that surveys complexities affecting how vulnerable youth grow into resilience.

The literature on resilience indicates this is still a construct under development. Moreover, other concepts in its constellation like protective factors and risk factors are nebulous in nature. For example, Sesma et al. (2005) provide this perspective:

> [There] are factors that, depending on the spectrum one chooses to emphasize, can either be a risk or a protective factor. For example, one of our assets is *family support*, which is defined in a way that emphasizes the positive end of the construct. However, other researchers can use the same global construct (a facet of family functioning) and focus on the negative pole (lack of family support; high degree of family conflict) and call this a risk factor. (p. 287; italics in original)

Recognizing such realities, and realizing a typology can suggest that growing into resilience is concretely understood, I offer this typology as an emergent configuration that positions growing in resilience as an intricate biopsychosocial process. What we know so far is that resilience, as a construct, is multidimensional and still indeterminate in nature (Grace, 2013a). With resilience understood as a multifaceted concept, construct, process, and outcome (Luthar et al., 2000), the typology presented here provides a synopsis of knowledge and consensus building around four key constructs that have been researched for several decades: stressors, risks, assets, and indicators of thriving.

Stressors

SGM youth live with adversity and trauma induced by an array of stressors including heterosexism, sexism, genderism, and homo/bi/transphobia. Since SGM youth are multiple subjects with socially and culturally determined positionalities, they may also experience discrimination and prejudice in intersections with other stressors, such as racism, ethnocentrism, classism, and ableism (Fassinger & Arseneau, 2007; Fieland et al., 2007; Grossman & D'Augelli, 2007; Meyer, 2007; Savin-Williams & Ream, 2003; Scourfield et al., 2008; Russell, 2002; Schindel, 2008; Trotter, 2009). SGM youth variously experience poverty; reduced feelings of safety and security, especially when they publicly self-identify at younger ages; internalized homo/bi/transphobia; harassment, abuse, and victimization through symbolic and physical violence; and neglect by key adults, which can include uncaring parents, school administrators, teachers, clinicians, and other professionals (Chesir-Teran, 2003; Freitas & Downey, 1998; Grace & Wells, 2005, 2009; Russell, 2002, 2005). Societal and cultural marginalization and disenfranchisement commonly lead to risk taking among SGM youth.

Inventory of Risks

Risk taking is associated with yielding to adversity and trauma (Doll & Lyon, 1998). In psychology and education, among other disciplines, the risk and resilience framework was developed to build understanding of the complexities of individual behaviour in terms of the balance of risks, which lead to negative outcomes, and resilience, which can grow when individuals have assets to protect them against risks (Corcoran & Nichols-Casebolt, 2004). However, there is a need to focus on the intricacies of researching risk and resilience, as Luthar and Zelazo (2003) point out:

> A methodological limitation common to both risk and resilience paradigms is lack of precision in measuring risk. Children with particular negative

life circumstances are treated as homogeneous groups despite possible
variations in the degree to which their lives are actually touched by the true
risk processes (e.g., supportive grandparents may shield some children
from maltreatment by alcoholic parents). (p. 512)

This concern can be extrapolated to emphasize the need to see vulnerable children and youth as individuals with multiple subjectivities
whose lives are complicated by the contexts, relationships of power,
and environments that shape them. Therefore, researching risk and
resilience requires an ecological approach that takes these complexities
into account. Moreover, in researching risk and resilience and the (im)
balance that marks their relationship, it is important to look at process
and investigate how individuals deal with risks by focusing on their
coping mechanisms, dispositional factors (mindset), and capacity to be
strategic change agents (Rutter, 2006).

What follows is an inventory of risks, as indicated in the research
literature in recent decades. It is not exhaustive, but it is representative.

Mental, Emotional, and Physical Health Risks

Aggression
McDaniel et al., 2001

Anxiety
Bolger & Patterson, 2003; Bringaze & White, 2001; D'Augelli, 2002;
    Luthar & Zigler, 1991

Apathy
Herrenkohl et al., 1994

Behavioural Problems
Bolger & Patterson, 2003; D'Augelli, 2002

Cognitive Dissonance (Between Religion and Sexuality or Gender
Identity)
Bringaze & White, 2001; D'Augelli, 2002

Coping Strain
Lock & Steiner, 1999

Depression
Bolger & Patterson, 2003; Hunter & Mallon, 2000; Luthar & Zigler,
   1991; Safren & Pantalone, 2006; Savin-Williams, 2008

Emotional Abuse and Emotional Health Problems
Chen-Hayes, 2001; Herrenkohl et al., 1994; Russell, 2005

Fear
Adams, 2006; Cramer & Roach, 1988; D'Augelli, 1998, 2002, 2003;
   D'Augelli et al., 2005; Elizur & Ziv, 2001; Fieland et al., 2007;
   Grossman et al., 2009; Hunter & Mallon, 2000; Rivers & Cowie, 2006;
   Sanders & Kroll, 2000; Travers & Paoletti, 1999

Identity Conflicts in Determining the Authentic Self
D'Augelli, 2003; Grossman & D'Augelli, 2007; Hunter & Mallon, 2000;
   McCready, 2004

Internalized Homophobia
Elizur & Ziv, 2001; D'Augelli, 1998; Meyer, 2007; Russell, 2005

Low Self-esteem
Bringaze & White, 2001; Callahan, 2001; Chen-Hayes, 2001; D'Augelli,
   2006a; Garmezy, 1991; Grossman & D'Augelli, 2007; Henning-Stout
   et al., 2000; Perrin et al., 2004

Negative Self-concept
Balsam, 2003; Bolger & Patterson, 2003; Herrenkohl et al., 1994

Physical Health Problems
Perrin et al., 2004

Psychological Distress
D'Augelli, 2002, 2003, 2006a; Hunter & Mallon, 2000; Perrin et al., 2004;
   Russell, 2005; Tharinger & Wells, 2000

Self-destructive Behaviour
Balsam, 2003; D'Augelli, 2006a; Ginsberg, 1998; Grossman &
   D'Augelli, 2007; Henning-Stout et al., 2000; Herrenkohl et al., 1994;
   Hunter & Mallon, 2000

Self-doubt
D'Augelli, 1998

Self-mutilation
Chen-Hayes, 2001; Hunter & Mallon, 2000

Sense of Hopelessness
Herrenkohl et al., 1994; Safren & Pantalone, 2006

Shame
Balsam, 2003

Suicidality
Callahan, 2001; Chen-Hayes, 2001; D'Augelli, 2002, 2003; Ginsberg,
    1998; Grossman & D'Augelli, 2007; Henning-Stout et al., 2000;
    Holmes & Cahill, 2004; McDaniel et al., 2001; Perrin et al., 2004;
    Russell, 2002, 2005; Safren & Pantalone, 2006; Scourfield et al.,
    2008

Victim Mentality
Balsam, 2003

Individual Risks

Academic Difficulties
D'Augelli, 2002; Garmezy, 1991; Grossman et al., 2009; Trotter, 2009

Bullying
Grossman & D'Augelli, 2007; Grossman et al., 2009; Scourfield et al.,
    2008; Trotter, 2009

Developmental Opportunity Loss
D'Augelli, 1998; Hunter & Mallon, 2000

Hiding
Adams, 2006; Callahan, 2001; Bringaze & White, 2001; D'Augelli,
    2002, 2003, 2006a; Fassinger & Arseneau, 2007; Hunter &
    Mallon, 2000; Rivers & Cowie, 2006; Sanders & Kroll, 2000;
    Trotter, 2009

Hypervigilance
Cagle, 2007; Chen-Hayes, 2001; Hunter & Mallon, 2000

Isolation
Bringaze & White, 2001; Cagle, 2007; Callahan, 2001; D'Augelli, 2002;
    Fassinger & Arseneau, 2007; Fieland et al., 2007; Griffin et al., 2004;
    Grossman et al., 2009; Hunter & Mallon, 2000; McCready, 2004;
    Perrin et al., 2004; Russell, 2002; Scourfield et al., 2008; Tharinger &
    Wells, 2000; Travers & Paoletti, 1999; Trotter, 2009

Lack of Agency
Grossman et al., 2009

Truancy and Dropping Out of School
Callahan, 2001; D'Augelli, 2002; Holmes & Cahill, 2004; McCready,
    2004; Russell, 2002, 2005; Trotter, 2009

Sexual Risk Taking
Callahan, 2001; Chesir-Teran, 2003; Henning-Stout et al., 2000; Hunter
    & Mallon, 2000; Perrin et al., 2004; Russell, 2005

Substance Abuse (Drugs and Alcohol)
Callahan, 2001; Chen-Hayes, 2001; D'Augelli, 2006a; Forman &
    Kalafat, 1998; Grossman & D'Augelli, 2007; Holmes & Cahill, 2004;
    Hunter & Mallon, 2000; McDaniel et al., 2001; Perrin et al., 2004;
    Russell, 2002

Environmental Risks

Coercive Mental Health Practices
Chen-Hayes, 2001; D'Augelli et al., 2006; Perrin et al., 2004; Travers &
    Paoletti, 1999

Coercive Religious Practices
Chen-Hayes, 2001

Demonization
Russell, 2002

Exploitation
Perrin et al., 2004

Family Strain
Cramer & Roach, 1988; D'Augelli, 1994, 1998, 2002, 2006b; D'Augelli et al.,
    2006; Elizur & Ziv, 2001; Grossman & D'Augelli, 2007; Herrenkohl
    et al., 1994; Luthar & Zigler, 1991; O'Conor, 1994; Perrin et al., 2004;
    Scourfield et al., 2008; Travers & Paoletti, 1999; Zucker et al., 2012

Family Rejection
Ejected from Home and Homelessness
    Henning-Stout et al., 2000; Hunter & Mallon, 2000; Perrin et al.,
        2004; Savin-Williams, 2008; Travers & Paoletti, 1999

Running Away
Callahan, 2001; Henning-Stout et al., 2000; Holmes & Cahill, 2004;
    Russell, 2005

Family Violence
D'Augelli, 2006b; D'Augelli et al., 2005; Grossman & D'Augelli, 2007;
    Travers & Paoletti, 1999

Gay Bashing (Physical Abuse and Physical Assault)
Chen-Hayes, 2001; Fieland et al., 2007; Grossman & D'Augelli, 2007;
    Grossman et al., 2009; Herrenkohl et al., 1994; Holmes & Cahill,
    2004; Meyer, 2007; O'Conor, 1994; Perrin et al., 2004; Sanders &
    Kroll, 2000; Savin-Williams, 1994; Schindel, 2008; Trotter, 2009

Harassment and Hostility
Chen-Hayes, 2001; Henning-Stout et al., 2000; Holmes & Cahill, 2004;
    Grossman et al., 2009; Perrin et al., 2004; Russell, 2002, 2005; Savin-
    Williams & Ream, 2003; Trotter, 2009; Savin-Williams, 1994; Travers
    & Paoletti, 1999

Homophobic Language
Ginsberg, 1998; Grossman et al., 2009; Holmes & Cahill, 2004;
    O'Conor, 1994; Perrin et al., 2004; Sanders & Kroll, 2000; Savin-
    Williams, 1994

Humiliation
Chen-Hayes, 2001

Lack of Role Models
Chen-Hayes, 2001

Marginalization
Aisenberg & Herrenkohl, 2008; Fassinger & Arseneau, 2007

Oppression
Alessi, 2014; Arrington & Wilson, 2000; Dane, 2005; Fassinger &
    Arseneau, 2007; Singh, 2012; Wexler et al., 2009

Peer Pressure
Chen-Hayes, 2001

Political Acts of Erasure
Russell, 2002; Sanders & Kroll, 2000

Problems in Peer Relationships
Bolger & Patterson, 2003; Chesir-Teran, 2003; D'Augelli, 2002; Freitas
    & Downey, 1998; Travers & Paoletti, 1999

Rigid Dress Codes
Chen-Hayes, 2001

Sexual Abuse
Chen-Hayes, 2001

Social Incompetence
Garmezy, 1991; Trotter, 2009

Societal Ambivalence
Russell, 2002

Stigmatization
Hunter & Mallon, 2000; Meyer, 2007

Verbal Abuse
Grossman & D'Augelli, 2007

Victimization
D'Augelli, 1998, 2002, 2003, 2006a; D'Augelli et al., 2005; Grossman
    et al., 2009; McDaniel et al., 2001; Russell, 2005; Savin-Williams,
    2008; Savin-Williams & Ream, 2003; Russell, 2002

Inventory of Assets

Assets enable individuals to develop a resilient mindset, which is a dynamic, reflexive process that hope energizes (Brooks, 2005; Goldstein & Brooks, 2005a, 2005b). Other characteristics of a resilient mindset include "empathy, a sense of satisfaction in the positive impacts of one's behaviors, a more confident outlook as islands of competence are displayed, and the use of problem-solving skills" (Brooks, 2005, p. 310). When individuals have a resilient mindset, they also have a sense of self-worth, feel appreciated, set achievable goals, can interact with others, can seek support, have coping strategies and the ability to make good decisions, and can identify both their strengths and areas for improvement (Brooks, 2005).

Resilient individuals use their assets to confront their problems (Brooks, 2005). As risk and resilience research indicates, assets that protect children and youth from adversity and trauma can be found in individuals, families, and communities (Yates et al., 2003). In contrasting assets and indicators of thriving conceptually, Sesma et al. (2005) describe assets "as *building blocks* of success, whereas thriving indicators are seen as *signs or markers* of success" (p. 289, italics in original). They locate the power of assets "in the cumulative pile-up of effects across multiple contexts" (p. 285). By this they mean there is no one asset or set of assets that can be singled out to account for enhanced development or growing into resilience. In the context of individuals, Sesma et al. (2005) define developmental assets "as a set of interrelated experiences, relationships, skills, and values that are known to enhance a broad range of youth outcomes" (p. 282). Assets, which do not necessarily insulate an individual from risk, are variously viewed as protective, promotive, compensatory, salutary, and beneficial (Luthar & Zelazo, 2003; Sameroff, Gutman, & Peck, 2003). The degree to which assets protect an individual from the effects of risk is apparently predicated on a person's vulnerability, the level of adversity or trauma, and environmental influences (Carbonell et al., 2002; Masten et al., 1990).

Individual Assets

Autonomy, Resourcefulness, Independence, and Integrity
Beardslee, 1989; Forman & Kalafat, 1998; Carbonell et al., 1998;
  Garmezy, 1991; Rak & Patterson, 1996; Sameroff et al., 2003

Cognitive Skills, Good Intellectual Functioning, Insightfulness, and Reflectiveness
Doll & Lyon, 1998; Forman & Kalafat, 1998; Herrenkohl et al., 1994; Lock & Steiner, 1999; Masten, 2001; Masten et al., 1990; Masten & Coatsworth, 1998; Sameroff et al., 2003; Sesma et al., 2005; Tharinger & Wells, 2000

Competence, Positive Self-perception and Self-efficacy, and Social Proficiency
Anderson, 1998; Bowleg et al., 2003; Carbonell et al., 2002; Doll & Lyon, 1998; Forman & Kalafat, 1998; Garmezy, 1991; Luthar & Zigler, 1991; Masten et al., 1990; Rutter, 1985; Sesma et al., 2005

Determination, Perseverance, and a Sense of Agency to Act in the World
Beardslee, 1989; Forman & Kalafat, 1998; Herrenkohl et al., 1994; Massey, Cameron, Ouellette, & Fine, 1998; Sesma et al., 2005

Good Communication Skills and Responsiveness
Brooks, 2005; Herrenkohl et al., 1994; Sameroff et al., 2003; Werner, 1995

Hobbies, Interests, and Talents
Garmezy, 1991; Herrenkohl et al., 1994; Tharinger & Wells, 2000; Werner, 1995

Internal Locus of Control and Capability to Deal with Power Issues
Anderson, 1998; Bolger & Patterson, 2003; Brooks, 2005; Cicchetti & Rogosch, 1997; Doll & Lyon, 1998; Herrenkohl et al., 1994; Luthar, 1993; Luthar & Zigler, 1991; Masten, 2001; Masten et al., 1990; Masten & Coatsworth, 1998; O'Grady & Metz, 1987; Ungar et al., 2007; Werner, 1995

Positive Identification and Openness about Sexual Orientation
Adams, 2006; Anderson, 1998; Bringaze & White, 2001; Clauss-Ehlers, 2008; Cramer & Roach, 1988; D'Augelli, 2002; Meyer, 2007; O'Conor, 1994; Perrin et al., 2004; Scourfield et al., 2008; Sesma et al., 2005

Repertoire of Coping Strategies
Hunter & Mallon, 2000; Rutter, 1999

Sense of Self-worth, a Positive Disposition, and the Capacity to Resolve Problems

Anderson, 1998; Beardslee, 1989; Bernard, 1992; Bowleg et al., 2003; Brooks, 2005; Carbonell et al., 2002; Cicchetti & Rogosch, 1997; Cowen et al., 1997; Cramer & Roach, 1988; Doll & Lyon, 1998; Forman & Kalafat, 1998; Galligan et al., 2010; Garmezy, 1991; Herrenkohl et al., 1994; Lock & Steiner, 1999; Luthar et al., 2000; Luthar & Zigler, 1991; Masten et al., 1990; Masten & Coatsworth, 1998; Poorman, 2002; Rak & Patterson, 1996; Russell, 2002, 2005; Rutter, 1985; Sameroff et al., 2003; Sanders & Kroll, 2000; Sesma et al., 2005; te Riele, 2006; Tharinger & Wells, 2000; Ungar et al., 2007; Valentine & Feinauer, 1993; Werner, 1995; Wolkow & Ferguson, 2001; Yates et al., 2003

Socioeconomic Resources and Work Experience
Carbonell et al., 2002; Masten & Coatsworth, 1998

Caregiver and Family Assets

Good Relationships with Parent(s) and Family
Adams, 2006; Angell, 2000; Bolger & Patterson, 2003; Brokenleg, 2010; Brooks, 2005; Carbonell et al., 1998; Carbonell et al., 2002; Cowen et al., 1997; D'Augelli, 2003, 2006b; D'Augelli et al., 2005; de Vries & Cohen-Kettenis, 2012; Doll & Lyon, 1998; Drescher & Byne, 2012; Elizur & Ziv, 2001; Fausto-Sterling, 2012; Fergusson & Lynskey, 1996; Forman & Kalafat, 1998; Herrenkohl et al., 1994; Hill & Menvielle, 2009; Hsieh & Leung, 2009; Johnson et al., 2014; Luecke, 2011; Luthar & Zigler, 1991; Luthar & Zelazo, 2003; Masten et al., 1990; Masten & Coatsworth, 1998; Rak & Patterson, 1996; Riley et al., 2011; Rivers & Cowie, 2006; Russell, 2002, 2005; Sameroff et al., 2003; Scharrón-del Río et al., 2014; Sesma et al., 2005; Tharinger & Wells, 2000; Ungar et al., 2007; Wolkow & Ferguson, 2001

Supportive and Effective Caregivers
Doll & Lyon, 1998; Garmezy, 1991; Herrenkohl et al., 1994; Masten et al., 1990; Masten & Coatsworth, 1998

Community Assets

Access to Counsellors Knowledgeable about Sexual and Gender Minorities
Bernal & Coolhart, 2012; Bringaze & White, 2001; Case & Meier, 2014; Edwards-Leeper & Spack, 2012; Ehrensaft, 2011, 2012, 2013; Heck

et al., 2014; McCabe, 2014; Minter, 2012; Scharrón-del Río et al., 2014; Stein, 2012

Access to Information, Resources, and Educational and Intervention Programs
Adams, 2006; Bowleg et al., 2003; Bringaze & White, 2001; Corcoran & Nichols-Casebolt, 2004; Grossman & D'Augelli, 2007; James, 2010; Lock & Steiner, 1999; Russell, 2002; Ungar et al., 2007

Connections, Mentors, Role Models, Quality Attachments, and Community, Cultural, and Environmental Supports
Cagle, 2007; Carbonell et al., 2002; Cowen et al., 1997; D'Augelli, 1994, 2002; Doll & Lyon, 1998; Forman & Kalafat, 1998; Garmezy, 1991; Hunter & Mallon, 2000; Luthar & Zelazo, 2003; Luthar & Zigler, 1991; Philip, 2008; Rak & Patterson, 1996; Russell, 2002; Sameroff et al., 2003; Sesma et al., 2005; Southwick et al., 2007; Tharinger & Wells, 2000; Werner, 1995; Wolkow & Ferguson, 2001

Effective Schools and Connectedness including GSAs, School Counselling Supports, Library Supports, SGM-inclusive Curriculum, and SGM-specific Anti-discrimination and Harassment Policies
Aisenberg & Herrenkohl, 2008; Bernard, 1992; Callahan, 2001; Chen-Hayes, 2001; Chesir-Teran, 2003; Corcoran & Nichols-Casebolt, 2004; Cowen et al., 1997; DiFulvio, 2011; Forman & Kalafat, 1998; Garmezy, 1991; Gastic & Johnson, 2009; Greytak et al., 2013; Grossman et al., 2009; Heck et al., 2014; Johnson, 2008; Luecke, 2011; Luthar et al., 2000; McCabe, 2014; McCready, 2004; Quasha et al., 2014; Reyes & Elias, 2011; Rivers & Cowie; 2006; Russell, 2005; Scharrón-del Río et al., 2014; St. John et al., 2014; Tharinger & Wells, 2000; Werner, 1995; Wexler et al., 2009

Positive Media Imagery
D'Augelli, 1994

Positive Relationships and Affectional Ties that Affirm, Enable Safety, and Encourage Trust, Autonomy, and Initiative
Beardslee, 1989; Bowleg et al., 2003; Carbonell et al., 2002; D'Augelli, 2006b; Luthar & Zelazo, 2003; Sanders & Kroll, 2000; Tharinger & Wells, 2000; Ungar et al., 2007; Ungar, 2011; Werner, 1995

Peer Relationships and Peer Support
Anderson 1998; Bernard, 1992; Bolger & Patterson, 2003; Bringaze &
    White, 2001; Carbonell et al., 2002; Dane, 2005; D'Augelli, 1998, 2002;
    Doll & Lyon, 1998; Elizur & Ziv, 2001; Garmezy, 1991; Hunter &
    Mallon, 2000; Lock & Steiner, 1999; Luthar & Zelazo, 2003; Mustanski,
    Newcomb, & Garofalo, 2011; O'Grady & Metz, 1987; Perrin et al.,
    2004; Rak & Patterson, 1996; Rivers & Cowie, 2006; Russell, 2005

Positive Relationship with (At Least One) Competent Adult
Adams, 2006; Bolger & Patterson, 2003; Brooks, 2005; Forman &
    Kalafat, 1998; Jessor et al., 1998; Luthar et al., 2000; Luthar & Zelazo,
    2003; Masten, 2001; Masten et al., 1990; Pianta & Walsh, 1998

Supportive Faith Groups and Other Institutional Ties
Bowleg et al., 2003; Cagle, 2007; Doll & Lyon; 1998; Garmezy, 1991;
    Herrenkohl et al., 1994; Masten et al., 1990; Tharinger & Wells, 2000

Indicators of Thriving

Noting that research has largely focused on risks behaviours that
impede adolescent growth into resilience, Sesma et al. (2005) relate, "[T]
here is a relative paucity of research around what constitutes thriving in
adolescence" (p. 289). As well, what it means to thrive is "more rooted
in moral worldviews and more culturally contextualized than are ideas
about risk" (p. 290). Thus, when reviewing the following list of indicators of thriving, it is important to ask how the list would vary based
on the sex, sexual, gender, ethnic, racial, and other differences marking
vulnerable youth (Ungar et al., 2007). In a generic context, Pianta and
Walsh (1998) conceptualize thriving as a dynamic and variable process
that works towards life balances; it is a "specific type of life energy
indicating movement and growth – an enhanced level of functioning
with creative and generative functions that cycle through periods of
rest, activity, and stasis" (p. 55). Behavioural indicators are key markers of thriving, and they complement assets in reflecting optimal individual and social development of SGM youth (Sesma et al., 2005). There
are numerous indicators of SGM youth thriving after learning to handle adversity, as indicated in the list that follows. Indeed experiences
of adversity, which can be rearticulated as challenges to overcome in
order to live a full and satisfying life, can have steeling effects against

the hurt, harm, and humiliation of living with heterosexism, sexism, genderism, and homo/bi/transphobia (Rak & Patterson, 1996; Rutter, 1985). Rutter (1987) concludes, "[P]rotection may lie in the 'steeling' qualities that derive from successful coping with the hazards when the exposure is of a type and degree that is manageable in the context of the child's capacities and social situation" (p. 326).

While the challenges that vulnerable SGM youth face must not be minimized in terms of the assault on their ability to cope, the power of youth agency wanting to blossom should not be underestimated either. SGM youth do not want to give up. They want to thrive. Having allies, role models, and resources for support are vital elements in an ecology of thriving that transcends just coping. Here resources are broadly understood "as the availability of structural provisions, including financial assistance and education, as well as basic instrumental needs, such as food, shelter, and clothing" (Ungar et al., 2007, p. 296). As youth demonstrate indicators of thriving, they are building the capacity to be problem solvers and change agents in their own lives and social networks. In the process they become happier, healthier, and more hopeful in the face of any setbacks that life brings their way.

Inventory of Indicators

Actively Seeks SGM Peers
Bringaze & White, 2001

Attachment to Family
Ungar et al., 2007

Believing in Community
Adams, 2006

Challenging Heterosexist Messages
Bringaze & White, 2001

Civic Engagement
Russell, 2002; Ungar et al., 2007

Coming Out, as One Is Comfortable
Massey et al., 1998

Coping
Bottrell, 2007; Butler & Astbury, 2008; Jaffee & Gallop, 2007;
    Lock & Steiner, 1999; Masten et al., 1990; Rutter, 1999;
    Ungar, 2010

Cultural Adherence
Ungar et al., 2007

Dealing with Internalized Myths about Heterosexuality
D'Augelli, 1994

Delaying Gratification
Sesma et al., 2005

Developing a Network to (Re)Construct and Support SGM Identity
Development
Bringaze & White, 2001; D'Augelli, 1994

Exhibiting Leadership
Sesma et al., 2005; Kress, 2006

Exhibiting Self-esteem
Ungar et al., 2007

Extending Time and Succeeding in Formal Education
Luthar & Zelazo, 2003; Massey et al., 1998; Sesma et al., 2005; Ungar
    et al., 2007

Finding Shelter
Massey et al., 1998

GSA Involvement
GSA Network, 2013; Mercier, 2009; Wells, 2006

Helping Others
Sesma et al., 2005

Joining Social Movements
Massey et al., 1998; Jones & Hillier, 2013

Leaving an Abusive Home
Massey et al., 1998

Maintaining Physical Health
Sesma et al., 2005

Mediating Societal and/or Cultural Expectations
Masten, 2001

Not Internalizing Heterosexism
Bringaze & White, 2001

Overcoming Adversity
Sesma et al., 2005

Seeing Choices
Massey et al., 1998

Seeking Out Resources
Bowleg et al., 2003

Seeking Out Role Models
Luthar & Zigler, 1991

Significant Attachment with Understanding Peers
Adams, 2006

SGM Activity Involvement
Adams, 2006; Massey et al., 1998

Steeling Effects
Pianta & Walsh, 1998; Rak & Patterson, 1996; Rutter, 1985

Valuing Diversity
Sesma et al., 2005

Willingness to Admit Setbacks
Massey et al., 1998

References

Adams, E.M., Cahill, B.J., & Ackerlind, S.J. (2005). A qualitative study of Latino lesbian and gay youths' experiences with discrimination and the career development process. *Journal of Vocational Behavior, 66*(2), 199–218. http://dx.doi.org/10.1016/j.jvb.2004.11.002

Adams, L.L. (2006). *Resilience in lesbian, gay and bisexual adult college students: A retrospective study* (Doctoral dissertation). Retrieved from ProQuest. (AAT 3240342)

Aisenberg, E., & Herrenkohl, T. (2008). Community violence in context: Risk and resilience in children and families. *Journal of Interpersonal Violence, 23*(3), 296–315. http://dx.doi.org/10.1177/0886260507312287

Alberta Health. (2013). HIV in Alberta: A brief epi update; A PowerPoint prepared by Kimberley Simmonds. Epidemiologist, Alberta Health.

Alberta's Education Partners. (2000). *A vision and agenda for public education.* Edmonton, AB: Author.

Alessi, E.J. (2014). A framework for incorporating minority stress theory into treatment with sexual minority clients. *Journal of Gay & Lesbian Mental Health, 18*(1), 47–66. http://dx.doi.org/10.1080/19359705.2013.789811

Alfonso, J.T., Diaz, N.V., Andujar-Bello, I., & Rosa, L.E.N. (2006). Strengths and vulnerabilities of a sample of gay and bisexual male adolescents in Puerto Rico. *Revista Interamericana de Psicología, 40*(1), 55–64.

Allman, P. (1999). *Revolutionary social transformation: Democratic hopes, political possibilities and critical education.* Westport, CT: Bergin & Garvey.

American Psychiatric Association (APA). (2013). *Gender dysphoria.* Retrieved from http://www.dsm5.org/Documents/Gender Dysphoria Fact Sheet.pdf

American Psychological Association. (2000). Guidelines for psychotherapy with lesbian, gay, and bisexual clients. *American Psychologist, 55*(12), 1440–51. http://dx.doi.org/10.1037/0003-066X.55.12.1440

Anderson, A.L. (1998). Strengths of gay male youth: An untold story. *Child & Adolescent Social Work Journal, 15*(1), 55–71. http://dx.doi.org/10.1023/A:1022245504871

Andrews, G.A. (2002, 8 April). *Durham Catholic District School Board confirms principal's decision.* Retrieved from http://www.durhamrc.edu.on.ca/html/pr-04-08-02.html (site discontinued)

Angell, G.B. (2000). Cultural resilience in North American Indian First Nations: The story of Little Turtle. *Critical Social Work, 1*(1), 1–14.

Anonymous Queers. (1999). Queers read this: I hate straights. In L. Gross & J.D. Woods (Eds.), *The Columbia reader on lesbians and gay men in media, society, and politics* (pp. 588–94). New York, NY: Columbia University Press.

Arana, G. (2012). My so-called ex-gay life. *The American Prospect.* Retrieved 10 April 2013 from http://prospect.org/article/my-so-called-ex-gay-life

Armstrong, L. (2014, 25 June). Pride abbreviation covers colours of the rainbow – and then some. *Toronto Star*, pp. A1, A4.

Arrington, E.G., & Wilson, M.N. (2000). A re-examination of risk and resilience during adolescence: Incorporating culture and diversity. *Journal of Child and Family Studies, 9*(2), 221–30. http://dx.doi.org/10.1023/A:1009423106045

Artuso, A. (2012, 5 June). Ontario MPPs pass anti-bullying bill. *Toronto Sun.* Retrieved from http://www.torontosun.com/2012/06/05/ontario-mpps-pass-anti-bullying-bill

Baird, V. (2007). *The no-nonsense guide to sexual diversity.* Toronto, ON: New Internationalist Publications & Between the Lines.

Balsam, K.F. (2003). Trauma, stress, and resilience among sexual minority women: Rising like the phoenix. *Journal of Lesbian Studies, 7*(4), 1–8. http://dx.doi.org/10.1300/J155v07n04_01

Baluja, T. (2011a, 21 March). Banning gay-straight alliances goes against equity grain, McGuinty warns. *Globe and Mail.* Retrieved from http://www.theglobeandmail.com/news/toronto/banning-gay-straight-alliances-goes-against-equity-grain-mcguinty-warns/article1949974/

Baluja, T. (2011b, 29 March). Principal takes over first gay alliance meeting, group says. *Globe and Mail.* Retrieved from http://www.theglobeandmail.com/news/toronto/principal-takes-over-first-gay-alliance-meeting-group-says/article1962144/

Baluja, T. (2012, 29 May). Catholic trustees prefer "Respecting Differences" clubs to gay-straight alliances. *Globe and Mail.* Retrieved from http://www.theglobeandmail.com/news/toronto/catholic-trustees-prefer-respecting-differences-clubs-to-gay-straight-alliances/article4216611/

Bancroft, J. (2003). Can sexual orientation change? A long-running saga. *Archives of Sexual Behavior, 32*(5), 419–21.

Barry, R. (2000). Sheltered "children": The self-creation of a safe space by gay, lesbian, and bisexual students. In L. Weis & M. Fine (Eds.), *Construction site: Evacuating race, class, and gender among urban youth* (pp. 84–99). New York, NY: Teachers College Press.

Beardslee, W.R. (1989). The role of self-understanding in resilient individuals: The development of a perspective. *American Journal of Orthopsychiatry, 59*(2), 266–78. http://dx.doi.org/10.1111/j.1939-0025.1989.tb01659.x

Beauchamp, D.L. (2008). *Sexual orientation and victimization 2004.* Ottawa, ON: Canadian Centre for Justice Statistics.

Becker, J.M. (2012, 17 May). World Health Organization's Americas Office condemns reparative therapy. *Truth Wins Out.* Retrieved from http://www.truthwinsout.org/blog/2012/05/25276/

Berghe, W.V., Dewaele, A., Cox, N., & Vincke, J. (2010). Minority-specific determinants of mental well-being among lesbian, gay, and bisexual youth. *Journal of Applied Social Psychology, 40*(1), 153–66. http://dx.doi.org/10.1111/j.1559-1816.2009.00567.x

Bernal, A.T., & Coolhart, D. (2012). Treatment and ethical considerations with transgender children and youth in family therapy. *Journal of Family Psychotherapy, 23*(4), 287–303. http://dx.doi.org/10.1080/08975353.2012.735594

Bernard, B. (1992). Peer programs: A major strategy for fostering resiliency in kids. *Peer Facilitator Quarterly, 9*(3), 14–17.

Biesta, G.J.J. (2003). Jacques Derrida: Deconstruction = justice. In M. Peters, M. Olssen, & C. Lankshear (Eds.), *Futures of critical theory: Dreams of difference* (pp. 141–54). Lanham, MD: Rowman & Littlefield.

Blackburn, M.V. (2004). Understanding agency beyond school-sanctioned activities. *Theory into Practice, 43*(2), 102–10.

Blackwell, C.W. (2008). Nursing implications in the application of conversion therapies on gay, lesbian, bisexual, and transgender clients. *Issues in Mental Health Nursing, 29*(6), 651–65. http://dx.doi.org/10.1080/01612840802048915

Blewitt, J. (2011). Lifelong learning and environmental sustainability. In S. Jackson (Ed.), *Lifelong learning and social justice: Communities, work and identities in a globalised world* (pp. 18–41). Leicester, UK: National Institute of Adult Continuing Education.

Blumenfeld, W.J. (1995). "Gay/straight" alliances. In G. Unks (Ed.), *The gay teenager* (pp. 211–24). New York, NY: Routledge.

Bogar, C.B., & Hulse-Killacky, D. (2006). Resiliency determinants and resiliency processes among female adult survivors of childhood sexual abuse. *Journal of Counseling and Development, 84*(3), 318–27. http://dx.doi.org/10.1002/j.1556-6678.2006.tb00411.x

Bolger, K.E., & Patterson, C.J. (2003). Sequelae of child maltreatment: Vulnerability and resistance. In S.S. Luthar (Ed.), *Resilience and vulnerability: Adaptation in the context of childhood adversities* (pp. 156–81). New York, NY: Cambridge University Press. http://dx.doi.org/10.1017/CBO9780511615788.009

Bottrell, D. (2007). Resistance, resilience and social identities: Reframing "problem youth" and the problem of schooling. *Journal of Youth Studies, 10*(5), 597–616. http://dx.doi.org/10.1080/13676260701602662

Bowleg, L., Huang, J., Brooks, K., Black, A., & Burkholder, G. (2003). Triple jeopardy and beyond: Multiple minority stress and resilience among black lesbians. *Journal of Lesbian Studies, 7*(4), 87–108. http://dx.doi.org/10.1300/J155v07n04_06

Brill, S., & Pepper, R. (2008). *The transgender child: A handbook for families and professionals.* San Francisco, CA: Cleis Press.

Bringaze, T.B., & White, L.J. (2001). Living out proud: Factors contributing to healthy identity development in lesbian leaders. *Journal of Mental Health Counseling, 23*(2), 162–73.

Britzman, D.P. (1995). Is there a queer pedagogy? Or, stop reading straight. *Educational Theory, 45*(2), 151–65. http://dx.doi.org/10.1111/j.1741-5446.1995.00151.x

Britzman, D.P. (1997). What is this thing called love? New discourses for understanding gay and lesbian youth. In S. de Castell & M. Bryson (Eds.), *Radical in<ter>ventions: Identity, politics, and differences in educational praxis* (pp. 183–207). Albany, NY: State University of New York Press.

Brokenleg, M. (2010). The resilience revolution: Our original collaboration. *Reclaiming Children and Youth, 18*(4), 8–11.

Bronfenbrenner, U. (1979). *The ecology of human development: Experiments by nature and design.* Cambridge, MA: Harvard University Press.

Brooks, R.B. (2005). The power of parenting. In S. Goldstein & R.B. Brooks (Eds.), *Handbook of resilience in children* (pp. 297–314). New York, NY: Kluwer. http://dx.doi.org/10.1007/0-306-48572-9_18

Brown, L. (2011, 23 March). Halton Catholic board committee rejects gay-straight alliances. *Toronto Star.* Retrieved from http://www.insidehalton.com/community-story/2988412-halton-catholic-board-committee-rejects-gay-straight-alliances/

Brown, M., & Colbourne, M. (2005). Bent but not broken: Exploring queer youth resilience. In M. Ungar (Ed.), *Handbook for working with children and youth: Pathways to resilience across cultures and contexts* (pp. 263–77). Thousand Oaks, CA: SAGE. http://dx.doi.org/10.4135/9781412976312.n16

Butler, A., & Astbury, G. (2008). The use of defence mechanisms as precursors to coming out in post-apartheid South Africa: A gay and lesbian youth perspective. *Journal of Homosexuality, 55*(2), 223–44. http://dx.doi.org/10.1080/00918360802129485

Butler, J. (1993). *Bodies that matter*. New York, NY: Routledge.

Butler, J. (2002). Capacity. In S.M. Barber & D.L. Clark (Eds.), *Regarding Sedgwick: Essays on queer culture and critical theory* (pp. 109–19). New York, NY: Routledge.

Butler, J. (2004). *Undoing gender*. New York, NY: Routledge.

Byne, W., Bradley, S.J., Coleman, E., Eyler, A.E., Green, R., Menvielle, E.J., … Tompkins, D.A. (2012). Report of the American Psychiatric Association task force on treatment of gender identity disorder. *Archives of Sexual Behavior, 41*(4), 759–96. http://dx.doi.org/10.1007/s10508-012-9975-x

Byrd, A.D. (2003). The malleability of homosexuality: A debate long overdue. *Archives of Sexual Behavior, 32*(5), 423–5.

Cagle, B.E. (2007). *Gay young men transitioning to adulthood: Resilience, resources, and the larger social environment* (Doctoral dissertation). Retrieved from ProQuest. (AAT 3280304)

Callahan, C.J. (2001). Protecting and counseling gay and lesbian students. *Journal of Humanistic Counseling, Education and Development, 40*(1), 5–10. http://dx.doi.org/10.1002/j.2164-490X.2001.tb00097.x

Camp, S., & Huggins, D. (2004, 27 November). *Hate and bias crime*. Presentation at the 4th annual Agape: Sex, Sexual, and Gender Differences in Education and Culture Conference, Faculty of Education, University of Alberta, Edmonton, Alberta.

Canadian Conference of Catholic Bishops (CCCB). (1994). *Catechism of the Catholic Church*. Ottawa, ON: Publications Service, CCCB.

Canadian Press (CP). (2002, 7 May). *Catholic board says gay teen can go to public school if he doesn't like rules*. Reprinted in *Sentinel-Review*, 8 May 2002. Retrieved from https://news.google.com/newspapers?nid=2710&dat=20020508&id=-Wg5AAAAIBAJ&sjid=USkMAAAAIBAJ&pg=1177,6270481&hl=en

Canadian Press (CP). (2005, 29 June). Gay student drops court battle over same-sex prom date. *The Edmonton Journal*, p. A13.

Canadian Press (CP). (2012a, 5 June). Ontario anti-bullying bill passed. Retrieved from http://www.cbc.ca/news/canada/ottawa/ontario-anti-bullying-bill-passed-1.1253806

Canadian Press (CP). (2012b, 5 June). Ontario anti-bullying bill passes third and final reading with NDP support. Retrieved from http://news.nationalpost.com/2012/06/05/ontario-anti-bullying-bill-passes-third-and-final-reading-with-ndp-support/

Canadian Teachers' Federation (CTF) (Ed.). (2004). *Policy on anti-homophobia and anti-heterosexism*. Retrieved from http://www.ctf-fce.ca/Documents/BGLTTPolicies -English.pdf

Canadian Teachers' Federation (CTF) (Ed.). (2005). *Lessons learned: A collection of stories and articles about bisexual, gay, lesbian, and transgender issues*. Ottawa, ON: CTF.

Canadian Teachers' Federation (CTF) & Elementary Teachers' Federation of Ontario (ETFO) (Eds.). (2002). *Seeing the rainbow: Teachers talk about bisexual, gay, lesbian, transgender and two-spirited realities*. Ottawa, ON: Authors.

Cannella, G.S., & Lincoln, Y.S. (2011). Ethics, research regulations, and critical social science. In N.K. Denzin & Y.S. Lincoln (Eds.), *The SAGE handbook of qualitative research* (4th ed., pp. 81–9). Thousand Oaks, CA: SAGE.

Carbonell, D.M., Reinherz, H.Z., & Giaconia, R.M. (1998). Risk and resilience in late adolescence. *Child & Adolescent Social Work Journal, 15*(4), 251–72. http://dx.doi.org/10.1023/A:1025107827111

Carbonell, D.M., Reinherz, H.Z., Giaconia, R.M., Stashwick, C.K., Paradis, A.D., & Beardslee, W.R. (2002). Adolescent protective factors promoting resilience in young adults at risk for depression. *Child & Adolescent Social Work Journal, 19*(5), 393–412. http://dx.doi.org/10.1023/A:1020274531345

Carey, B. (2012, 18 May). Leading psychiatrist apologizes for study supporting gay "cure." *The New York Times*. Retrieved from http://www.nytimes.com/2012/05/19/health/dr-robert-l-spitzer-noted-psychiatrist-apologizes-for-study-on-gay-cure.html?pagewanted=all&_r=2&

Carrette, J.R. (Ed.). (1999). *Religion and culture: Michel Foucault*. New York, NY: Routledge.

Case, K.A., & Meier, S.C. (2014). Developing allies to transgender and gender-nonconforming youth: Training for counselors and educators. *Journal of LGBT Youth, 11*(1), 62–82. http://dx.doi.org/10.1080/19361653.2014.840764

Casper, R.F. (1991). Clinical uses of gonadotropin-releasing hormone analogues. *Canadian Medical Association Journal, 144*(2), 153–8.

CBC News. (2002a, 26 March). *Catholic board meeting disrupted by gay student's supporters*. Retrieved from http://www.cbc.ca/news/canada/catholic-board-meeting-disrupted-by-gay-student-s-supporters-1.325527

CBC News. (2002b, 9 April). *Catholic school board rules against gay prom date*. Retrieved from http://www.cbc.ca/news/canada/catholic-school-board-rules-against-gay-prom-date-1.336629

CBC News. (2002c, 22 May). *Gay teen wins fight over Catholic prom*. Retrieved from http://www.cbc.ca/news/canada/gay-teen-wins-fight-over-catholic-prom-1.348831

CBC News. (2002d, 7 May). *Gay student a "bad example" says school board.* Retrieved from http://www.cbc.ca/news/canada/gay-student-a-bad-example-says-school-board-1.334498

CBC Toronto. (2002, 9 April). *Board refuses bid for same-sex prom date.* Retrieved from http://toronto.cbc.ca/regional/servlet/View?filename=prom_090502 (site discontinued)

Central Toronto Youth Services (CTYS). (2008). *Families in transition: A resource guide for parents of trans youth.* Toronto, ON: Author.

Chen-Hayes, S.F. (2001). Counseling and advocacy with transgendered and gender-variant persons in schools and families. *Journal of Humanistic Counseling, Education and Development, 40*(1), 34–48. http://dx.doi.org/10.1002/j.2164-490X.2001.tb00100.x

Chesir-Teran, D. (2003). Conceptualizing and assessing heterosexism in high schools: A setting-level approach. *American Journal of Community Psychology, 31*(3/4), 267–79. http://dx.doi.org/10.1023/A:1023910820994

Chief Public Health Officer (CPHO). (2011). *The Chief Public Health Officer's report on the state of public health in Canada 2011: Youth and young adults – life in transition.* Ottawa, ON: Office of the CPHO. Available at http://www.phac-aspc.gc.ca/cphorsphc-respcacsp/2011/index-eng.php

Chief Public Health Officer (CPHO). (2012). *The Chief Public Health Officer's report on the state of public health in Canada 2012: Influencing health – the importance of sex and gender.* Ottawa, ON: Office of the CPHO. Available at http://www.phac-aspc.gc.ca/cphorsphc-respcacsp/2012/index-eng.php

Children's Aid Society of Toronto. (2012). *Out and proud affirmation guidelines: Practice guidelines for equity in gender and sexual diversity.* Toronto, ON: Author.

Cianciotto, J., & Cahill, S. (2006). *Youth in the crosshairs: The third wave of ex-gay activism.* New York, NY: National Gay and Lesbian Task Force Policy Institute.

Cicchetti, D., & Rogosch, F.A. (1997). The role of self-organization in the promotion of resilience in maltreated children. *Development and Psychopathology, 9*(4), 797–815. http://dx.doi.org/10.1017/S0954579497001442

Clauss-Ehlers, C.S. (2008). Sociocultural factors, resilience, and coping: Support for a culturally sensitive measure of resilience. *Journal of Applied Developmental Psychology, 29*(3), 197–212. http://dx.doi.org/10.1016/j.appdev.2008.02.004

Clements-Nolle, K., Marx, R., & Katz, M. (2006). Attempted suicide among transgender persons: The influence of gender-based discrimination and victimization. *Journal of Homosexuality, 51*(3), 53–69. http://dx.doi.org/10.1300/J082v51n03_04

Cloud, J. (2005, 2 October). The battle over gay teens. *Time Magazine.* Retrieved from http://content.time.com/time/magazine/article/0,9171,1112856,00.html

Congregation for the Doctrine of the Faith (CDF). (1986). Letter to the bishops of the Catholic church on the pastoral care of homosexual persons. Retrieved from

http://www.vatican.va/roman_curia/congregations/cfaith/documents/
rc_con_cfaith_doc_19861001_homosexual-persons_en.html

Corcoran, J., & Nichols-Casebolt, A. (2004). Risk and resilience ecological
framework for assessment and goal formulation. *Child & Adolescent Social
Work Journal, 21*(3), 211–35. http://dx.doi.org/10.1023/B:CASW.
0000028453.79719.65

Courage. (n.d.). *Courage: Pastoral care for homosexual persons.* Retrieved from
http://www.ewtn.com/library/ISSUES/COURAGE.TXT

Courage. (2000a). *Courage apostolate.* Retrieved from http://couragerc.org

Courage. (2000b). *Canadian chapters.* Retrieved from http://couragerc.org

Cowen, E.L., Wyman, P.A., Work, W.C., Kim, J.Y., Fagen, D.B., & Magnus, K.B.
(1997). Follow-up study of young stress-affected and stress-resilient urban
children. *Development and Psychopathology, 9*(3), 565–77. http://dx.doi.
org/10.1017/S0954579497001326

Coyote, I. (2012). What I wish I knew. In D. Savage & T. Miller (Eds.), *It gets
better: Coming out, overcoming bullying, and creating a life worth living* (pp.
87–90). New York, NY: Plume.

Cramer, D.W., & Roach, A.J. (1988). Coming out to mom and dad: A
study of gay males and their relationships with their parents. *Journal of
Homosexuality, 15*(3–4), 79–92. http://dx.doi.org/10.1300/J082v15n03_04

Cronin, M., & McNinch, J. (2004). Introduction. In J. McNinch & M. Cronin
(Eds.), *I could not speak my heart: Education and social justice for gay and lesbian
youth* (pp. ix–xvi). Regina, SK: Canadian Plains Research Centre, University
of Regina Press.

Dane, S. (2005). The importance of out-group acceptance in addition to in-
group support in predicting the well-being of same-sex attracted youth. *Gay
& Lesbian Issues and Psychology Review, 1*(1), 23–9.

D'Augelli, A.R. (1994). Identity development and sexual orientation: Toward a
model of lesbian, gay, and bisexual development. In E.J. Trickett, R.J. Watts,
& D. Birman (Eds.), *Human diversity: Perspectives on people in context* (pp.
312–33). San Francisco, CA: Jossey-Bass.

D'Augelli, A.R. (1998). Developmental implications of victimization of lesbian,
gay, and bisexual youths. In G.M. Herek (Ed.), *Stigma and sexual orientation:
Understanding prejudice against lesbians, gay men, and bisexuals* (pp. 187–210).
Thousand Oaks, CA: SAGE. http://dx.doi.org/10.4135/9781452243818.n9

D'Augelli, A.R. (2002). Mental health problems among lesbian, gay, and
bisexual youth ages 14 to 21. *Clinical Child Psychology and Psychiatry, 7,* 439–62.

D'Augelli, A.R. (2003). Lesbian and bisexual female youths aged 14 to 21:
Developmental challenges and victimization experiences. *Journal of Lesbian
Studies, 7*(4), 9–29. http://dx.doi.org/10.1300/J155v07n04_02

D'Augelli, A.R. (2006a). Developmental and contextual factors and mental health among lesbian, gay, and bisexual youths. In A.M. Omoto & H.S. Kurtzman (Eds.), *Sexual orientation and mental health: Examining identity and development in lesbian, gay, and bisexual people* (pp. 37–53). Washington, DC: American Psychological Association. http://dx.doi.org/10.1037/11261-002

D'Augelli, A.R. (2006b). Stress and adaptation among families of lesbian, gay, and bisexual youth: Research challenges. In J.J. Bigner (Ed.), *An introduction to GLBT family studies* (pp. 135–57). New York, NY: Haworth Press.

D'Augelli, A.R., Grossman, A.H., & Starks, M.T. (2005). Parents' awareness of lesbian, gay, and bisexual youths' sexual orientation. *Journal of Marriage and the Family, 67*(2), 474–82. http://dx.doi.org/10.1111/j.0022-2445.2005.00129.x

D'Augelli, A.R., Grossman, A.H., & Starks, M.T. (2006). Childhood gender atypicality, victimization, and PTSD among lesbian, gay, and bisexual youth. *Journal of Interpersonal Violence, 21*(11), 1462–82. http://dx.doi.org/10.1177/0886260506293482

Deater-Deckard, K., Ivy, L., & Smith, J. (2005). Resilience in gene-environment transactions. In S. Goldstein & R.B. Brooks (Eds.), *Handbook of resilience in children* (pp. 49–63). New York, NY: Kluwer. http://dx.doi.org/10.1007/0-306-48572-9_4

de Lauretis, T. (1991). Queer theory: Lesbian and gay sexualities – an introduction. *Differences: A Journal of Feminist Cultural Studies, 3*(2), iii–xviii.

D'Emilio, J. (1992). *Making trouble*. New York, NY: Routledge.

Denzin, N.K., & Lincoln, Y.S. (2005). Introduction: The discipline and practice of qualitative research. In N.K. Denzin & Y.S. Lincoln (Eds.), *The SAGE handbook of qualitative research* (3rd ed., pp. 1–32). Thousand Oaks, CA: SAGE.

Denzin, N.K., & Lincoln, Y.S. (Eds.). (2011). *The SAGE handbook of qualitative research* (4th ed.). Thousand Oaks, CA: SAGE.

Department of Justice Canada (DJC). (2003). Canadian Charter of Rights and Freedoms. Retrieved from http://laws-lois.justice.gc.ca/eng/Const/index.html

de Vries, A.L.C., & Cohen-Kettenis, P.T. (2012). Clinical management of gender dysphoria in children and adolescents: The Dutch approach. *Journal of Homosexuality, 59*(3), 301–20. http://dx.doi.org/10.1080/00918369.2012.653300

DiFulvio, G.T. (2011). Sexual minority youth, social connection and resilience: From personal struggle to collective identity. *Social Science & Medicine, 72*(10), 1611–17. http://dx.doi.org/10.1016/j.socscimed.2011.02.045

Dignity Canada Dignité (DCD). (n.d.). *Vatican "Halloween Letter" 1986: Letter to the bishops of the Catholic Church on the pastoral care of homosexual persons.* Retrieved from http://dignitycanada.org/halloweenletter.html

Dilley, P. (1999). Queer theory: Under construction. *International Journal of Qualitative Studies in Education*, *12*(5), 457–72. http://dx.doi.org/10.1080/095183999235890

Doll, B., & Lyon, M.A. (1998). Risk and resilience: Implications for the delivery of educational and mental health services in schools. *School Psychology Review*, *27*, 348–63.

Drescher, J., & Byne, W. (2012). Gender dysphoric/gender variant (GD/GV) children and adolescents: Summarizing what we know and what we have yet to learn. *Journal of Homosexuality*, *59*(3), 501–10. http://dx.doi.org/10.1080/00918369.2012.653317

Driskill, Q.-L., Finley, C., Gilley, B.J., & Morgensen, S.L. (Eds.). (2011). *Queer indigenous studies: Critical interventions in theory, politics, and literature.* Tucson, AZ: University of Arizona Press.

Driskill, Q.-L., Justice, D.H., Mirandi, D., & Tatonetti, L. (Eds.). (2011). *Sovereign erotics: A collection of Two-Spirit literature.* Tucson, AZ: University of Arizona Press.

Durham Catholic District School Board (DCDSB). (n.d.). *Durham Catholic District School Board.* Retrieved from http://www.oshawa.ca/com_res/drrsccb.asp (currently http://dcdsb.ca)

Dysart-Gale, D. (2010). Social justice and social determinants of health: Lesbian, gay, bisexual, transgendered, intersexed, and queer youth in Canada. *Journal of Child and Adolescent Psychiatric Nursing*, *23*(1), 23–8. http://dx.doi.org/10.1111/j.1744-6171.2009.00213.x

Edmonton Public School Board (EPSB). (2013a). *Code: HFA.BP. Topic: Sexual Orientation and Gender Identity. Effective date: 29-11-2011.* Retrieved from http://www.epsb.ca/ourdistrict/policy/h/hfa-bp/

Edmonton Public School Board (EPSB). (2013b). *Code: HFA.AR. Topic: Sexual Orientation and Gender Identity. Effective date: 13-11-2012.* Retrieved from http://www.epsb.ca/ourdistrict/policy/h/hfa-ar/

Edmonton Public Schools. (2013). *Sexual orientation and gender identity: Overview.* Retrieved from http://www.epsb.ca/ourdistrict/topics/sexualorientationandgenderidentity/

Edwards, P. (2011, 16 February). Halton Catholic board sits on gay-straight fence. *Toronto Star.* Retrieved from http://www.insidehalton.com/community/education/article/955602--halton-catholic-board-sits-on-gay-straight-fence

Edwards-Leeper, L., & Spack, N.P. (2012). Psychological evaluation and medical treatment of transgender youth in an interdisciplinary "Gender Management Service" (GeMS) in a major pediatric center. *Journal of Homosexuality*, *59*(3), 321–36. http://dx.doi.org/10.1080/00918369.2012.653302

Egale Canada. (2002, Summer). Court upholds gay student's bid to attend prom. *INFO-EGALE*, 1.

Egale Canada. (2009). *Youth speak up about homophobia and transphobia: The first national climate survey on homophobia in Canadian schools*. Retrieved from http://egale.ca/

Egale Canada. (2011). *Egale's comments on the TCDSB's draft policy statement [on equity and inclusive education]*. Retrieved from http://egale.ca/

Egale Canada. (2013). *My GSA*. Retrieved from http://mygsa.ca

Ehrensaft, D. (2011). *Gender born, gender made: Raising healthy gender-nonconforming children*. New York, NY: The Experiment.

Ehrensaft, D. (2012). From gender identity disorder to gender identity creativity: True gender self child therapy. *Journal of Homosexuality, 59*(3), 337–56. http://dx.doi.org/10.1080/00918369.2012.653303

Ehrensaft, D. (2013). Look, mom, I'm a boy – don't tell anyone I was a girl. *Journal of LGBT Youth, 10*(1–2), 9–28. http://dx.doi.org/10.1080/19361653.2012.717474

Elementary Teachers' Federation of Ontario (ETFO). (2012, 5 June). *Bill 13 – minority government works to prevent, stop bullying in schools*. Toronto, ON: ETFO Media Relations.

Elias, M.J., Parker, S., & Rosenblatt, J.L. (2005). Building educational opportunity. In S. Goldstein & R.B. Brooks (Eds.), *Handbook of resilience in children* (pp. 315–36). New York, NY: Kluwer. http://dx.doi.org/10.1007/0-306-48572-9_19

Elizur, Y., & Ziv, M. (2001). Family support and acceptance, gay male identity formation, and psychological adjustment: A path model. *Family Process, 40*(2), 125–44. http://dx.doi.org/10.1111/j.1545-5300.2001.4020100125.x

Elliott, D., & Paris, V. (2002, 6 May). *Legal factum for the Coalition for Marc Hall*. Toronto, ON: Authors.

Ellis, C., & Berger, L. (2003). Their story/my story/our story: Including the researcher's experience in interview research. In J.A. Holstein & J.F. Gubrium (Eds.), *Inside interviewing: New lenses, new concerns* (pp. 467–93). Thousand Oaks, CA: SAGE.

Ellis, V., & High, S. (2004). Something more to tell you: Gay, lesbian or bisexual young people's experiences of secondary schooling. *British Educational Research Journal, 30*(2), 213–25. http://dx.doi.org/10.1080/0141192042000195281

Episcopal Commission for Doctrine of the Canadian Conference of Catholic Bishops (ECD-CCCB). (2011). *Pastoral ministry to young people with same-sex attraction*. Ottawa, ON: Concacan.

Epstein, D., & Johnson, R. (1994). On the straight and the narrow: The heterosexual presumption, homophobias and schools. In D. Epstein (Ed.), *Challenging lesbian and gay inequalities in education* (pp. 197–230). Bristol, PA: Open University Press.

Epstein, D., & Johnson, R. (1998). *Schooling sexualities*. Buckingham, UK: Open University Press.

Epstein, D., O'Flynn, S., & Telford, D. (2001). "Othering" education: Sexualities, silences, and schooling. In W.G. Secada (Ed.), *Review of research in education 25, 2000–2001* (pp. 127–79). Washington, DC: American Educational Research Association.

Epstein, D., O'Flynn, S., & Telford, D. (2003). *Silenced sexualities in schools and universities*. Stoke-on-Trent, Staffordshire, UK: Trentham Books.

Epstein, D., & Sears, J.T. (1999). Introduction: Knowing dangerously. In D. Epstein & J.T. Sears (Eds.), *A dangerous knowing: Sexuality, pedagogy and popular culture* (pp. 1–7). New York, NY: Cassell.

Este, D., Sitter, K., & MacLaurin, B. (2009). Using mixed methods to understand resilience. In L. Liebenberg & M. Ungar (Eds.), *Researching resilience* (pp. 201–24). Toronto, ON: University of Toronto Press.

Fassinger, R.E., & Arseneau, J.R. (2007). "I'd rather get wet than be under that umbrella": Differentiating the experiences and identities of lesbian, gay, bisexual, and transgender people. In K.J. Bieschke, R.M. Perez, & K.A. DeBord (Eds.), *Handbook of counseling and psychotherapy with lesbian, gay, bisexual, and transgender clients* (2nd ed., pp. 19–49). Washington, DC: American Psychological Association. http://dx.doi.org/10.1037/11482-001

Fausto-Sterling, A. (2012). The dynamic development of gender variability. *Journal of Homosexuality, 59*(3), 398–421. http://dx.doi.org/10.1080/0091836 9.2012.653310

Feinberg, L. (1996). *Transgender warriors: Making history from Joan of Arc to Dennis Rodman*. Boston, MA: Beacon Press.

Fenaughty, J., & Harré, N. (2003). Life on the seesaw: A qualitative study of suicide resiliency factors for young gay men. *Journal of Homosexuality, 45*(1), 1–22. http://dx.doi.org/10.1300/J082v45n01_01

Fergusson, D.M., & Horwood, J.L. (2003). Resilience to childhood adversity: Results of a 21-year study. In S.S. Luthar (Ed.), *Resilience and vulnerability: Adaptation in the context of childhood adversities* (pp. 130–55). New York, NY: Cambridge University Press. http://dx.doi.org/10.1017/CBO9780511615788.008

Fergusson, D.M., & Lynskey, M.T. (1996). Adolescent resiliency to family adversity. *Journal of Child Psychology and Psychiatry, and Allied Disciplines, 37*(3), 281–92. http://dx.doi.org/10.1111/j.1469-7610.1996.tb01405.x

Fetner, T., & Kush, K. (2008). Gay-straight alliances in high schools: Social predictors of early adoption. *Youth & Society, 40*(1), 114–30. http://dx.doi.org/10.1177/0044118X07308073

Fieland, K.C., Walters, K.L., & Simoni, J.M. (2007). Determinants of health among two-spirit American Indians and Alaska Natives. In I.H. Meyer & M.E. Northridge (Eds.), *The health of sexual minorities: Public health perspectives on lesbian, gay, bisexual, and transgender populations* (pp. 268–300). New York, NY: Springer. http://dx.doi.org/10.1007/978-0-387-31334-4_11

Filbert, K.M., & Flynn, R.J. (2010). Developmental and cultural assets and resilient outcomes in First Nations young people in care: An initial test of an explanatory model. *Children and Youth Services Review, 32*(4), 560–4. http://dx.doi.org/10.1016/j.childyouth.2009.12.002

Fine, M., & Bertram, C. (1999). Sexing the globe. In D. Epstein & J.T. Sears (Eds.), *A dangerous knowing: Sexuality, pedagogy and popular culture* (pp. 153–63). New York, NY: Cassell.

Fine, M., & Weis, L. (2005). Compositional studies, in two parts: Critical theorizing and analysis on social (in)justice. In N.K. Denzin & Y.S. Lincoln (Eds.), *The SAGE handbook of qualitative research* (3rd ed., pp. 65–84). Thousand Oaks, CA: SAGE.

Fine, M., Weis, L., Centrie, C., & Roberts, R. (2000). Educating beyond the borders of schooling. *Anthropology & Education Quarterly, 31*(2), 131–51. http://dx.doi.org/10.1525/aeq.2000.31.2.131

Fisher, J. (2002, 9 April). *Open letter to EGALE Educators' Network.* Ottawa, ON: Author.

Flicker, S., Travers, R., Flynn, S., Larkin, J., Guta, A., Salehi, R., Pole, J.D., & Layne, C. (2010). Sexual health research for and with urban youth: The Toronto Teen Survey story. *Canadian Journal of Human Sexuality, 19*(4), 133–44.

Foley, D., & Valenzuela, A. (2005). Critical ethnography: The politics of collaboration. In N.K. Denzin & Y.S. Lincoln (Eds.), *The SAGE handbook of qualitative research* (3rd ed., pp. 217–34). Thousand Oaks, CA: SAGE.

Fone, B. (2000). *Homophobia: A history.* New York, NY: Metropolitan Books, Henry Holt & Co.

Fontana, A., & Frey, J.H. (2005). The interview: From neutral stance to political involvement. In N.K. Denzin & Y.S. Lincoln (Eds.), *The SAGE handbook of qualitative research* (3rd ed., pp. 695–727). Thousand Oaks, CA: SAGE.

Forman, S.G., & Kalafat, J. (1998). Substance abuse and suicide: Promoting resilience against self-destructive behavior in youth. *School Psychology Review, 27*(3), 398–406.

Foster, K.R., & Spencer, D. (2011). At risk of what? Possibilities over probabilities in the study of young lives. *Journal of Youth Studies, 14*(1), 125–43. http://dx.doi.org/10.1080/13676261.2010.506527

Frankham, J. (2001). The "open secret": Limitations on the expression of same-sex desire. *International Journal of Qualitative Studies in Education, 14*(4), 457–69. http://dx.doi.org/10.1080/095183901100446-9

Fraser, N. (1993). Rethinking the public sphere: A contribution to the critique on actually existing democracy. In B. Robbins (Ed.), *The phantom public sphere* (pp. 1–32). Minneapolis, MN: University of Minnesota Press.

Freire, P. (1998). *Teachers as cultural workers: Letters to those who dare teach* (D. Macedo, D. Koike, & A. Oliveira, Trans.). Boulder, CO: Westview Press.

Freire, P. (2004). *Pedagogy of indignation.* Boulder, CO: Paradigm Publishers.

Freitas, A.L., & Downey, G. (1998). Resilience: A dynamic perspective. *International Journal of Behavioral Development, 22*(2), 263–85. http://dx.doi.org/10.1080/016502598384379

Friedman-Nimz, R., Altman, J., Cain, S., Korn, S., Karger, M.J., Witsch, M.J., & Weiss, M. (2006). Blending support and social action: The power of a gay-straight alliance and PrideWorks conference. *Journal of Secondary Gifted Education, 17,* 258–64. http://dx.doi.org/10.4219/jsge-2006-412

Friend, R.A. (1993). Choices, not closets: Heterosexism and homophobia in schools. In L. Weis & M. Fine (Eds.), *Beyond silenced voices: Class, race, gender in the United States* (pp. 209–35). New York, NY: State University of New York Press.

Friend, R.A. (1998). Heterosexism, homophobia, and the culture of schooling. In S. Brooks (Ed.), *Invisible children in the society and its schools* (pp. 137–66). Mahwah, NJ: Lawrence Erlbaum Associates.

Gabarino, J. (2005). Foreword. In M. Ungar (Ed.), *Handbook for working with children and youth: Pathways to resilience across cultures and contexts* (pp. xi–xiii). Thousand Oaks, CA: SAGE.

Gager, P.J., & Elias, M.J. (1997). Implementing prevention programs in high-risk environments: Application of the resiliency paradigm. *American Journal of Orthopsychiatry, 67*(3), 363–73. http://dx.doi.org/10.1037/h0080239

Galligan, S.B., Barnett, R.V., Brennan, M.A., & Israel, G.D. (2010). Understanding the link between gender role conflict, resilience, and propensity for suicide in adolescent and emerging adult males. *International Journal of Men's Health, 9*(3), 201–10. http://dx.doi.org/10.3149/jmh.0903.201

Garmezy, N. (1991). Resiliency and vulnerability to adverse developmental outcomes associated with poverty. *American Behavioral Scientist, 34*(4), 416–30. http://dx.doi.org/10.1177/0002764291034004003

Gaskell, J. (2001). The "public" in public schools: A school board debate. *Canadian Journal of Education, 26*(1), 19–36. http://dx.doi.org/10.2307/1602143

Gastic, B., & Johnson, D. (2009). Teacher-mentors and the educational resilience of sexual minority youth. *Journal of Gay & Lesbian Social Services, 21*(2–3), 219–31. http://dx.doi.org/10.1080/10538720902772139

Gay & Lesbian Educators of British Columbia (GALE-BC). (2002, April). Student prevented from attending high school prom. *Gale Force, 12*(4), 4.

Gay-Straight Alliance Network (GSA Network). (2013). *About Us.* Retrieved from http://www.gsanetwork.org/

Ginsberg, R.W. (1998). Silenced voices inside our schools. *Initiatives, 58,* 1–15.

Ginsburg, K.R., Winn, R.J., Rudy, B.J., Crawford, J., Zhao, H., & Schwarz, D.F. (2002). How to reach sexual minority youth in the health care setting: The teens offer guidance. *Journal of Adolescent Health, 31*(5), 407–16. http://dx.doi.org/10.1016/S1054-139X(02)00419-6

Giroux, H.A. (1992). *Border crossings.* New York, NY: Routledge.

Glicken, M.D. (2006). *Learning from resilient people: Lessons we can apply to counseling and psychotherapy.* Thousand Oaks, CA: SAGE.

Gold, M. (2012, 18 November). Push is on to develop more gay-straight alliances in Alberta schools. *Edmonton Journal.* Retrieved from https://groups.google.com/forum/#!topic/transgender-news/jviLw2igM_Q

Goldie, T. (Ed.). (2001a). *In a queer country: Gay & lesbian studies in the Canadian context.* Vancouver, BC: Arsenal Pulp Press.

Goldie, T. (2001b). Queer nation? In T. Goldie (Ed.), *In a queer country: Gay and lesbian studies in the Canadian context* (pp. 7–26). Vancouver, BC: Arsenal Pulp Press.

Goldstein, S., & Brooks, R.B. (2005a). The future of children today. In S. Goldstein & R.B. Brooks (Eds.), *Handbook of resilience in children* (pp. 397–400). New York, NY: Kluwer. http://dx.doi.org/10.1007/0-306-48572-9_23

Goldstein, S., & Brooks, R.B. (2005b). Why study resilience? In S. Goldstein & R.B. Brooks (Eds.), *Handbook of resilience in children* (pp. 3–15). New York, NY: Kluwer. http://dx.doi.org/10.1007/0-306-48572-9_1

Goodenow, C., Szalacha, L., & Westheimer, K. (2006). School support groups, other school factors, and the safety of sexual minority adolescents. *Psychology in the Schools, 43*(5), 573–89. http://dx.doi.org/10.1002/pits.20173

Gore, F.M., Bloem, P.J.N., Patton, G.C., Ferguson, J., Joseph, V., Coffey, C., . . ., & Mathers, C.D. (2011). Global burden of disease in young people aged 10–24 years: A systematic analysis. *The Lancet, 377*(9783), 2093–102. http://dx.doi.org/10.1016/S0140-6736(11)60512-6

Gore, J.M. (1998). Disciplining bodies: On the continuity of power relations in pedagogy. In T.S. Popkewitz & M. Brennan (Eds.), *Foucault's challenge: Discourse, knowledge, and power in education* (pp. 231–51). New York, NY: Teachers College Press.

Grace, A.P. (2005a). LGBT issues in Canada. In J.T. Sears (Ed.), *Youth, education, and sexualities: An international encyclopedia* (pp. 122–6). Westport, CT: Greenwood Publishing.

Grace, A.P. (2005b). Reparative therapies: A contemporary clear and present danger across minority sex, sexual, and gender differences. *Canadian Woman Studies, 24*(2, 3), 145–51.

Grace, A.P. (2005c). Lesbian, gay, bisexual, and trans-identified (LGBT) teachers and students and the post-Charter quest for ethical and just treatment in Canadian schools. Featured paper presented at the Building Inclusive Schools: A Search for Solutions – A Canadian Teachers' Federation Conference, Ottawa Marriott Hotel, Ottawa, ON, 17–19 November 2005. (Available at http://www.teachers.ab.ca/For Members/ Professional Development/Diversity and Human Rights/Sexual Orientation/ Publications/Articles/Pages/LGBT.aspx)

Grace, A.P. (2007a). In your care: School administrators and their ethical and professional responsibility toward students across sexual-minority differences. In W. Smale & K. Young (Eds.), *Approaches to educational leadership and practice* (pp. 16–40). Calgary, AB: Detselig Enterprises/ Temeron Books.

Grace, A.P. (2007b). Envisioning a critical social pedagogy of learning and work in a contemporary culture of cyclical lifelong learning. *Studies in Continuing Education, 29*(1), 85–103. http://dx.doi. org/10.1080/01580370601146361

Grace, A.P. (2008a). Psychotherapy. In J.T. Sears (Ed.), *The Greenwood encyclopedia of love, courtship, and sexuality through history: The modern world* (Vol. 6, pp. 212–15). Westport, CT: Greenwood Publishing Group.

Grace, A.P. (2008b). The charisma and deception of reparative therapies: When medical science beds religion. *Journal of Homosexuality, 55*(4), 545–80. http:// dx.doi.org/10.1080/00918360802421676

Grace, A.P. (2008c). Respondent's text: Situating contemporary educational research as a traversing and transformative practice. In R. Henderson & P.A. Danaher (Eds.), *Troubling terrains: Tactics for traversing and transforming contemporary educational research* (pp. 223–9). Teneriffe, Queensland, Australia: Post Pressed.

Grace, A.P. (2009a). Resilient sexual-minority youth as fugitive lifelong learners: Engaging in a strategic, asset-creating, community-based learning process to counter exclusion and trauma in formal schooling. In J. Field (Ed.), *Proceedings of the Lifelong Learning Revisited: What Next? Conference of the Scottish Centre for Research in Lifelong Learning,* University of Stirling, Stirling, UK (CD format, 4,041 words).

Grace, A.P. (2009b). A view of Canadian lifelong-learning policy culture through a critical lens. In J. Field, J. Gallacher, & R. Ingram (Eds.), *Researching transitions in lifelong learning* (pp. 28–39). London, UK: Routledge.

Grace, A.P. (2010). Space matters: Lifelong learning, sexual minorities, and realities of adult education as social education. *Proceedings of the 40th Annual Standing Conference on University Teaching and Research in the Education of Adults,* University of Warwick, Coventry, UK (CD format, 3509 words). British Education Index ID: 191624.

Grace, A.P. (2012). The emergence of North American adult education (1947–1970): With a reflection on creating critically progressive education. *Studies in the Education of Adults*, 44(2), 225–44.

Grace, A.P. (2013a). Researching sexual minority and gender variant youth and their growth into resilience. In W. Midgley, P.A. Danaher, & M. Baguley (Eds.), *The role of participants in education research: Ethics, epistemologies, and methods* (pp. 15–28). New York, NY: Routledge.

Grace, A.P. (2013b). Camp fYrefly: Linking research to advocacy in community work with sexual and gender minority youth. In W. Pearce & J. Hillabold (Eds.), *OUT SPOKEN: Perspectives on queer identities* (pp. 127–42). Regina, SK: University of Regina Press.

Grace, A.P. (2013c). *Lifelong learning as critical action: International perspectives on people, politics, policy, and practice.* Toronto, ON: Canadian Scholars' Press.

Grace, A.P., & Benson, F.J. (2000). Using autobiographical queer life narratives of teachers to connect personal, political, and pedagogical spaces. *International Journal of Inclusive Education*, 4(2), 89–109. http://dx.doi.org/10.1080/136031100284830

Grace, A.P., Dawson, C.M., & Hillyard, A.K. (2010). Sexual minority youth and building assets for resilience. In A. P. Grace, C. M. Dawson, & A. K. Hillyard (Eds.), *Proceedings of Queer Issues in the Study of Education and Culture II, the 2nd Queer Pre-Conference at the 38th Annual Conference of the Canadian Society for the Study of Education,* Concordia University, Montreal, QC, 21–5.

Grace, A.P., & Hill, R.J. (2004). Positioning queer in adult education: Intervening in politics and praxis in North America. *Studies in the Education of Adults*, 36(2), 167–89.

Grace, A.P., Hill, R.J., Johnson, C.W., & Lewis, J.B. (2004). In other words: Queer voices/dissident subjectivities impelling social change. *International Journal of Qualitative Studies in Education*, 17(3), 301–23. http://dx.doi.org/10.1080/0951839042000204670

Grace, A.P., & Wells, K. (2001). Getting an education in Edmonton, Alberta: The case of queer youth. *Torquere: Journal of the Canadian Lesbian and Gay Studies Association*, 3, 137–51.

Grace, A.P., & Wells, K. (2004). Engaging sex-and-gender differences: Educational and cultural change initiatives in Alberta. In J. McNinch & M. Cronin (Eds.), *I could not speak my heart: Education and social justice for gay and lesbian youth* (pp. 289–307). Regina, SK: Canadian Plains Research Centre, University of Regina.

Grace, A.P., & Wells, K. (2005). The Marc Hall prom predicament: Queer individual rights v. institutional church rights in Canadian education. *Canadian Journal of Education, 28*(3), 237–70. http://dx.doi. org/10.2307/4126470

Grace, A.P., & Wells, K. (2007a). Everyone performs, everyone has a place: Camp fYrefly and arts-informed, community-based education, cultural work, and inquiry. In D. Clover & J. Stalker (Eds.), *The art of social justice: Re-crafting activist adult education and community leadership* (pp. 61–82). Leicester, UK: NIACE.

Grace, A.P., & Wells, K. (2007b). Victims no more: Trends enabling resilience in sexual-minority students. *Proceedings of the Education for Social Justice: From the Margin to the Mainstream – A Canadian Teachers' Federation Conference,* Ottawa Marriott Hotel, Ottawa, ON, 79–88.

Grace, A.P., & Wells, K. (2007c). Using Freirean pedagogy of just ire to inform critical social learning in arts-informed community education for sexual minorities. *Adult Education Quarterly, 57*(2), 95–114. http://dx.doi. org/10.1177/0741713606294539

Grace, A.P., & Wells, K. (2009). Gay and bisexual male youth as educator activists and cultural workers: The queer critical praxis of three Canadian high-school students. *International Journal of Inclusive Education, 13*(1), 23–44. http://dx.doi.org/10.1080/13603110701254121

Greene, J.C. (2007). *Mixed methods in social inquiry.* San Francisco, CA: Jossey-Bass.

Greene, M. (2000). Lived spaces, shared spaces, public spaces. In L. Weis & M. Fine (Eds.), *Construction site: Evacuating race, class, and gender among urban youth* (pp. 293–303). New York, NY: Teachers College Press.

Greytak, E.A., Kosciw, J.G., & Boesen, M.J. (2013). Putting the "T" in "resource": The benefits of LGBT-related school resources for transgender youth. *Journal of LGBT Youth, 10*(1–2), 45–63. http://dx.doi.org/10.1080/193 61653.2012.718522

Griffin, P., Lee, C., Waugh, J., & Beyer, C. (2004). Describing roles that gay-straight alliances play in schools: From individual support to social change. *Journal of Gay & Lesbian Issues in Education, 1*(3), 7–22. http://dx.doi. org/10.1300/J367v01n03_03

Griffin, P., & Ouellett, M.L. (2002). Going beyond gay-straight alliances to make schools safe for lesbian, gay, bisexual, and transgender students. *Policy Journal of the Institute for Gay and Lesbian Strategic Studies, 6*(1), 1–8.

Grossman, A.H., & D'Augelli, A.R. (2006). Transgender youth: Invisible and vulnerable. *Journal of Homosexuality, 51*(1), 111–28. http://dx.doi. org/10.1300/J082v51n01_06

Grossman, A.H., & D'Augelli, A.R. (2007). Transgender youth and life-threatening behaviors. *Suicide & Life-Threatening Behavior, 37*(5), 527–37. http://dx.doi.org/10.1521/suli.2007.37.5.527

Grossman, A.H., D'Augelli, A.R., & Frank, J.K. (2011). Aspects of psychological resilience among transgender youth. *Journal of LGBT Youth, 8*(2), 103–15. http://dx.doi.org/10.1080/19361653.2011.541347

Grossman, A.H., Haney, A.P., Edwards, P., Alessi, E.J., Ardon, M., & Howell, T.J. (2009). Lesbian, gay, bisexual and transgender youth talk about experiencing and coping with school violence: A qualitative study. *Journal of LGBT Youth, 6*(1), 24–46. http://dx.doi.org/10.1080/19361650802379748

Gulli, C. (2014, 13 January). What happens when your son tells you he's really a girl. *Maclean's.* Retrieved from http://www.macleans.ca/society/health/what-happens-when-your-son-tells-you-hes-really-a-girl/

Haas, A.P., Eliason, M., Mays, V.M., Mathy, R.M., Cochran, S.D., D'Augelli, A.R., . . ., & Clayton, P.J. (2010). Suicide and suicide risk in lesbian, gay, bisexual, and transgender populations: Review and recommendations. *Journal of Homosexuality, 58*(1), 10–51. http://dx.doi.org/10.1080/00918369.2011.534038

Haberland, N., & Rogow, R. (Eds.). (2011). *It's all one curriculum: Guidelines and activities for a unified approach to sexuality, gender, HIV, and human rights education* (Revised ed.). Retrieved from http://www.popcouncil.org/uploads/pdfs/2011PGY_ItsAllOneGuidelines_en.pdf

Haldeman, D.C. (2002). Gay rights, patient rights: The implications of sexual orientation conversion therapy. *Professional Psychology, Research and Practice, 33*(3), 260–4. http://dx.doi.org/10.1037/0735-7028.33.3.260

Hall, H.R. (2007). Poetic expressions: Students of color express resiliency through metaphors and similes. *Journal of Advanced Academics, 18*, 216–44.

Halpert, S.C. (2000). "If it ain't broke, don't fix it": Ethical considerations regarding conversion therapies. *International Journal of Sexuality and Gender Studies, 5*(1), 19–35. http://dx.doi.org/10.1023/A:1010133501054

Hammer, K., & Howlett, K. (2012, June 4). Catholic school trustees fear fallout over gay-straight alliance furor. *The Globe and Mail.* Retrieved from http://www.theglobeandmail.com/news/politics/catholic-school-trustees-fear-fallout-over-gay-straight-alliance-furor/article4230933/

Haraldsen, I., Ehrbar, R.D., Gorton, R.N., & Menvielle, E. (2010). Recommendations for revision of the DSM diagnosis of gender identity disorder in adolescents. *International Journal of Transgenderism, 12*(2), 75–9. http://dx.doi.org/10.1080/15532739.2010.509201

Haskell, R., & Burtch, B. (2010). *Get that freak: Homophobia and transphobia in high schools.* Halifax, NS, and Winnipeg, MB: Fernwood Publishing.

Hatzenbuehler, M.L. (2011). The social environment and suicide attempts in lesbian, gay, and bisexual youth. *Pediatrics, 127*(5), 896–903. http://dx.doi.org/10.1542/peds.2010-3020

Hauser, S.T. (1999). Understanding resilient outcomes: Adolescent lives across time and generations. *Journal of Research on Adolescence, 9*(1), 1–24. http://dx.doi.org/10.1207/s15327795jra0901_1

Heck, N.C., Lindquist, L.M., Machek, G.R., & Cochran, B.N. (2014). School belonging, school victimization, and the mental health of LGBT young adults: Implications for school psychologists. *School Psychology Forum: Research in Practice, 8*(1), 28–37.

Hein, L.C., & Matthews, A.K. (2010). Reparative therapy: The adolescent, the psych nurse, and the issues. *Journal of Child and Adolescent Psychiatric Nursing, 23*(1), 29–35. http://dx.doi.org/10.1111/j.1744-6171.2009.00214.x

Helminiak, D.A. (2000). *What the Bible really says about homosexuality (Millennium Edition).* Tajique, NM: Alamo Square Press.

Henning-Stout, M., James, S., & Macintosh, S. (2000). Reducing harassment of lesbian, gay, bisexual, transgender, and questioning youth in schools. *School Psychology Review, 29*, 180–92.

Herdt, G. (1995). The protection of lesbian and gay youth. *Harvard Educational Review, 65*(2), 315–21.

Herrenkohl, E.C., Herrenkohl, R.C., & Egolf, B. (1994). Resilient early school-age children from maltreating homes: Outcomes in late adolescence. *American Journal of Orthopsychiatry, 64*(2), 301–9. http://dx.doi.org/10.1037/h0079517

Hicks, K.A. (2000). "Reparative" therapy: Whether parental attempts to change a child's sexual orientation can legally constitute child abuse. *American University Law Review, 49*, 505–47.

Hilfinger Messias, D.K., Jennings, L.B., Fore, M.E., McLoughlin, K., & Parra-Medina, D. (2008). Societal images of youth: Representations and interpretations by youth actively engaged in their communities. *International Journal of Qualitative Studies in Education, 21*(2), 159–78. http://dx.doi.org/10.1080/09518390701217466

Hill, D., & Menvielle, E. (2009). "You have to give them a place where they feel protected and safe and loved": The views of parents who have gender-variant children and adolescents. *Journal of LGBT Youth, 6*(2–3), 243–71. http://dx.doi.org/10.1080/19361650903013527

Hill, R.J. (2010). Policy and adult learning and education. In C.E. Kasworm, A.D. Rose, & J.M. Ross-Gordon (Eds.), *Handbook of adult and continuing education: 2010 edition* (pp. 103–12). Los Angeles, CA: SAGE.

Hill, R.J. (2012). Crisis in adult learning and education in the United States – and a postscript of hope. *Voices Rising, 10*(432), 1–20. Retrieved 13 March 2013 from http://www.icae2.org/?q=en/node/1686; also available at http://files.eric.ed.gov/fulltext/ED539407.pdf

Hill, R.J., & Grace, A.P. (Eds.). (2009). *Adult and higher education in queer contexts: Power, politics, and pedagogy.* Chicago, IL: Discovery Association Publishing House.

Hirsch, A.J., Carlson, J.S., & Crowl, A.L. (2010). Promoting positive development outcomes in sexual minority youth through best practices in clinic-school consultation. *Journal of Child and Adolescent Psychiatric Nursing, 23*(1), 17–22. http://dx.doi.org/10.1111/j.1744-6171.2009.00212.x

Holmes, S.E., & Cahill, S. (2004). School experiences of gay, lesbian, bisexual and transgender youth. *Journal of Gay & Lesbian Issues in Education, 1*(3), 53–66. http://dx.doi.org/10.1300/J367v01n03_06

Honeychurch, K.G. (1996). Researching dissident subjectivities: Queering the grounds of theory and practice. *Harvard Educational Review, 66*(2), 339–55.

Houston, A. (2011a, 6 January). Halton Catholic schools ban gay-straight alliance groups. *Xtra! Canada's Gay & Lesbian News.* Retrieved from http://www.xtra.ca/public/Toronto/Halton_Catholic_schools_ban_GayStraight_Alliance_groups-9611.aspx

Houston, A. (2011b, 10 January). Xtra story on Halton Catholic GSA ban sparks outrage. *Xtra! Canada's Gay & Lesbian News.* Retrieved from http://www.xtra.ca/public/Toronto/Xtra_story_on_Halton_Catholic_GSA_ban_sparks_outrage-9621.aspx.

Houston, A. (2011c, 2 July). Ontario to mandate "LGBT support groups" in Catholic schools. *Xtra! Canada's Gay & Lesbian News.* Retrieved from http://www.xtra.ca/public/National/Ontario_to_mandate_LGBT_support_groups_in_Catholic_schools-10425.aspx

Howlett, K. (2012, 5 June). Ontario anti-bullying bill passes, clearing way for gay-straight alliance groups in schools. *The Globe and Mail.* Retrieved from http://www.theglobeandmail.com/news/politics/ontario-anti-bullying-bill-that-has-catholics-upset-faces-final-vote/article4231542/

Human Rights Watch (2001). *Hatred in the hallways: Violence and discrimination against lesbian, gay, bisexual, and transgender students in U.S. schools.* Retrieved from http://www.hrw.org/reports/2001/uslgbt/

Hunter, J., & Mallon, G. (2000). Lesbian, gay and bisexual adolescent development: Dancing with your feet tied together. In B. Greene & G.L. Croom (Eds.), *Education, research and practice in lesbian, gay, bisexual, and transgendered psychology: A resource manual* (pp. 226–43). Thousand Oaks, CA: SAGE. http://dx.doi.org/10.4135/9781452233697.n9

Hsieh, M.-O., & Leung, P. (2009). Protective factors for adolescents among divorced single-parent families from Taiwan. *Social Work in Health Care, 48*(3), 298–320. http://dx.doi.org/10.1080/00981380802599216

Jaffee, S.R., & Gallop, R. (2007). Social, emotional, and academic competence among children who have had contact with child protective services: Prevalence and stability estimates. *Journal of the American Academy of Child and Adolescent Psychiatry, 46*(6), 757–65. http://dx.doi.org/10.1097/chi.0b013e318040b247

James, A.B. (2010). Reclaiming deep democracy. *Reclaiming Children and Youth, 19*(3), 16–19.

Janoff, D.V. (2005). *Pink blood: Homophobic violence in Canada*. Toronto, ON: University of Toronto Press.

Jessor, R., Turbin, M.S., & Costa, F.M. (1998). Risk and protection in successful outcomes among disadvantaged adolescents. *Applied Developmental Science, 2*(4), 194–208. http://dx.doi.org/10.1207/s1532480xads0204_3

Jones, T., & Hillier, L. (2013). Comparing trans-spectrum and same-sex-attracted youth in Australia: Increased risks, increased activisms. *Journal of LGBT Youth, 10*(4), 287–307. http://dx.doi.org/10.1080/19361653.2013.825197

Johnson, B. (2008). Teacher-student relationships which promote resilience at school: A micro-level analysis of students' views. *British Journal of Guidance & Counselling, 36*(4), 385–98. http://dx.doi.org/10.1080/03069880802364528

Johnson, D., Sikorski, J., Savage, T.A., & Woitaszewski, S.A. (2014). Parents of youth who identify as transgender: An exploratory study. *School Psychology Forum: Research in Practice, 8*(1), 56–74.

Jordan, J.V. (2005). Relational resilience in girls. In S. Goldstein & R.B. Brooks (Eds.), *Handbook of resilience in children* (pp. 79–90). New York, NY: Kluwer. http://dx.doi.org/10.1007/0-306-48572-9_6

Kamberelis, G., & Dimitriadis, G. (2005). Focus groups: Strategic articulations of pedagogy, politics, and inquiry. In N.K. Denzin & Y.S. Lincoln (Eds.), *The SAGE handbook of qualitative research* (3rd ed., pp. 887–907). Thousand Oaks, CA: SAGE.

Kidd, J.R. (1961). Editor's preface. In E.C. Lindeman (Ed.), *The meaning of adult education (1926)* (pp. xiii–xxiv). Montreal, QC: Harvest House.

Kincheloe, J.L., & McLaren, P. (2005). Rethinking critical theory and qualitative research. In N.K. Denzin & Y.S. Lincoln (Eds.), *The SAGE handbook of qualitative research* (3rd ed., pp. 303–42). Thousand Oaks, CA: SAGE.

Kincheloe, J.L., McLaren, P., & Steinberg, S.R. (2011). Critical pedagogy and qualitative research: Moving to the bricolage. In N.K. Denzin & Y.S. Lincoln (Eds.), *The SAGE handbook of qualitative research* (4th ed., pp. 163–78). Thousand Oaks, CA: SAGE.

Kirsch, M.H. (2000). *Queer theory and social change*. New York, NY: Routledge.

Kissen, R.M. (Ed.). (2002). *Getting ready for Benjamin: Preparing teachers for sexual diversity in the classroom*. Lanham, MD: Rowman & Littlefield Publishers.

Kong, T.S.K., Mahoney, D., & Plummer, K. (2001). Queering the interview. In J.F. Gubrium & J.A. Holstein (Eds.), *Handbook of interview research: Context and method* (pp. 239–58). Thousand Oaks, CA: SAGE. http://dx.doi.org/10.4135/9781412973588.d16

Koro-Ljungberg, M., Bussing, R., & Cornwell, L. (2010). Framework for the analysis of teenagers' agency and self-disclosure and methodological reflections on knowledge production during qualitative research. *Qualitative Research in Psychology, 7*(3), 193–213. http://dx.doi.org/10.1080/14780880802641516

Kosciw, J.G., Diaz, E.M., & Greytak, E.A. (2008). *2007 National School Climate Survey: The experiences of lesbian, gay, bisexual and transgender youth in our nation's schools*. New York, NY: GLSEN.

Kress, C.A. (2006). Youth leadership and youth development: Connections and questions. *New Directions for Youth Development, 2006*(109), 45–56. http://dx.doi.org/10.1002/yd.154

Krieger, I. (2011). *Helping your transgender teen: A guide for parents*. New Haven, CT: Genderwise Press.

Kumashiro, K.K. (Ed.). (2001). *Troubling intersections of race and sexuality: Queer students of color and anti-oppressive education*. Lanham, MD: Rowman & Littlefield Publishers.

Lahey, K.A. (1999). *Are we persons yet? Law and sexuality in Canada*. Toronto, ON: University of Toronto Press.

Lambda Legal. (2012). *Working with transgender youth*. Retrieved from http://www.lambdalegal.org/know-your-rights/working-with-transgender-youth

The Lancet. (2011). Health concerns of adolescents who are in a sexual minority. *The Lancet, 377*(9783), 2056. http://dx.doi.org/10.1016/S0140-6736(11)60902-1

Lather, P.A., & Smithies, C.S. (1997). *Troubling the angels: Women living with HIV/AIDS*. Boulder, CO: Westview Press.

Lee, C. (2002). The impact of belonging to a high school gay/straight alliance. *High School Journal, 85*(3), 13–26. http://dx.doi.org/10.1353/hsj.2002.0005

Leech, N.L. (2010). Interviews with the early developers of mixed methods research. In A. Tashakkori & C. Teddlie (Eds.), *SAGE handbook of mixed methods in social & behavioral research* (2nd ed., pp. 253–72). Thousand Oaks, CA: SAGE.

Lewis, C. (2012a, 28 May). Church rejects Ontario's gay-straight club decision, accuses government of "micromanagement." *National Post*. Retrieved from http://news.nationalpost.com/2012/05/28/church-rejects-ontarios-gay-straight-club-decision-accuses-government-of-micromanagement/

Lewis, C. (2012b, 28 May). Ontario Catholic schools struggle to get their point across on gay-straight alliances during press call. *National Post*. Retrieved from http://news.nationalpost.com/2012/05/28/ontario-catholic-schools-struggle-to-get-their-point-across-on-gay-straight-alliances-during-press-call/

Lewis, C. (2012c, 30 May). Catholic schools' opposition to gay clubs revives public-funding debate. *National Post*. Retrieved from http://news.nationalpost.com/2012/05/30/catholic-schools-opposition-to-gay-clubs-revives-public-funding-debate/

Lewis, C., & Perkel, C. (2012, 25 May). Church blindsided by Ontario government over gay-straight alliances: Catholic sources. *National Post*. Retrieved from http://news.nationalpost.com/2012/05/25/church-blindsided-by-ontario-government-over-gay-straight-alliances-catholic-sources/

Liebenberg, L., & Ungar, M. (2008). Introduction: Understanding youth resilience in action: The way forward. In L. Liebenberg & M. Ungar (Eds.), *Resilience in action* (pp. 3–16). Toronto, ON: University of Toronto Press.

Liebenberg, L., & Ungar, M. (2009). Introduction: The challenges in researching resilience. In L. Liebenberg & M. Ungar (Eds.), *Researching resilience* (pp. 3–25). Toronto, ON: University of Toronto Press.

Lindeman, E.C. (1961). *The meaning of adult education*. Montreal, QC: Harvest House (originally published in 1926).

Lipkin, A. (2004). *Beyond diversity day: A Q&A on gay and lesbian issues in schools*. Lanham, MD: Rowman & Littlefield Publishers.

Lock, J., & Steiner, H. (1999). Relationships between sexual orientation and coping styles of gay, lesbian, and bisexual adolescents from a community high school. *Journal of the Gay and Lesbian Medical Association, 3*(3), 77–82. http://dx.doi.org/10.1023/A:1022235910749

Luecke, J.C. (2011). Working with transgender children and their classmates pre-adolescence: Just be supportive. *Journal of LGBT Youth, 8*(2), 116–56. http://dx.doi.org/10.1080/19361653.2011.544941

Luthar, S.S. (1993). Methodological and conceptual issues in research on childhood resilience. *Journal of Child Psychology and Psychiatry, and Allied Disciplines, 34*(4), 441–53. http://dx.doi.org/10.1111/j.1469-7610.1993.tb01030.x

Luthar, S.S., Cicchetti, D., & Becker, B. (2000). The construct of resilience: A critical evaluation and guidelines for future work. *Child Development, 71*(3), 543–62. http://dx.doi.org/10.1111/1467-8624.00164

Luthar, S.S., & Zelazo, L.B. (2003). Research on resilience: An integrative review. In S.S. Luthar (Ed.), *Resilience and vulnerability: Adaptation in the context of childhood adversities* (pp. 510–50). New York, NY: Cambridge University Press. http://dx.doi.org/10.1017/CBO9780511615788.023

Luthar, S.S., & Zigler, E. (1991). Vulnerability and competence: A review of research on resilience in childhood. *American Journal of Orthopsychiatry, 61*(1), 6–22. http://dx.doi.org/10.1037/h0079218

MacDougall, B. (2000). *Queer judgments: Homosexuality, expression, and the courts in Canada*. Toronto, ON: University of Toronto Press.

Macgillivray, I.K. (2007). *Gay-straight alliances: A handbook for students, educators, and parents*. New York, NY: Harrington Park Press.

MacKinnon, Justice R. (2002, 10 May). *Smitherman v. Powers and the Durham Catholic District School Board*. (Court File No. 12-CV-227705CM3). Whitby, ON: Ontario Superior Court of Justice.

Mark, R. (2011). Literacy, lifelong learning and social inclusion: Empowering learners to learn about equality and reconciliation through lived experiences. In S. Jackson (Ed.), *Lifelong learning and social justice: Communities, work and identities in a globalised world* (pp. 42–58). Leicester, UK: National Institute of Adult Continuing Education.

Marksamer, J. (2011). *A place of respect: A guide for group care facilities serving transgender and gender non-conforming youth*. Washington, DC: National Center for Lesbian Rights and Sylvia Rivera Law Project.

Marshall, D. (2010). Popular culture, the "victim" trope and queer youth analytics. *International Journal of Qualitative Studies in Education, 23*(1), 65–85. http://dx.doi.org/10.1080/09518390903447176

Marshall, E.A., & Leadbeater, B.L. (2008). Policy responses to youth in adversity: An integrated, strengths-based approach. In L. Liebenberg & M. Ungar (Eds.), *Resilience in action* (pp. 380–99). Toronto, ON: University of Toronto Press.

Marwick, A. (1998). *The sixties: Cultural revolution in Britain, France, Italy, and the United States, c.1958–c. 1974*. Oxford, UK: Oxford University Press.

Marx, R. (2011). *"I want them to know who they are is ok": Supporting trans and gender nonconforming students: A guide for primary and secondary school educators*. Retrieved from: http://www.scribd.com/doc/87592428/I-Want-Them-To-Know-Who-They-Are-Is-OK

Massey, S., Cameron, A., Ouellette, S., & Fine, M. (1998). Qualitative approaches to the study of thriving: What can be learned? *Journal of Social Issues, 54*(2), 337–55. http://dx.doi.org/10.1111/j.1540-4560.1998.tb01222.x

Masten, A.S. (2001). Ordinary magic: Resilience processes and development. *American Psychologist, 56*(3), 227–38. http://dx.doi.org/10.1037/0003-066X.56.3.227

Masten, A.S., Best, K.M., & Garmezy, N. (1990). Resilience and development: Contributions from the study of children who overcome adversity. *Development and Psychopathology, 2*(04), 425–44. http://dx.doi.org/10.1017/S0954579400005812

Masten, A.S., & Coatsworth, J.D. (1998). The development of competence in favorable and unfavorable environments: Lessons from research on successful children. *American Psychologist, 53*(2), 205–20. http://dx.doi.org/10.1037/0003-066X.53.2.205

Mayberry, M. (2006). The story of a Salt Lake City gay-straight alliance: Identity work and LGBT youth. *Journal of Gay & Lesbian Issues in Education, 4*(1), 13–31. http://dx.doi.org/10.1300/J367v04n01_03

McCabe, P.C. (2014). The r(ally) cry: School psychologists as allies and advocates for the LGBTQ community. *School Psychology Forum: Research in Practice, 8*(1), 1–9.

McCready, L.T. (2004). Some challenges facing queer youth programs in urban high schools: Racial segregation and de-normalizing whiteness. *Journal of Gay & Lesbian Issues in Education, 1*(3), 37–51. http://dx.doi.org/10.1300/J367v01n03_05

McCreary Centre Society. (1999). *Being out: Lesbian, gay, bisexual, & transgender youth in BC: An adolescent health survey*. Burnaby, BC: Author.

McDaniel, J.S., Purcell, D., & D'Augelli, A.R. (2001). The relationship between sexual orientation and risk for suicide: Research findings and future directions for research and prevention. *Suicide & Life-Threatening Behavior, 31*(Suppl. 1), 84–105. http://dx.doi.org/10.1521/suli.31.1.5.84.24224

McKay, A. (1998). *Sexual ideology and schooling: Towards democratic sexuality education*. London, ON: The Althouse Press.

Meagher, Most Reverend A.G. (2002, 4 April). *Open letter faxed to Mr. Dalton McGuinty, MPP*. Barrie, ON: Author.

Menvielle, E. (2011). Foreword. In D. Ehrensaft (Ed.), *Gender born, gender made: Raising healthy gender-nonconforming children* (pp. ix–xi). New York, NY: The Experiment.

Menvielle, E. (2012). A comprehensive program for children with gender variant behaviors and gender identity disorders. *Journal of Homosexuality, 59*(3), 357–68. http://dx.doi.org/10.1080/00918369.2012.653305

Mercier, M.T. (2009). Fighting to fit in: Gay-straight alliances in schools under United States jurisprudence. *International Journal of Human Rights, 13*(2–3), 177–91. http://dx.doi.org/10.1080/13642980902758101

Meyer, I.H. (2007). Prejudice and discrimination as social stressors. In I.H. Meyer & M.E. Northridge (Eds.), *The health of sexual minorities: Public health perspectives in lesbian, gay, bisexual and transgender populations* (pp. 242–67). New York, NY: Springer. http://dx.doi.org/10.1007/978-0-387-31334-4_10

Miceli, M. (2005). *Standing out, standing together: The social and political impact of gay-straight alliances*. New York, NY: Routledge.

Minter, S.P. (2012). Supporting transgender children: New legal, social, and medical approaches. *Journal of Homosexuality, 59*(3), 422–33. http://dx.doi.org/10.1080/00918369.2012.653311

Morgan, D.L. (2001). Focus group interviewing. In J.F. Gubrium & J.A. Holstein (Eds.), *Handbook of interview research: Context and method* (pp. 141–59). Thousand Oaks, CA: SAGE. http://dx.doi.org/10.4135/9781412973588.d10

Morrison, L.L., & L'Heureux, J. (2001). Suicide and gay/lesbian/bisexual youth: Implications for clinicians. *Journal of Adolescence, 24*(1), 39–49. http://dx.doi.org/10.1006/jado.2000.0361

Munns, G. (2007). A sense of wonder: Pedagogies to engage students who live in poverty. *International Journal of Inclusive Education, 11*(3), 301–15. http://dx.doi.org/10.1080/13603110701237571

Murphy, H.E. (2012). Improving the lives of students, gay and straight alike: Gay-straight alliances and the role of school psychologists. *Psychology in the Schools, 49*(9), 883–91. http://dx.doi.org/10.1002/pits.21643

Mustanski, B.S., Newcomb, M.E., Du Bois, S.N., Garcia, S.C., & Grov, C. (2011). HIV in young men who have sex with men: A review of epidemiology, risk and protective factors, and interventions. *Journal of Sex Research, 48*(2–3), 218–53. http://dx.doi.org/10.1080/00224499.2011.558645

Mustanski, B., Newcomb, M.E., & Garofalo, R. (2011). Mental health of lesbian, gay, and bisexual youths: A developmental resiliency perspective. *Journal of Gay & Lesbian Social Services, 23*(2), 204–25. http://dx.doi.org/10.1080/1053 8720.2011.561474

Nemoto, T., Bodeker, B., & Iwamoto, I. (2011). Social support, exposure to violence and transphobia, and correlates of depression among male-to-female transgender women with a history of sex work. [Advance online publication]. *American Journal of Public Health, 101*(10), 1980–8. http://dx.doi.org/10.2105/AJPH.2010.197285

O'Conor, A. (1994). Who gets called queer in school? Lesbian, gay and bisexual teenagers, homophobia and high school. *High School Journal, 77*, 7–12.

O'Dougherty Wright, M., & Masten, A.S. (2005). Resilience processes in development: Fostering positive adaptation in the context of adversity. In S. Goldstein & R.B. Brooks (Eds.), *Handbook of resilience in children* (pp. 17–37). New York, NY: Kluwer. http://dx.doi.org/10.1007/0-306-48572-9_2

O'Grady, D., & Metz, J.R. (1987). Resilience in children at high risk for psychological disorder. *Journal of Pediatric Psychology, 12*(1), 3–23. http://dx.doi.org/10.1093/jpepsy/12.1.3

Ontario Ministry of Education (OME). (2009). Equity and inclusive education in Ontario schools – realizing the promise of diversity: Guidelines for policy development and implementation. Retrieved from www.edu.gov.on.ca/eng/policyfunding/inclusiveguide.pdf

Pearson, K. (2012). Foreword. In R. Pepper (Ed.), *Transitions of the heart: Stories of love, struggle and acceptance by mothers of transgender and gender variant children* (pp. xiii–xv). Berkeley, CA: Cleis Press.

Pepper, R. (Ed.). (2012). *Transitions of the heart: Stories of love, struggle and acceptance by mothers of transgender and gender variant children*. Berkeley, CA: Cleis Press.

Perrin, E.C., Cohen, K.M., Gold, M., Ryan, C., Savin-Williams, R.C., & Schorzman, C.M. (2004). Gay and lesbian issues in pediatric health care. *Current Problems in Pediatric and Adolescent Health Care, 34*(10), 355–98. http://dx.doi.org/10.1016/j.cppeds.2004.08.001

Perrotti, J., & Westheimer, K. (2001). *When the drama club is not enough: Lessons from the Massachusetts Safe Schools Program for Gay and Lesbian Students.* Boston, MA: Beacon Press.

Peterkin, A., & Risdon, C. (2003). *Caring for lesbian and gay people: A clinical guide*. Toronto, ON: University of Toronto Press.

Philip, K. (2008). She's my second mum: Young people building relationships in uncertain circumstances. *Child Care in Practice, 14*(1), 19–33. http://dx.doi.org/10.1080/13575270701733674

Pianta, R.C., & Walsh, D.J. (1998). Applying the construct of resilience in schools: Cautions from a developmental systems perspective. *School Psychology Review, 27*(3), 407–17.

Plummer, K. (2005). Critical humanism and queer theory: Living with the tension. In N.K. Denzin & Y.S. Lincoln (Eds.), *The SAGE handbook of qualitative research* (3rd ed., pp. 357–73). Thousand Oaks, CA: SAGE.

Plummer, K. (2011a). Critical humanism and queer theory: Living with the tensions. In N.K. Denzin & Y.S. Lincoln (Eds.), *The SAGE handbook of qualitative research* (4th ed., pp. 195–207). Thousand Oaks, CA: SAGE.

Plummer, K. (2011b). Postscript 2011 to living with the contradictions – Moving on: Generations, cultures, and methodological cosmopolitanism. In N.K. Denzin & Y.S. Lincoln (Eds.), *The SAGE handbook of qualitative research* (4th ed., pp. 208–11). Thousand Oaks, CA: SAGE.

Podgorski, J. (Ed.). (2001). *Homosexuality and the Catholic high school: A compilation of newsletters with new material.* Ottawa, ON: Ontario Family Life Educators Network (OCFLEN).

Pollack, W.S. (2005). Sustaining and reframing vulnerability and connection: Creating genuine resilience in boys and young males. In S. Goldstein & R.B. Brooks (Eds.), *Handbook of resilience in children* (pp. 65–77). New York, NY: Kluwer. http://dx.doi.org/10.1007/0-306-48572-9_5

Poorman, P.B. (2002). Perceptions of thriving by women who have experienced abuse or status-related oppression. *Psychology of Women Quarterly, 26*(1), 51–62. http://dx.doi.org/10.1111/1471-6402.00043

Pruegger, V. (2009). *Alberta hate/bias crime report.* Calgary, AB: Alberta Hate Crimes Committee and the City of Calgary.

Public Health Agency of Canada (PHAC) (2006). *Youth and violence.* Retrieved from http://www.phac-aspc.gc.ca/ncfv-cnivf/familyviolence/html/nfntsyjviolence_e.html#8

Public Health Agency of Canada (PHAC) (2008). *Canadian guidelines for sexual health education.* Retrieved from http://www.phac-aspc.gc.ca/publicat/cgshe-ldnemss/index-eng.php

Public Health Agency of Canada (PHAC). (2010a, July). *HIV/AIDS epi update: HIV/AIDS among youth in Canada.* Ottawa, ON: Author.

Public Health Agency of Canada (PHAC). (2012, August). *Fact sheet: Gay, bisexual, two-spirit and other men who have sex with men.* Ottawa, ON: Author.

Public Health Agency of Canada (PHAC) (2014a). *Questions & answers: Sexual orientation in schools.* Retrieved from http://www.phac-aspc.gc.ca/std-mts/rp/so-os/index-eng.php

Public Health Agency of Canada (PHAC) (2014b). *Questions & answers: Gender identity in schools.* Retrieved from http://www.phac-aspc.gc.ca/std-mts/rp/gi-is/index-eng.php

Quasha, S., McCabe, P.C., & Ortiz, S.O. (2014). A program review of a middle school gay-straight alliance club. *School Psychology Forum: Research in Practice, 8*(1), 91–102.

Quinlivan, K., & Town, S. (1999). Queer pedagogy, educational practice and lesbian and gay youth. *International Journal of Qualitative Studies in Education, 12*(5), 509–24. http://dx.doi.org/10.1080/095183999235926

Rainbow Health Ontario. (2012). *RHO fact sheet: Supporting gender independent children and their families.* Retrieved from http://www.rainbowhealthontario.ca/resources/

Rak, C.F., & Patterson, L.E. (1996). Promoting resilience in at-risk children. *Journal of Counseling and Development, 74*(4), 368–73. http://dx.doi.org/10.1002/j.1556-6676.1996.tb01881.x

Rasmussen, M.L., Rofes, E., & Talburt, S. (Eds.). (2004). *Youth and sexualities: Pleasure, subversion and insubordination in and out of schools.* New York, NY: Palgrave Macmillan. http://dx.doi.org/10.1057/9781403981912

Rayside, D. (2008). *Queer inclusions, continental divisions: Public recognition of sexual diversity in Canada and the United States.* Toronto, ON: University of Toronto Press.

REAL Women of Canada. (2013, 4 June). *There is something peculiar about the bill on the transgendered (Bill C-279).* Retrieved from http://www.realwomenofcanada.ca/wp-content/uploads/2013/10/june42013M-E-D-I-A-release-on-C-279.pdf

REAL Women of Canada. (2014). *REAL Women of Canada*. Retrieved from
http://www.realwomenofcanada.ca/

Reiner, W.G., & Reiner, D.T. (2012). Thoughts on the nature of identity: How
disorders of sex development inform clinical research about gender identity
disorders. *Journal of Homosexuality, 59*(3), 434–49. http://dx.doi.org/10.1080
/00918369.2012.653312

Remafedi, G. (Ed.). (1994). *Death by denial: Studies of suicide in gay and lesbian
teenagers*. Boston, MA: Alyson Publications.

Rettew, D.C. (2012). Apples to committee consensus: The challenge of gender
identity classification. *Journal of Homosexuality, 59*(3), 450–9. http://dx.doi.or
g/10.1080/00918369.2012.653313

Reyes, J.A., & Elias, M.J. (2011). Fostering social-emotional resilience among
Latino youth. *Psychology in the Schools, 48*(7), 723–37. http://dx.doi.
org/10.1002/pits.20580

Reygan, F.C.G. (2009). The school-based lives of LGBT youth in the
republic of Ireland. *Journal of LGBT Youth, 6*(1), 80–9. http://dx.doi.
org/10.1080/19361650802379789

Rich, A. (1980). Compulsory heterosexuality and lesbian existence. *Signs
(Chicago, Ill.), 5*(4), 631–60. http://dx.doi.org/10.1086/493756

Richardson, L., & St. Pierre, E.A. (2005). Writing: A method of inquiry. In
N.K. Denzin & Y.S. Lincoln (Eds.), *The SAGE handbook of qualitative research*
(3rd ed., pp. 959–78). Thousand Oaks, CA: SAGE.

Riley, E.A., Sitharthan, G., Clemson, L., & Diamond, M. (2011). The needs of
gender-variant children and their parents according to health professionals.
International Journal of Transgenderism, 13(2), 54–63. http://dx.doi.org/10.1080/
15532739.2011.622121

Rind, B. (2003). Sexual orientation change and informed consent in reparative
therapy. *Archives of Sexual Behavior, 32*(5), 447–9.

Rivers, I., & Cowie, H. (2006). Bullying and homophobia in UK schools:
A perspective on factors, affecting resilience and recovery. *Journal of Gay
& Lesbian Issues in Education, 3*(4), 11–43. http://dx.doi.org/10.1300/
J367v03n04_03

Robinson, G. (2012). God believes in you: Introduction. In D. Savage & T.
Miller (Eds.), *It gets better: Coming out, overcoming bullying, and creating a life
worth living* (pp. 30–1). New York, NY: Plume.

Rodan, G. (2011, July 3). Ontario reaffirms support for gay support groups
in schools. *The Star*. Retrieved from http://www.thestar.com/news/
gta/2011/07/03/ontario_reaffirms_support_for_gay_support_groups_in_
schools.html

Russell, S.T. (2002). Queer in America: Citizenship for sexual minority youth. *Applied Developmental Science*, 6(4), 258–63. http://dx.doi.org/10.1207/S1532480XADS0604_13

Russell, S.T. (2005). Beyond risk: Resilience in the lives of sexual minority youth. *Journal of Gay & Lesbian Issues in Education*, 2(3), 5–18. http://dx.doi.org/10.1300/J367v02n03_02

Russell, S.T., Horn, S., Kosciw, J., & Saewyc, E. (2010). Safe schools policy for LGBTQ students. *Social Policy Report*, 24(4), 1–25.

Russell, S.T., & Joyner, K. (2001). Adolescent sexual orientation and suicide risk: Evidence from a national study. *American Journal of Public Health*, 91(8), 1276–81. http://dx.doi.org/10.2105/AJPH.91.8.1276

Russell, S.T., Muraco, A., Subramaniam, A., & Laub, C. (2009). Youth empowerment and high school gay-straight alliances. *Journal of Youth and Adolescence*, 38(7), 891–903. http://dx.doi.org/10.1007/s10964-008-9382-8

Rutter, M. (1985). Resilience in the face of adversity: Protective factors and resistance to psychiatric disorder. *British Journal of Psychiatry*, 147(6), 598–611. http://dx.doi.org/10.1192/bjp.147.6.598

Rutter, M. (1987). Psychosocial resilience and protective mechanisms. *American Journal of Orthopsychiatry*, 57(3), 316–31. http://dx.doi.org/10.1111/j.1939-0025.1987.tb03541.x

Rutter, M. (1993). Resilience: Some conceptual considerations. *Journal of Adolescent Health*, 14(8), 626–31. http://dx.doi.org/10.1016/1054-139X(93)90196-V

Rutter, M. (1999). Resilience concepts and findings: Implications for family therapy. *Journal of Family Therapy*, 21(2), 119–44. http://dx.doi.org/10.1111/1467-6427.00108

Rutter, M. (2006). Implications of resilience concepts for scientific understanding. *Annals of the New York Academy of Sciences*, 1094(1), 1–12. http://dx.doi.org/10.1196/annals.1376.002

Rutter, M. (2012). Resilience as a dynamic concept. *Development and Psychopathology*, 24(02), 335–44. http://dx.doi.org/10.1017/S0954579412000028

Ryan, C. (2010). Engaging families to support lesbian, gay, bisexual, and transgender youth: The Family Acceptance Project. *Prevention Researcher*, 17(4), 11–13.

Ryan, C., & Futterman, D. (1998). *Lesbian and gay youth: Care & counseling*. New York, NY: Columbia University Press.

Ryan, L., Hood, C., & Hall, M. (n.d.). *Have your voice heard*. Retrieved from http://geocities.com/rights_and_freedoms/ (site discontinued)

Saewyc, E.M. (2011). Research on adolescent sexual orientation: Development, health disparities, stigma, and resilience. *Journal of Research on Adolescence*, 21(1), 256–72. http://dx.doi.org/10.1111/j.1532-7795.2010.00727.x

Saewyc, E.M., Poon, C.S., Homma, Y., & Skay, C.L. (2008). Stigma management? The links between enacted stigma and teen pregnancy trends among gay, lesbian, and bisexual students in British Columbia. *Canadian Journal of Human Sexuality*, 17(3), 123–39.

Saewyc, E.M., Wang, N., Chittenden, M., Murphy, A., & The McCreary Centre Society (2006). *Building resilience in vulnerable youth*. Retrieved from http://www.mcs.bc.ca

Safren, S.A., & Pantalone, D.W. (2006). Social anxiety and barriers to resilience among lesbian, gay, and bisexual adolescents. In A.M. Omoto & H.S. Kurtzman (Eds.), *Sexual orientation and mental health: Examining identity and development in lesbian, gay, and bisexual people* (pp. 55–71). Washington, DC: American Psychological Association. http://dx.doi.org/10.1037/11261-003

Sameroff, A., Gutman, L.M., & Peck, S.C. (2003). Adaptation among youth facing multiple risks: Prospective research findings. In S.S. Luthar (Ed.), *Resilience and vulnerability: Adaptation in the context of childhood adversities* (pp. 364–91). New York, NY: Cambridge University Press. http://dx.doi.org/10.1017/CBO9780511615788.017

Sanders, G.L., & Kroll, I.T. (2000). Generating stories of resilience: Helping gay and lesbian youth and their families. *Journal of Marital and Family Therapy*, 26(4), 433–42. http://dx.doi.org/10.1111/j.1752-0606.2000.tb00314.x

Savage, D. (2012). Introduction. In D. Savage & T. Miller (Eds.), *It gets better: Coming out, overcoming bullying, and creating a life worth living* (pp. 1–8). New York, NY: Plume.

Savage, D., & Miller, T. (Eds.). (2012). *It gets better: Coming out, overcoming bullying, and creating a life worth living*. New York, NY: Plume.

Savin-Williams, R.C. (1994). Verbal and physical abuse as stressors in the lives of lesbian, gay male, and bisexual youths: Associations with school problems, running away, substance abuse, prostitution, and suicide. *Journal of Consulting and Clinical Psychology*, 62(2), 261–9. http://dx.doi.org/10.1037/0022-006X.62.2.261

Savin-Williams, R.C. (2005). *The new gay teenager*. Cambridge, MA: Harvard University Press.

Savin-Williams, R.C. (2008). Then and now: Recruitment, definition, diversity, and positive attributes of same-sex populations. *Developmental Psychology*, 44(1), 135–8. http://dx.doi.org/10.1037/0012-1649.44.1.135

Savin-Williams, R.C., & Ream, G.L. (2003). Suicide attempts among sexual-minority male youth. *Journal of Clinical Child and Adolescent Psychology*, *32*(4), 509–22. http://dx.doi.org/10.1207/S15374424JCCP3204_3

Scharrón-del Río, M.R., Dragowski, E.A., & Phillips, J.J. (2014). Therapeutic work with gender-variant children: What school psychologists need to know. *School Psychology Forum: Research in Practice*, *8*(1), 38–55.

Schindel, J.E. (2008). Gender 101 – beyond the binary: Gay-straight alliances and gender activism. *Sexuality Research & Social Policy*, *5*(2), 56–70. http://dx.doi.org/10.1525/srsp.2008.5.2.56

Schneider, M.S. (Ed.). (1997). *Pride and prejudice: Working with lesbian, gay and bisexual youth*. Toronto, ON: Central Toronto Youth Services.

Schrader, A.M., & Wells, K. (2007). *Challenging silence, challenging censorship: Inclusive resources, strategies and policy directives for addressing BGLTT realities in school and public libraries*. Ottawa, ON: Canadian Teachers' Federation.

Schuller, T., & Watson, D. (2009). *Learning through life: Inquiry into the future for lifelong learning*. Leicester, UK: NIACE.

Schulman, M. (2013, 9 January). Generation LGBTQIA. *The New York Times*. Retrieved from http://www.nytimes.com/2013/01/10/fashion/generation-lgbtqia.html?pagewanted=1&src=dayp&_r=1

Schwartz, D. (2012). Listening to children imagining gender: Observing the inflation of an idea. *Journal of Homosexuality*, *59*(3), 460–79. http://dx.doi.org/10.1080/00918369.2012.653314

Scourfield, J., Roen, K., & McDermott, L. (2008). Lesbian, gay, bisexual and transgender young people's experiences of distress: Resilience, ambivalence and self-destructive behaviour. *Health & Social Care in the Community*, *16*(3), 329–36. http://dx.doi.org/10.1111/j.1365-2524.2008.00769.x

Sedgwick, E.K. (1990). *Epistemology of the closet*. Los Angeles, CA: University of California Press.

Sedgwick, E.K. (1993). *Tendencies*. Durham, NC: Duke University Press.

Serovich, J.M., Craft, S.M., Toviessi, P., Gangamma, R., McDowell, T., & Grafsky, E.L. (2008). A systematic review of the research base on sexual reorientation therapies. *Journal of Marital and Family Therapy*, *34*(2), 227–38. http://dx.doi.org/10.1111/j.1752-0606.2008.00065.x

Sesma, A., Mannes, M., & Scales, P.C. (2005). Positive adaptation, resilience, and the developmental asset framework. In S. Goldstein & R.B. Brooks (Eds.), *Handbook of resilience in children* (pp. 281–96). New York, NY: Kluwer. http://dx.doi.org/10.1007/0-306-48572-9_17

Sharkey, J.D., You, S., & Schnoebelen, K. (2008). Relations among school assets, individual resilience, and student engagement for youth grouped by level of family functioning. *Psychology in the Schools*, *45*(5), 402–18. http://dx.doi.org/10.1002/pits.20305

Shelley, C.A. (2008). *Transpeople: Repudiation, trauma, healing*. Toronto, ON: University of Toronto Press.

Shelton, M. (2013). *Family pride: What LGBT families should know about navigating home, school, and safety in their neighbourhoods*. Boston, MA: Beacon Press.

Silin, J.G. (1992). What AIDS teaches us about the education of children. *Educational Theory*, *42*(3), 253–69. http://dx.doi.org/10.1111/j.1741-5446.1992.00253.x

Simon, R.I. (1992). *Teaching against the grain: Texts for a pedagogy of possibility*. New York, NY: Bergin & Garvey.

Simons, P. (2009, 9 May). Homophobic activists the bullies of the legislature. *Edmonton Journal*. Retrieved from https://groups.yahoo.com/neo/groups/TNUKdigest/conversations/messages/46301

Simpson, J. (2004, 20 March). The formation of the first high-school GSA and the education of an administrator. A keynote presentation at the 7th annual *Breaking the Silence Conference: Gays and Lesbians in our Schools*, College of Education, University of Saskatchewan, Saskatoon, Canada.

Singh, A. (2012). Transgender youth of color and resilience: Negotiating oppression and finding support. *Sex Roles*. Advance online publication. http://dx.doi.org/10.1007/s11199-012-0149-z

Siu, J. (2002a, 10 May). *Off to the prom!* Retrieved from http://365gay.com (no longer accessible)

Siu, J. (2002b, 11 May). *Prom fight not over*. Retrieved from http://365gay.com/newscontent/051102marcProm.htm (no longer accessible)

Snyder, J.E. (2011). Trend analysis of medical publications about LGBT persons: 1950–2007. *Journal of Homosexuality*, *58*(2), 164–88. http://dx.doi.org/10.1080/00918369.2011.540171

Southwick, S.M., Morgan, C.A., III, Vythilingam, M., & Charney, D. (2007). Mentors enhance resilience in at-risk children and adolescents. *Psychoanalytic Inquiry*, *26*(4), 577–84. http://dx.doi.org/10.1080/07351690701310631

Spack, N.P. (2008). Foreword. In S. Brill & R. Pepper (Eds.), *The transgender child: A handbook for families and professionals* (pp. ix–xi). San Francisco, CA: Cleis Press.

Spitzer, R.L. (2003a). Can some gay men and lesbians change their sexual orientation? 200 participants reporting a change from homosexual to heterosexual orientation. *Archives of Sexual Behavior*, *32*(5), 403–17. http://dx.doi.org/10.1023/A:1025647527010

Spitzer, R.L. (2003b). Reply: Study results should not be dismissed and justify further research on the efficacy of sexual reorientation therapy. *Archives of Sexual Behavior, 32*(5), 469–72. http://dx.doi.org/10.1023/A:1025651627919

Spoon, R., & Coyote, I.E. (2014). *Gender failure.* Vancouver, BC: Arsenal Pulp Press.

Stanley, E.A. (2011). Fugitive flesh: Gender self-determination, queer abolition, and trans resistance. In E.A. Stanley & N. Smith (Eds.), *Captive genders: Trans embodiment and the prison industrial complex* (pp. 1–11). Oakland, CA: AK Press.

Statistics Canada. (2010, 14 June). *Police-reported hate crimes, 2008.* Ottawa, ON: Communications and Library Services Division, Statistics Canada.

Steensma, T., Biemond, R., de Boer, F., & Cohen-Kettenis, P. (2011). Desisting and persisting gender dysphoria after childhood: A qualitative follow-up study. *Clinical Child Psychology and Psychiatry, 16*(4), 499–516. http://dx.doi.org/10.1177/1359104510378303

Stein, E. (2012). Commentary on the treatment of gender variant and gender dysphoric children and adolescents: Common themes and ethical reflections. *Journal of Homosexuality, 59*(3), 480–500. http://dx.doi.org/10.1080/00918369.2012.653316

Stewart, C. (2007). *Combating hate and bias crime and incidents in Alberta: Current responses and recommendations for the future – July 2007.* Calgary, AB: Alberta Hate and Bias Crime and Incidents Committee.

St. John, A., Travers, R., Munro, L., Liboro, R., Schneider, M., & Greig, C.L. (2014). The success of gay-straight alliances in Waterloo region, Ontario: A confluence of political and social factors. *Journal of LGBT Youth, 11*(2), 150–70. http://dx.doi.org/10.1080/19361653.2014.878564

Strassberg, D.S. (2003). A candle in the wind: Spitzer's study on reparative therapy. *Archives of Sexual Behavior, 32*(5), 451–2.

Stryker, S. (2008). *Transgender history.* Berkeley, CA: Seal Press.

Supreme Court of Canada (SCC) (2004, 9 December). *Reference re same-sex marriage (2004 SCC 79; file no.: 29866).* Retrieved from http://www.canlii.org/en/ca/scc/doc/2004/2004scc79/2004scc79.pdf

Supreme Court Judgments. (2001). *Trinity Western University (TWU) v. British Columbia College of Teachers (BCCT),* 1 S.C.R. 772, 2001 SCC 31. Retrieved from http://scc-csc.lexum.com/scc-csc/scc-csc/en/item/1867/index.do

Surrey Teachers' Association (STA). (2000). *"Moving beyond silence": Addressing homophobia in elementary schools.* Surrey, BC: Author.

Swan, M. (2004, 6 December). Ont. offers help for gay students. *Western Catholic Reporter,* p. 4.

Szalacha, L.A. (2003). Safer sexual diversity climates: Lessons learned from an evaluation of Massachusetts Safe Schools Program for Gay and Lesbian Students. *American Journal of Education, 110*(1), 58–88. http://dx.doi.org/10.1086/377673

Talburt, S. (2000). Introduction: Some contradictions and possibilities of thinking queer. In S. Talburt & S.R. Steinberg (Eds.), *Thinking queer: Sexuality, culture, and education* (pp. 3–13). New York, NY: Peter Lang.

Talburt, S. (2004). Constructions of LGBT youth: Opening up subject positions. *Theory into Practice, 43*(2), 116–21. http://dx.doi.org/10.1207/s15430421tip4302_4

Taylor, C. (2010). Facts of life in homophobia high: Findings of the first national climate survey on homophobia and transphobia in Canadian schools. In A.P. Grace, C.M. Dawson, & A.K. Hillyard (Eds.), Proceedings of Queer Issues in the Study of Education and Culture II, the 2nd Queer Pre-Conference at the 38th Annual Conference of the Canadian Society for the Study of Education, Concordia University, Montreal, QC, 55–62.

Taylor, C., & Peter, T., with McMinn, T.L., Schachter, K., Beldom, S., Ferry, A., Gross, Z., & Paquin, S. (2011). *Every class in every school: The first national climate survey on homophobia, biphobia, and transphobia in Canadian schools; Final report.* Toronto, ON: Egale Canada Human Rights Trust.

Tedlock, B. (2000). Ethnography and ethnographic representation. In N.K. Denzin & Y.S. Lincoln (Eds.), *The SAGE handbook of qualitative research* (2nd ed., pp. 455–86). Thousand Oaks, CA: SAGE.

Teich, N.M., & Green, J. (2012). *Transgender 101: A simple guide to a complex issue.* New York, NY: Columbia University Press.

te Riele, K. (2006). Schooling practices for marginalized students – practice-with-hope. *International Journal of Inclusive Education, 10*(1), 59–74. http://dx.doi.org/10.1080/13603110500221750

Testa, R.J., Jimenez, C.L., & Rankin, S. (2014). Risk and resilience during transgender identity development: The effects of awareness and engagement with other transgender people on affect. *Journal of Gay & Lesbian Mental Health, 18*(1), 31–46. http://dx.doi.org/10.1080/19359705.2013.805177

Tharinger, D., & Wells, G. (2000). An attachment perspective on the developmental challenges of gay and lesbian adolescents: The need for continuity of caregiving from family and schools. *School Psychology Review, 29*(2), 158–72.

Thompson, R.A. (2006). *Nurturing future generations: Promoting resilience in children and adolescents through social, emotional, and cognitive skills.* New York, NY: Routledge.

365Gay.com. (2002). *Prom date battle draws support from one of Canada's most powerful union bosses.* Retrieved from http://www.thebacklot.com/

Throckmorton, W. (2002). Initial empirical and clinical findings concerning the change process for ex-gays. *Professional Psychology, Research and Practice, 33*(3), 242–8. http://dx.doi.org/10.1037/0735-7028.33.3.242

Timmons, V. (2006). Impact of a multipronged approach to inclusion: Having all partners on side. *International Journal of Inclusive Education, 10*(4–5), 469–80. http://dx.doi.org/10.1080/13603110500392726

Tolman, D.L., & McClelland, S.I. (2011). Normative sexuality development in adolescence: A decade review, 2000–2009. *Journal of Research on Adolescence, 21*(1), 242–55. http://dx.doi.org/10.1111/j.1532-7795.2010.00726.x

Tonkin, R.S., Murphy, A., Lees, Z., Saewyc, E., & The McCreary Centre Society. (2005). *British Columbia youth health trends: A retrospective, 1992–2003.* Vancouver, BC: The McCreary Centre Society.

Toomey, R.B., Ryan, C., Diaz, R.M., & Russell, S.T. (2011). High school gay-straight alliances (GSAs) and young adult well-being: An examination of GSA presence, participation, and perceived effectiveness. *Applied Developmental Science, 15*(4), 175–85. http://dx.doi.org/10.1080/10888691.2011.607378

Toronto Police Service. (n.d.). *Report homophobic violence, period (RHVP).* Retrieved from http://www.torontopolice.on.ca/rhvp/

Trans PULSE Project. (2012). *Impacts of strong parental support for trans youth.* Retrieved 5 November 2012 from http://transpulseproject.ca/research/impacts-of-strong-parental-support-for-trans-youth/

Travers, R., & Paoletti, D. (1999). The Lesbian, Gay, and Bisexual Youth Program (LGBYP): A model for communities seeking to improve quality of life for lesbian, gay and bisexual youth. *Canadian Journal of Human Sexuality, 8,* 293–303.

Trotter, J. (2009). Ambiguities around sexuality: An approach to understanding harassment and bullying of young people in British schools. *Journal of LGBT Youth, 6*(1), 7–23. http://dx.doi.org/10.1080/19361650802377700

Ungar, M. (2005). Introduction: Resilience across cultures and contexts. In M. Ungar (Ed.), *Handbook for working with children and youth: Pathways to resilience across cultures and contexts* (pp. xv–xxxix). Thousand Oaks, CA: SAGE.

Ungar, M. (2008). Putting resilience theory into action: Five principles for intervention. In L. Liebenberg & M. Ungar (Eds.), *Resilience in action* (pp. 17–36). Toronto, ON: University of Toronto Press.

Ungar, M. (2010). Families as navigators and negotiators: Facilitating culturally and contextually specific expressions of resilience. *Family Process, 49*(3), 421–35. http://dx.doi.org/10.1111/j.1545-5300.2010.01331.x

Ungar, M. (2011). Community resilience for youth and families: Facilitative physical and social capital in contexts of adversity. *Children and Youth Services Review, 33*(9), 1742–8. http://dx.doi.org/10.1016/j.childyouth.2011.04.027

Ungar, M., Brown, M., Liebenberg, L., & Othman, R. (2007). Unique pathways to resilience across cultures. *Adolescence, 42*(166), 287–310.

United Nations Educational, Scientific, and Cultural Organization (UNESCO). (2009). *International technical guidance on sexuality education: An evidence-informed approach for schools, teachers, and health educators.* Retrieved from http://hivhealthclearinghouse.unesco.org/sites/default/files/media/content/migrated/user/pdf/2009/20091210_international_guidance_sexuality_education_vol_1_en.pdf

Unks, G. (Ed.). (1995). *The gay teen: Educational practice and theory for lesbian, gay, and bisexual adolescents.* New York, NY: Routledge.

Uribe, V. (1994). Project 10: A school-based outreach to gay and lesbian youth. *High School Journal, 77,* 108–12.

Valenti, M., & Campbell, R. (2009). Working with youth on LGBT issues: Why gay-straight alliance advisors become involved. *Journal of Community Psychology, 37*(2), 228–48. http://dx.doi.org/10.1002/jcop.20290

Valentine, D. (2007). *Imagining transgender: An ethnography of a category.* Durham, NC: Duke University Press. http://dx.doi.org/10.1215/9780822390213

Valentine, L., & Feinauer, L.L. (1993). Resilience factors associated with female survivors of childhood sexual abuse. *American Journal of Family Therapy, 21*(3), 216–24. http://dx.doi.org/10.1080/01926189308250920

Vasey, P.L. (2003). Sexual diversity and change along a continuum of bisexual desire. *Archives of Sexual Behavior, 32*(5), 453–5.

Victor, J.M. (2014, 12 February). Ending "gay conversion" for good. *The New York Times.* Retrieved from http://www.nytimes.com/2014/02/13/opinion/ending-gay-conversion-for-good.html

Wallace, R., & Russell, H. (2013). Attachment and shame in gender-nonconforming children and their families: Toward a theoretical framework for evaluating clinical interventions. *International Journal of Transgenderism, 14*(3), 113–26. http://dx.doi.org/10.1080/15532739.2013.824845

Walls, N.E., Kane, S.B., & Wisnesk, H. (2010). Gay-straight alliances and school experiences of sexual minority youth. *Youth & Sexuality, 41*(3), 307–32. http://dx.doi.org/10.1177/0044118X09334957

Warner, T. (2002). *Never going back: A history of queer activism in Canada.* Toronto, ON: University of Toronto Press.

Webb, S. (2011). Community engagement and the idea of a "good university." In S. Jackson (Ed.), *Lifelong learning and social justice: Communities, work and identities in a globalised world* (pp. 82–101). Leicester, UK: NIACE.

Weber, S., & Poster, E.C. (2010). Guest editorial: Special issue on mental health nursing care of LGBT adolescents and young adults. *Journal of Child and Adolescent Psychiatric Nursing, 23*(1), 1–2. http://dx.doi.org/10.1111/j.1744-6171.2009.00209.x

We*Happy*Trans*. (2013). *About*. Retrieved from http://wehappytrans.com

Weis, L., & Fine, M. (2001). Extraordinary conversations in public schools. *International Journal of Qualitative Studies in Education, 14*(4), 497–523. http://dx.doi.org/10.1080/09518390110046355

Wells, K. (2006). *The gay-straight student alliance handbook: A comprehensive resource for Canadian K-12 teachers, administrators, and school counsellors*. Ottawa, ON: Canadian Teachers' Federation.

Wells, K. (2008, Winter). *Homophobic bullying* [Fact Sheet]. Edmonton, AB. Government of Alberta.

Wells, K., Roberts, G., & Allan, C. (2012). *Supporting transsexual and transgender students in K-12 schools: A guide for educators*. Ottawa, ON: Canadian Teachers' Federation.

Wells, K., & Tsutsumi, L.M. (2005). *Creating safe and caring schools for lesbian, gay, bisexual, and trans-identified students: A guide for counsellors*. Edmonton, AB: The Society for Safe and Caring Schools and Communities.

Werner, E.E. (1995). Resilience in development. *Current Directions in Psychological Science, 4*(3), 81–5. http://dx.doi.org/10.1111/1467-8721.ep10772327

West, C. (1996). Cornell West on heterosexism and transformation: An interview. *Harvard Educational Review, 66*(2), 356–67.

Wexler, L.M., DiFulvio, G., & Burke, T.K. (2009). Resilience and marginalized youth: Making a case for personal and collective meaning-making as part of resilience research in public health. *Social Science & Medicine, 69*(4), 565–70. http://dx.doi.org/10.1016/j.socscimed.2009.06.022

White Holman, C., & Goldberg, J.M. (2006). Ethical, legal, and psychosocial issues in care of transgender adolescents. *International Journal of Transgenderism, 9*(3–4), 95–110. http://dx.doi.org/10.1300/J485v09n03_05

Whitnell, T. (2011a, 16 February). Board's equity policy change criticized by gay trustee. *Independent Free Press*. Retrieved from http://www.theifp.ca/community-story/5363733-board-s-equity-policy-change-criticized-by-gay-trustee/

Whitnell, T. (2011b, 8 April). Catholic board still finalizing equity, inclusivity policy. *Burlington Post*. Retrieved from http://www.insidehalton.com/community-story/2989129-catholic-board-still-finalizing-equity-inclusivity-policy/

Whitnell, T. (2011c, 6 May). Halton Catholic school board finalizes equity policy. *Burlington Post*. Retrieved from http://www.insidehalton.com/community-story/2884973-halton-catholic-school-board-finalizes-equity-policy/

Whittaker, K.R. (2009). Gay-straight alliances and free speech: Are parental consent laws constitutional? *Berkeley Journal of Gender Law & Justice, 24*(1), 48–67.

Wilber, S., Ryan, C., & Marksamer, J. (2006). *CWLA best practice guidelines: Serving LGBT youth in out-of-home care*. Washington, DC: Child Welfare League of America.

Wildemeersch, D., & Salling Olesen, H. (2012). Editorial: The effects of policies for the education and learning of adults – from "adult education" to "lifelong learning," from "emancipation" to "empowerment." *European Journal for Research on the Education and Learning of Adults, 3*(2), 97–101. http://dx.doi.org/10.3384/rela.2000-7426.relae5

Wolkow, K.E., & Ferguson, H.B. (2001). Community factors in the development of resiliency: Considerations and future directions. *Community Mental Health Journal, 37*(6), 489–98. http://dx.doi.org/10.1023/A:1017574028567

Worthington, R.L. (2003). Heterosexual identities, sexual reorientation therapies, and science. *Archives of Sexual Behavior, 32*(5), 460–1.

Yates, T.M., Egeland, B., & Sroufe, L.A. (2003). Rethinking resilience: A developmental process perspective. In S.S. Luthar (Ed.), *Resilience and vulnerability: Adaptation in the context of childhood adversities* (pp. 243–66). New York, NY: Cambridge University Press. http://dx.doi.org/10.1017/CBO9780511615788.012

Youth-Gender Action Project (Y-GAP). (2009a). *Trans youth accessing health and social services*. Toronto, ON: Author.

Youth-Gender Action Project (Y-GAP). (2009b). *Trans youth at school*. Toronto, ON: Author.

Zucker, K.J. (2006). The politics and science of "reparative therapy." In J. Drescher & K.J. Zucker (Eds.), *Ex-gay research: Analyzing the Spitzer study and its relation to science, religion, politics, and culture* (pp. 3–6). New York, NY: Harrington Park Press.

Zucker, K.J., & Cohen-Kettenis, P.Y. (2008). Gender identity disorder in children and adolescents. In D.L. Rowland & L. Incrocci (Eds.), *Handbook of sexual and gender identity disorders* (pp. 376–422). Hoboken, NJ: Wiley. http://dx.doi.org/10.1002/9781118269978.ch13

Zucker, K.J., Wood, H., Singh, D., & Bradley, S. (2012). A developmental, biopsychosocial model for the treatment of children with gender identity disorder. *Journal of Homosexuality, 59*(3), 369–97. http://dx.doi.org/10.1080/00918369.2012.653309

Index

Page numbers followed by (s) refer to a narrative entry, such as an InterText or vignette.

155–6. *See also* Hall, Marc, and his
Ontario high school prom
Catholic schools: Bill 13 passage, 23,
274–5, 276; By Your SIDE Spaces,
271–2; and divided Catholic
opinion, 276; Dufferin-Peel
Catholic District School Board
(DPCDSB), 273–4; Episcopal
Commission for Doctrine of the
Canadian Conference of Catholic
Bishops (ECD-CCCB), 271, 273,
274; equity and inclusivity policy,
270, 272; GSA name recognition,
270, 272–3, 274, 275; Leanne
Iskander and Open Arms club
name, 274; Marai, Paul, 272;
Ontario Catholic School Trustees'
Association, 272, 275, 276; and
Ontario GSA clubs, 269–77;
original outright GSA ban (Halton
region), 270–2; province-wide
GSA-equivalent groups, 272;
"Respecting Differences" name
proposal, 275; and sexual minority
youth invisibility, 23, 271, 272, 274
Catholics for Free Choice, 145, 271
Central Toronto Youth Services
(CTYS), 59, 76
Centre for Addiction and Mental
Health (Toronto), 67–8, 71
Charter rights. *See* Canadian Charter
of Rights and Freedoms
Chief Public Health Officer's
(CPHO) 2011 Report, 118–19,
127–8
Chief Public Health Officer's
(CPHO) 2012 Report: basic scope
of report, 118; mental health
issues, 120–1; sexual and gender
diversity and health, 119–21;

transgendered and transsexual
youth and adults, 121, 125
cisgender people, 51, 261–2
Coalition in Support of Marc Hall,
145, 148, 159, 165, 166, 271
Cohen-Kettenis, P.Y., 69
Collins, Thomas, 276
coming out (disclosure): advice
for professionals, 134–5; and the
choice to stay closeted in high
school, 260; family response to
disclosure, 78, 230, 232–3; gender
self-identification and disclosure,
216–17, 219; Marc Hall's parents'
reaction, 154–5; negative parental
reaction, 155; and psychosocial
difficulties, 193–4; vignettes:
Jeremy, Ryan, and Bruce,
189–90(s), 190–3(s); at younger
and younger ages, 11(s), 189
comprehensive health and
education: Camp fYrefly, 93–4;
Chief Public Health Officer's
(CPHO) 2011 Report, 118–19,
127–8; Chief Public Health
Officer's (CPHO) 2012 Report,
118–21; community peer-to-
peer programs, 102–3(s), 260–1;
professional best practices, 131–5
comprehensive health and SGM
family factors: ethnocultural
environment, 230; families of
choice/families of origin, 227;
family response to disclosure,
78, 230, 232–3; interactive,
communicative parents, 232;
reasons for disclosing or not
disclosing, 231–2; reparative
therapy, 233–6; SGM youth
family stories, 227–9; and youth

179, 258; and staff psychologists, 58, 212–13; and student coping strategies, 261; and teacher training, xviii, 163; trans children and youth, 74–6, 119–20, 122, 124–5; Youth-Gender Action Project (Y-GAP) study, 54–5, 122. *See also* bullying; Camp fYrefly; Catholic schooling; Edmonton Public Schools; GSA clubs; SGM students as activists and cultural workers

Schuller, T., 94
Schulman, M., 47–8
Sears, J.T., 156
Sesma, A., 95, 289, 297, 301
sexual orientation: definition of, 16; and Supreme Court of Canada, ix–x, xiii, 146–7, 157, 162–4, 184
Sexual Orientation and Gender Identity policy (Edmonton Public School Board), 128–9
SGM students as activists and cultural workers: interviewing Ryan, Jeremy, and Bruce, 182–3; queer critical praxis of Ryan, Jeremy, and Bruce, 25, 179–80, 194–5, 196, 200–2; vignettes by Bruce, 185–6, 193, 198–200, 203; vignettes by Jeremy, 185, 189–91, 197–8, 203; vignettes by Ryan, 186, 191–3, 196, 203. *See also* GSA clubs
SGM youth: "at promise" and "at risk," 21–2; intervention and prevention, 131–5 (*see also* comprehensive health, intervention and prevention); and isolation, 118; as a multivariate population, 16, 119, 215–18, 219–20; "naming and labelling,"

132–3; role models and mentors, 19–20, 28, 33, 82, 226
SGM Youth Intervention and Outreach Worker (YIOW) program, 241–2
Shelley, C.A., 50, 83–4
Shelton, M., xviii, 17–18, 23, 123
Shields, Mike, 159
Simons, P., 25
Simpson, John, 200–1
Singh, A., 231
Smitherman, George, 157(s), 160, 162
Socarides, Charles, 58
social education, 92
Social Sciences and Humanities Research Council of Canada, 100
Spack, N.P., 86
Spitzer, Robert, 236
Spoon, Rae, 82–3, 288
Stanley, E.A., 53–4
Statistics Canada, hate crimes, 188
Stein, E., 66
Stewart, C., 186–7
St. John, A., 257–8
Stryker, S., 50, 51
suicide: Chief Public Health Officer's (CPHO) 2011 report, 118; Colby's story, 209–10(s); despite GSA support, 267; of gay males, 180, 209; *It Gets Better* campaign, 19; research coverage, 213–14; research statistics, 194, 215, 279; and the role of parents, 231, 232; and trans youth, 49, 60, 73, 223, 224
supportive/affirming vs. corrective treatment for trans and gender-nonconforming children and youth, 57–8. *See also* developmental, biopsychosocial treatment model (Zucker);